TACHS and HSPT® Exams Skills and Drills Workbook

1st Edition

About Peterson's®

Peterson's has been your trusted educational publisher for over 50 years. It's a milestone we're quite proud of, as we continue to offer the most accurate, dependable, high-quality educational content in the field, providing you with everything you need to succeed. No matter where you are on your academic or professional path, you can rely on Peterson's for its books, online information, expert test-prep tools, the most up-to-date education exploration data, and the highest quality career success resources—everything you need to achieve your education goals. For our complete line of products, visit **www.petersons.com**.

For more information, contact Peterson's, 8740 Lucent Blvd., Suite 400, Highlands Ranch, CO 80129, or find us online at **www.petersons.com**.

ISBN: 978-0-7689-4368-9

Printed in the United States of America

10 9 8 7 6 5 4 3 2 1 21 20 19

First Edition

Peterson's Updates

Check out our website at **www.petersonspublishing.com/publishingupdates** to see if there is any new information regarding the test and any revisions or corrections to the content of this book. We've made sure the information in this book is accurate and up-to-date; however, the test format or content may have changed since the time of publication.

CONTENTS

Before You Begin

Why You Should Use This Book

If you're graduating from junior high or middle school and exploring your options for high school, it's an exciting time in your life. This may be your first opportunity to make a big decision about your education—and if you've purchased this book to enhance that process, you're taking that responsibility seriously.

Because you have this book in your hands, it's likely that you're considering continuing your education at a Catholic high school. An essential part of getting into the Catholic high school of your choice is not only passing an entrance exam but earning a score that sets you apart from the other students with similar goals. Peterson's *TACHS and HSPT® Exams Skills and Drills Workbook* is the tool that can help you do both.

While Peterson's *Master the*™ *Catholic High School Entrance Exams* is the best book to use to **begin** your test prep journey, Peterson's *TACHS and HSPT® Exams Skills and Drills Workbook* is designed by test experts and educators to further prepare you for test-day success, whether you're planning to take the TACHS (Test for Admission into Catholic High Schools) or the HSPT (High School Placement Test) entrance exam. This helpful workbook is filled with the extra exercises that can enhance your knowledge and test-taking skills beyond what a traditional test prep book would. The drills provided are designed to give you the extra practice that will not only boost your confidence but also significantly impact your test score for the better!

We know that doing well on your Catholic high school entrance exam is important, both to you and your family—and we're here to help you through every step of your journey. If you haven't already done so, consider investing in a copy of Peterson's *Master the*™ *Catholic High School Entrance Exams.* It offers an all-in-one test preparation package to familiarize you with and get you through the exam and on your way to the Catholic high school of your choice.

However, if you're comfortable with the concepts that will be assessed on the exam and what you *really* want is to focus on answering practice questions to sharpen your test-taking skills, this workbook is exactly what you need. Peterson's *TACHS and HSPT® Exams Skills and Drills Workbook* is designed to help you dive deeper into your test preparation. Start by taking the diagnostic test in Chapter 1 and use your test score to determine what subject areas you need to work on the most. By taking the drills, you will be able to target and strengthen your skills in the individual content sections of the entrance exams.

This workbook includes the following:

- A diagnostic test to help you determine on which subject areas you need to focus
- Overviews of each subject area with examples of the various types of questions you will encounter on the exams
- Drills built specifically for each subject area (including two Reading Comprehension and Math drill sets)
- Removable skill-building study guides that you can refer to before taking the drills and take with you for on-the-go memorization practice

How This Book Is Organized

Peterson's *TACHS and HSPT® Exams Skills and Drills Workbook* is divided into six chapters, all designed to give you focused practice in all subject areas covered on the TACHS and HSPT exams. The appendixes are included to give you extra study support.

- **Chapter 1: Diagnostic Test**—The diagnostic test is designed to give you a sample of the types of questions you may find on the TACHS and HSPT exams. Use it to pinpoint the subject areas in in which you need more practice.
- **Chapter 2: Reading**—Two reading comprehension drill sets present questions based on reading passages. You will be asked questions about main ideas, details, inferences, and vocabulary in context. In addition, this chapter includes a drill to prepare you for the HSPT Reading Vocabulary section.
- **Chapter 3: Written Expression/Language**—The four drills in this chapter are designed to prepare you for the English language skills assessed on the exams: spelling, capitalization, punctuation, usage, and composition and expression.
- **Chapter 4: Math**—Two math drills present questions covering a wide range of question types, such as algebra, arithmetic, geometry, number sense, and statistics. Space is provided right next to the questions for you to work out the problems as you go, so you can compare your work step-by step to the correct answer explanations after scoring your drill.
- **Chapter 5: HSPT® Verbal Skills**—This chapter provides four drills that focus on the Verbal Skills portion of the HSPT exam: Analogies, Antonyms, Synonyms, and Verbal Classification/Logic. While this section is specific to the HSPT, mastery of these question types can boost your verbal reasoning skills, which will be valuable during your high school years and beyond.

- **Chapter 6: Quantitative Skills/Ability Questions**—The two drills in this chapter focus on two unique skill sets assessed on the entrance exams: HSPT Quantitative Skills and TACHS Ability. The quantitative skills questions include sequences, quantitative reasoning, and geometric and nongeometric reasoning. The TACHS ability questions ask you to solve figure classification, figure matrix, and paper-folding problems. This small but challenging section will help sharpen your cognitive skills for test day.
- **Appendixes**—The appendixes will help you prepare with skill-building resources, such as a list of approximately 500 commonly used words that may appear on the exams, including hundreds of related words that are variants of the primary words or that share a common word root; a list of synonyms and antonyms for many of the terms on the word list, as well as additional terms; a list of capitalization rules, comma rules, and other important grammar tips to review before test day; a list of 20 must-know spelling rules; and a sheet of math formulas. In addition, you'll find answer sheets for the drills that you can use to simulate the test-taking experience.

Tips for Test-Taking Success

No test-preparation book would be complete without a rundown of surefire test-taking techniques. Some of the techniques and tips listed here are common sense, but it never hurts to be reminded.

Getting Ready

- **Gather your gear.** Always assemble everything you will need the night before the exam. You will need a few #2 pencils and a watch (calculator watches are not permitted). Bring a sweater or sweatshirt in case the room is air conditioned.
- **Bring only what you need.** The only materials you need to bring to your exam are a few sharpened #2 pencils with clean erasers, positive identification, and your admission ticket (if you were issued one).
- **Rest up.** Get a good night's sleep and get up early enough so you can eat breakfast, so you don't have to rush, and so you can arrive at the testing center with plenty of time to spare. Enter the room early enough to find a comfortable seat and relax.
- **Do not bring a calculator.** Unless you were expressly instructed to bring a calculator, do not bring one to your exam. Calculators are not permitted on most high school entrance exams.

- **If permitted to do so, wear a watch.** It is important to wear a watch even though the room will most likely have a clock. The clock might not be conveniently located to keep track of time. Since calculators are not allowed, be sure that your watch is not a calculator watch, because all calculator watches will be confiscated for the duration of the exam. If your watch has an alarm, be sure to turn it off. (**Note:** You are *not* permitted to wear a watch for the HSPT exam.)
- **Enter the room early enough to choose a comfortable seat.** After you're settled, relax. You'll concentrate more and perform better on the test if you're relaxed and comfortable. Besides, you studied hard for the exam, so what do you have to worry about, right?

Answering Questions

When it comes to answering exam questions, one of the best test tips we can offer is this: Try to answer every question on the exam. To do this might mean you have to guess. If you answer every question—even if you guess wildly—you are more likely to earn a higher score. There is no penalty for wrong answers on the TACHS or HSPT, so even a wild guess gives you a 20 or 25 percent chance for credit!

If you're uncertain of the correct answer to a question, guess—you can always mark the question and return to it for another try later if you have the time. If you're running out of time, start guessing. Here are two solid tips to remember about guessing on an exam:

1. **An educated guess is worth more than a random guess.** To make an educated guess, look carefully at the question and eliminate any answers that you are sure are wrong. Chances are that you can spot some obviously wrong answers among the choices for vocabulary, reading, and language questions. You will probably find some of the choices for math questions to be so far off as to make you chuckle. When it comes right down to it, you have a better chance of guessing correctly when you have three options instead of four or five. Your odds improve even more if you can guess between two choices.
2. **When time is short, pick a response and stick with it.** Be mindful of the time so you know when the exam period is close to ending. In those last few seconds, pick one response—preferably not the first, because the first answer tends to be the correct one less often than the others—and mark all remaining blanks on your answer sheet with that same answer. By the law of averages, you should pick up a free point or two.

Avoiding Careless Mistakes

To do well on your exam, make sure that you don't lose any points through carelessness. The following eleven suggestions apply to any paper-and-pencil standardized exam, including the TACHS and HSPT:

1. **Take aim.** Mark your answers by completely blackening the answer space of your choice. Be sure not to make any marks outside the lines.
2. **Be decisive.** Mark only **one** answer for each question, even if you think that more than one answer is correct. If you mark more than one answer, you will receive no credit for that question.
3. **Erase completely.** If you change your mind, erase the answer completely. Leave no doubt as to which answer you mean.
4. **Follow the dotted rows.** Answer every question in the right place on the answer sheet. Make sure that the number of the answer blank matches the number of the question you are answering. You could lose valuable time if you must go back and change a lot of answers.
5. **Manage your time wisely.** Don't spend too much time on any question, even if it poses an interesting challenge. Pick an answer and move on. You can always mark the question in your test booklet and go back to it later if time permits.
6. **Skip carefully, or just guess.** You are not required to answer every question; however, if you do skip one, **be sure to skip its answer space**. Otherwise, you might throw off your entire answer sheet. For that reason, it's safer to guess than to skip. Just mark the guesses in your test booklet so that you can go back and deliberate some more if you have time.
7. **Make your answers count.** If you use scratch paper (you may on the HSPT), be sure to mark the answer on the answer sheet. Only the answer sheet is scored; the test booklet and the scratch paper are not.
8. **Stay alert.** Getting a good night's sleep the night before and eating breakfast on the morning of the test will help you to be alert.
9. **Can't finish? Don't panic.** If you don't finish a section before the time is up, don't worry. Few people can answer every question. If you are accurate, you might earn a high score even without finishing every test section.
10. **Look forward, not back.** Don't let your performance on a section affect your performance on any other part of the exam. For example, if you don't think you did very well on mathematics, forget about that section after you are finished and start on the next section. Worrying about a previous section could cause you a lot of stress and negatively impact your performance on the sections that follow.
11. **Check and recheck.** If you finish any part before the time is up, go back and check to be sure that each question is answered in the right space and that there is only one answer for each question. Return to the difficult questions and rethink them.

What to Expect When You Take the Exam

Now that you're well prepared for the exam, have the right tools, and have arrived in plenty of time, the first thing you will do in the exam room is fill out forms. You will be given detailed instructions for this procedure. Listen, read, and follow the directions; filling out forms is not timed, so don't rush. The exam will not begin until everyone has finished.

Next, the administrator will give you general instructions for taking the exam. You will be told how to recognize the stop and start signals. You will also find out what to do if you have a problem, such as if all your pencil leads break or you discover a page missing from your test booklet. Pay attention to the instructions. If you have any questions, ask them before the test begins.

When the signal is given, open your test booklet and read:

- **Read all directions carefully.** The directions will probably be very similar to those in this book, but don't take anything for granted. Test makers do periodically change the exams.
- **Read every word of every question.** Be alert for little words that might have a big effect on your answer—for example, words such as *not*, *most*, *all*, *every*, and *except*.
- **Read all the answer choices before you select an answer.** It is statistically true that the most errors are made when the correct answer is the last choice given. Too many people mark the first answer that seems correct without reading through all the choices to find out which answer is best.

Using Peterson's *TACHS and HSPT® Exams Skills and Drills Workbook* as a Companion to Peterson's *Master the™ Catholic Entrance Exams*: Ten Steps to Raise Your Score

When it comes to taking your high school entrance exam, some test-taking skills will benefit you more than others. There are concepts you can learn, techniques you can follow, and tricks you can use that will help you to do your very best. Using Peterson's *TACHS and HSPT® Exams Skills and Drills Workbook* is a great way to polish your skills if you're looking for straightforward drill practice. But if you're planning to use this workbook in conjunction with Peterson's *Master the™ Catholic High School Entrance Exams*, follow the 10-step plan on the next page to get the most out of your preparation and raise your score.

1. **Diagnose your knowledge needs.** Regardless of which study plan in Peterson's *Master the™ Catholic High School Entrance Exams* you will follow, get started by completing the diagnostic test found in Chapter 1 of this workbook or taking either the TACHS or HSPT diagnostic test in Part 1 of Peterson's *Master the™ Catholic High School Entrance Exams.* These diagnostic tests will point you in the right direction to focus your studying.
2. **Study, then exercise.** Once you know what you need to work on, study the appropriate review chapters in Peterson's *Master the™ Catholic High School Entrance Exams.* Complete the exercises at the end of each chapter to confirm your understanding.
3. **Take a practice test.** When you are one third of the way through your preparation, take a practice test. Make sure you are applying new test-taking strategies.
4. **Use your study resources as you review.** Keep a **dictionary** nearby while taking the practice tests or studying the review sections in Peterson's *Master the™ Catholic High School Entrance Exams.* If you come across a word you don't know, circle it and look it up later. In addition, keep the **workbook study guides** handy to review math formulas and basic rules for spelling and grammar.
5. **Revisit problematic chapters and topics.** Use the related drills in Peterson's *TACHS and HSPT® Exams Skills and Drills Workbook* to get more practice with the question types that are giving you trouble.
6. **Take a practice test.** After you have completed all the study sections in Peterson's *Master the™ Catholic High School Entrance Exams*, take your second practice test. After studying and practicing, you should find the second practice test much easier, and you should be able to answer more questions than you could on the first practice test. Continue this review-and-test sequence for the remaining practice tests in Peterson's *Master the™ Catholic High School Entrance Exams.* If you have the time, you might find it instructive to take the practice tests for the other exams. For example, if you're required to take the TACHS, you might also test yourself with the HSPT exam.
7. **Complete all the drills in this workbook.** The extra practice will build your test-taking confidence and solidify your skills across the test subject areas.
8. **Do a final review.** During the last phase of your study, review the practice tests and the completed workbook drills. Look closely at the answer explanations to reinforce concepts and remind yourself of common mistakes to avoid.
9. **Reread the test-taking tips.** Be sure to reread the test-taking tips and techniques provided here to help you on the day of the exam. Whether it's a reminder to bring your pencils, a trick to help you keep track of the correct answer row, or help with how to make an educated guess, these proven tips and techniques, in combination with the knowledge skills you've strengthened, will get you through test day with confidence.
10. **Rest your mind.** The night before your exam, **RELAX**. You'll be prepared.

You're Well On Your Way To Success!

Again, congratulations on taking the steps to help **increase your score** on your Catholic high school entrance exam. Whether you're taking the TACHS, HSPT, CHSEE, SSAT, or any other high school entrance or placement exam, utilizing the prep material found in Peterson's *TACHS and HSPT® Exams Skills and Drills Workbook* (either as a stand-alone resource or paired with Peterson's *Master the™ Catholic High School Entrance Exams*) will help you achieve your goal.

Chapter 1
Diagnostic Test

Appendix Alert

The answer sheet for the diagnostic test is located in Appendix C, on page 511.

75 Questions—Untimed

This diagnostic test contains questions that reflect the subjects and styles of the questions presented on the TACHS and HSPT exams. Although the test is divided by subject matter, the sections are not individually timed. After taking and grading this test, refer to the scoring grid to help you determine on which areas you need to focus.

Reading

Comprehension

Directions: Read the passage carefully. Then mark one answer on your answer sheet—the answer you think is best—for each item.

Questions 1–8 refer to the following passage.

Many people do not realize that plants are alive. This mistake is due to the fact that plants are not so noisy and quick in their ways as animals, and therefore do not attract so much attention to themselves, their lives, and their <u>occupations</u>.

Line

When we look at a sunflower, surrounded by its leaves and standing still and upright in the sunlight, we do not realize at first that it is doing work; we do not connect the idea of work with such a thing of beauty, but look on it as we should on a picture or a statue. Yet all the time that plant is not only living its own life, but is doing work of a kind which animals cannot do. Its green leaves in the light are manufacturing food for the whole plant out of such simple materials that an animal could not use them at all as food. Even its beautiful flower is creating and building up the seeds which will form the sunflowers of the future. All animals directly or indirectly make use of the work done by plants in manufacturing food, for they either live on plants themselves, or eat other animals which do so.

Plants are living, and therefore require food of some kind as well as air and water in the same way, and for the same purposes as do animals. As a rule, we cannot see them breathing and eating, but that is because we do not look in the right way. In our study of plants we must first learn how to see and question them properly, and when we have done this they will show themselves to us and tell us stories of their lives which are quite as interesting as any animal stories.

—Excerpt from *The Study of Plant Life*, by M. C. Stopes

1. Which of the following would be the best title for this passage?

A. "How to Grow Sunflowers"

B. "Those Lively Plants"

C. "Plants and Animals: A Study in Contrasts"

D. "All Living Things"

2. The purpose of the flower part of a sunflower plant is to

A. generate seeds.

B. manufacture food.

C. feed animals.

D. take in oxygen.

3. According to the passage, what effect does sunlight have on plants?

A. It keeps them warm.

B. It makes them edible.

C. It nourishes them.

D. It makes plants reproduce.

4. Based on the passage, some people do not realize plants are living because

A. plants are too perfect to seem alive.

B. plants actually are not alive.

C. plants perform all of their work below the soil.

D. plants perform work that cannot be observed easily.

5. What is the author's purpose in writing this passage?

A. To convince the reader that plants are alive and hardworking

B. To prove that plants and animals are very similar

C. To show why some animals eat plants

D. To prove that people cannot live without plants

6. The word occupations, as underlined and used in this passage, most nearly means

A. employments.

B. activities.

C. games.

D. possesses.

7. After reading this passage, a person who takes its advice is most likely to

A. learn how to observe plants.

B. stop eating plants.

C. grow a garden.

D. write a book about plants.

8. In what way are plants and art alike?

A. They are both immobile.

B. They are both beautiful.

C. They are both easily observed.

D. They are both open to interpretation.

Questions 9–12 refer to the following passage.

As in the United States today, ancient Athens had courts where a wrong might be righted. Since any citizen might accuse another of a crime, the Athenian courts of law were very busy.

At a trial, both the accuser and the person accused were allowed a certain time to speak. The length of time was marked by a water clock. Free men testified under oath as they do today, but the oath of a slave was counted as worthless.

To judge a trial, a jury was chosen from the members of the assembly who had reached 30 years of age. The Athenian juries were very large, often consisting of 201, 401, 501, 1,001, or more men, depending upon the importance of the case being tried. Each juryman gave his decision by depositing a white or black stone in a box. To keep citizens from being too careless in accusing each other, there was a rule that if the person accused did not receive a certain number of negative votes, the accuser was condemned instead.

9. Which title best fits this passage?

A. "Athens and the United States"

B. "Justice in Ancient Athens"

C. "Testifying Under Oath"

D. "The Duties of Juries"

10. People in Athens were frequently on trial in a court of law because

A. they liked to serve on juries.

B. a juryman agreed to listen to both sides.

C. any person might accuse another of a crime.

D. the slaves were troublesome.

11. An Athenian was likely to avoid accusing another without a good reason because

A. the jury might condemn the accuser instead of the accused.

B. the jury might be very large.

C. cases were judged by men over 30 years old.

D. there was a limit on the time a trial could take.

12. Which statement is *true* according to the selection?

A. An accused person was denied the privilege of telling his side of the case.

B. The importance of the case determined the number of jurors.

C. A jury's decision was handed down in writing.

D. A citizen had to appear in court every few years.

Questions 13–15 refer to the following passage.

The Tribe of Goats sent a message to the Tribe of Leopards, saying, "Let us have a Wrestling Match, in an effort to see which is the stronger." Then Leopard took counsel with his Tribe, "This Tribe of Goats! I do not see that they have any strength. Let us agree to the contest; for, they can do nothing to me."

So, the Goat Tribe gathered all together; and the Leopard Tribe all together; and they met in a street of a town, to engage in the drumming and dancing and singing usually preceding such contests.

For the wrestling, they joined in thirty pairs, one from each tribe. The first pair wrestled; and the representative of the Leopards was overcome and thrown to the ground. Another pair joined; and again the Leopard champion was overcome. A third pair joined and wrestled, contesting desperately; the Leopard in shame, and the Goat in exultation. Again the Leopard was overcome.

There was, during all this time, drumming by the adherents of both parties. The Leopard drum was now beaten fiercely to encourage their side, as they had already been overcome three times in succession.

Then, on the fourth effort, the Leopard succeeded in overcoming. Again a pair fought; and Leopard overcame a second time. The sixth pair joined; and Leopard said, "Today we wrestle to settle that doubt as to which of us is the stronger."

So, pair after pair wrestled, until all of the thirty arranged pairs had contested. Of these, the Leopard Tribe were victors ten times; and the Goat Tribe twenty times.

Then the Leopard Tribe said, "We are ashamed that the report should go out among all the animals that we beat only ten times, and the Tomba [Goats] twenty times. So, we will not stay any longer here, with their and our towns near together," for they knew that their Leopard Tribe would always be angry when they should see a company of Goats passing, remembering how often they were beaten. So, they moved away into the forest distant from their hated rivals. In their cherished anger at being beaten, and to cover their shame, Leopard attacks a Goat when he meets him alone, or any other single beast known to be friendly to the Goats, *e.g.*, Oxen or Antelopes.

—Excerpt from *Where Animals Talk*, by Robert Hamill Nassau

13. Which of the following best describes the Leopard Tribe?

A. They are extremely dignified.

B. They are sore losers.

C. They are very generous.

D. They are frustrated but understanding.

14. Which literary technique is used throughout the passage?

A. allusion

B. metaphor

C. foreshadowing

D. personification

15. The main irony of this passage is that

A. leopards are usually considered to be fiercer than goats.

B. no goat has ever defeated a leopard in real life.

C. the leopards seem as though they will win at first, but the goats win in the end.

D. the goats seem angrier than the leopards, but the leopards act out of anger in the end.

Vocabulary

Directions: For questions 16–20, choose the word that means the same or about the same as the underlined word.

16. an arid climate

- **A.** moist
- **B.** uncomfortable
- **C.** dry
- **D.** sweltering

17. a consummated business deal

- **A.** troubled
- **B.** postponed
- **C.** forced
- **D.** completed

18. a tentative agreement

- **A.** assured
- **B.** beneficial
- **C.** planned
- **D.** uncertain

19. a heinous man

- **A.** attractive
- **B.** intellectual
- **C.** calculating
- **D.** evil

20. a sedentary lifestyle

- **A.** busy
- **B.** inactive
- **C.** exciting
- **D.** creative

Verbal Skills

Directions: For questions 21–35, choose the best answer and mark the corresponding letter on your answer sheet.

21. Knife is to cut as razor is to

A. shave.

B. stubble.

C. blade.

D. smooth.

22. Sand is to beach as grass is to

A. green.

B. grain.

C. lawn.

D. plant.

23. Exhausted is to energized as upset is to

A. distraught.

B. careless.

C. excited.

D. soothed.

24. Belt is to waist as tie is to

A. pants.

B. neck.

C. collar.

D. bow.

25. Liana is smarter than Merry. Merry is smarter than Darius. Darius is smarter than Liara. If the first two statements are true, the third is

A. true.

B. false.

C. uncertain.

26. Grant has black hair. Sarah has black hair. All of the kids on Grant's soccer team have black hair. If the first two statements are true, the third is

A. true.

B. false.

C. uncertain.

27. Aria has more berries than Drue. Yoko has fewer berries than Drue. Aria has more berries than Yoko. If the first two statements are true, the third is

A. true.

B. false.

C. uncertain.

28. A *superfluous* detail is

A. important.

B. long.

C. beautiful.

D. unnecessary.

29. Transient means the *opposite* of

A. permanent.

B. temporary.

C. territory.

D. sudden.

30. Insular means the *opposite* of

A. expansive.

B. private.

C. total.

D. impressive.

31. An *insipid* story is

A. fascinating.

B. complex.

C. uninteresting.

D. nonsensical.

32. Which word does not belong with the others?

A. Clarinet

B. Saxophone

C. Oboe

D. Harp

33. Which word does not belong with the others?

A. Happiness

B. Kindness

C. Sadness

D. Anger

34. Which word does not belong with the others?

A. Broccoli

B. Asparagus

C. Eggplant

D. Artichoke

35. Which word does not belong with the others?

A. Freezing

B. Snow

C. Rain

D. Sleet

Written Expression/Language

Directions: In questions 36–45, look for errors in capitalization, punctuation, spelling, and usage. Some of the questions will consist of full sentences to compare; others will provide a short piece of writing to evaluate. Choose the letter of the answer choice that contains the error and mark it on your answer sheet.

36. **A.** The screenwriter concieved a very original plot.
B. He was punished for committing an act of deceit.
C. Be sure to keep your receipt in case you need to return your purchase.
D. *No mistakes*

37. **A.** "If you want to come with us," Bea began, "just call me."
B. "When the bell rings", the teacher explained, "take your seats."
C. "With a little luck," Trey said, "I'll see you next weekend."
D. *No mistakes*

38. **A.** The puppy's hyperactivity seemed to exasperate the cat.
B. You should stretch before exercising.
C. Our first guest needs no intraductions.
D. *No mistakes*

39. **A.** My one regret about last summer
B. is that I missed seeing *Incredibles 2*, which
C. I would of seen if it had stayed in the theaters a little longer.
D. *No mistakes*

40. **A.** We watched President Barack Obama's inauguration speech in social studies class.
B. My former neighbor's name is Mr. McCree, but my new neighbor is Ms. Holoway.
C. I just got a message from my Aunt, who is coming to visit me next week.
D. *No mistakes*

41. **A.** When you see Trudy next, please told her I miss her.
B. I wanted to see her this afternoon, but
C. she is practicing for the game she will play tomorrow.
D. *No mistakes*

42. **A.** You need to bring the following items to tomorrow's test: a pencil, a piece of scrap paper, and an eraser.

B. Mom is taking a nap on the sofa; Dad is busy cooking dinner.

C. You'll have to walk your bike instead of riding it home—it has a flat tire.

D. *No mistakes*

43. **A.** Xena is hosting the party at she house

B. because the venue we wanted to rent

C. was already booked.

D. *No mistakes*

44. **A.** Either you want to join my team nor you do not.

B. Deandra plans to major in political science when she gets to college, but Yolanda wants to major in art.

C. The math test was super easy; however, the English test was rather challenging.

D. *No mistakes*

45. **A.** This Saturday I am going to see a movie called *How to Train Your Dragon.*

B. Have you read the *Lord Of The Rings* books?

C. Have you ever driven across the Golden Gate Bridge?

D. *No mistakes*

Math

Directions: For questions 46–65, chose the correct answer and mark the corresponding letter on your answer sheet.

SHOW YOUR WORK HERE

46. A robotic vacuum cleaner can vacuum an entire room in $\frac{3}{4}$ hour. A newer version can vacuum $1\frac{2}{3}$ rooms of the same size in the same amount of time. How long would it take the newer model to vacuum one such room?

A. 15 minutes

B. 27 minutes

C. 40 minutes

D. 45 minutes

47. Solve for x: $\frac{2}{3}x = -9$

A. $-\frac{29}{3}$

B. −6

C. $-\frac{27}{2}$

D. $-\frac{25}{3}$

48. The volume of a rectangular box that measures 1.5 feet thick, 5 feet long, and 30 inches wide is

A. 225 cubic feet.

B. 150 cubic feet.

C. 18.75 cubic feet.

D. 36.5 cubic feet.

SHOW YOUR WORK HERE

49. The members of a peewee baseball team sell pendants at their games to raise money for new uniforms. They pay $4 for each pendant, but then mark up the price 250% over cost. If they sell 100 pendants, how much money will they raise?

A. $400

B. $500

C. $1,000

D. $1,450

50. A contractor needs 12 paving stones to cover 3 square feet of flooring. How many are needed to cover 140 square feet?

A. 280

B. 560

C. 1,120

D. 2,240

51. Mall patrons are asked to indicate their preference of five different restaurants in the food court. The results are summarized on the following bar graph:

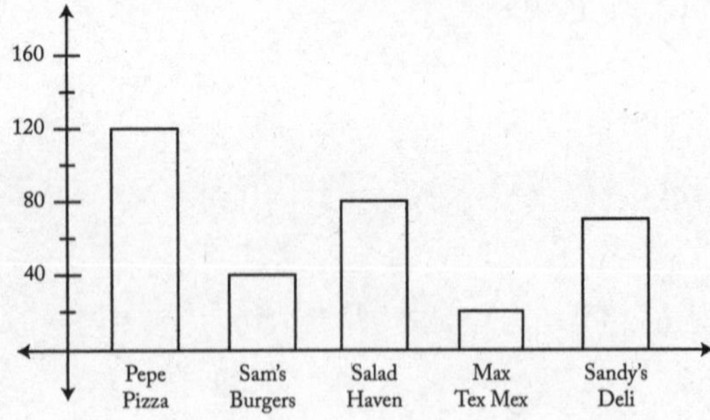

How many mall patrons answered the survey?

A. 120

B. 340

C. 400

D. 500

52. A can-labeling machine can affix labels to 300 cans every 20 seconds. How long does it take for it to affix labels to 4,500 cans?

A. 5 minutes

B. 10 minutes

C. 15 minutes

D. 20 minutes

53. The total worth of *a* 15-cent stamps, *b* 32-cent stamps, *c* 44-cent stamps, and *d* 60-cent stamps is _______ dollars.

A. $abcd$

B. $a + b + c + d$

C. $0.15a + 0.32b + 0.44c + 0.60d$

D. $(0.15 + 0.32 + 0.44 + 0.60) \cdot (a + b + c + d)$

54. Which of these points has coordinates (–2, 4)?

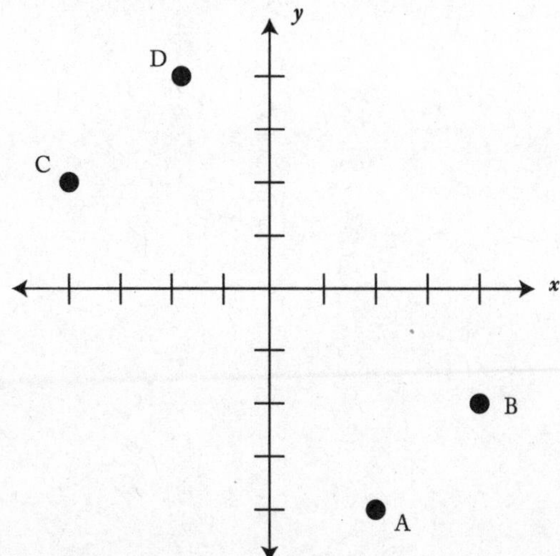

A. Point A

B. Point B

C. Point C

D. Point D

SHOW YOUR WORK HERE

Diagnostic Test

SHOW YOUR WORK HERE

55. There are two sump pumps in opposite corners of a basement. During a rainstorm, the probability of sump pump 1 triggering is 35%, and the probability that neither sump pump 1 nor sump pump 2 triggers is 41%. What is the probability that sump pump 2 will trigger?

A. 0.24

B. 0.50

C. 0.51

D. 0.65

56. Which of the following is equivalent to $2 \cdot (8-5)^2$?

A. 6

B. 18

C. 36

D. 39

57. The number of 200 m sprints the members of the tennis team complete in 15 minutes is recorded in this data set:

8, 11, 7, 7, 6, 8, 12, 5, 9, 7

What is the mean number of sprints run by this group?

A. 5

B. 7

C. 8

D. 12

SHOW YOUR WORK HERE

58. To convert from centimeters to meters, you would

A. multiply by 100.

B. multiply by 10.

C. divide by 10.

D. divide by 100.

59. In a county prone to severe weather, a meteorologist records the number of lightning strikes each day during a two-week period. The results are as follows:

Week 1	50	120	10	0	35	0	80
Week 2	40	55	0	5	40	10	0

Which of these statements is true?

A. mode < median < mean

B. mode = median = mean

C. mean = median > mode

D. mode < mean < median

60. If the area of a square is 169 square feet, what is its perimeter?

A. 13 feet

B. 52 feet

C. 104 feet

D. 338 feet

61. Which of the following numbers is prime?

A. 21

B. 51

C. 71

D. 121

SHOW YOUR WORK HERE

62. What is the approximate circumference of the circle with a diameter of 12 centimeters? (Round your answer to the nearest hundredth of a centimeter.)

A. 18.85 centimeters

B. 37.70 centimeters

C. 75.40 centimeters

D. 113.10 centimeters

63. Solve for c: $(5c - 1)(4c + 7) = 0$

A. $c = \frac{1}{5}$ and $c = -\frac{7}{4}$

B. $c = -\frac{1}{5}$ and $c = \frac{7}{4}$

C. $c = 5$ and $c = -\frac{4}{7}$

D. $c = -5$ and $c = \frac{4}{7}$

64. Compute:

	3 yards, 1 foot, 9 inches
+	6 feet, 5 inches

A. 3 yards, 1 foot, 5 inches

B. 5 yards, 2 feet

C. 5 yards, 2 feet, 2 inches

D. 4 yards, 1 foot, 2 inches

65. If $a = \frac{2}{3}$ and $b = \frac{3}{4}$, determine the value of $\frac{(b-a)^2}{a \cdot b}$.

A. 2

B. $\frac{1}{12}$

C. $\frac{1}{288}$

D. $\frac{1}{72}$

Quantitative Skills

Directions: For questions 66–75, select the correct answer and mark the corresponding letter on your answer sheet.

SHOW YOUR WORK HERE

66. Examine A, B, and C and choose the best answer.

- **A.** $4 \cdot (5-2)^2$
- **B.** $4^2 \cdot 3^2$
- **C.** 36

A. A < B < C

B. A < C < B

C. A = B and C < B

D. A = C and C < B

67. Consider the following series. What should the next two terms be?

$$\frac{2}{A}, \frac{D}{4}, \frac{8}{G}, \_\_\_, \_\_\_, \ldots$$

A. $\frac{16}{I}, \frac{L}{32}$

B. $\frac{I}{16}, \frac{32}{L}$

C. $\frac{16}{J}, \frac{M}{32}$

D. $\frac{J}{16}, \frac{32}{M}$

68. Eighty percent of what number is the product of 35 and 0.4?

A. 14

B. 17.5

C. 28

D. 32.5

SHOW YOUR WORK HERE

69. Examine A, B, and C, and choose the best answer.

A. 2^5

B. 5^2

C. $2 \cdot 5$

A. A = B = C

B. C < B < A

C. C < A < B

D. B = C and A < B

70. Consider the following diagram:

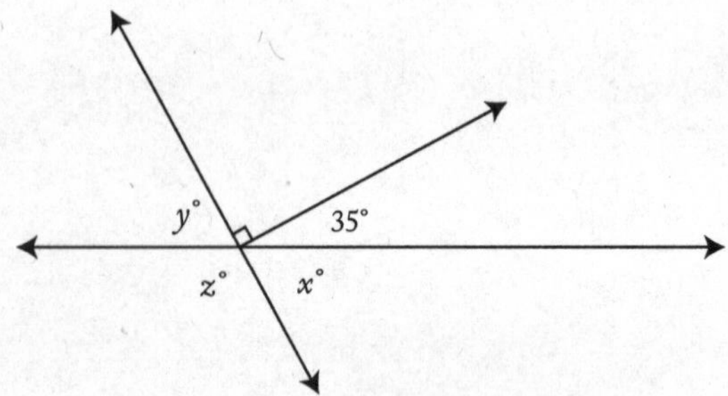

Choose the best answer.

A. $y + z = 90$

B. $x = y$

C. $x = 65$

D. $x + y + z = 270$

71. Consider the following series. What term should fill in the blank?

8, 17, 26, _____, 44, …

A. 35

B. 37

C. 39

D. 41

Ability

Directions: For question 72, look at the top row to see how a square piece of paper is folded and where holes are punched into it. Then look at the bottom row and choose which answer choice shows how the paper will look when it is completely unfolded.

72.

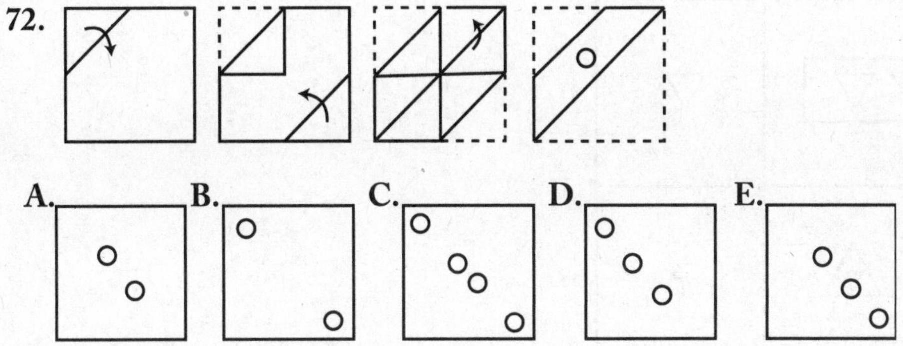

Directions: In questions 73 and 74, the first three figures are alike in certain ways. Choose the answer choice that corresponds to the first three figures.

73.

74.

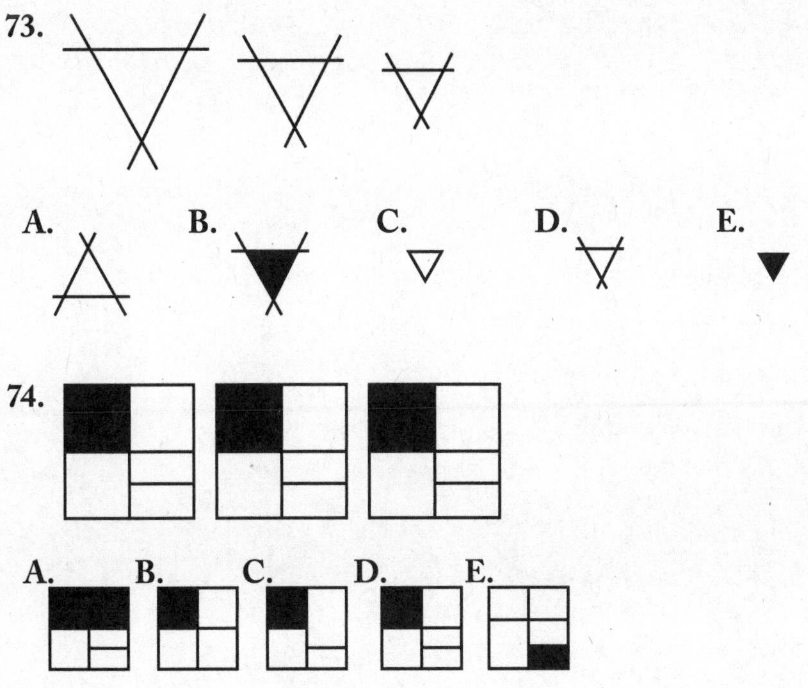

Directions: For question 75, find the figure that completes the puzzle.

75.

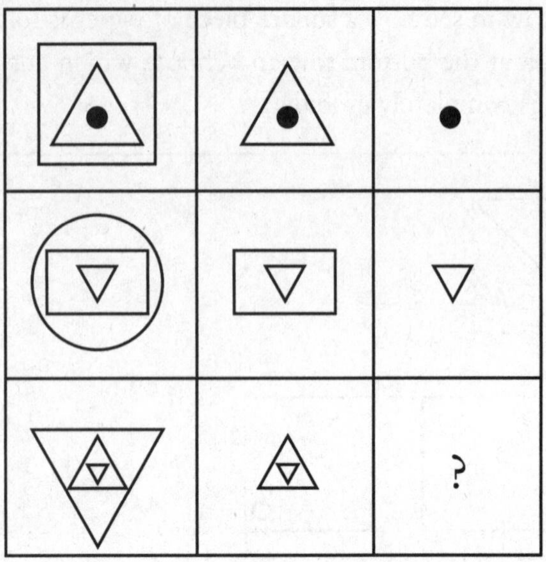

?

A. B. C.  D.  E.

Answer Key and Explanations

1. B	16. C	31. C	46. B	61. C
2. A	17. D	32. D	47. C	62. B
3. C	18. D	33. B	48. C	63. A
4. D	19. D	34. C	49. C	64. C
5. A	20. B	35. A	50. B	65. D
6. B	21. A	36. A	51. B	66. D
7. A	22. C	37. B	52. A	67. D
8. B	23. D	38. C	53. C	68. B
9. B	24. B	39. C	54. D	69. B
10. C	25. B	40. C	55. A	70. B
11. A	26. C	41. A	56. B	71. A
12. B	27. A	42. D	57. C	72. C
13. B	28. D	43. A	58. D	73. D
14. D	29. A	44. A	59. A	74. D
15. A	30. A	45. B	60. B	75. A

1. **The correct answer is B.** The focus of this passage is on how plants are living things that perform various functions even though most people do not notice. Therefore, "Those Lively Plants" would be an appropriate title for this passage. While the passage does use sunflowers as an example of lively plants, it does not provide instructions for growing sunflowers, so choice A would not be the best title. The passage draws both comparisons and contrasts between plants and animals, so choice C is a misleading title. The passage specifically focuses on plants, but choice D implies that it focuses on a variety of living things, which is inaccurate.

2. **The correct answer is A.** According to the passage, "its beautiful flower is creating and building up the seeds which will form the sunflowers of the future." The leaves are responsible for manufacturing food (choice B). While the passage suggests that animals eat plants, it does not specifically state that they eat the flowers of sunflower plants, nor does it imply that being eaten is the purpose of the flowers, so choice C is not the best answer. The passage also states that flowers breathe, but it does not suggest that sunflowers take in oxygen through their flowers, so choice D is incorrect.

3. **The correct answer is C.** The passage suggests that plants convert light into food, so sunlight nourishes them. While sunlight may keep plants warm (choice A) that fact is not really suggested in the passage. While animals eat plants, the passage never implies that light is what makes plants edible (choice B). Seeds are the means by which plants reproduce, so choice D is incorrect.

4. **The correct answer is D.** The author compares plants to nonliving artwork such as pictures and statues, which do not move, and describes how plants are usually observed "standing still." The author also explains that plants are neither noisy nor "quick in their ways." Based on this information, the reader can infer that some people do not realize plants are living because the work those plants perform cannot be observed easily. While the author comments on the beauty of plants while discussing how some people do not realize that plants are alive, he does not imply that it is the plants' perfection (choice A) that leads these people to that opinion. Choice B contradicts the main discussion about how plants are alive. The author suggests that the leaves and flowers of plants, which are above, not below, the soil (choice C), do perform work.

5. **The correct answer is A.** The author's main intent is convincing the reader that plants are alive and hardworking and does so with numerous examples of how they function. While the author does imply some similarities between plants and animals (choice B), proving these similarities is not the purpose of the passage as a whole. Choice C refers to only one detail in the passage that is too minor to capture the main purpose of the passage as a whole. Choice D is true in itself, but the author does not discuss how people benefit from plants much, so it is not the best answer.

6. **The correct answer is B.** While each answer choice can be used as a synonym for *occupations*, choice B makes the most sense because the author describes the various activities of plants throughout the passage. A plant does perform work, but it cannot really be employed as a human is, so choice A is not the best answer. A plant neither plays games (choice C) nor possesses (choice D) things.

7. **The correct answer is A.** At the end of the passage (lines 16–19), the author explains the importance of beginning a study of plants by learning "how to see and question them properly," so choice A is the best answer. The author is not arguing that people should stop eating plants (choice B). The purpose of this passage is to understand plants; it does not provide instructions for growing a garden (choice C), and it does not encourage writing a book about plants (choice D) either.

8. **The correct answer is B.** In lines 5–7 in the second paragraph, the author suggests that people view plants as they view art because both are so beautiful. However, the author contradicts the notion that plants are immobile (choice A) by discussing how hard they work. The author also explains that it is not easy to observe how plants perform their functions, so choice C is not the best answer. While art may be open to interpretation, there is nothing in the passage that suggests plants are also open to interpretation, so choice D is not a strong answer.

9. **The correct answer is B.** Remember that a "best title" question is asking you to identify the main idea of a passage. This passage provides an overview about court practices—how justice was carried out—in ancient Athens. Although a comparison between the courts of the United States and ancient Athens serves as an introduction to the passage, this comparison goes no further, so choice A is not the best fit. The passage briefly mentions the procedure for testifying under oath (choice C) and the process of how juries came to a verdict (choice D), but these topics are details that are included to support the main idea.

10. **The correct answer is C.** Line 2 of the passage (lines 10–13) states that any citizen might accuse another of a crime, which kept the Athenian courts very busy. Members of the juries were selected from the assembly, but the passage does not state that it was something they enjoyed (choice A). The passage does not address whether a juryman would be an impartial listener (choice B), and it doesn't say anything about the behavior of slaves, only that their oaths were worthless in the court, so D is not the best answer.

11. **The correct answer is A.** The last sentence of the passage states that a rule existed that if the person accused did not receive a certain number of negative votes from the jury, the accuser was condemned instead. This rule was in place to keep citizens from being too careless in accusing each other. The potential size of the jury (choice B), age of the jury members (choice C), and time limits for testifying (choice D) were not factors in a citizen's caution when taking another citizen to court.

12. **The correct answer is B.** Of the statements given, only one can be supported in the passage: the importance of a case determined the number of jurors. This information is found in lines 8 and 9 in the third paragraph. The passage states that both the accuser and the accused were given an opportunity to speak and that jury verdicts were determined by counting black and white stones placed in a box, so both choices A and C contradict what's in the passage. The passage does not mention anything about the number of times a citizen had to appear in court (choice D).

13. **The correct answer is B.** The Leopard Tribe is so angry about losing the wrestling matches with the Goat Tribe that, in addition to relocating to the forest to avoid seeing the Goats, they made a practice of attacking lone goats and any other single beast that the Leopards knew to be friendly to the Goats. That they did so with "cherished anger" implies that they were very sore losers. This fact also somewhat contradicts the idea that they are extremely dignified (choice A). There is no evidence that supports that they are generous (choice C). While the Leopard Tribe is clearly frustrated by their loss to the Goat Tribe, they are far from understanding (choice D).

14. **The correct answer is D.** Personification is a figure of speech used when a writer describes something that is not human as having human character traits. Throughout this passage, the animals are described as feeling human emotions, such as desperation, exultation, shame, and anger. An allusion (choice A) refers to another work, but that does not happen in this passage. A metaphor (choice B) makes a comparison between two unlike things, but that does not occur in this passage. Foreshadowing (choice C) signals future events before they occur, but that technique is not used in this passage.

15. **The correct answer is A.** People generally think of carnivorous leopards as being fiercer than herbivorous goats, but in this passage, the goats are ultimately better fighters than the leopards. Choice B is an extreme and impossible-to-prove assumption, and such answer choices are best avoided. The Leopard Tribe loses the first three wrestling matches, so choice C is incorrect. The leopards seem angrier than the goats throughout the passage, so choice D is incorrect as well.

16. **The correct answer is C.** *Dry* is a synonym for *arid.* Other synonyms are *waterless* and *desertlike.*

17. **The correct answer is D.** *Completed* is a synonym for *consummated.* Other synonyms are *finalized*, *finished*, and *accomplished.*

18. **The correct answer is D.** *Uncertain* is a synonym for *tentative.* Other synonyms are *conditional* and *dependent.*

19. **The correct answer is D.** *Evil* is a synonym for *heinous*. Other synonyms are *monstrous* and *horrifying*.

20. **The correct answer is B.** *Inactive* is a synonym for *sedentary*. Other synonyms are *stationary* and *idle*.

21. **The correct answer is A.** This analogy is an object-purpose relationship. The purpose of a knife is to cut. The purpose of a razor is to shave.

22. **The correct answer is C.** This analogy is a part-whole relationship. Sand is part of a beach. Grass is part of a lawn.

23. **The correct answer is D.** This analogy is an antonym relationship. *Exhausted* is the opposite of *energized*. *Upset* is the opposite of *soothed*.

24. **The correct answer is B.** This analogy is an association relationship. A belt is fastened around one's waist. A tie is fastened around one's neck.

25. **The correct answer is B.** If Liana is taller than Merry, and she is taller than Darius, then Darius can't be taller than Liana. Therefore, the third statement is false.

26. **The correct answer is C.** We do not know if Grant and Sarah are on the same soccer team, or anything about the other children on Grant's team, so there is no way to know if the final statement is true.

27. **The correct answer is A.** Yoko has the fewest berries, so Aria must have more berries than she does. Therefore, the third statement is true.

28. **The correct answer is D.** A superfluous detail is unnecessary.

29. **The correct answer is A.** *Transient* means "passing quickly"; the opposite is *permanent*.

30. **The correct answer is A.** *Insular* means "narrow"; the opposite is *expansive*.

31. **The correct answer is C.** An insipid story is uninteresting.

32. **The correct answer is D.** A clarinet, a saxophone, and an oboe are all woodwind instruments. A harp is a stringed instrument.

33. **The correct answer is B.** Happiness, sadness, and anger are all emotions. Kindness is a personality quality.

34. **The correct answer is C.** Broccoli, asparagus, and artichokes are all green vegetables. An eggplant is not green; it is purple.

35. **The correct answer is A.** Snow, rain, and sleet are forms of precipitation. Freezing is a description of temperature.

36. **The correct answer is A.** The correct spelling is *conceived.*

37. **The correct answer is B.** The comma following *rings* belongs within the quotation marks.

38. **The correct answer is C.** The correct spelling is *introductions.*

39. **The correct answer is C.** This sentence contains a word choice error. It uses the preposition *of* as a helping verb incorrectly. It should use *have*, not *of.*

40. **The correct answer is C.** The word *aunt* should be capitalized only if it is the first word of a sentence, or if it is used as a title before a proper name, such as *Aunt Eunice.* Since this sentence does not use *aunt* in either of those ways, *aunt* should not be capitalized.

41. **The correct answer is A.** In this complex sentence, the introductory phrase describes something that will happen in the future. However, in the second clause, the verb *told* is in the past tense. It should have been *tell* instead of *told.*

42. **The correct answer is D.** There are no errors in these sentences.

43. **The correct answer is A.** The house belongs to Xena, so the sentence requires the possessive form of the pronoun *she*, which is *her.*

44. **The correct answer is A.** There is no such thing as an *either/nor* construction. This sentence should use the conjunction *or* instead of *nor.*

45. **The correct answer is B.** Prepositions such as *of* and articles such as *the* should not be capitalized in the middle of titles such as *Lord of the Rings.*

46. The correct answer is B. Let x be the time it takes (in hours) for the newer model to vacuum one room. Set up the proportion:

$$\frac{\frac{3}{4}\text{ hour}}{1\frac{2}{3}\text{ rooms}} = \frac{x\text{ hour}}{1\text{ room}}$$

$$\frac{3}{4} = \left(1\frac{2}{3}\right)x$$

$$x = \frac{\frac{3}{4}}{\frac{5}{3}} = \frac{3}{4} \cdot \frac{3}{5} = \frac{9}{20}\text{ hour}$$

Since there are 60 minutes in one hour, this is equivalent to $\frac{9}{20} \cdot 60$ minutes = 27 minutes.

47. The correct answer is C. Divide both sides of the equation by $\frac{2}{3}$, which is equivalent to multiplying by $\frac{3}{2}$, to get $x = (-9) \cdot \frac{3}{2} = -\frac{27}{2}$.

48. The correct answer is C. First, make sure that all units are the same. To this end, convert 30 inches to feet: 30 inches $\cdot \frac{1\text{ foot}}{12\text{ inches}} = 2.5$ feet. The volume is $(1.5)\cdot(5)\cdot(2.5) = 18.75$ cubic feet.

49. The correct answer is C. 250% of \$4 = 2.5(\$4) = \$10, so, they sell a pendant for \$4 + \$10 = \$14. If they sell 100 pendants, they collect 100(\$14) = \$1,400. The cost for making 100 pendants is 100(\$4) = \$400. The amount they collect for their new uniforms is \$1,400 – \$400 = \$1,000.

50. The correct answer is B. Let x be the number of paving stones needed. Set up and solve the following proportion:

$$\frac{12\text{ paving stones}}{3\text{ square feet of flooring}} = \frac{x\text{ paving stones}}{140\text{ square feet of flooring}}$$

$$3x = 12(140)$$

$$x = \frac{12(140)}{3}$$

$$x = 560$$

51. The correct answer is B. Add the heights of all five bars to get 340.

52. The correct answer is A. The can labeling machine can affix 300(3) = 900 labels to cans every minute. So the number of minutes it takes to label 4,500 cans is $\frac{4,500}{900} = 5$ minutes.

Answers Diagnostic Test

53. The correct answer is C. The value of *a* 15-cent stamps is $0.15a$, *b* 32-cent stamps is $0.32b$, *c* 44-cent stamps is $0.44c$, and *d* 60-cent stamps is $0.60d$. The total worth is $(0.15a + 0.32b + 0.44c + 0.60d)$ dollars.

54. The correct answer is D. For the point (–2, 4) the *x*-value is –2 and the *y*-value is 4. This places the location of this point at D.

55. The correct answer is A. The probability that sump pump 2 triggers is $1 - (0.35 + 0.41) = 1 - 0.76 = 0.24$.

56. The correct answer is B. Use the order of operations to compute:

$$2 \cdot (8-5)^2 = 2 \cdot (3)^2 = 2 \cdot 9 = 18$$

57. The correct answer is C. Remember, the mean is also known as the average. Add the 10 numbers and divide the sum by 10 to get 8.

58. The correct answer is D. Since 1 meter is equal to 100 centimeters, to convert from centimeters to meters, you must divide by 100.

59. The correct answer is A. Arrange the data in increasing order:

0, 0, 0, 0, 5, 10, 10, 35, 40, 40, 50, 55, 80, 120

The mode is 0 since it occurs more often than any other value in the data set. The median is the average of the 7th and 8th values, so $\frac{10+35}{2} = 22.5$. The mean is the average of all 14 data values (obtained by adding all the data values and dividing the sum by 14), which yields approximately 31.8. So, mode < median < mean.

60. The correct answer is B. The area of a square equals s^2, where *s* is the length of a side.

$$s^2 = 169$$

$$s = 13 \text{ feet}$$

Hence, the perimeter is 4(13) = 52 feet.

61. The correct answer is C. 21 = 3(7), 51 = 3(17), and 121 = 11(11). The only number left is 71, which has only 1 and 71 as its factors, making it a prime number.

62. The correct answer is B. The radius of the circle is 6 centimeters. Its circumference is $2\pi \cdot 6 = 12\pi \approx 37.70$ centimeters.

63. **The correct answer is A.** Set each factor equal to zero and solve for c: $5c - 1 = 0$ when $c = \frac{1}{5}$ and $4c + 7 = 0$ when $c = -\frac{7}{4}$.

64. **The correct answer is C.** Adding like units initially gives 3 yards, 7 feet, 14 inches. Since 1 foot equals 12 inches, this is equivalent to 3 yards, 8 feet, 2 inches. Then, since 1 yard equals 3 feet, this is equivalent to 5 yards, 2 feet, 2 inches.

65. **The correct answer is D.** Substitute the given values of a and b into the expression and simplify using the order of operations:

$$\frac{(b-a)^2}{a \bullet b} = \frac{\left(\frac{3}{4} - \frac{2}{3}\right)^2}{\frac{2}{3} \bullet \frac{3}{4}} = \frac{\left(\frac{3(3) - 2(4)}{12}\right)^2}{\frac{1}{2}} = \frac{\left(\frac{1}{12}\right)^2}{\frac{1}{2}} = \frac{\frac{1}{144}}{\frac{1}{2}} = \frac{1}{72}$$

66. **The correct answer is D.** Simplify the expressions as follows:

A: $4 \bullet (5-2)^2 = 4 \bullet 3^2 = 4 \bullet 9 = 36$
B: $4^2 \bullet 3^2 = 16 \bullet 9 = 144$
C: 36

A = C and C < B.

67. **The correct answer is D.** The pattern is to increase the number by a power of 2 for each term and to skip two letters. The position of the number and the letter in the fraction oscillates every term. So, the next two terms should be $\frac{J}{16}, \frac{32}{M}$.

68. **The correct answer is B.** Let x be the number. Since 80% = 0.80, x satisfies the equation $0.80x = 35(0.4)$. Solve for x:

$$\begin{aligned} 0.80x &= 35(0.4) \\ 0.80x &= 14 \\ x &= \frac{14}{0.80} \\ x &= 17.5 \end{aligned}$$

69. **The correct answer is B.** Note that $2^5 = (2)(2)(2)(2)(2) = 32$, and $5^2 = (5)(5) = 25$, and $2 \bullet 5 = 10$, so C < B < A.

70. **The correct answer is B.** Vertical angles are congruent, so x must equal y.

71. **The correct answer is A.** The pattern is to add 9 to a number in the series to get the next number. Adding 9 to 26 yields 35.

72. **The correct answer is C.** The holes are punched in the locations "second row, second column" and "third row, third column" in the 4 × 4 grid of holes. Since the corners are bent over, they too are punched, creating holes in the top left and bottom right corners.

73. **The correct answer is D.** The figures are comprised of unshaded triangles with edges that extend past their vertices, and the figures get smaller from left to right. The next figure in the sequence would be a smaller version of the third one in the row, which is choice D.

74. **The correct answer is D.** The three figures are identical. The figure that matches this sequence should be an exact copy of them.

75. **The correct answer is A.** The rule for each row is to remove the outermost part of the previous figure. To determine the missing figure, remove the outer triangle from the figure in the center of the bottom row, leaving just the small inverted triangle. To solve the puzzle using the rule of the columns, each figure in each column has the same number of components—three in the first column, two in the second, and one in the third. Only choice A follows the rules for both the rows and columns.

Diagnostic Test Scoring Grid

Although your actual exam scores will not be reported as percentages, it might be helpful to convert your test scores to percentages so that you can see at a glance where your strengths and weaknesses lie.

Subject	Number Correct	÷ Number of Questions	× 100 = __%
Reading			
Comprehension		÷ 15	× 100 = ___%
Vocabulary		÷ 5	× 100 = ___%
TOTAL		÷ 20	× 100 = ___%
Verbal Skills			
Analogy		÷ 4	× 100 = ___%
Verbal Logic		÷ 3	× 100 = ___%
Synonym/Antonym		÷ 4	× 100 = ___%
Verbal Classification		÷ 4	× 100 = ___%
TOTAL		÷ 15	× 100 = ___%
Written Expression			
Spelling		÷ 2	× 100 = ___%
Punctuation		÷ 2	× 100 = ___%
Capitalization		÷ 2	× 100 = ___%
Usage & Composition		÷ 4	× 100 = ___%
TOTAL		÷ 10	× 100 = ___%
Math			
Number Sense		÷ 6	× 100 = ___%
Algebra		÷ 4	× 100 = ___%
Geometry		÷ 4	× 100 = ___%
Measurement		÷ 3	× 100 = ___%
Data Analysis/Statistics		÷ 3	× 100 = ___%
TOTAL		÷ 20	× 100 = ___%

Subject	Number Correct	÷ Number of Questions	× 100 = ___%
Quantitative Skills/Ability			
Non-geometric Comparison		÷ 2	× 100 = ___%
Sequence		÷ 2	× 100 = ___%
Reasoning		÷ 1	× 100 = ___%
Geometric Comparison		÷ 1	× 100 = ___%
Paper Folding		÷ 1	× 100 = ___%
Figure Classification		÷ 2	× 100 = ___%
Figure Matrices		÷ 1	× 100 = ___%
TOTAL		÷ 10	× 100 = ___%
GRAND TOTAL		÷ 75	× 100 = ___%

Chapter 2
Reading

Introduction to Reading Questions

The Reading section is an important part of both the TACHS and the HSPT because reading is such a vital part of everyday life. The Reading section on the HSPT includes both reading comprehension and stand-alone vocabulary questions.

In the TACHS **Reading** or HSPT exam **Reading–Comprehension** sections, you will be reading both literary (fiction and nonfiction) and informational (nonfiction) texts. Informational texts may involve topics related to science, social studies, history, or humanities and the arts.

Although the TACHS passages tend to be shorter and its questions focus more on main idea and detail questions than those on the HSPT exam, you will not merely be expected to remember details from the reading passages on either test. You will also have to think deeply about the texts to consider what is not directly stated in them.

Informational and literary texts each come with their own question types.

The questions that accompany informational texts may assess your ability to exercise these reading skills:

- Identify details and events explicitly stated in a passage
- Identify the main idea of a passage
- Identify a title for a passage that best reflects that passage's main idea
- Understand the purpose of a passage
- Draw conclusions and make inferences based on explicitly stated evidence
- Compare and contrast different elements in a passage
- Understand cause-and-effect relationships between details in a passage
- Identify reasons why events occurred
- Make thoughtful predictions about what will happen beyond the conclusion of a passage
- Identify potentially unfamiliar vocabulary words based on how they are used within the context of a passage

The questions that accompany literary texts may require you to identify the following:

- Details and events explicitly stated in a passage
- The main plot, important themes, and central setting of a passages
- The personality traits of characters
- The point of view and essential style of a passage
- The author's use of literary techniques such as flashback (the temporary shift to the past), foreshadowing (the suggestion of events that have not occurred yet), paradox (ideas that are seemingly illogical but true), repetition (the repetition of ideas, language, and other elements), and satire (the use of humorous exaggeration or ridicule to make a philosophical point)
- The author's use of irony (the contrast between how things seem and how they really are), personification (the application of human traits to animals and objects), and metaphor (the suggestion that two unlike things are similar)
- The author's use of imagery (the use of descriptive language to appeal to the reader's senses) and symbolism (the representation of abstract ideas)

The stand-alone vocabulary questions in the HSPT exam **Reading–Vocabulary** section are not associated with any passages and will test your ability to identify complex, potentially unfamiliar words based on their use in brief phrases.

Reading Question Preview

Now we'll walk you through examples of both reading comprehension and vocabulary questions.

Take a look at the following excerpt from a nonfiction piece of writing.

> Science is knowledge; it is what we know. But mere knowledge is not science. For a bit of knowledge to become a part of science, its relation to other bits of knowledge must be found. In botany, for example, bits of knowledge about plants do not make a science of botany. To have a science of botany, we must not only know about leaves, roots, flowers, seeds, etc., but we must know the relations of these parts and of all the parts of a plant to one another. In other words, in science, we must not only *know*, we must not only have *knowledge*, but we must know the significance of the knowledge, must know its *meaning*. This is only another way of saying that we must have knowledge and know its relation to other knowledge.
>
> —Excerpt from *The Science of Human Nature*, by William Henry Pyle

Which of the following would be the best title for this passage?

A. "Science is Knowledge"

B. "Understanding Relationships: The Key to Science"

C. "Studying the Science of Botany"

D. "Why We All Must Have Knowledge"

The correct answer is B. When you encounter questions that require you to select a title for an informational passage such as this one, you are essentially being asked to identify the passage's main idea and express that main idea as a title. What is this passage's main idea? It is mainly that important relationships between bits of knowledge are crucial if that knowledge is to be scientific. Does choice A reflect that main idea? While it does reflect the very first fact in this passage, it does not say anything about relationships, so it may not be the very best answer. Don't select this choice just yet. How about choice B? It does refer to the scientific importance of understanding relationships, so it is certainly a better answer than choice A. Choice C implies that the passage is mainly about botany, which is mentioned only briefly as part of an example in the passage. Botany is not central enough to the main idea for choice C to be an adequate title for the passage. Eliminate it. Choice D refers to neither science nor relationships. Eliminate this one too. That leaves choice B as the best title and the best answer.

Now let's look at an excerpt from a work of fiction.

One morning, when Gregor Samsa woke from troubled dreams, he found himself transformed in his bed into a horrible vermin. He lay on his armour-like back, and if he lifted his head a little he could see his brown belly, slightly domed and divided by arches into stiff sections. The bedding was hardly able to cover it and seemed ready to slide off any moment. His many legs, pitifully thin compared with the size of the rest of him, waved about helplessly as he looked.

"What's happened to me?" he thought. It wasn't a dream. His room, a proper human room although a little too small, lay peacefully between its four familiar walls. A collection of textile samples lay spread out on the table—Samsa was a traveling salesman—and above it there hung a picture that he had recently cut out of an illustrated magazine and housed in a nice, gilded frame. It showed a lady fitted out with a fur hat and fur boa who sat upright, raising a heavy fur muff that covered the whole of her lower arm towards the viewer.

—Excerpt from *Metamorphosis*, by Franz Kafka

Which of the following best describes Gregor Samsa?

A. Angry

B. Confused

C. Bemused

D. Depressed

The correct answer is B. The key to answering this question is considering Gregor Samsa's situation and his reaction to it. What has happened to Gregor in this literary passage? He has transformed into a "vermin"—an insect. How does he react? He says, "What's happened to me?" His reaction is sufficient evidence that he is confused by his bizarre situation, so choice B seems like the best answer, but let's examine the other answer choices before making our final selection. Gregor certainly would be right to be angry to discover that he has been transformed into a giant insect, but he does not behave in an angry manner in this passage. All answers must be based on evidence rather than assumptions, and there simply is no evidence to support choice A. *Bemused* (choice C) and *depressed* (choice D) also describe appropriate reactions to this strange turn of events, but they similarly lack evidence in the text. Therefore, you can eliminate choices A, C, and D and select *confused* (choice B) with confidence.

Now, let's look at an HSPT-style vocabulary question.

a <u>florid</u> design

A. plain

B. sleepy

C. simple

D. fancy

The correct answer is D. Have you ever heard the word *florid* before? Do you know its meaning? Don't worry if you are not familiar with it, because there are still ways to decode it. Think about the word. Does it remind you of any other words? How about *floral*, which refers to flowers? *Florid* and *floral* do sound as though they derive from the same root word. Flowers are pretty fancy, so maybe *florid* means "fancy" (choice D). Let's check out the other answer choices. Choice A is *plain*, which is the opposite of *fancy.* A design certainly can be plain, so this answer choice may make sense. However, if we zip down to the word *simple* (choice C), you may realize that *simple* essentially has the same meaning as *plain*, and synonyms tend to cancel each other out in vocabulary questions. Go ahead and eliminate choices A and C. So how about choice B? Can a design be sleepy? Not really. Eliminate that one too and select choice D. It's the correct answer.

The Reading sections make up a large portion of the of the TACHS and HSPT exams, and scoring well on them will go a long way toward earning a competitive score on your entrance exam, so we've included two sets of drills in this workbook. There are no time limits on the drills, so take your time and familiarize yourself with the structure of the questions as they relate to the different texts. That way, when you face the time limit on test day, you will know what to look for as you read and how to quickly recognize or methodically eliminate incorrect answer choices.

Appendix Alert

If you're taking the HSPT exam, be especially sure to check out Appendixes A and B starting on page 455 to boost your vocabulary and get familiar with synonyms and antonyms. We've compiled two comprehensive resources for you—a list of vocabulary words and their meanings, and a list of antonyms and synonyms. These lists will help you get through any vocabulary questions you will encounter on both the HSPT and TACHS entrance exams on test day.

You will also find answer sheets for these drills in Appendix C, starting on page 512.

Reading–Comprehension Drill 1

75 Questions

Directions: Read each passage carefully. Then mark one answer on your answer sheet—the answer you think is best—for each item.

Questions 1–4 refer to the following passage.

The peopling of the Northwest Territory by companies from the eastern states, such as the Ohio Company under the leadership of Reverend Manasseh Cutler of Ipswich, Massachusetts, furnishes us with many interesting historical tales.

The first towns to be established were Marietta, Zanesville, Chillocothe, and Cincinnati. After the Ohio Company came the Connecticut Company, which secured all the territory bordering Lake Erie save a small portion known as fire lands and another portion known as Congress lands. The land taken up by the Connecticut people was called the Western Reserve and was settled almost entirely by New England people. The remainder of the state of Ohio was settled by Virginians and Pennsylvanians. Because the British controlled Lakes Ontario and Erie, the Massachusetts and Connecticut people made their journey into the Western Reserve through the southern part of the state. General Moses Cleaveland, the agent for the Connecticut Land Company, led a body of surveyors to the tract, proceeding by way of Lake Ontario. He quieted the Indian claims to the eastern portion of the reserve by giving them five hundred pounds, two heads of cattle, and one hundred gallons of whiskey. Landing at the mouth of the Conneaut River, General Moses Cleaveland and his party of fifty, including two women, celebrated Independence Day, 1796, with a feast of pork and beans with bread. A little later, a village was established at the mouth of the Cuyahoga River and was given the name of Cleaveland in honor of the agent of the company. It is related that the name was afterward shortened to Cleveland by one of the early editors because he could not get so many letters into the heading of his newspaper.

1. Reverend Manasseh Cutler
   - **A.** led the Ohio Company.
   - **B.** owned the Western Reserve.
   - **C.** led the Connecticut Land Company.
   - **D.** settled the Congress lands.

2. The title that best expresses the main idea of this selection is
   - **A.** "Control of the Great Lake Region."
   - **B.** "The Accomplishments of Reverend Manasseh Cutler."
   - **C.** "The Naming of Cleveland, Ohio."
   - **D.** "The Settling of the Northwest Territory."

3. The word related, as underlined and used in the passage, most nearly means
   - **A.** associated with.
   - **B.** rumored.
   - **C.** reported.
   - **D.** thought.

4. The selection suggests that General Cleaveland at first found the Indians to be
   - **A.** extremely noisy people.
   - **B.** hostile to his party of strangers.
   - **C.** starving.
   - **D.** eager to work with him.

Questions 5–9 refer to the following passage.

"There are many things from which I might have derived good, by which I have not profited, I dare say, Christmas among the rest. But I am sure I have always thought of Christmastime, when it has come round—apart from the veneration due to its sacred origin, if anything belonging to it *can* be apart from that—as a good time; a kind, forgiving, charitable, pleasant time; the only time I know of, in the long calendar of the year, when men and women seem by one consent to open their shut-up hearts freely and to think of people below them as if they really were fellow travelers to the grave, and not another race of creatures bound on other journeys. And therefore, Uncle, though it has never put a scrap of gold or silver in my pocket, I believe that it *has* done me good, and *will* do me good; and I say, God bless it!" The clerk in the tank involuntarily applauded.

"Let me hear another sound from *you*," said Scrooge, "and you'll keep your Christmas by losing your situation! You're quite a powerful speaker, sir," he added, turning to his nephew. "I wonder you don't go into Parliament."

—From *A Christmas Carol*, by Charles Dickens

5. The word veneration, as underlined and used in the passage, most nearly means

A. worship.

B. disapproval.

C. agreement.

D. love.

6. The first speaker

A. is a very religious person.

B. enjoys and celebrates Christmas.

C. is defending Christmas.

D. has been fired by Scrooge.

7. The first speaker believes that Christmas

A. is a pleasant nuisance.

B. brings out the best in people.

C. has been separated from its religious origin.

D. could be a profitable time of year.

8. The words by one consent, as underlined and used in the passage, most nearly means

A. affirmatively.

B. contractually.

C. partially.

D. unanimously.

9. Scrooge probably is angry with

A. the speaker and the clerk.

B. only the speaker.

C. only the clerk.

D. people who celebrate Christmas.

Questions 10–14 refer to the following passage.

When an art form—any art form—becomes widespread, it usually becomes the subject of scholarly study. Scholars examine the art form to understand its roots and its history. The art form of hip-hop music is no exception.

Author John Richardson discusses how hip-hop has continued as a music form, even though it has been mass-produced. The style first emerged to reflect the views of a specific minority group. It was a type of "underground" music, as Richardson states. It followed a similar path as did punk rock and other underground music styles.

First, it was supported by major corporations who realized they could make a great profit from it. Then, hip-hop became mainstream. Next, it became standardized and mass-produced. Through this process, hip-hop lost some of its subtle qualities. It also lost some of its originality.

Normally, in a path such as this, underground forms of music would lose their uniqueness as well, states Richardson. Eventually, the music form would lose its identity entirely. It would fall out of favor as a popular style and would disappear. This never happened to hip-hop, however. It has continued to maintain its emphasis on the underground, focusing on "the street" and on "keeping it real."

10. When does an art form usually become the subject of scholarly study?

A. When it begins to generate profits

B. When it becomes widespread

C. When it is one century old

D. When it disappears from public view

11. According to the passage, which of the following happened to hip-hop?

A. It lost its popularity and disappeared.

B. It became standardized and mass-produced.

C. It developed a sound similar to punk rock.

D. It maintained an emphasis on big business.

12. According to John Richardson, why has hip-hop music not lost its identity entirely?

A. It has become standardized and highly uniform.

B. It has shifted its focus away from "the street."

C. It has continued to maintain its emphasis on the underground.

D. It has been supported by major corporations

13. According to the passage, hip-hop first developed to express the views and experiences of

A. the mainstream public.

B. a major corporation.

C. an underground music business.

D. a minority group.

14. What happened after hip-hop became a mainstream form of music?

A. Hip-hop lost some of its subtle qualities.

B. Hip-hop gained more originality.

C. Hip-hop stopped being mass-produced.

D. Hip-hop fell out of favor as a popular style.

Questions 15 and 16 refer to the following passage.

There is evidence that the usual variety of high blood pressure is, in part, a familial disease. Since families have similar genes as well as similar environment, familial diseases could be due to shared genetic influences, to shared environmental factors, or both. For some years, the role of one environmental factor commonly shared by families, namely dietary salt, has been studied at Brookhaven National Laboratory. The studies suggest that excessive ingestion of salt can lead to high blood pressure in man and animals. Some individuals and some rats, however, consume large amounts of salt without developing high blood pressure. No matter how strictly all environmental factors were controlled in these experiments, some salt-fed animals never developed hypertension, whereas a few rapidly developed very severe hypertension followed by early death. These marked variations were interpreted to result from differences in genetic makeup.

15. The main idea of this article is that

A. research is desperately needed in the field of medicine.

B. a cure for high blood pressure is near.

C. research shows salt to be a major cause of high blood pressure.

D. a tendency toward high blood pressure may be inherited.

16. According to the article, high blood pressure is

A. strictly a genetic disease.

B. strictly an environmental disease.

C. due to both genetic and environmental factors.

D. caused only by dietary salt.

Questions 17–20 refer to the following passage.

While the Europeans were still creeping cautiously along their coasts, Polynesians were making trips between Hawaii and New Zealand, a distance of 3,800 miles, in frail canoes. These fearless sailors of the Pacific explored every island in their vast domain without even the simplest of navigational tools.

In the daytime, the Polynesians guided their craft by the position of the sun, the trend of the waves and wind, and the flight of seabirds.

Stars were used during long trips between island groups. Youths studying navigation were taught to view the heavens as a cylinder on which the highways of navigation were marked. An invisible line bisected the sky from the North Star to the Southern Cross.

In addition to single canoes, the Polynesians often used twin canoes for transpacific voyages. The two boats were fastened together by canopied platforms that shielded passengers from sun and rain. Such crafts were remarkably seaworthy and could accommodate 60 to 80 people, in addition to water, food, and domestic animals. Some of these vessels had as many as three masts.

These Pacific <u>mariners</u> used paddles to propel and steer their canoes. The steering paddle was so important that it was always given a personal name. Polynesian legends not only recite the names of the canoe and the hero who discovered a new island but also the name of the steering paddle he used.

17. Which title is best for this selection?

A. "European Sailors"

B. "The History of the Pacific Ocean"

C. "The Study of Navigation"

D. "Early Polynesian Navigation"

18. The Polynesians made trips to

A. New Zealand.

B. the Atlantic.

C. the Southern Cross.

D. Europe.

19. The word <u>mariners</u>, as underlined and used in the passage, most nearly means

A. propellers.

B. seamen.

C. paddles.

D. journeys.

20. This passage suggests that the Polynesians

A. trained seabirds to guide their canoes.

B. had seen a line in the sky that was invisible to others.

C. used a primitive telescope to view the heavens.

D. were astronomers as well as explorers.

Questions 21–25 refer to the following passage.

On May 8, 1939, folk song collector and scholar Herbert Halpert arrived in Mississippi to document folklore and folk music during a recording tour of the South sponsored by the Joint Committee on the Arts of the Works Progress Administration (WPA). The WPA was one of many New Deal agencies created by President Franklin D. Roosevelt to help boost the country's economy after the setbacks of the Great Depression.

To conduct the tour, Halpert drove into Mississippi in an old ambulance outfitted with cabinets, a small cot, food, and clothes. The ambulance also had specially built shelves for the latest in recording equipment—an acetate disc recorder lent by the Archive of American Folk Song at the Library of Congress.

To take full advantage of Halpert's short visit, local WPA workers acted as intermediaries, preceding the recording truck to make arrangements with the folk musicians he would visit and grouping artists in convenient places to minimize travel and maximize recording time. Following their schedule, with a few side trips to pursue a couple of leads of his own, Halpert cut 168 records between May 8 and June 11, 1939.

Halpert was assisted by Abbott Ferriss, a Mississippi native, who later went on to become a sociologist at Columbia University. Ferriss was employed at the time by another New Deal program known as the Federal Writers' Project. He used the experience to gather sociological information about Southern folk music communities that would eventually influence some of his academic contributions to the field.

In addition to helping with the actual recording, Ferriss kept field notes on the trip and took photographs of the musicians, their families, homes, and surroundings. At the project's conclusion, the recordings became part of the folk-music collections at the Library of Congress. The photographs and much of the manuscript material related to the project were retained in Mississippi.

21. According to the passage, the purpose of Halpert's journey to Mississippi was to

A. make arrangements for the writing of folk songs.

B. consult with a local native.

C. record the folk music of Mississippi performers.

D. photograph the Mississippi landscape.

22. Which of the following can be reasonably inferred about the WPA?

A. It was only interested in folk music.

B. It took full advantage of short visits to the Library of Congress.

C. It was a national organization with local offices.

D. It was sponsored by the Joint Committee on the Arts.

23. According to the passage, Abbott Ferriss was originally from

A. Columbia.

B. Mississippi.

C. New York.

D. London.

24. During the time of the Mississippi recordings in 1939, Abbott Ferriss was employed by

A. the Federal Writers' Project.

B. the Library of Congress.

C. Columbia University.

D. folk music communities.

25. The word <u>retained</u>, as underlined and used in the passage, most nearly means

A. lost

B. repaired

C. grown

D. kept

Questions 26–28 refer to the following passage.

Now and then, in the haste of business, it had been my habit to assist in comparing some brief document myself, calling Turkey or Nippers for this purpose. One object I had in placing Bartleby so handy to me behind the screen, was to avail myself of his services on such trivial occasions. It was on the third day, I think, of his being with me, and before any necessity had arisen for having his own writing examined, that, being much hurried to complete a small affair I had in hand, I abruptly called to Bartleby. In my haste and natural expectancy of instant compliance, I sat with my head bent over the original on my desk, and my right hand sideways, and somewhat nervously extended with the copy, so that immediately upon emerging from his retreat, Bartleby might snatch it and proceed to business without the least delay.

In this very attitude did I sit when I called to him, rapidly stating what it was I wanted him to do—namely, to examine a small paper with me. Imagine my surprise, nay, my consternation, when without moving from his privacy, Bartleby in a singularly mild, firm voice, replied, "I would prefer not to."

I sat awhile in perfect silence, rallying my stunned faculties. Immediately it occurred to me that my ears had deceived me, or Bartleby had entirely misunderstood my meaning. I repeated my request in the clearest tone I could assume. But in quite as clear a one came the previous reply, "I would prefer not to."

"Prefer not to," echoed I, rising in high excitement, and crossing the room with a stride. "What do you mean? Are you moon-struck? I want you to help me compare this sheet here—take it," and I thrust it towards him.

"I would prefer not to," said he.

I looked at him steadfastly. His face was leanly composed; his gray eye dimly calm. Not a wrinkle of agitation rippled him. Had there been the least uneasiness, anger, impatience or impertinence in his manner; in other words, had there been any thing ordinarily human about him, doubtless I should have violently dismissed him from the premises. But as it was, I should have as soon thought of turning my pale plaster-of-Paris bust of Cicero out of doors. I stood gazing at him awhile, as he went on with his own writing, and then reseated myself at my desk. This is very strange, thought I. What had one best do? But my business hurried me. I concluded to forget the matter for the present, reserving it for my future leisure. So calling Nippers from the other room, the paper was speedily examined.

—Excerpt from *Bartleby the Scrivener: A Story of Wall Street,* by Herman Melville

26. Which of the following *best* describes the tone of this passage?
    A. Hostile
    B. Wry
    C. Romantic
    D. Playful

27. A theme of this passage is the
    A. beauty of simplicity.
    B. power of change.
    C. illusion of power.
    D. necessity of work.

28. Which of the following *best* describes Bartleby?
    A. Easily bullied
    B. Intimidating
    C. Self-assured
    D. Belligerent

Questions 29–38 refer to the following passage.

Litterbugs have a bad reputation, but the biggest litterbugs in history have, in fact, been very helpful to mankind.

For glaciers, in ancient times and today, are the greatest creators and distributors of litter. Of course, they don't drop tin cans, paper cups, and pop bottles; they dump rocks, boulders, sand, gravel, and mud all over the landscape, and it's this glacial debris that has helped create some of the world's most fertile farmland, such as that in America's Midwest.

Geologists describe glacial ice as true rock, different only in that it melts more easily than other rock. Because glacial ice is moving rock, it scrapes, bangs, and tears at the terrain over which it moves, breaking off chunks of all sizes. When the ice melts, the debris drops, and, if it is rich in minerals, creates fertile soil when it erodes.

It's too bad human litterbugs aren't as useful!

29. The richness of the soil in America's Midwest can be attributed, in part, to

A. heavy annual rainfalls.

B. scientific analysis.

C. human litterbugs.

D. ancient glacial debris.

30. Although the author of this passage describes glaciers as litterbugs, his attitude toward glaciers is one of

A. love.

B. gratitude.

C. disgust.

D. fear.

31. Which of the following is correct?

A. Glacial ice is full of pop bottles.

B. Glaciers are harmful.

C. Glaciers erode the terrain.

D. Glacial ice may be full of fertile soil.

32. According to this passage, history's biggest litterbugs are

A. glaciers.

B. people.

C. rocks.

D. bulldozers.

33. The words <u>most fertile</u>, as underlined and used in the passage, most nearly mean

A. most icy.

B. flattest.

C. most rocky.

D. best growing.

34. Good soil contains

A. rocks.

B. minerals.

C. vitamins.

D. melted ice.

35. A good title for this passage might be

A. "A Lovely Litterbug."

B. "The Destructive Forces of Glaciers."

C. "Glaciers—Then and Now."

D. "The History of Glaciers."

36. This passage implies that the litter human beings drop is

A. useless.

B. ugly.

C. uninteresting.

D. unimportant.

37. The word <u>terrain</u>, as underlined and used in the passage, most nearly means

A. rock.

B. terror.

C. view.

D. land.

38. On the basis of this passage, it could be said that glaciers change the

A. earth's atmosphere.

B. pollution rate.

C. mineral content of rocks.

D. earth's geography.

Questions 39 and 40 refer to the following passage.

"Lefty" Gordon was an obscure outfielder who had a brief major league career with the Cleveland Indians in the 1960s. He never hit dozens of home runs in a single season, he never stole many bases, he didn't have blazing speed, and he didn't have the flashy style that many modern players have. What Lefty did have, though, was a connection with the fans, particularly the ones in the cheap seats behind the centerfield wall. For one particular fan, Lefty Gordon was the greatest baseball player ever.

Mitchell Haskins was just a kid in the 1960s. Mitchell's family had very little money, but he was fortunate enough to be able to attend a few Indians games, in the cheap seats, as a kid. One warm June afternoon in the final inning of a lopsided game, Lefty Gordon made his first appearance of the game in centerfield. On the final out of the game, Gordon chased down a fly ball and made a nice catch. Mitchell, just a kid then, applauded wildly. Gordon saw Mitchell cheering, climbed the fence, and tossed Mitchell the ball. As he climbed down from the fence, he said to Mitchell, "If every fan cheered as hard as you, we'd win every game. Thanks, kid!"

39. Why didn't Lefty Gordon get into the game until the final innings?

A. He was left-handed.

B. The game was lopsided, so the Indians didn't want to run up the score on the visiting team.

C. The coaches didn't like Lefty.

D. Lefty was not good enough to start the game and probably played only as a reserve player.

40. Why did Mitchell think Lefty was one of the greatest players?

A. Lefty had amazing skills.

B. Lefty wasn't being treated fairly.

C. Mitchell saw talent in Lefty that the coaches didn't see.

D. Lefty made a personal connection with Mitchell and the fans that other players didn't make.

Questions 41–50 refer to the following passage.

A vast stretch of land lies untouched by civilization in the back country of the Eastern portion of the African continent. With the occasional exception of a big-game hunter, foreigners never penetrate this area. Aside from the Wandorobo tribe, even the natives shun its confines because it harbors the deadly tsetse fly. The Wandorobo nomads depend on the forest for their lives, eating its roots and fruits, and making their homes wherever they find themselves at the end of the day.

One of the staples of their primitive diet, and their only sweet, is honey. They obtain it through an ancient, symbiotic relationship with a bird known as the Indicator. The scientific community finally confirmed the report, at first discredited, that this bird purposefully led the natives to trees containing the honeycombs of wild bees. Other species of honey guides are also known to take advantage of the foraging efforts of some animals in much the same way that the Indicator uses men.

This amazing bird settles in a tree near a Wandorobo encampment and chatters incessantly until the men answer it with whistles. It then begins its leading flight. Chattering, it hops from tree to tree, while the men continue their musical answering call. When the bird reaches the tree, its chatter becomes shriller and its followers examine the tree carefully. The Indicator usually perches just over the honeycomb, and the men hear the humming of the bees in the hollow trunk. Using torches, they smoke most of the bees out of the tree, but those that escape the nullifying effects of the smoke sting the men viciously. Undaunted, the Wandorobos free the nest, gather the honey, and leave a small offering for their bird guide.

41. The title that best expresses the topic of this selection is

A. "Life in the African Backwoods."

B. "The Wandorobo Tribe."

C. "Locating a Honeycomb."

D. "Men and Birds Working Together."

42. Most people avoid the back country of Eastern Africa because they

A. dislike honey.

B. fear the cannibalistic Wandorobo.

C. fear bee stings.

D. fear the tsetse fly.

43. The Wandorobo communicate with the Indicator bird by

A. whistling.

B. chattering.

C. playing musical instruments.

D. smoke signals.

44. The Indicator bird's name stems from the fact that it

A. always flies in a northward line.

B. points out locations of tsetse fly nests.

C. leads the Wandorobo to trees containing wild bee honeycombs.

D. uses smoke to indicate the location of bees.

45. The reward of the Indicator bird is

A. a symbiotic relationship.

B. a musical concert.

C. roots and fruits.

D. some honey.

46. Smoke causes bees to

A. fly away.

B. sting viciously.

C. hum.

D. make honey.

47. Scientists at first discredited reports of the purposeful behavior of the Indicator bird because

A. the Wandorobo are known to exaggerate in their stories.

B. birds do not eat honey.

C. honey guides take advantage of others of their own species only.

D. the arrangement seemed so farfetched that they waited to confirm the reports scientifically.

48. The response of the Wandorobo toward bee stings is to

A. ignore them.

B. smoke the bees out.

C. eat roots to nullify the effects of the stings.

D. fear them.

49. The word incessantly, as underlined and used in the passage, most nearly means

A. meaninglessly.

B. continuously.

C. raucously.

D. softly.

50. According to the selection, one characteristic of the Wandorobo tribe is that its members

A. avoid the country of the tsetse fly.

B. have no permanent homes.

C. lack physical courage.

D. live entirely on a diet of honey.

Questions 51 and 52 refer to the following passage.

In ancient Egypt, there once was a pharaoh who turned the entire kingdom upside down. The ancient Egyptians believed that many deities existed and that these deities controlled all of nature and human activity. For example, there were deities who controlled the flood stages of the Nile, the stars in the sky, and the weather. Others had responsibilities in the afterlife. Egyptians never questioned this system until Amenhotep IV took the throne.

Amenhotep IV, who changed his name to Akhenaton, did away with the system of worshipping many deities and replaced it with the worship of a single deity, Aton, who was the sun god. Historians debate Akhenaton's motives. Some argue that he was mentally disturbed and obsessed with the sun. Others argue that he made a brilliant political move by taking power away from the kingdom's many priests who were loyal to various deities. Regardless of his motives, Akhenaton's bold decision temporarily altered life for everyone in Egypt.

51. Which of the following, based on the information in the passage, is most likely true?

A. Egyptians never worshipped the sun until Akhenaton changed the religion.

B. There may have been a power struggle between kings and priests before Akhenaton ruled.

C. Akhenaton hoped to make Egypt's climate warmer by worshipping the sun.

D. Akhenaton hoped to confuse historians.

52. Using context clues, the word *pharaoh* is most closely defined as which of the following?

A. Governor

B. King

C. Mayor

D. Priest

Questions 53–57 refer to the following passage.

Our planet is made up of three separate layers, known as the crust, mantle, and core. The core of the earth is also made up of two layers, an outer core and an inner core.

Just as the earth rotates on its axis, the parts of the earth also move over time. This movement occurs in a horizontal direction and is very slow. Most parts of the earth are believed to move at a rate of only 10 centimeters per year—about the same rate as the growth of a human fingernail, according to writer David Schneider.

Recently, scientists investigating the inner core of the earth have discovered that this part of the earth moves much faster than the surrounding parts. Exactly how fast the inner core moves, however, is still a subject of debate.

Up until recently, most of our knowledge about the content of the earth's inner core has come through using scientific logic. Scientists deduced that the earth's core was composed mainly of iron. In addition to using logic, scientists have gathered some direct evidence regarding the earth's core. This evidence comes from seismic studies, which investigate waves traveling through the earth from earthquakes and explosives. Seismic studies show that the earth contains not just iron, but a lighter element as well. Scientists aren't sure which lighter element is contained in the core, but they have narrowed down the possibilities. They believe it could be one of these five: oxygen, sulfur, silicon, hydrogen, or carbon.

Recently, new experiments show that silicon may be the key element. These studies, conducted at the University of Chicago, encouraged scientists to pinpoint silicon as the most likely light element for three reasons. First, like iron, silicon is very abundant in our solar system. Second, it combines easily with iron to create an iron alloy. Third, silicon lowers the density of iron when the two elements are placed together under high pressure conditions.

53. The inner core of the earth is most likely made up mainly of

A. iron and silicon.

B. iron and oxygen.

C. silicon and sulfur.

D. oxygen and hydrogen.

54. Which statement best describes the inner core of the earth?

A. It moves at a rate of about 10 centimeters per year.

B. It is divided into two layers: crust and mantle.

C. It moves at a rate of about 10 kilometers per year.

D. It moves faster than the other parts of the earth.

55. The earth is made up of three separate layers called the
    A. outer core, the inner core, and the iron core.
    B. surface, spindle, and core.
    C. crust, mantle, and core.
    D. crust, the outer core, and the inner core.

56. Scientists have been learning about the earth's core by analyzing waves traveling through the earth caused by
    A. explosives and earthquakes.
    B. explosives and volcanoes.
    C. earthquakes and asteroids.
    D. explosives and meteors.

57. According to the passage, what effect does silicon have upon iron when the two are placed together under high pressure?
    A. Silicon increases the specific gravity of iron.
    B. Silicon makes iron more explosive.
    C. Silicon decreases the temperature of iron.
    D. Silicon decreases the density of iron.

Questions 58–61 refer to the following passage.

From Gettysburg to the Battle of the Bulge, carrier pigeons have winged their way through skies fair and foul to deliver the vital messages of battle. Today, in spite of electronics and atomic weapons, these feathered heroes are still an important communication link in any army.

No one could be surer of this than the men at Fort Monmouth, New Jersey, the sole Army pigeon breeding and training center in this country. On the roosts at Fort Monmouth perch many genuine battle heroes, among them veteran G. I. Joe.

In 1943, 1,000 British troops moved speedily ahead of the Allied advance in Italy to take the small town of Colvi Vecchia. Since communications could not be established in time to relay the victory to headquarters, the troops were due for a previously planned Allied bombing raid. Then one of the men released carrier pigeon G. I. Joe. With a warning message on his back, he flew 20 miles in 20 minutes, arriving just as the bombers were warming up their engines. For saving the day for the British, the Lord Mayor of London later awarded G. I. Joe the Dickin Medal, England's highest award to an animal.

Even when regular message channels are set up, equipment can break or be overloaded, or radio silence must be observed. Then the carrier pigeon comes into his own. Ninety-nine times out of a hundred, he completes his mission. In Korea, Homer the homing pigeon was flying from the front to a rear command post when he developed wing trouble. Undaunted, Homer made a forced landing, hopped the last two miles, and delivered his message. For initiative and loyalty, Homer was promoted to Pfc.—Pigeon First Class!

58. The writer of this selection evidently believes that carrier pigeons

A. have no usefulness in modern warfare.

B. should be forced to fly only in emergencies.

C. are remarkably reliable as message carriers.

D. should receive regular promotions.

59. G. I. Joe was rewarded for

A. preventing unnecessary loss of life.

B. guiding a bomber's flight.

C. returning in spite of an injured wing.

D. bringing the news of an allied victory.

60. G. I. Joe's reward was a

A. promotion.

B. reception given by the Lord Mayor.

C. chance to retire to Fort Monmouth.

D. medal.

61. The word undaunted, as underlined and used in the passage, most nearly means

A. tired.

B. determined.

C. lost.

D. angry.

Questions 62–66 refer to the following passage.

In today's digital world, almost all graphic art is created on the computer. Computer-aided drawing programs enable graphic artists to reproduce images using lines, shapes, and even paintbrushes and drawing tools. Artists have had to work to learn how to use these computerized tools, however, and sometimes this process hasn't been easy. To generate their works of art, artists must use computerized paintbrushes or pens that are controlled by moving a computer mouse. The mouse, however, feels much different than an actual paintbrush or pen. Artists who work with paint on paper, for example, can sense how much paint they are applying by feeling the pressure of their brushstroke. Computer artists, on the other hand, don't have the luxury of sensing the pressure of their brushstrokes. They can only alter the heaviness of the color in their art by giving the computer a command.

This predicament may be changing with the invention of a new tool known as the Proactive Desktop. Created by a team of developers from Kyoto, Japan, the Proactive Desktop looks like a computer screen, but it lies flat on a table top. Using the Proactive Desktop, artists can grasp an actual tool shaped like a pen or a paintbrush and use this tool to create their designs. The Proactive Desktop enables the artist to "feel" the sensations of working with an actual pen or paintbrush, such as the pressure of his or her fingers on the tool. Painters, for instance, can then benefit from much of the information that they normally use when painting on a canvas: the thickness of the paint, the texture of the canvas, and the movement of the canvas as they paint, to name a few.

The Proactive Desktop may also change the way that artistic techniques are taught to students. Not only does it allow the user to "feel" sensations as they are transmitted to the computer—it also allows users to experience physical sensations transmitted *by* the computer! Using this technology, an art teacher might use her desktop to show students how to make a particular stroke with a paintbrush. Students could grasp their paintbrush tools and feel the sensations of the brush exactly as the instructor moves it.

62. What is the main advantage of the Proactive Desktop compared to regular computers?

A. It allows artists to see through the different layers of an object to the parts underneath.

B. It allows artists to control a computerized art tool by moving a computer mouse.

C. It allows artists to grasp an actual art tool and to feel the sensations of working with that tool.

D. It allows artists to change the amount of color in their art by giving the computer a command.

63. According to paragraph 1, computer artists

A. cannot sense the pressure of their brushstrokes.

B. cannot alter the amount of color in their art.

C. easily learn how to use computerized tools.

D. prefer using a computer mouse to a brush.

64. The Proactive Desktop was created by which of the following?

A. A large American computer manufacturer

B. A team of American entrepreneurs

C. Graphic artists from France

D. A group of Japanese developers

65. Each of the following is mentioned in the passage as information that painters normally use when painting on a canvas *except*

A. paint thickness.

B. canvas size.

C. canvas movement.

D. canvas texture.

66. The Proactive Desktop looks like which of the following?

A. A computer screen lying flat on a table

B. An artist's paint palette

C. A computer screen positioned upright

D. An art canvas on an easel

Questions 67–70 refer to the following passage.

Nine-banded armadillos, the only type of armadillo that lives in the United States, are fascinating and unusual mammals. Originally located in South America, armadillos have gradually extended their geographical range northward, and they can now be found across the southeastern United States and as far north as Kansas. The armadillo is particularly popular in Texas, where it is the official state small mammal.

Instead of being covered with skin, the armadillo's body is covered with hard, bony plates, reminiscent of armor. These plates gave the armadillo its name, which means "little armored one" in Spanish. Nine-banded armadillos have nine separate segments of bony plate around their midsections. This allows them to bend.

About the size of large house cats, armadillos have poor eyesight but a superb sense of smell. Their strong legs and extra-large front claws make them excellent diggers, a trait they use to build underground burrow homes. Their digging skills, plus their long, sticky tongues, enable armadillos to search for and trap insects, one of their favorite foods.

Because of their heavy outer covering, it would be easy to assume that armadillos cannot function in water. However, this is far from the truth. An armadillo can hold its breath for four to six minutes. If it needs to cross a small body of water, it simply holds its breath and walks across the bottom. For longer aquatic encounters, the armadillo gulps in air to inflate its intestines. This makes its body quite buoyant, enabling the armadillo to become a capable swimmer.

Shy creatures, armadillos prefer to escape rather than face confrontation. When frightened, they have the rather strange ability to jump, straight up, three to four feet in the air. This propensity makes armadillos a roadway hazard, both to drivers and themselves. An armadillo senses a moving vehicle and leaps just high enough to be struck by the vehicle's bumper.

67. According to the article, a nine-banded armadillo would be least likely to be found in

A. Texas.

B. Florida.

C. Michigan.

D. Oklahoma.

68. Nine-banded armadillos can bend in the middle because their armor

A. is flexible.

B. has nine sections.

C. has hinges.

D. is bony and thick.

69. When an armadillo faces danger, it will most likely not
    - A. stand and fight.
    - B. jump high in the air.
    - C. dig a hole to hide in.
    - D. run away quickly.

70. Although it seems unlikely, the armadillo is a good swimmer because its
    - A. oversized front claws make it excellent at paddling.
    - B. poor eyesight and keen sense of smell are assets in the water.
    - C. bony plates are lightweight and act like a boat in the water.
    - D. ability to fill its intestines with air enables it to float easily.

Questions 71–75 refer to the following passage.

Ages ago, when that part of our earth was cut off from the Asian mainland, this fantastic animal from nature's long-ago was also isolated. There are about two dozen species distributed through Australasia, southward to Tasmania and northward to New Guinea and neighboring islands. Some are no bigger than rabbits; some can climb trees. They are known by a variety of picturesque names: wallabies, wallaroos, potoroos, boongaries, and paddymelons. But the kangaroo—the one that is Australia's national symbol—is the great grey kangaroo of the plains, admiringly known throughout the island continent as the Old Man, and also as Boomer, Forester, and Man of the Woods. His smaller mate, in Australian talk, is called a flyer. Their baby is known as a joey.

A full-grown kangaroo stands taller than a man and commonly weighs 200 pounds. Even when he sits in his favorite position, reposing on his haunches and tilting back on the propping support of his "third leg"—his tail—his head is five feet or more above the ground. His huge hind legs, with steel-spring power, can send him sailing over a ten-foot fence with ease, or in a fight can beat off a dozen dogs. A twitch of his tail can break a man's leg like a matchstick.

Kangaroos provide an endless supply of tall tales to which wide-eyed visitors are treated in the land Down Under. The beauty of the tall tales about the kangaroos is that they can be almost as tall as you please and still be close to fact.

71. Choose the best topic sentence for this passage.

A. The kangaroo is found nowhere in the world but in Australia.

B. Kangaroos are popular throughout the world.

C. "Joeys" are kangaroo babies.

D. Kangaroos don't make very good pets.

72. The amazing jumping power of the kangaroo is chiefly due to

A. the power of his hind legs.

B. the support of his tail.

C. his size.

D. his weight.

73. Australasia is
   A. another name for Australia.
   B. an area that includes Australia and part of the continent of Asia.
   C. Australia and some surrounding islands to the north and south of it.
   D. all of the land in the Southern Hemisphere.

74. Which statement is true according to the passage?
   A. The name "Old Man" shows the people's dislike of kangaroos.
   B. Visitors to Australia hear very little about kangaroos.
   C. A kangaroo's tail is a powerful weapon.
   D. The most widely known species of kangaroo is no larger than a rabbit.

75. The author believes that the stories told about kangaroos are generally
   A. harmful.
   B. true.
   C. suspicious.
   D. beautiful.

Answer Key and Explanations

1. A	16. C	31. D	46. A	61. A
2. D	17. D	32. A	47. D	62. C
3. C	18. A	33. D	48. A	63. A
4. B	19. B	34. B	49. B	64. D
5. A	20. D	35. A	50. B	65. B
6. C	21. C	36. A	51. B	66. A
7. B	22. C	37. D	52. B	67. C
8. D	23. B	38. D	53. A	68. B
9. A	24. A	39. D	54. A	69. A
10. C	25. D	40. D	55. C	70. D
11. B	26. B	41. D	56. B	71. A
12. C	27. C	42. D	57. D	72. A
13. D	28. C	43. A	58. C	73. C
14. A	29. D	44. C	59. A	74. C
15. D	30. B	45. D	60. D	75. D

1. **The correct answer is A.** The answer to this question of fact is in the first sentence, where it states that the Ohio Company was "under the leadership of Reverend Manasseh Cutler."

2. **The correct answer is D.** Do not be misled by the first sentence, which introduces Reverend Manasseh Cutler, nor by the last portion of the selection, which discusses the naming of Cleveland. The entire selection has to do with the settling of the Northwest Territory.

3. **The correct answer is C.** In this context, the word *related* means "reported" or "told."

4. **The correct answer is B.** Read carefully. General Cleaveland quieted the Indian *claims*; he did not quiet the Indians. If the Indians were making claims, they were not eager to work with him. The selection suggests that General Cleaveland bought off the Indians with money, cattle, and whiskey.

5. **The correct answer is A.** The context in which it is used should help you to choose this answer. ". . . veneration due to its sacred origin . . ." implies something religious and related to worship.

6. **The correct answer is C.** The speaker probably does celebrate and enjoy Christmas, but the primary reason for this speech is to defend the holiday to Scrooge by listing its advantages to mankind.

7. **The correct answer is B.** In lines 4–8, the first speaker states that, in his opinion, Christmastime is a good, kind, forgiving, charitable, and pleasant time when men and women open their hearts and think of others as equals.

8. **The correct answer is D.** Again, use of the words in context should lead you to their meaning. The paragraph speaks of goodwill among all men and women. This *one consent* therefore is a unanimously good feeling.

9. **The correct answer is A.** Read the last paragraph carefully. Scrooge is first reacting to the clerk who has just applauded the speech in defense of Christmas. Scrooge threatens the clerk with firing. He then turns and makes a sarcastic remark to his nephew. It can be assumed that he is angry with both characters.

10. **The correct answer is C.** The first sentence explains that an art form will become the subject of scholarly study when it becomes a century old or disappears from public view. Choices A, B, and D are incorrect because they contain ideas that are not mentioned in the passage.

11. **The correct answer is B.** According to the third paragraph, after hip-hop became mainstream, the music then became standardized and mass-produced. Choice A is incorrect because the author makes it clear that although some music loses popularity and disappears after becoming mass-produced, this did not happen to hip-hop.

12. **The correct answer is C.** This question is a "cause and effect" question. It asks you to identify the *reason why* hip-hop music has not lost its identity, according to John Richardson. The answer to this question can be found in the last paragraph of the passage. Here, we are told that, in Richardson's view, part of the reason why hip-hop did not lose its identity entirely is because it kept its emphasis on the underground.

13. **The correct answer is D.** The second paragraph states that hip-hop originally reflected the view of a specific minority group. Choice C is incorrect because, although hip-hop is a form of underground music, the passage indicates that it first emerged to express the views of a minority group, not a business.

14. **The correct answer is A.** In paragraph 3 we are told that when hip-hop became mainstream, it lost some of its subtle qualities. Choice A states accurately that hip-hop lost some of its subtle qualities in the process of becoming mainstream. Choices B, C, and D are incorrect because they contradict the information in the passage. According to the third paragraph, when hip-hop became mainstream, it *lost* some of its originality. Also, once hip-hop became mainstream, it next became "standardized and mass-produced." Finally, the last paragraph states that hip-hop never fell out of favor as a popular style.

15. **The correct answer is D.** The article discusses high blood pressure as a familial disease, a disease that runs in families. It goes on to discuss the role of genetic makeup in determining reaction to dietary factors. "Genetic makeup" refers to hereditary factors.

16. **The correct answer is C.** This is a main idea question. The main point of the selection is that there is an interplay of genetic and environmental factors influencing the development of high blood pressure.

17. **The correct answer is D.** A title should reflect the main idea of a passage. From its outset, the passage focuses on how Polynesian sailors traveled among the Pacific islands. It highlights their use of simple navigational tools but doesn't present any study material about navigation, and it compares the Polynesians' travels in the Pacific Ocean with those of the early European sailors, but these are all details that support the main idea of early Polynesian navigation.

18. **The correct answer is A.** The first sentence states that the Polynesians made trips to New Zealand. Their travels were in the Pacific, not the Atlantic Ocean (choice B) or in Europe (choice D). The Southern Cross (choice C) is a constellation they used for navigation.

19. **The correct answer is B.** The first sentence of the last paragraph makes clear that mariners are people.

20. **The correct answer is D.** The third paragraph states how the Polynesians used the stars for navigation. People who study and understand movements of the stars are astronomers. Although the Polynesians used movements of seabirds as a guide during the daytime, they had not trained the birds (choice A). The "line" that bisected the sky (choice B) was invisible to everyone; youths studying navigation were taught to view this line mentally. There is no mention of telescopes (choice C).

21. **The correct answer is C.** The first sentence states that Herbert Halpert arrived in Mississippi to document folklore and folk music during a WPA-sponsored recording tour of the South.

22. **The correct answer is C.** The second paragraph tells of local WPA workers and the assistance they gave.

23. **The correct answer is B.** In paragraph 4, Ferriss is described as a Mississippi native. This means that he was originally from Mississippi.

24. **The correct answer is A.** The passage mentions in paragraph 4 that Ferriss was employed by the Federal Writers' Project during the time that he assisted Halpert in 1939.

25. **The correct answer is D.** The last paragraph states that the recordings went to the Library of Congress, and the photographs and manuscript materials were *retained* in Mississippi. From the context, we can infer that even though the recordings went elsewhere, the photographs and manuscript materials stayed in Mississippi. *Kept* (choice D) best reflects this meaning. Nothing in the passage suggests that the photographs and manuscript material were *lost*, so choice A is incorrect.

26. **The correct answer is B.** Only choice B identifies the tone of this passage. *Wry* describes a twisted and ironic humor, and Bartleby's strange behavior and refusal to explain himself contributes to the passage's wry tone.

27. **The correct answer is C.** Only choice C identifies a theme of this passage. Bartleby's boss thinks he has power over his employees, but this illusion is shattered when Bartleby refuses to do the task his boss asks him to do.

28. **The correct answer is C.** Only choice C describes Bartleby. Bartleby is so self-assured that he refuses to do his job without losing his calm at all.

29. **The correct answer is D.** The richness of the soil in America's Midwest can be attributed, in part, to ancient glacial debris. See paragraph 2, sentence 2.

30. **The correct answer is B.** Nothing in the passage indicates that the author feels affection for glaciers, so *love* (choice A) is not the best choice. The tone of the passage is positive, so neither *disgust* (choice C) nor *fear* (choice D) describe the author's attitude.

31. **The correct answer is D.** In paragraph 3 the passage states that when the glacial ice melts, if the debris it drops is rich in minerals, it creates fertile soil when it erodes.

32. **The correct answer is A.** According to this passage, *glaciers* are history's biggest litterbugs (lines 1–4).

33. **The correct answer is D.** In the context of the passage, *most fertile* means "best growing."

34. The correct answer is B. You can infer from the sentence, "When the ice melts, the debris drops, and, if it is rich in minerals, creates fertile soil when it erodes" (lines 10 and 11) that fertile soil contains minerals, and fertile soil is "good" for growing.

35. The correct answer is A. The author refers to glaciers as litterbugs and then relates the benefits of glacial "littering," so "A Lovely Litterbug" is the best choice for the passage title. While the passage describes how glaciers move and interact with the terrain around them, it does not call them a destructive force; in fact, the glacier is what gets broken apart, so choice B is not the best answer. The passage doesn't address the history of glaciers or provide an in-depth comparison of ancient and modern-day glaciers, so choices C and D are incorrect.

36. The correct answer is A. By comparing human litterbugs to glaciers in the closing sentence of the passage, the author implies that the litter humans drop is useless.

37. The correct answer is D. *Terrain* most nearly means "land."

38. The correct answer is D. On the basis of this passage, it could be said that glaciers change the earth's geography. Because glacial ice is moving rock that interacts with the earth around it (lines 9 and 10), it can be said that glaciers change the earth's geography. To conclude that glaciers change the earth's atmosphere (choice A), the pollution rate (choice B), or the mineral content of rocks (choice C) would go beyond the scope of what's discussed in the passage.

39. The correct answer is D. Based on the description given about Lefty in the first paragraph, it can be inferred that Lefty was not good enough to start the game and probably played only as a reserve player. The passage points out that Lefty wasn't a standout player, so it is reasonable that the weakest players are the last to play on a professional team.

40. The correct answer is D. Lefty made a personal connection with Mitchell and the fans that other players didn't make. Lefty was outgoing and friendly toward Mitchell, and that allowed Mitchell to connect to and identify with Lefty. It was Lefty's personality, not his physical ability, that made him likable to Mitchell.

41. The correct answer is D. Although the selection does describe the Wandorobo tribe in some detail, the main topic of the selection is the manner in which birds and men work together in their quest for honey.

42. The correct answer is D. People fear the tsetse fly because it carries the blood parasite that causes the often-fatal African sleeping sickness.

43. **The correct answer is A.** The Wandorobo whistle. The bird chatters.

44. **The correct answer is C.** The Indicator bird indicates the location of trees containing honeybee hives. Men use the smoke to dislodge the bees.

45. **The correct answer is D.** The small offering of honey left by the Wandorobo is the bird's reward. A symbiotic relationship is the association of two dissimilar organisms for their mutual benefit.

46. **The correct answer is A.** Bees do not like smoke. The Wandorobo use torch smoke to chase the bees out of the trees. When the bees leave, the Wandorobo collect the honey. Those few bees that somehow avoid the effects of the smoke, perhaps by being outside the tree trunk at the time, sting viciously (choice B). Humming (choice C) and making honey (choice D) are natural bee behaviors and have nothing to do with smoke.

47. **The correct answer is D.** The scientific community would be reluctant to believe such a close symbiotic relationship between man and bird existed without proof. There is no support for the other choices in this passage.

48. **The correct answer is A.** If the Wandorobo are undaunted (line 20) by bee stings, they ignore the stings.

49. **The correct answer is B.** The bird chatters continuously without stopping until the men answer it with whistles and begin to follow (lines 13–15).

50. **The correct answer is B.** The last sentence of the first paragraph states that the Wandorobo are nomads who make their homes wherever they find themselves at the end of the day. The Wandorobo are the only tribe that travels in the forest infested with the tsetse fly. Their diet is roots and fruits. They are very courageous, even in the face of stinging bees.

51. **The correct answer is B.** There may have been a power struggle between kings and priests before Akhenaton ruled. The second paragraph indicates that he took power away from the priests and that this may have been a politically motivated move. This is the clue that there may have been political competition between priests and other kings like Akhenaton.

52. **The correct answer is B.** The context clues that point to a pharaoh being a king are the references to the kingdom, the throne, and the idea that Akhenaton's decision affected everyone in Egypt.

53. The correct answer is A. Paragraph 5 states that in addition to iron, silicon may be the key element in the earth's core. Oxygen (choice B) is not an element in the earth's inner core. In paragraph 4, the passage states that the earth's inner core is made up mainly of iron and a lighter element, so choices C and D can be eliminated.

54. The correct answer is A. The passage states that most parts of the earth move at a rate of about 10 centimeters per year. Paragraph 3 states that the inner core moves faster than the other parts of the earth, but the exact speed of the inner core is not mentioned.

55. The correct answer is C. The first paragraph of the passage states that the earth has three separate layers and that these are the crust, mantle, and core.

56. The correct answer is B. The fourth paragraph states the scientists have learned about the earth's core through seismic studies, which investigate waves traveling through the earth caused by earthquakes and explosives.

57. The correct answer is D. The last paragraph states that silicon lowers the density of iron when the two elements are placed together under high pressure conditions. Silicon does not make iron ore more explosive (choice B), nor does it decrease iron's temperature (choice C) or density (choice D).

58. The correct answer is C. Clearly the writer of the selection is an admirer of carrier pigeons, praising their usefulness and reliability.

59. The correct answer is A. G. I. Joe brought the news of an allied victory, but he was rewarded for the results of his bringing the news, for preventing unnecessary loss of life. If the British had not received news that their troops were already in the town of Colvi Vecchia, they would have sent out the raid and bombed their own soldiers. When two answers to a question seem right, you must choose the one that more specifically answers what is asked.

60. The correct answer is D. At the end of paragraph 3, the passage states that the Lord Mayor of London gave G. I. Joe the Dickin Medal, England's highest award given to an animal.

61. The correct answer is A. *Undaunted* means "unafraid and determined."

62. **The correct answer is C.** This question is a "compare and contrast" question. It requires you to compare the Proactive Desktop and regular computers. Specifically, the question asks you to identify why Proactive Desktops are *better* for graphic artists than regular computers. The second paragraph describes the main benefit of the Proactive Desktop. It states that the Desktop allows artists to work with art tools on the computer in a more realistic way. In comparison, the first paragraph describes the disadvantages for graphic artists of working with regular computers. Paragraph 1 states that when an artist works with a regular computer, he or she must use a computer mouse, which can be awkward to work with, since it doesn't feel like an actual art tool. Choice C best describes the advantage of the Proactive Desktop over regular computers.

63. **The correct answer is A.** Paragraph 1 states that, unlike artists who work with paint on paper, computer artists "don't have the luxury of sensing the pressure of their brushstrokes." Choice B is incorrect because the last sentence of the paragraph states that artists can change the heaviness of the color they apply by using a computer command.

64. **The correct answer is D.** The second sentence of paragraph 2 states that the Proactive Desktop was created by a team of developers from Kyoto, Japan.

65. **The correct answer is B.** The last sentence of paragraph 2 describes the information that painters normally use when painting on a canvas. Paint thickness (choice A), canvas movement (choice C), and canvas texture (choice D) are all mentioned in this sentence. Canvas size is not mentioned in the passage.

66. **The correct answer is A.** The answer to this question is given in paragraph 2. Sentence 2 of the paragraph states that the Proactive Desktop looks like a computer screen, but it lies flat on a tabletop.

67. **The correct answer is C.** The first paragraph of the article states that armadillos are found in the southeastern United States and as far north as Kansas. Michigan is on the northern border of the United States.

68. **The correct answer is B.** This information is found in the third and fourth sentences of paragraph 2: "Nine-banded armadillos have nine separate segments of bony plate around their midsections. This allows them to bend."

69. **The correct answer is A.** Line 20 states that armadillos prefer escape to confrontation, so they are not likely to stand their ground when threatened.

70. The correct answer is D. In paragraph 4, lines 17–19 explain how an armadillo inflates its intestines when it has a need to swim: "For longer aquatic encounters, the armadillo gulps in air to inflate its intestines. This makes its body quite buoyant, enabling the armadillo to become a capable swimmer."

71. The correct answer is A. By introducing the subject of the passage, the kangaroo, stating a fact that makes it unique (they are found nowhere in the world but Australia), and leading to the next sentence about how the geographic isolation affected this animal, this sentence is the best topic sentence of the choices given.

72. The correct answer is A. The kangaroo's hind legs are described as having "steel-spring power" (line 13).

73. The correct answer is C. The first paragraph states that kangaroos are found only in Australasia and that this part of the earth was cut off from the Asian mainland. Specifically, kangaroos are found in Australia, Tasmania to the south, and New Guinea to the north.

74. The correct answer is C. Lines 14 and 15 state that "A twitch of [a kangaroo's] tail can break a man's leg like a matchstick," making it a highly effective weapon. The other statements contradict what is stated in the passage: the name "Old Man" is a term of admiration for kangaroos (line 8); kangaroos provide an "endless supply of tall tales to wide-eyed visitors" (line 16); and the most widely known species of kangaroo stands "taller than a man" (line 10).

75. The correct answer is D. The author states that the "beauty" of the stories—the tall tales in particular—is that no matter how exaggerated they may be, they can still be close to the truth. That the author said the tales can be "close to fact" indicates that he or she does not believe the tales to be generally true (choice B). The author does not feel the stories are harmful (choice A) or suspicious (choice C).

Reading–Comprehension Drill 2

75 Questions

Directions: Read each passage carefully. Then mark one answer on your answer sheet—the answer you think is best—for each item.

Questions 1 and 2 refer to the following passage.

The impressions that an individual gets from his environment are greatly influenced by his emotional state. When he is happy, objects and people present themselves to him in a favorable aspect; when he is depressed, he views the same things in an entirely different light. It has been said that a person's moods are the lenses that color life with many different hues. Not only does mood affect impression, but impression also affects mood. The beauty of a spring morning might dissipate the gloom of a great sorrow, the good-natured chuckle of a fat man might turn anger into a smile, or a telegram might transform a house of mirth into a house of mourning.

1. According to the passage, an individual's perception of his environment
   A. depends on the amount of light available.
   B. is greatly influenced by his emotional state.
   C. is affected by color.
   D. is usually favorable.

2. The word dissipate, as underlined and used in the passage, most nearly means
   A. condense.
   B. draw out.
   C. melt away.
   D. inflate.

Questions 3–9 refer to the following passage.

A phase of my life which has lost something through refinement is the game of croquet. We used to have an old croquet set whose wooden balls, having been chewed by dogs, were no rounder than eggs. Paint had faded; wickets were askew. The course had been laid out haphazardly and eagerly by a child, and we all used to go out there on summer nights and play good-naturedly, with the dogs romping on the lawn in the beautiful light, and the mosquitoes sniping at us, and everyone in good spirits, racing after balls and making split shots for the sheer love of battle. Last spring, we decided the croquet set was beyond use and invested in a rather fancy new one with hoops set in small wooden sockets, and mallets with rubber faces. The course is now exactly seventy-two feet long and we lined the wickets up with a string, but the little boy is less fond of it now, for we make him keep still while we are shooting. A dog isn't even allowed to cast his shadow across the line of play. There are frequent quarrels of a minor nature, and it seems to me we return from the field of honor tense and out of sorts.

3. The word refinement, as underlined and used in the passage, most nearly means

A. politeness.

B. distinction.

C. improvement.

D. his own dignity.

4. The author of the paragraph is

A. very angry.

B. deeply grieved.

C. indifferent.

D. mildly regretful.

5. The mood of the paragraph is

A. dogmatic.

B. very earnest.

C. wistful.

D. belligerent.

6. In comparing the earlier and later ways in which they played croquet, the author considers the new way more

A. exact and less amusing.

B. beneficial for children.

C. conducive to family life.

D. fun for the dogs.

7. The "quarrels of a minor nature" occur because

A. the dog chases the croquet balls.

B. the balls do not roll well.

C. efficiency has become more important than sociability.

D. the little boy interrupts the game with his shouts.

8. The author

A. is opposed to all progress.

B. is very exact in everything he does.

C. dislikes games.

D. feels that undue attention to detail can lessen enjoyment.

9. The author thinks that

A. children should be seen and not heard.

B. dogs are pleasant companions.

C. dogs are a nuisance.

D. children should not be trusted to arrange croquet wickets.

Questions 10–15 refer to the following passage.

Powdered zirconium is more fiery and violent than the magnesium powder that went into wartime incendiary bombs. Under some conditions, it can be ignited with a kitchen match, and it cannot be extinguished with water. Munitions makers once tried to incorporate it into explosives but turned it down as too dangerous even for them to handle.

But when this strange metal is transformed into a solid bar or sheet or tube as lustrous as burnished silver, its temper changes. It is so <u>docile</u> that it can be used by surgeons as a safe covering plate for sensitive brain tissues. It is almost as strong as steel, and it can be exposed to hydrochloric acid or nitric acid without corroding.

Zirconium is also safe and stable when it is bound up with other elements to form mineral compounds, which occur in abundant deposits in North and South America, India, and Australia. Although it is classified as a rare metal, it is more abundant in the earth's crust than nickel, copper, tungsten, tin, or lead. Until a few years ago, scarcely a dozen men had ever seen zirconium in pure form, but today it is the wonder metal of a fantastic new industry, a vital component of television, radar, and radio sets, an exciting structural material for chemical equipment and for super rockets and jet engines, and a key metal for nuclear reactors.

10. The title that best expresses the main idea of this selection is

A. "A Vital Substance."

B. "A Safe, Stable Substance."

C. "Zirconium's Uses in Surgery."

D. "Characteristics of Zirconium."

11. The word *docile* in the second paragraph means

A. stable.

B. pliable.

C. strong.

D. profuse.

12. The selection emphasizes that
    - A. zirconium rusts easily.
    - B. chemists are finding uses for zirconium.
    - C. keys are often made of zirconium.
    - D. zirconium is less abundant in the earth's crust than lead.

13. Zirconium is *not* safe to handle when it is
    - A. lustrous.
    - B. in powdered form.
    - C. in tubes.
    - D. in bar form.

14. The selection states that zirconium
    - A. is a metal.
    - B. is fireproof.
    - C. dissolves in water.
    - D. is stronger than steel.

15. Zirconium is likely to be useful in all these fields *except*
    - A. surgery.
    - B. television.
    - C. atomic research.
    - D. the manufacture of fireworks.

Questions 16–20 refer to the following passage.

In August of 1814, when news came that the British were advancing on Washington, three State Department clerks stuffed all records and valuable papers—including the Articles of Confederation, the Declaration of Independence, and the Constitution—into coarse linen sacks and smuggled them in carts to an unoccupied gristmill on the Virginia side of the Potomac. Later, fearing that a cannon factory nearby might attract a raiding party of the enemy, the clerks procured wagons from neighboring farmers, took the papers 35 miles away to Leesburg, and locked them in an empty house. It was not until the British fleet had left the waters of the Chesapeake that it was considered safe to return the papers to Washington.

On December 26, 1941, the five pages of the Constitution together with the single leaf of the Declaration of Independence were taken from the Library of Congress, where they had been kept for many years, and were stored in the vaults of the United States Bullion Depository at Fort Knox, Kentucky. Here they "rode out the war" safely.

Since 1952, visitors to Washington may view these historic documents at the Exhibition Hall of the National Archives. Sealed in bronze and glass cases filled with helium, the documents are protected from touch, light, heat, dust, and moisture. At a moment's notice, they can be lowered into a large safe that is bombproof, shockproof, and fireproof.

16. The title that best expresses the main idea of this selection is

A. "Three Courageous Clerks."

B. "The Constitution and Other Documents."

C. "How to Exhibit Valuables."

D. "Preserving America's Documents of Freedom."

17. Before the War of 1812, the Constitution and the Declaration of Independence were apparently kept in

A. Independence Hall.

B. Fort Knox, Kentucky.

C. the office of the State Department.

D. a gristmill in Virginia.

18. Nowadays, these documents are on view in the
   - A. National Archives' Exhibition Hall.
   - B. Library of Congress.
   - C. United States Bullion Depository.
   - D. United States Treasury Building.

19. An important reason for the installation of an apparatus for quick removal of the documents is the
   - A. possibility of a sudden disaster.
   - B. increasing number of tourists.
   - C. need for more storage space.
   - D. lack of respect for the documents.

20. The documents have been removed from Washington at least twice in order to preserve them from
   - A. dust, heat, and moisture.
   - B. careless handling.
   - C. possible war damage.
   - D. sale to foreign governments.

Questions 21–26 refer to the following passage.

The fall American History midterm was coming up fast. It was a huge test, covering the American Revolution and the beginning of the new United States. Tyler knew he needed to study, but there were so many things he'd rather do. Besides, all that history was back in the 1700s. What could the American Revolution possibly have to do with his life in the twenty-first century?

After school, Tyler went to soccer practice. He could have studied afterwards while he waited for his mother, but he didn't. He could have studied in the car. But he didn't. He went home and had dinner. Then he procrastinated a while longer, watching a TV show he had already seen at least five times. Finally, his mother said, "Tyler, shouldn't you be studying for that humongous history test?"

Tyler sighed. "Yes, Mom, but I'm frustrated that we have to learn all these irrelevant facts about a bunch of dead guys and events that happened more than two hundred years ago. Nothing I am learning impacts our lives today."

Mom shook her head. "That's where you're mistaken, Tyler, and I can give you an example. You have the freedom to complain about this test because a bunch of dead guys drafted the United States Constitution with a Bill of Rights. Number one on that Bill of Rights guarantees your freedom of speech.

"Seriously?" Tyler asked.

"Yes," Mom replied. "Those guys also wrote the Declaration of Independence, which says we are entitled to 'life, liberty, and the pursuit of happiness.' And that's just the tip of the iceberg. The American revolutionaries from the 1700s designed the country we have today. So let's pretend for now that happiness is a good grade, and the pursuit of happiness means studying!"

21. According to the passage, Tyler had opportunities to study at each of these times *except*

A. in the car.

B. after dinner.

C. before school.

D. after soccer.

22. Tyler was annoyed with studying American history primarily because

A. it took too much time away from other things he wanted to do.

B. he found it impossible to remember all the necessary facts.

C. his mother kept insisting that it was highly important.

D. he didn't understand how it related to his everyday life.

Reading Comprehension Drill 2

23. Each of these documents from early American history is mentioned in the story *except* the

- **A.** Declaration of Independence.
- **B.** Bill of Rights.
- **C.** United States Constitution.
- **D.** Federalist Papers.

24. In paragraph 6 (lines 20–21), when Tyler's mom says, "And that's just the tip of the iceberg," she means

- **A.** Tyler will be in major trouble if he doesn't study.
- **B.** there is much more to know about American history.
- **C.** icebergs were more common before global warming.
- **D.** procrastination will affect Tyler's history grades.

Questions 25–28 refer to the following passage.

Cotton fabrics treated with the XYZ Process have features that make them far superior to any previously known cotton fabrics treated with flame retardant. XYZ Process-treated fabrics are durable to repeated laundering and dry cleaning and are glow resistant as well as flame resistant; when exposed to flames or intense heat, they form tough, pliable, and protective barriers; are inert physiologically to persons handling or exposed to the fabric; are only slightly heavier than untreated fabrics; and are susceptible to further wet and dry finishing treatments. In addition, the treated fabrics exhibit little or no adverse change in feel, texture, and appearance, and are shrink-, rot-, and mildew resistant. The treatment reduces strength only slightly. Finished fabrics have "easy care" properties in that they are wrinkle-resistant and dry rapidly.

25. The author in the passage presents

- **A.** facts, but reaches no conclusion concerning the value of the process.
- **B.** a conclusion concerning the value of the process and facts to support that conclusion.
- **C.** a conclusion concerning the value of the process, unsupported by facts.
- **D.** neither facts nor conclusions, but merely describes the process.

26. Which of the following articles would be most suitable for the XYZ Process?

- **A.** Nylon stockings
- **B.** Woolen shirt
- **C.** Polyester slacks
- **D.** Cotton bedsheet

27. The main reason for treating a fabric with the XYZ Process is to

A. prepare the fabric for other wet and dry finishing treatments.

B. render it shrink-, rot- and mildew resistant.

C. increase its weight and strength.

D. reduce the chance that it will catch fire.

28. Which of the following would be considered a minor drawback of the XYZ Process?

A. It forms barriers when exposed to flame.

B. It makes fabrics mildew resistant.

C. It adds to the weight of fabrics.

D. It does not wash out of the fabric.

Questions 29–32 refer to the following passage.

Pearl was growing weary of working in the hot sun, having been there since early that morning, nailing shingle after shingle into the new church roof. Every time Pearl found herself wishing that she'd volunteered to help with the kitchen crew instead, she looked over at Reverend Cartwright working hard on his pile of shingles, and she found her inspiration in him. He had been the first to arrive on the roof that morning, and she was sure that he'd be the last to leave. Pearl had always admired Rev. Cartwright for his moving sermons and his ability to uplift any crowd of people. No matter how she was feeling, his Sunday messages always brought her back to looking on the positive side again. Seeing his hard work and dedication to the church rebuilding effort had made Pearl realize that she had only known a portion of Rev. Cartwright's caring up until now.

Each day and each night, Reverend Cartwright and his wife Mattie stood watch over the volunteer teams and lent their hands to the physical work whenever they could—whenever they weren't busy checking in supplies or organizing crews of people to start a new phase of the project. Every Wednesday night, the volunteers would pile into the makeshift sanctuary set up at old Cutter's barn just down the road and listen as Rev. Cartwright encouraged them to look for the silver lining in every cloud. He and Mattie refused to see the burning of their church as a setback. They chose instead, Rev. Cartwright preached, to see it as an opportunity: an opportunity to bring the congregation together in a united effort, which in fact was exactly what had happened.

29. Which word best describes the character of Reverend Cartwright in the story?
   - A. Playful
   - B. Angry
   - C. Dedicated
   - D. Frustrated

30. According to the passage, how was Pearl's church damaged?
   - A. By lightning
   - B. By a falling tree
   - C. By a flood
   - D. By a fire

31. In the opening of the passage, which of the following most likely explains why Pearl wishes she had volunteered for the kitchen crew instead of working on the roof?
   - A. She would meet more people on the kitchen crew.
   - B. The kitchen crew got to eat first.
   - C. Working on the kitchen crew was an easier job.
   - D. The kitchen crew held higher status.

32. Cutter's barn is used as a temporary
   - A. shelter for homeless people.
   - B. place of worship for the church members.
   - C. center for strategic planning.
   - D. kitchen for free meals.

Questions 33–37 refer to the following passage.

An excerpt from a Dead Sea Scroll describing Abraham's *sojourn* in Egypt and the beauty of Sarah, his wife, was recently made public for the first time. The 2,000-year-old scroll, badly preserved and extremely brittle, is the last of seven scrolls found in 1947 in the caves of the Judean desert south of Jericho. Scholars say that this scroll enlarges on the hitherto known Biblical tales of Lamech, Enoch, Noah, and Abraham.

This document of Hebrew University yielded *decipherable* contents only after months of exposure to controlled humidity. The centuries had compressed the leather scroll into a brittle, glued-together mass. After it had been rendered flexible, the scroll was folded into pages. Four complete pages, each with 34 lines of writing, resulted. Besides this, for their studies scholars had large sections of the decipherable writing on five other pages, and readable lines and words on additional pages. Scholars were delighted, for they had almost despaired of recovering the scroll as a readable document. The work of giving new life to the desiccated parchment and of unrolling it was done by an old German expert on ancient materials, under the supervision of two Israeli scholars.

33. As used in the passage, the word *sojourn* (line 1) most likely means

A. servitude.

B. stay.

C. flight.

D. difficulties.

34. As used in the passage, *decipherable* (line 6) means

A. intelligible.

B. durable.

C. exciting.

D. scholarly.

35. The scroll

A. was found in Egypt.

B. gives new details about people already known of.

C. tells of Abraham's life in the Judean desert.

D. is the first of seven found in 1947.

36. The scroll

A. belongs to an Israeli university.

B. is in Germany.

C. was deciphered by a German specialist.

D. was taken to Jericho.

37. The writing on the scroll

A. was finally legible throughout the document.

B. was legible on only four pages.

C. could be read on several pages.

D. was too damaged by age to be deciphered.

Questions 38–40 refer to the following passage.

In September 1953, a man in a ten-gallon hat appeared at the gate of New York's famous Bronx Zoo. "Just stopped by on my way through town," he told zoo officials. "I've got an animal outside I think you might like to see."

The officials raised their eyebrows and looked at each other meaningfully, but the man in the hat didn't seem to notice. He went on to introduce himself as Gene Holter. "I call it a Zonkey," he said calmly, "because it's a cross between a donkey and a zebra. I've got his parents out there, too."

The zoo officials didn't wait to hear about the parents. They left their desks and started for the gate. Outside, Mr. Holter opened the side door of a huge truck and reached inside. Calmly, he pulled out a gibbon, and hung it, by its tail, from a tree. Then he walked past five ostriches and carried out the baby Zonkey.

Just three weeks old, the only Zonkey in the world had long ears, a face and legs covered with candy stripes, and a body covered with brown baby fuzz. The parents were on hand, too. The father was no ordinary zebra. He was broken to ride, and one of the zoo officials realized a lifelong dream when he jumped on the zebra's back and cantered around.

When last seen, Mr. Holter and his caravan were on their way to Dayton and then to Anaheim, California, where they live year-round.

38. Mr. Holter's manner was

A. boastful.

B. excitable.

C. demanding.

D. matter-of-fact.

39. When Mr. Holter first approached the zoo officials, they

A. were excited about his announcement.

B. thought he was telling a tall tale.

C. thought he was an interesting person.

D. couldn't wait to realize a lifelong dream.

40. Mr. Holter probably made a living

A. as a veterinarian.

B. traveling and showing his animals.

C. breeding animals for scientific experiments.

D. working as a zoo official.

Questions 41–45 refer to the following passage.

Of all the characters in the legend of King Arthur, perhaps the one who has received least credit for his achievements is the knight Perceval. Perceval is a relatively obscure knight compared to other famous characters such as Lancelot or Galahad. Nonetheless, he accomplished very lofty goals during his service to King Arthur.

The story of Perceval appears first in a work entitled *The Story of the Grail*, written by a French author named Chrétien de Troyes. According to author and translator Kirk McElhearn, who specializes in the Perceval literature, Chrétien de Troyes died sometime in the 1180s, and the date of his birth remains unknown. His work, according to McElhearn, "marks the beginning of the Arthurian Legend, at least in what we know today."

Chrétien de Troyes' work tells the story of a young lad named Perceval, the son of a great warrior who was wounded in battle and later died of grief after his two oldest sons were killed in battle. Perceval at the time was very young, and his mother became determined that she would not lose her only remaining son. She lived with Perceval in the forest and tried to protect him from ever learning about knights, horses, armor, and battle.

As Perceval grows, he soon learns of knights who pass by on their way through the forest. He chooses to accompany the knights to learn of the world, much to his mother's sorrow. During his travels, Perceval gets a glimpse of the Holy Grail by chance in a castle. He does not understand the significance of the grail, and he neglects to ask about it. He later realizes that he has missed his opportunity to learn about the grail, so he sets off on a quest to find it again.

Unfortunately, we never learn what happens to Perceval in Chrétien de Troyes' version of the story. Chrétien died before the story was finished, so the ending of his text remains a mystery. According to other versions of the legend, however, Perceval was extremely noble and pure of heart, and these qualities eventually caused him to be granted guardianship of the Holy Grail.

41. Which statement best reflects the main idea of the passage?

A. Perceval is a less well-known character in the Arthurian legends who accomplished important goals for King Arthur.

B. Perceval is an important character in the Arthurian legends who has received the least credit for his accomplishments.

C. The legend of King Arthur's court emphasizes loyalty, courageousness, and honor.

D. The story of Perceval concerns a knight who misses his opportunity to learn about the Holy Grail.

42. Kirk McElhearn is a(n)

A. translator who translated the works of Chrétien de Troyes.

B. translator who translated the Arthurian legends from English to French.

C. author and translator who specializes in the Perceval literature.

D. author who has published a book regarding Chrétien de Troyes.

43. In *The Story of the Grail*, why does Perceval's mother keep him from learning about knights, horses, armor, and battle?

A. She wants to honor the memory of Perceval's father, who was opposed to war.

B. She wants to protect Perceval, because he is her only remaining son.

C. She feels that Perceval is too young to begin learning about these things.

D. She would prefer for Perceval to be a poet or a scholar instead of a warrior.

44. As used in the passage, the word *obscure* most likely means

A. not very capable.

B. not very confident.

C. not well-known.

D. not very likable.

45. According to the passage, Chrétien de Troyes

A. completed the story of Perceval in the 1190s.

B. saw the Holy Grail himself.

C. died before completing the story of Perceval.

D. was unknown until his work was translated.

Questions 46–49 refer to the following passage.

When we say a snake "glides," we have already persuaded ourselves to shiver a little. If we say that it "slithers," we are as good as undone. To avoid unsettling ourselves, we should state the simple fact—a snake walks.

A snake doesn't have any breastbone. The tips of its ribs are free-moving and amount, so to speak, to its feet. A snake walks along on its rib tips, pushing forward its ventral scutes at each "step," and it speeds up this mode of progress by undulating from side to side and by taking advantage of every rough "toehold" it can find in the terrain. Let's look at it this way: A human or other animal going forward on all fours is using a sort of locomotion that's familiar enough to all of us and isn't at all dismaying. Now: Suppose this walker is enclosed inside some sort of pliable encasement like a sacking. The front "feet" will still step forward, the "hind legs" still hitch along afterward. It will still be a standard enough sort of animal walking, only all we'll see now is a sort of wiggling of the sacking without visible feet. That's the snake way. A snake has its covering outside its feet, as an insect has its skeleton on its outside with no bones in the interior. There's nothing more "horrid" about the one arrangement than about the other.

46. The title below that expresses the main idea of this selection is

A. "Snake's Legs."

B. "Comparing Snakes to People."

C. "The Movement of a Snake."

D. "A Slimy Animal."

47. A snake's "feet" are its

A. toes.

B. ribs.

C. side.

D. breastbone.

48. The word *terrain* (line 7) means

A. terraced.

B. rocky ledge.

C. vertical hole.

D. ground areas.

49. We may conclude that the author

A. raises reptiles.

B. dislikes snakes.

C. is well informed about snakes.

D. thinks snakes move better than humans.

Questions 50–55 refer to the following passage.

Coming into the relay station with a rush, the Pony Express rider swung down from his exhausted mount and up onto a fresh horse with his precious *mochilla*, the saddle bag containing the mail. He was off again without a moment's delay. He was expected to reach the next station, and he did, or he died trying.

A rider might come into a station at dawn only to find that the station had been burned, the keepers killed, and the horses run off by attacking Indians. In that case he would continue to the next station without food or rest.

"Buffalo Bill," a boy of 18, made the longest continuous run in the history of the Pony Express, 384 miles. By riding 280 miles in just 22 hours, Jim Moore earned the distinction of having made the fastest run.

Ninety riders covered the trail at all times of the day and night, often risking their lives to get the mail through within the ten-day limit. Most made it in eight days.

On the average, the riders could travel 11 miles an hour, a quick pace over terrain that might require the horse to swim rivers or cat-foot its way along narrow cliff trails.

The pace of the mail delivery by Pony Express was snail-like by today's standards, but at the time of its commencement in 1860, it offered the fastest cross-country communication that had ever been achieved. Abraham Lincoln was elected president during that year, and thanks to the Pony Express, residents of California received news of Lincoln's victory in just over a week.

The Pony Express riders carried the mail between Missouri and California for less than two years. They stopped riding in 1861 when a telegraph line offered a swifter means of communication. The efforts of the riders are memorialized at the Pony Express National Museum, established in St. Joseph, Missouri. According to the records of the museum, the Pony Express lost only a single delivery of mail during the entire period of its operation.

Reading Comprehension Drill 2

50. The Pony Express rider stopped at a station to

A. get a few hours of sleep.

B. get a fresh mount.

C. sort the mail.

D. escape Native American attacks.

51. The *mochila* (line 2) refers to the

A. Pony Express rider's saddle bags.

B. Pony Express horses.

C. stations.

D. trails.

52. This passage implies that most of the Pony Express riders were

A. sure-footed.

B. faithful to their jobs.

C. mountain-bred.

D. killed.

53. Those sending mail by Pony Express could expect that it would reach its destination within

A. ten days.

B. five days.

C. a month.

D. before dawn.

54. The longest continuous run was

A. completed within 22 hours.

B. 280 miles.

C. made by traveling 11 miles per hour.

D. 384 miles.

55. Which of the following statements is most likely true, based on the passage?

A. The Pony Express was reliable at delivering the mail.

B. The Pony Express was operational throughout the 1860s.

C. Mail was delivered by Pony Express from east coast to west coast.

D. The Pony Express was less expensive than other forms of mail delivery.

Questions 56–59 refer to the following passage.

A list of America's top tourist destinations would probably not include Collinsville, Illinois. However, Collinsville boasts one distinctive attraction tourists will find nowhere else. It is the home of the world's largest catsup bottle.

Catsup was manufactured in Collinsville from around the turn of the twentieth century until the early 1960s. Although the catsup factory had several different owners, the product was known for most of its history as Brooks Catsup. Brooks often advertised its catsup using oversized bottles mounted on poles.

When the manufacturing plant needed a new water tower in 1947, the president of the company decided to take oversized bottle advertising to a new extreme. He had the water tower designed in the shape of a giant Brooks Catsup bottle. The 170-foot tall tower, a 70-foot ketchup bottle on a 100-foot platform, loomed over Collinsville, a constant reminder of the product being created nearby.

After the catsup factory shut down, the enormous tribute to America's favorite French fry sauce remained. Over the years, though, it fell into disrepair until, in the early 1990s, the town of Collinsville decided it couldn't afford to keep the tower and planned to demolish it. Enter a determined group of preservationists who held bake sales and sold thousands of T-shirts and sweatshirts to raise funds to refurbish the massive icon. They acquired enough money not only to fix up the bottle, but also to purchase a floodlight to illuminate it at night, and to create a maintenance fund for the bottle's future.

Today, the bottle is on the National Register of Historic Places. It has its own fan club, and Collinsville holds a festival each summer to continue raising money for the landmark that makes the town unique.

56. According to this article, the world's largest catsup bottle was not kept in good repair because

A. the catsup factory was closed.

B. catsup was no longer popular.

C. Collinsville became bankrupt.

D. the company got new advertising.

Reading Comprehension Drill 2

57. The world's largest catsup bottle was designed to function as

A. a tourist attraction.

B. a manufacturing plant.

C. an advertisement.

D. a water tower.

58. Someone who chose to vacation in Collinsville would most likely

A. want to learn about catsup manufacturing.

B. enjoy visiting unusual roadside attractions.

C. have a keen interest in national parks.

D. travel to a different festival each summer.

59. According to the passage, preservationists have done everything to raise money for the bottle except

A. sell sweatshirts.

B. have bake sales.

C. offer catsup samples.

D. hold summer festivals.

Questions 60–63 refer to the following passage.

American inventor Dean Kamen began his career at an early age. His first invention, at age five, was a gadget that assisted him with making his bed in the mornings.

As an adult, Kamen said, "Education is . . . the most important thing you can do with your life." As a child, though, he didn't care much for school. He felt bored because his classes did not address the subjects he was interested in. So, he educated himself by reading all he could about the questions he wanted to answer.

In high school, Kamen converted his parents' basement into a workshop for his projects. By the time he graduated, he was making a living as an inventor. In fact, he made more money than his mother, a teacher, and his father, a comic book artist, put together.

Making money is not the primary force behind Kamen's work, however. When he discovers something the world needs, he does his best to create it. His inventions have included a high-tech prosthetic arm, a portable kidney dialysis machine, and a low-cost water-purifying system for people in developing countries.

Seeing a wheelchair user struggle to leap a curb inspired Kamen to invent a wheelchair that climbs stairs. The chair has six wheels, four large and two small. All four large wheels are powered. To ascend stairs, the large wheels roll up and over each other, while a gyroscope adjusts the balance of the chair to keep it upright.

Kamen believes scientists and engineers should be considered stars, like athletes and actors. To encourage young people's interest in science, he founded a robotics program for kids. Teams compete to develop the best robot for a given task, such as shooting hoops. The robot competitions are run like sporting events, complete with mascots and cheering crowds.

60. The wheelchair Kamen invented is extraordinary because it

A. holds the user in a standing position.

B. goes up and down stairs.

C. does not leap curbs.

D. has large wheels.

61. According to this article, Dean Kamen

A. was not concerned about his own education.

B. wants to increase student interest in athletics.

C. stopped attending school at an early age.

D. believes education is of the utmost importance.

62. Dean Kamen is inspired to be an inventor primarily because he wants

A. to earn a great deal of money.

B. to be treated like a movie star.

C. to solve problems he sees in the world.

D. young people to become interested in science.

63. All of the following are inventions by Kamen mentioned in the passage *except* a

A. prosthetic arm.

B. dialysis machine.

C. water purifier.

D. robotic athlete.

Questions 64–66 refer to the following passage.

As he threw his head back in the chair, his glance happened to rest upon a bell, a disused bell, that hung in the room and communicated, for some purpose now forgotten, with a chamber in the highest story of the building. It was with great astonishment, and with a strange inexplicable dread, that, as he looked, he saw this bell begin to swing. Soon it rang out loudly, and so did every bell in the house.

This was succeeded by a clanking noise, deep down below as if some person were dragging a heavy chain over the casks in the wine merchant's cellar. Then he heard the noise much louder on the floors below; then coming up the stairs; then coming straight toward his door.

It came in through the heavy door, and a specter passed into the room before his eyes. And upon its coming in, the dying flame leaped up, as though it cried, "I know him! Marley's ghost!"

—from *A Christmas Carol,* by Charles Dickens

64. The bell that began ringing

A. was large and heavy.

B. did so by itself.

C. was attached to every bell in the house.

D. rested first on his glance.

65. The man who was listening to the bell

A. dragged a chain across the wine casks.

B. sat perfectly still.

C. was apparently very frightened.

D. is Marley's ghost.

66. The man in the story

A. first heard noises in his room.

B. is probably a wine merchant.

C. recognized Marley's ghost.

D. set the room on fire.

Questions 67–72 refer to the following passage.

"Sophistication by the reel" is the motto of Peretz Johannes, who selects juvenile films for Saturday viewing at the Museum of the City of New York. Sampling the intellectual climate of the young fans in this city for the past two years has convinced him that many people underestimate the taste level of young New Yorkers. Consequently, a year ago he began to show films ordinarily restricted to art movie distribution. The series proved enormously successful, and in September, when the program commenced for this season, youngsters from the five boroughs filled the theater.

As a student of history, Mr. Johannes has not confined himself to productions given awards in recent years, but he has spent many hours among dusty reels ferreting out such prewar favorites as the silhouette films Lotte Reiniger made in Germany. One program included two films based on children's stories, *The Little Red Lighthouse* and *Mike Mulligan and His Steam Shovel.* The movies are shown at 11 a.m. and 3 p.m., with a short program of stories and a demonstration of toys presented during the intermission.

67. Mr. Johannes is a

A. filmmaker.

B. film critic.

C. film selector.

D. student of film.

68. Admission to the program described is

A. limited to children in the neighborhood of the museum.

B. for Manhattan only.

C. available for all the city.

D. for teenagers only.

69. As used in the passage, the phrase *ferreting out* most nearly means

A. searching out.

B. dusting off.

C. editing.

D. protesting against.

70. The films are shown

A. year-round.

B. twice every day.

C. at the Museum of Modern Art.

D. on Saturday.

71. Mr. Johannes

A. followed an established policy in planning his programs.

B. has failed so far to secure a good audience.

C. limits his programs to the newest award-winning pictures.

D. evidently is a good judge of children's tastes.

72. Mr. Johannes found that children's taste in motion pictures

A. was more varied than had been thought.

B. ruled out pictures made before their own day.

C. was limited to cartoons.

D. was even poorer than adults had suspected.

Questions 73–75 refer to the following passage.

When Jason, the son of the dethroned king of Solcus, was a little boy, he was sent away from his parents and placed under the queerest schoolmaster that ever you heard of. This learned person was one of the people, or *quadrupeds*, called Centaurs. He lived in a cavern and had the body and legs of a white horse, with the head and shoulders of a man. His name was Chiron; and, in spite of his odd appearance, he was a very excellent teacher and had several scholars who afterward did him credit by making great figures in the world. The famous Hercules was one, and so was Achilles, and Philoctetes, likewise, and Aesculapius, who acquired immense repute as a doctor. The good Chiron taught his pupils how to play upon the harp and how to cure diseases and how to use the sword and shield, together with various other branches of education in which the lads of those days used to be instructed, instead of writing and arithmetic.

—from *The Golden Fleece*, by Nathaniel Hawthorne

73. The main purpose of this passage is to

A. describe Jason.

B. describe Chiron.

C. describe Jason's education.

D. name the scholars taught by Chiron.

74. The word *quadruped* probably means a(n)

A. creature with four feet.

B. creature with two feet.

C. strange schoolmaster.

D. educated person.

75. Chiron

A. taught writing and arithmetic to his pupils.

B. instructed the centaurs.

C. was the son of Solcus.

D. had the body and legs of a horse and the head and shoulders of a man.

Answer Key and Explanations

1. B	**16.** D	**31.** C	**46.** C	**61.** D
2. C	**17.** C	**32.** B	**47.** B	**62.** C
3. C	**18.** A	**33.** B	**48.** D	**63.** D
4. D	**19.** A	**34.** A	**49.** C	**64.** B
5. C	**20.** C	**35.** B	**50.** B	**65.** C
6. A	**21.** C	**36.** A	**51.** A	**66.** C
7. C	**22.** D	**37.** C	**52.** B	**67.** C
8. D	**23.** D	**38.** D	**53.** A	**68.** C
9. B	**24.** B	**39.** B	**54.** D	**69.** A
10. D	**25.** B	**40.** B	**55.** A	**70.** D
11. A	**26.** D	**41.** A	**56.** A	**71.** D
12. B	**27.** D	**42.** C	**57.** D	**72.** A
13. B	**28.** C	**43.** B	**58.** B	**73.** B
14. A	**29.** C	**44.** C	**59.** C	**74.** A
15. D	**30.** D	**45.** C	**60.** B	**75.** D

1. **The correct answer is B.** The first sentence of the passage (lines 1–2) makes the point that one's perceptions are influenced by one's emotional state.

2. **The correct answer is C.** Other synonyms for *dissipate* are *scatter*, *dissolve*, and *evaporate.*

3. **The correct answer is C.** Find this answer by substituting the choices for the word *refinement.* Then continue reading the passage following the substituted word, and the correct contextual meaning should be clear: "A phase of my life which has lost something through *improvement* is the game of croquet." The irony of this statement is that the improvement of the game has led to a less enjoyable experience for the author when playing it.

4. **The correct answer is D.** The author's emotions don't appear to be extreme, as they would if he or she were *very* angry (choice A) or *terribly* grieved (choice B), but the fact that the author considers a phase of his or her life as "lost" shows that he or she is not indifferent (choice C) to the situation. The author seems to regret the changes that have been made.

5. **The correct answer is C.** To answer this question, you need to first figure out how you would describe the mood of the paragraph in your own words. The author seems regretful that the way the croquet gameplay has changed and wishes for the experiences from the past. Which of the given words best fits that definition? *Dogmatic* (choice A), *very earnest* (choice B), and *belligerent* (choice D) all describe strong, opinionated writing, but the passage has a gentler, more nostalgic feel. *Wistful* is the best choice.

6. **The correct answer is A.** The author's description of the new set and new croquet course as compared to the old makes it clear that the new arrangement is far more exact. On the other hand, all concerned seem to have less fun.

7. **The correct answer is C.** Now that the course of play is measured exactly and the playful spontaneity that the dog and the little boy brought to the game is no longer a part of the experience, the environment is more tense and leads to minor quarrels. The balls are new and roll perfectly, so choice B is incorrect. The dog cannot chase the balls because it is not allowed on the green, and the little boy is made to be quiet during play, so choices A and D are incorrect.

8. **The correct answer is D.** This answer can be inferred from the selection. The author compares the past experience of playing croquet with an old and worn set and haphazardly placed wickets, with "everyone in good spirits," to the current, more formalized and exactly measured game setup, which results in the players feeling "tense and out of sorts."

9. **The correct answer is B.** The author appears to be a genial sort who enjoys children, animals, sunsets, and sport for sport's sake. All of the other choices imply negativism on the part of the author.

10. **The correct answer is D.** The selection describes the properties of zirconium in its various forms, so "Characteristics of Zirconium" is an appropriate title. "A Vital Substance (choice A) is too vague because it doesn't specify what the substance is or what it is vital to; "A Safe, Stable Substance" (choice B) is less than accurate, because in its powdered form, zirconium is neither safe nor stable; and "Zirconium's Uses in Surgery" (choice C) highlights a minor detail in the passage.

11. **The correct answer is A.** In the context of the passage, *docile* means "stable." The author is using personification to describe the qualities of zirconium in two of its states. Recall that solid zirconium, which can be used in delicate brain surgeries, is called "docile" in contrast to the much more volatile powdered zirconium, which is described as "violent."

12. **The correct answer is B.** An emphasis of the selection is that increasing uses are being found for zirconium.

13. **The correct answer is B.** Paragraph 1 of the passage (lines 1–4) details the dangerous nature of powered zirconium, stating, among other things, that under some circumstances it cannot be extinguished with water and that munitions makers consider it to be too dangerous to work with.

14. **The correct answer is A.** In both the second and third paragraphs, zirconium is described as a metal.

15. **The correct answer is D.** If zirconium is too dangerous to be used in ammunition, it is most certainly too dangerous to be used in fireworks.

16. **The correct answer is D.** The selection traces the history of protection of our documents of freedom during times of war, so the title "Preserving America's Documents of Freedom" is the most appropriate. The other titles refer to details included in the passage but do not reflect its main idea.

17. **The correct answer is C.** If State Department clerks in Washington scooped up the documents and stuffed them into linen sacks, the documents must have been lying around the office.

18. **The correct answer is A.** According to the last paragraph, these historical documents have been on display at the Exhibition Hall of the National Archives since 1952.

19. **The correct answer is A.** Bombs, shock, and fire are sudden disasters against which the documents need protection.

20. **The correct answer is C.** The documents have been moved for their protection during times of war. The first time mentioned in the passage was when the British advanced on and burned Washington in 1814 during the War of 1812; the second time occurred during the opening days of World War II, on December 26, 1941, shortly after the Japanese attacked Pearl Harbor on December 7, 1941.

21. **The correct answer is C.** "Before school" is the only possible study time *not* mentioned in the story.

22. **The correct answer is D.** The last sentence in paragraph 1 ("What could the American Revolution possibly have to do with his life in the twenty-first century?") lets readers know the main reason Tyler is not happy studying American history. He didn't understand how it related to his everyday life, making choice D the best answer.

23. **The correct answer is D.** The Federalist Papers are not mentioned in the story. The other three answer choices are documents from early American history that Tyler's mother mentions.

24. **The correct answer is B.** After Tyler's mom says, "And that's just the tip of the iceberg," she implies that there is much more to know in the next sentence of that paragraph.

25. **The correct answer is B.** This is a combination main idea and interpretation question. If you cannot answer this question readily, reread the selection. The author clearly thinks that the XYZ Process is terrific and says so in the first sentence. The rest of the selection presents a wealth of facts to support the initial claim.

26. **The correct answer is D.** At first glance, you might think that this is an inference question requiring you to make a judgment based upon the few drawbacks of the process. Closer reading, however, shows you that there is no contest for the correct answer here. This is a simple question of fact. The XYZ Process is a treatment for cotton fabrics.

27. **The correct answer is D.** This is a main idea question. You must distinguish between the main idea and the supporting and incidental facts. The passage begins by comparing XYZ Process-treated fabrics to other cotton fabrics treated with flame retardant, and then later goes into detail about their flame resistance—when exposed to flames or intense heat, they form tough, pliable, and protective barriers.

28. **The correct answer is C.** A drawback is a negative feature. The selection mentions only two negative features. The treatment reduces strength slightly, and it makes fabrics slightly heavier than untreated fabrics. Only one of these negative features is offered among the answer choices.

29. **The correct answer is C.** Reverend Cartwright is described throughout the story as someone who is a hard worker and who is very devoted to his church. The passage states in paragraph 1 (lines 4–6), for instance, that Reverend Cartwright has spent the entire day working hard on the roof and that he will continue to work until all the volunteers have left. In the last paragraph, the passage states that Reverend Cartwright and his wife always help with the volunteer efforts themselves, doing the actual work when they are not coordinating projects. These descriptions of Reverend Cartwright show that he is very dedicated to the church. Choice A is incorrect because nothing in the passage suggests that Reverend Cartwright is particularly playful (choice A). He is not described as joking or humorous, but as a hard worker who is very positive. Choices B and D are also incorrect because they express negative qualities, while Reverend Cartwright is described in the story in a very positive manner. He doesn't appear to be angry (choice B) or frustrated (choice D) about the damage to their church, for example; instead, he sees this as a positive opportunity.

30. **The correct answer is D.** The answer to this question is buried a little bit in the passage, but it is still there. The last paragraph briefly mentions that Reverend Cartwright and his wife "refused to see the burning of their church as a setback." Thus, we know that the church was damaged by a fire.

31. **The correct answer is C.** In the opening of the passage, Pearl is described as very tired and weary as she works on the roof. We can infer that she momentarily wishes she had been assigned to the kitchen crew because it is an easier job.

32. **The correct answer is B.** The barn is described as a makeshift sanctuary. *Sanctuary*, in this case, means a holy place or a place of worship.

33. **The correct answer is B.** A sojourn is a visit or a temporary stay.

34. **The correct answer is A.** The context of the second paragraph should help you to figure out the meaning of this word. In other contexts, *decipher* may mean "to decode." Here it means "to make out the meaning of," in this case, ancient, nearly illegible, inscriptions or writings.

35. **The correct answer is B.** See the last sentence of the first paragraph (lines 4–5). By enlarging on hitherto known tales of the named persons, the scroll is giving new details about persons already known of. The scroll is the last of the seven found in 1947, not the first. It tells of Abraham's stay in Egypt, but it was found in the Judean desert of Israel.

36. **The correct answer is A.** The second paragraph opens by telling us that the scroll belongs to Hebrew University. If you were not certain that Hebrew University is an Israeli university, the statement that the work is being done under the supervision of Israeli scholars (line 14) should confirm this.

37. **The correct answer is C.** If this question gives you trouble, reread the middle of the second paragraph (lines 9–11). The readable material included four full pages, legible parts of five other pages, and some lines and words on additional pages.

38. **The correct answer is D.** "Just stopped by..." (line 2) is quite a matter-of-fact way of speaking.

39. **The correct answer is B.** The officials' raised eyebrows (line 4) imply disbelief.

40. **The correct answer is B.** Mr. Holter had a caravan of animals; was in New York on his way to Dayton, Ohio; and resided in Anaheim, California. You can infer that he made his living traveling and showing his animals.

41. **The correct answer is A.** The correct answer to a "main idea" question will always summarize the main idea that the author was trying to get across in writing the passage. In this case, the author starts the passage by telling us of the importance of Perceval's contributions to King Arthur's court. Then, he explains Perceval's story and states that in some versions of the story, Perceval was awarded the position of guardian of the Holy Grail. The passage does not focus mainly on how little credit Perceval received (choice B) but instead describes his accomplishments. Choice C is too broad, and choice D is too narrow to reflect the main idea.

42. **The correct answer is C.** In paragraph 2 we are told that McElhearn is an author and a translator who specializes in the Perceval literature. The passage never mentions that McElhearn has translated the works of Chrétien de Troyes (choice A) or the Arthurian legends (choice B). In addition, although McElhearn does seem knowledgeable about Chrétien de Troyes, we are never told that McElhearn has published a book regarding him (choice D).

43. **The correct answer is B.** The answer to this question can be found in paragraph 3, which explains that Perceval's mother kept him sheltered because she wished to protect him. Perceval's mother did not want to lose her only remaining son, so she kept him from learning about the aspects of war.

44. **The correct answer is C.** To answer this vocabulary question, it is helpful to look for clues in the sentence and the paragraph around it that might help you to understand the meaning of the word *obscure*. The second sentence of Paragraph 1 states that Perceval is *obscure* compared to other famous characters such as Lancelot or Galahad (lines 2–3). Lancelot and Galahad are knights that many people know about. Perceval is being compared to them, and the sentence gives us the sense that Perceval doesn't quite measure up. The sentence prior to this one also states that Perceval hasn't been given much credit for his accomplishments—in other words, people don't recognize him for what he achieved. This must mean that Perceval is not very famous, like Lancelot and Galahad are. The clues from the sentence and the paragraph suggest that the word *obscure* must mean the opposite of *famous*, so "not well-known" is the correct choice.

45. **The correct answer is C.** The last paragraph of the passage states that Chrétien de Troyes died before completing the story of Perceval (line 23). We know from paragraph 2 that he died in the 1180s (line 8), so choice A cannot be correct. Choice D is incorrect because the passage does not address how well known his work was before it was translated. The Holy Grail is a mythical object, so it would have been impossible for Chrétien de Troyes to have seen it, making choice B incorrect as well.

46. **The correct answer is C.** The selection graphically details the movement of a snake. While much of the description is in terms of legs and feet, the point of the selection is to fully describe the means of locomotion.

47. **The correct answer is B.** The second sentence of the second paragraph makes this statement. The remainder of the paragraph expands on the theme.

48. **The correct answer is D.** This word appears in line 7. Read carefully and you can figure out the meaning from the context. *Terrain* means "earth," with reference to its topographical features.

49. **The correct answer is C.** The detail in this selection indicates that the author knows a good deal about snakes.

50. **The correct answer is B.** The first sentence of the passage states that the Pony Express rider swung down from his exhausted mount and up onto a fresh horse in order to make the mail delivery.

51. **The correct answer is A.** This definition of the mochila is given at the end of the first sentence (line 2).

52. **The correct answer is B.** The entire selection extols the dedication of the Pony Express riders in the face of the hazards they met.

53. **The correct answer is A.** Paragraph 4 (line 12) states that there was a ten-day limit in which the route must be covered.

54. **The correct answer is D.** Buffalo Bill made the longest continuous run of 384 miles; Jim Moore made the fastest run, 280 miles in 22 hours.

55. **The correct answer is A.** The last sentence of the passage states that the Pony Express lost only a single delivery of mail during the entire period of its operation. Thus, we can infer that mail sent by Pony Express got through to its destination reliably.

56. **The correct answer is A.** Paragraph 4, lines 13–15, state that the world's biggest catsup bottle fell into poor repair after the catsup factory closed.

57. **The correct answer is D.** This information is found in the first and second sentences of paragraph 3: "When the manufacturing plant needed a new water tower in 1947, the president of the company … had the water tower designed in the shape of a giant Brooks Catsup bottle."

58. **The correct answer is B.** The world's biggest catsup bottle is popular because it is odd and one-of-a-kind. Clearly, someone who enjoyed visiting unusual roadside attractions would choose to vacation in Collinsville.

59. **The correct answer is C.** The passage does not state that preservationists offered catsup samples as part of their fundraising.

60. **The correct answer is B.** Kamen's wheelchair invention was designed with the ability to climb stairs. The article does not say the chair holds the user in a standing position (choice A). Choice C is also incorrect; if the chair climbs stairs, it could definitely leap a curb. All wheelchairs have at least one set of large wheels (choice D) so the fact Kamen's invention has them would not make it extraordinary.

61. **The correct answer is D.** The quote by Dean Kamen in lines 3–4 states his belief in the importance of education.

62. **The correct answer is C.** Paragraph 4, sentence 2 states, "When he [Kamen] discovers something the world needs, he does his best to create it."

63. **The correct answer is D.** Paragraph 4 lists the items invented by Kamen. This list rules out each answer except robotic athlete.

64. **The correct answer is B.** The bell began to ring by itself. The bell might have been large and heavy, but we have no way of knowing this from the passage. The ringing of every bell in the house would likely be due to the same supernatural factors that caused the first bell to ring.

65. **The correct answer is C.** Obviously, this was a frightening experience. Also, "inexplicable dread" indicates fear.

66. **The correct answer is C.** If the man imagined the flame crying out the identity of the specter, he must have recognized it himself.

67. **The correct answer is C.** Mr. Johannes selects films for showing. He is a student of history.

68. **The correct answer is C.** The last sentence of the first paragraph states that youngsters from all five boroughs of the City of New York attend the program.

69. **The correct answer is A.** To *ferret out* is to "dig" or to "search out." A ferret is a weasel-like animal that hunts out small rodents by flushing them out of their burrows.

70. **The correct answer is D.** Read carefully. The film series begins in September. The films are shown at the Museum of the City of New York at 11 a.m. and 3 p.m. on Saturdays only.

71. **The correct answer is D.** Because Mr. Johannes chooses a wide variety of films and regularly fills his theater, he is obviously a good judge of children's tastes.

72. **The correct answer is A.** Mr. Johannes found that children's taste in motion pictures was more varied than had been thought. You can find the answer in paragraph 1 (lines 2–4).

73. **The correct answer is B.** This is a main idea question. The paragraph describes Chiron.

74. **The correct answer is A.** The paragraph states that Chiron had the legs of a horse; a horse has four legs. From basic etymology, you know that *quad* means "four" and that *ped* refers to feet.

75. **The correct answer is D.** Read carefully. The physical description is the only choice supported by the paragraph. The last sentence specifically states that Chiron did *not* teach writing and arithmetic (choice A). Chiron was a centaur, but the passage does not say that he taught centaurs (choice B); rather, his students included Hercules and Achilles. Jason, not Chiron, was the son of Solcus (choice C).

Reading–Vocabulary Drill

75 Questions

Directions: Choose the word that means the same or about the same as the underlined word.

1. a devout monk

A. reverent
B. lacking
C. growing
D. lonely

2. to abate the fury

A. minnow
B. grow
C. formula
D. ebb

3. an outcast of his community

A. paragon
B. parasite
C. pariah
D. pagan

4. an affable gentleman

A. appetizing
B. unappetizing
C. foolish
D. amiable

5. the mangled wreckage

A. intact
B. disfigured and torn
C. lost
D. faded

6. a weary runner

A. energetic

B. lost

C. tired

D. winning

7. the smallest hovel

A. hut

B. shovel

C. house

D. palace

8. to loathe the task

A. hate

B. love

C. help

D. lose

9. a deft move

A. skillful

B. dangerous

C. thoughtless

D. final

10. many diverse cultures

A. similar

B. valuable

C. ancient

D. varied

11. an infraction of the rules

A. violation

B. use

C. interpretation

D. part

12. an extensive search

A. complicated

B. superficial

C. thorough

D. leisurely

13. lofty goals

A. elevated

B. unworthy

C. apparent

D. confusing

14. a pleasing demeanor

A. smell

B. sight

C. behavior

D. understanding

15. a disheveled bedroom

A. large

B. messy

C. complicated

D. spacious

16. move hastily

A. slowly

B. deliberately

C. steadily

D. quickly

17. to achieve recognition

A. attain

B. deserve

C. seek

D. squander

18. placid waters

A. stormy

B. churning

C. muddied

D. peaceful

19. much rejoicing

A. celebrating

B. mourning

C. relaxing

D. studying

20. a large segment

A. hole

B. section

C. discussion

D. mystery

21. fascinating new developments

A. boring

B. important

C. confusing

D. interesting

22. highly anticipated arrival

A. expected

B. late

C. departed

D. unclear

23. decaying leaves

A. growing

B. falling

C. rotting

D. colorful

24. an alternate plan

A. replacement

B. ineffective

C. ambitious

D. inferior

25. estimate the cost

A. calculate approximately

B. approve of

C. discount

D. pay for

26. generic canned goods

A. individual

B. common

C. delicious

D. expensive

27. vibrant colors

A. drab and dull

B. bold and bright

C. transparent

D. black and white

28. a puzzling dilemma

A. explicable

B. definite

C. amusing

D. problematic

29. driving recklessly

A. easily

B. carelessly

C. carefully

D. for the first time

30. a rambling speaker

A. interesting

B. motivational

C. long-winded

D. loud

31. enormous buildings

A. intricate

B. close together

C. huge

D. stone

32. a full agenda

A. receipt

B. agent

C. combination

D. schedule

33. a credible witness

A. believable

B. untrue

C. correct

D. suitable

34. to intervene on her behalf

A. induce

B. invert

C. interfere

D. solve

35. a mundane task

A. stupid

B. extraordinary

C. weekly

D. commonplace

36. dehydrated food supplies
   A. airless
   B. deflated
   C. waterless
   D. worthless

37. the prevalent attitude among teens
   A. predating
   B. predominant
   C. preeminent
   D. prior

38. a succinct report
   A. concise
   B. superfluous
   C. despicable
   D. fearful

39. nocturnal creatures
   A. by night
   B. by day
   C. alternating
   D. frequent

40. an equitable distribution
   A. preferential
   B. fair
   C. unreasonable
   D. biased

41. expedite the shipment
   A. hinder
   B. harm
   C. send
   D. hasten

42. a <u>turbulent</u> struggle
    A. authentic
    B. tranquil
    C. violent
    D. tamed

43. a <u>tenacious</u> salesman
    A. persistent
    B. thin
    C. timid
    D. divisive

44. <u>pertinent</u> information
    A. applicable
    B. truthful
    C. irreverent
    D. irrelevant

45. <u>dogmatic</u> views on music
    A. bovine
    B. canine
    C. opinionated
    D. traditional

46. <u>unscrupulous</u> business practices
    A. dirty
    B. honest
    C. austere
    D. unprincipled

47. a <u>wily</u> opponent
    A. crooked
    B. narrow
    C. cunning
    D. blunt

48. blatant spelling error
- **A.** insipid
- **B.** obvious
- **C.** shining
- **D.** secret

49. a pretext of a headache
- **A.** excuse
- **B.** preface
- **C.** answer
- **D.** doubt

50. evasion of the topic
- **A.** attack
- **B.** displeasure
- **C.** avoidance
- **D.** fatigue

51. an indispensable aid
- **A.** incontrovertible
- **B.** essential
- **C.** impetuous
- **D.** ungovernable

52. obliterate the evidence
- **A.** obligate
- **B.** subjugate
- **C.** erase
- **D.** maintain

53. an amiable hostess
- **A.** forgetful
- **B.** efficient
- **C.** friendly
- **D.** grumpy

54. writhe in pain
   A. strangle
   B. topple
   C. slide
   D. twist

55. a heartfelt endorsement
   A. inscription
   B. approval
   C. editorial
   D. signature

56. convert the room
   A. reform
   B. predict
   C. weave
   D. transform

57. an erudite lecture
   A. educated
   B. unrefined
   C. long-winded
   D. scintillating

58. endeavor to carry on
   A. expectation
   B. attempt
   C. tack
   D. necessity

59. feint with your right fist
   A. distract
   B. proclaim
   C. penalize
   D. scavenge

60. withstand peer pressure

A. external

B. beginner

C. equal

D. look

61. trite expressions

A. unskilled

B. common

C. unlikely

D. ignorant

62. a grimace of rage

A. scowl

B. grindstone

C. journal

D. treasure

63. compel you to attend

A. calculated

B. combined

C. collected

D. forced

64. an ally in times of need

A. opponent

B. passage

C. helper

D. preference

65. solicit assistance

A. consent

B. comfort

C. request

D. help

66. refute his claims

A. demolish

B. postpone

C. disprove

D. assist

67. explicit instructions

A. ambiguous

B. clearly stated

C. give information about

D. to blow out

68. retain your receipt

A. pay out

B. play

C. keep

D. inquire

69. confidential correspondence

A. letters

B. files

C. testimony

D. response

70. legitimate claim

A. democratic

B. legal

C. genealogical

D. underworld

71. deduct it from my paycheck

A. conceal

B. understand

C. subtract

D. terminate

72. return in a fortnight

A. two weeks

B. one week

C. two months

D. one month

73. preempt the scheduled programming

A. steal

B. empty

C. preview

D. appropriate

74. highest income per capita

A. for an entire population

B. by income

C. for each person

D. for every adult

75. optional features

A. not required

B. infrequent

C. choosy

D. for sale

Answer Key and Explanations

1. A	**16.** D	**31.** C	**46.** D	**61.** B
2. D	**17.** A	**32.** D	**47.** C	**62.** A
3. C	**18.** D	**33.** A	**48.** B	**63.** D
4. D	**19.** A	**34.** C	**49.** A	**64.** C
5. B	**20.** B	**35.** D	**50.** C	**65.** C
6. C	**21.** D	**36.** C	**51.** B	**66.** C
7. A	**22.** A	**37.** B	**52.** C	**67.** B
8. A	**23.** C	**38.** A	**53.** C	**68.** C
9. A	**24.** A	**39.** A	**54.** D	**69.** A
10. D	**25.** A	**40.** B	**55.** B	**70.** B
11. A	**26.** B	**41.** D	**56.** D	**71.** C
12. C	**27.** B	**42.** C	**57.** A	**72.** A
13. A	**28.** D	**43.** A	**58.** B	**73.** D
14. C	**29.** B	**44.** A	**59.** A	**74.** C
15. B	**30.** C	**45.** C	**60.** C	**75.** A

1. **The correct answer is A.** *Devout* means "reverent, religious, or pious."

2. **The correct answer is D.** *Abate* means "to subside, diminish, or ebb."

3. **The correct answer is C.** An outcast is a pariah. Other synonyms for *outcast* include *reject* and *persona non grata.*

4. **The correct answer is D.** *Affable* means "pleasant," "gracious," "sociable," and "amiable."

5. **The correct answer is B.** *Mangled* means "disfigured and torn." Other synonyms for *mangled* include *distorted* and *corrupted.*

6. **The correct answer is C.** *Weary* means "tired." Other synonyms for *weary* include *exhausted* and *fatigued.*

7. **The correct answer is A.** A *hovel* is a "cottage," a "hut," or a "cabin."

8. **The correct answer is A.** *Loathe* means to "detest," "abhor," or "hate."

9. **The correct answer is A.** *Deft* means "dexterous," "masterful," or "skillful."

10. **The correct answer is D.** *Diverse* means "varied." Other synonyms for *diverse* include *different*, *unalike*, or *distinct*.

11. **The correct answer is A.** *Infraction* means "a failure to follow the rules" or "a violation."

12. **The correct answer is C.** *Extensive* means "thorough," "comprehensive," or "far-reaching."

13. **The correct answer is A.** *Lofty* means "elevated." Other synonyms for *lofty* include *raised*, *high*, and *towering*.

14. **The correct answer is C.** *Demeanor* means "behavior," or "the way in which one conducts oneself." Other synonyms for *demeanor* include *manner* and *deportment*.

15. **The correct answer is B.** *Disheveled* and *messy* are synonyms, both meaning "not tidy."

16. **The correct answer is D.** *Hastily* means "quickly." Other synonyms for *hastily* include *swiftly* and *hurriedly*.

17. **The correct answer is A.** *Achieve* means "to attain." Other synonyms for *achieve* include *accomplish*, *gain*, and *reach*.

18. **The correct answer is D.** *Placid* means "peaceful." Other synonyms for *placid* include *calm* and *serene*.

19. **The correct answer is A.** *Rejoicing* means "celebrating." Other synonyms for *rejoicing* include *reveling* and *exulting*.

20. **The correct answer is B.** *Segment* means "section." Other synonyms for *segment* include *fragment* and *portion*.

21. **The correct answer is D.** *Fascinating* means "interesting." Other synonyms for *fascinating* include *intriguing*, *captivating*, and *enticing*.

22. **The correct answer is A.** *Anticipated* means "expected." Other synonyms for *anticipated* include *hoped for* and *awaited*.

23. **The correct answer is C.** *Decaying* means "rotting." Other synonyms for *decaying* include *decomposing* and *disintegrating*.

24. **The correct answer is A.** *Alternate* means "replacement." Other synonyms for *alternate* include *substitute* and *stand-in*.

25. **The correct answer is A.** *Estimate* means "to calculate approximately." Other synonyms for *estimate* include *approximate* and *reckon*.

26. **The correct answer is B.** *Generic* and *common* are synonyms, both meaning "part of a broad group," "not of a specific brand name," or without a distinct quality."

27. **The correct answer is B.** *Vibrant* means "bold and bright." Other synonyms for *vibrant* include *vivid* and *dazzling*.

28. **The correct answer is D.** *Puzzling* means "problematic." Other synonyms for *puzzling* include "perplexing" and "bewildering." Be careful to read the given word. *Explicable* (choice A) is an antonym for *puzzling*; *inexplicable* is its synonym.

29. **The correct answer is B.** *Recklessly* means "carelessly." Other synonyms for *recklessly* include *thoughtlessly* and *wildly*.

30. **The correct answer is C.** *Rambling* means "long-winded and wordy." Other synonyms for *rambling* include *verbose* and *garrulous*.

31. **The correct answer is C.** *Enormous* means "huge." Other synonyms for *enormous* include *gigantic*, *immense*, and *monstrous*.

32. **The correct answer is D.** An agenda is a program of things to be done, or a schedule.

33. **The correct answer is A.** *Credible* means "believable." Other synonyms for *credible* are *plausible* and *reliable*.

34. **The correct answer is C.** To intervene is to come between two people or things either to interfere or to influence positively.

35. **The correct answer is D.** *Mundane* means "commonplace," "earthly," or "ordinary."

36. **The correct answer is C.** To dehydrate is to remove water; therefore, *dehydrated* means "waterless."

37. **The correct answer is B.** *Prevalent* means "widely existing," "prevailing," or "generally accepted."

38. **The correct answer is A.** *Succinct* means "brief and to the point."

39. **The correct answer is A.** That which is nocturnal happens at night.

40. **The correct answer is B.** *Equitable* means "fair" and "just."

41. **The correct answer is D.** *Expedite* means "to accelerate the progress of" or "to speed up."

42. **The correct answer is C.** *Turbulent* means "marked by bursts of intense activity or destructive or violent force."

43. **The correct answer is A.** *Tenacious* means "persistent" or "unwaveringly determined."

44. **The correct answer is A.** *Pertinent* means "relevant" or "applicable."

45. **The correct answer is C.** *Dogmatic* means "dictatorial" or "opinionated." The word has to do with doctrine or dogma, not with dogs.

46. **The correct answer is D.** One who is unscrupulous is not restrained by ideas of right and wrong and thus would be considered unprincipled.

47. **The correct answer is C.** *Wily* means "cunning," "crafty," or "sly."

48. **The correct answer is B.** *Blatant* means "obvious" and "flagrant," or "glaring."

49. **The correct answer is A.** A pretext is a false reason or an excuse.

50. **The correct answer is C.** Evasion is subterfuge or avoidance.

51. **The correct answer is B.** That which is indispensable is absolutely essential.

52. **The correct answer is C.** To obliterate is to destroy without leaving a trace.

53. **The correct answer is C.** *Amiable* means "pleasant," "friendly," and "good-natured."

54. **The correct answer is D.** To writhe is to twist, squirm, or contort, usually in discomfort.

55. **The correct answer is B.** An endorsement is a statement of approval. Be sure to consider the context when answering the question. An endorsement can also be a signature (choice D) on the back of a check, but that definition would not make sense in this context.

56. **The correct answer is D.** To convert is to transform from one form, appearance, or use to another.

57. **The correct answer is A.** *Erudite* means "educated" or "scholarly."

58. **The correct answer is B.** To endeavor is to attempt or to try.

59. **The correct answer is A.** To feint is to distract or divert attention away from one's real intent, or to fool.

60. **The correct answer is C.** A peer is someone or something that is of equal standing to another. Be sure to consider the context when answering the question. To peer can also mean to look intently (choice D), but that definition would not make sense in this context.

61. **The correct answer is B.** *Trite* means "boring as a result of overuse," or "common."

62. **The correct answer is A.** A grimace is a scowling facial expression of disgust or displeasure.

63. **The correct answer is D.** To compel is to force. Other synonyms for *compel* are *coerce*, *make*, or *pressure*.

64. **The correct answer is C.** An ally is an associate of another with a common purpose, or a helper.

65. **The correct answer is C.** *Solicit* means "to approach with a request or plea."

66. **The correct answer is C.** To refute is to disprove or show something to be false.

67. **The correct answer is B.** *Explicit* means "distinct," "observable," or "clearly stated."

68. **The correct answer is C.** To retain is to hold on to or to keep.

69. **The correct answer is A.** Correspondence is an exchange of letters or the letters themselves.

70. **The correct answer is B.** *Legitimate* means "conforming to the law; legal" or "abiding by the rules."

71. **The correct answer is C.** To deduct is to subtract.

72. **The correct answer is A.** A fortnight (fourteen nights) is a period of two weeks.

73. **The correct answer is D.** To preempt is to replace one thing with something else, usually considered to be of higher priority or greater importance than what is replaced.

74. **The correct answer is C.** *Per capita* literally means "for each head," and therefore for each person, regardless of age.

75. **The correct answer is A.** That which is optional is left to one's choice and is therefore not required.

Chapter 3

Written Expression and Language

Introduction to Written Expression and Language Questions

There is a right way and a wrong way to express yourself formally. There are rules for spelling and capitalizing words, and forming those words into well-punctuated, grammatically correct, consistently styled, well-expressed sentences. Your ability to do so is measured in TACHS written expression and HSPT exam language questions. These questions include spelling, capitalization, punctuation, and usage and composition questions.

Spelling questions measure your ability to recognize words that are spelled incorrectly.

Capitalization questions measure your ability to recognize the correct ways to capitalize proper names and titles and to notice errors such as when the first words of sentences or the pronoun *I* are not capitalized.

Punctuation questions measure your ability to recognize when a sentence requires punctuation, contains unnecessary punctuation, or misuses punctuation. The punctuation may include marks such as periods, commas, quotation marks, question marks, exclamation marks, em dashes, hyphens, colons, semicolons, parentheses, and brackets.

Usage and composition questions measure your ability to recognize mistakes in grammar, expression, and style. Usage mistakes may involve problems with subject-verb agreement, pronoun agreement, adjective and adverb use, or commonly confused words. Composition mistakes may include problems with topic development, organization, and the appropriateness of language.

For each of these question types on the HSPT, you will be presented three sentences, one of which may contain a mistake in spelling, capitalization, punctuation, style, or grammar. The particular problem will not be explicitly identified for you. If you notice an error in the provided sentence, you must select the answer choice that corrects the error. If there is no error, select *No mistakes.*

Written Expression and Language Questions

Now we'll walk you through examples of each type of written expression and language question.

1. **A.** The child was being careless and dropped his glass.
   B. The airplane flys through the cloud-speckled sky.
   C. The young horse is unstable on its hooves.
   D. *No mistakes.*

Answering written expression and language questions can be tricky because you're looking for an error, but you don't know what kind of error you're looking for—or if there is even any error at all. So the best thing to do is to read each answer choice carefully and do your best to spot a mistake. The good news is that you will only have to read three answer choices since the fourth choice is always the same: *No mistake.*

The correct answer is B. Begin by reading choice A. Do you see any spelling errors? Hopefully you don't, because there are no spelling errors in this sentence. How about capitalization errors? Only the first word of the sentence is capitalized, and the first word of a sentence is always capitalized. There are also no proper names, titles, or uses of *I* that need to be capitalized. What about punctuation problems? This is a simple declarative statement that ends with a period correctly and requires no additional punctuation. It is also grammatically and stylistically strong. Therefore, choice A contains no errors. Let's move on to choice B. Any spelling errors? Well, the word *flys* should stop you in your tracks because *y* should be changed to *ie* in words such as *fly* that end with a consonant and a *y*. The correct spelling is *flies*, and choice B is the right answer. Choice C contains no mistakes.

2. **A.** Did you know that President Abraham Lincoln was born in Kentucky?
   B. The novella *The Strange Case of Dr. Jekyll and Mr. Hyde* is pretty scary.
   C. I saw Aunt Susan and my Uncle yesterday.
   D. *No mistakes.*

The correct answer is C. The fact that each of these answer choices contains several capitalized words is a little hint that this could be a capitalization question. But let's read the answer choices to make sure. Well, the first sentence looks correct: *President* is used as a title for the proper name *Abraham Lincoln*, and *Kentucky* is the proper name of a U.S. state, so all of these words should be capitalized, and they are. The italicized capitalized words in choice B form the title of a book. Since articles such as *the* should be capitalized when they are the first word of a title, and prepositions such as *of* and conjunctions such as *and* should not be capitalized in the middle of titles, there are no mistakes in the capitalizing of *The Strange Case of Dr. Jekyll and Mr. Hyde.* Choice B looks fine. Choice C, however, contains a problem. A person's title should be capitalized only when that title is attached to a proper name. The word *Aunt* should be capitalized because it is attached to the proper name *Susan*, but *uncle* is not part of a proper name. It should not be capitalized in this sentence.

3. **A.** My dinner was excellent; but I don't care for this dessert.
   B. The following items are in the refrigerator: milk, eggs, butter, and bread.
   C. You're walking on thin ice!
   D. *No mistakes.*

The correct answer is A. Read the first sentence. Do you notice any errors? Is that the correct way to use a semicolon? A semicolon is used to separate complete clauses in a sentence when those clauses are not separated with a conjunction. However, *but* is a conjunction. That means the semicolon is not needed. Choice A is the correct answer. Choice B uses a colon to introduce a list of items correctly. Choice D also uses its punctuation correctly; this urgent sentence ends with an appropriate exclamation mark.

Now we come to our last example, and the one thing we have not examined yet is a usage and composition question. That is exactly what the next two questions are.

4. A. He seems like a really nice person.

B. I wonder what she is thinking about?

C. They wants to know what they can bring to the party.

D. *No mistakes.*

The correct answer is C. As you read each answer choice, you should notice that there is a subject-verb agreement error in one of the sentences. The problem is not in choice A, which matches a singular subject (he) with a singular verb (seems). Choice B is fine too since the noun *I* and the verb *wonder* agree and the noun *she* and the verb *is* agree as well. The problem is in choice C because *They* is a plural noun and *wants* is a singular verb. If written correctly, choice C would read *They want to know what they can bring to the party.*

While they assess the same concepts as the HSPT Language questions, Written Expressions questions on the TACHS are formatted a bit differently. Instead of presenting three different and unrelated sentences, answer choices A through C are related and form a united thought.

A. The first day of school

B. always excites Candace

C. because it makes new friends.

D. *No mistakes.*

The correct answer is C. Again, as you read each answer choice, you should notice that there is a pronoun error in the clause that starts with *because* (choice C). As written, the pronoun *it* would seem to be referring to the first day of school, which makes no sense because a day cannot make friends. The person who makes new friends is Candace, so the way to solve the problem is to use the pronoun *she.* The combined answer choices should form the sentence, *The first day of school always excites Candace because she makes new friends.*

The preparation you do for the Written Expression and Language portions of the test will not only help improve your TACHS or HSPT exam score but also fine tune your English and writing skills, which will help you as you continue your studies and if you take other standardized tests, which often include an essay writing component.

Appendix Alert

For helpful reminders for spelling and grammar rules, check out Appendix C before starting the drills. You will find study guides for spelling (page 491) and grammar (page 495) that will refresh your English skills and get your mind ready to think like an editor as you tackle the drills in this chapter and when you take the language portion of your entrance exam on test day. These study guides can be removed from your workbook, so you can take them with you and review them anytime you like.

You will also find answer sheets for these drills in Appendix C, starting on page 515.

Spelling Drill

75 questions

Directions: For questions 1–37, find the sentence that has an error in spelling and mark the corresponding letter on your answer sheet. If you find no mistake, mark choice D as your answer.

1. A. The sailor shouted, "All ashore that are going ashore."
B. The turtle crawled accross the street.
C. For lunch, I ate a turkey sandwich.
D. *No mistakes*

2. A. It's a shame Anne can't attend the show with us.
B. Everyone voted except Mr. Jones.
C. They're always late for our group's meeting.
D. *No mistakes*

3. A. The soldier was given a medal for his courageous service.
B. Juliette offered her opinion about what I should wear to the party.
C. No one will be admited into the theater after the performance begins.
D. *No mistakes*

4. A. The general spoke of a possible winter offensive.
B. Ted finally succeded in solving the puzzle.
C. Thomas Alva Edison was a brilliant inventor.
D. *No mistakes*

5. A. The cirkumference of a circle is the distance around its outer edge.
B. Every accused individual is entitled to trial before an impartial jury.
C. Now that the snow has been cleared from the streets, the mayor is able to rescind the no-parking order.
D. *No mistakes*

6. A. A timid person is likely to be terrified of mysterious noises in the night.
   B. Persons who are taking certain medicines should confine themselves to drinking caffeine-free coffee.
   C. Examinations such as this one are, unfortunately, a necessary evil.
   D. *No mistakes*

7. A. We recieved a letter from the principal.
   B. The library closes at 5 o'clock tomorrow.
   C. I have an appointment with the doctor on Wednesday.
   D. *No mistakes*

8. A. The protesters had become a public nuisanse.
   B. The king mistook obedience for loyalty.
   C. Harold dismissed his debate opponent's point of view as nonsense.
   D. *No mistakes*

9. A. The matter was kept confidential.
   B. Her initial response was of horror.
   C. After the riots, the city was placed under marsial law.
   D. *No mistakes*

10. A. The party will be held on Saturday.
    B. We held a vigil last Thursday evening.
    C. I like to go a matinee every Wendsday.
    D. *No mistakes*

11. A. The story always ends with the guilty party confessing to the crime.
    B. Carrie spent hours plotting ways of aroussing the nosy neighbor's curiosity.
    C. It's a fact that caressing a beloved pet can relax you.
    D. *No mistakes*

12. A. Bob forgot to take his memory-enhancing medicine again.
    B. "This room needs a feminine touch," she hinted a little too enthusiastically.
    C. Most candles contain paraffin.
    D. *No mistakes*

13. **A.** It's always a pleasure to dine with Sandy.
    B. Stephen decided to measure the room before he ordered the carpet.
    C. Serafina dreamed of a life of liesure as she rode the subway to work.
    D. *No mistakes*

14. **A.** We celebrated the day the city opened a new libary on our side of town.
    B. Ian chose contemporary furniture for his mid-century home.
    C. The use of a canary as a warning signal in coal mines was a common practice until 1986.
    D. *No mistakes*

15. **A.** The investment group promised its clients prosperity if they invested wisely.
    B. Which university did Mari choose to attend?
    C. Her susceptibility to contagions made Jordi a shut-in during flu season.
    D. *No mistakes*

16. **A.** The lawyer objected to the question on the grounds that it was immaterial.
    B. The love the mother felt for her newborn was immeasurable.
    C. His look communicated an implicit threat.
    D. *No mistakes*

17. **A.** We often talk about exercising but do it only ocassionaly.
    B. It isn't necessarily so.
    C. The restaurant comes highly recommended.
    D. *No mistakes*

18. **A.** The feudal system existed in the Middle Ages.
    B. He lived most of his later years as a fugitive from justice.
    C. The oppressed sailors spoke of muetiny.
    D. *No mistakes*

19. **A.** Did you know that donkies are members of the horse family?
    B. Explorers penetrated territories previously undisturbed by humans.
    C. "Executives would be nothing without their secretaries," whispered Morgan to Leslie.
    D. *No mistakes*

20. **A.** The child often squashes his banana before eating it.

B. We built a special set of shelfs for Tobi's trophies.

C. Wearing contact lenses boosted Becca's self-confidence.

D. *No mistakes*

21. **A.** The defendant feels he is blamless.

B. Jorge was nervous going into the interview.

C. The immensity of the project was overwhelming.

D. *No mistakes*

22. **A.** The committee worked toward concurence of opinion.

B. Please enclose your remittance in the envelope provided.

C. Marc was pleased with his appearance after his surgery.

D. *No mistakes*

23. **A.** The starlet gracefully exited the limousine.

B. Hannah was intimately familiar with the situation.

C. Laird climbed steadyly up the hill, carrying both sleeping children.

D. *No mistakes*

24. **A.** Karina's food was deficient in taste, so she didn't win the contest.

B. It has been a wierd day!

C. He dreamed of being a high-powered financier after his graduation.

D. *No mistakes*

25. **A.** Jennifer began to feel the effects of not getting enough sleep.

B. B. Everyone crowded around the cast list posted on the auditoreum wall to see who would be in the play.

C. Andre had a note excusing him from the test because he had a doctor's appointment at the same time.

D. *No mistakes*

26. **A.** Mayor Jones said she would except the results of the election either way.

B. The line for concert tickets snaked all the way around the building and into the parking lot.

C. Maura assumes that the package will be delivered this afternoon.

D. *No mistakes*

27. A. Winning the spelling bee would be a pinnacle of success for me.
    B. During the ceremony, Principal Davis handed out diplomas and congratulated the new graduates.
    C. Jenny's grandmother is teaching her the fundamentals of cooking, in the hopes that she will someday keep the family's culinary traditions.
    D. *No mistakes*

28. A. Ringo's busy schedule meant that he had three classes before lunch: physics, calculus, and English.
    B. Paul's toddler sister went into hysterics when she was denied candy.
    C. It's bean about four years since we've eaten at that restaurant.
    D. *No mistakes*

29. A. The board was full of examples that showed how to do the commplex algebra problem.
    B. If chicken isn't cooked until the interior temperature is 165 degrees, it is too rare and could cause illness.
    C. Everyone in school attended an anti-bullying presentation that included skits starring students.
    D. *No mistakes*

30. A. Barrett's science fare project involved playing symphonies to plants to see if they would grow better than plants that grew without music.
    B. The mountain views are spectacular this time of day, especially just before the sun sets.
    C. Mary was fatigued and achy, so she could tell she was coming down with a cold.
    D. *No mistakes*

31. A. The most interesting point in the lecture was the discussion of global temperatures.
    B. She felt gullible for having beleived Jerome's outrageous story.
    C. The explorers checked their maps for reference, to confirm where the boundaries were.
    D. *No mistakes*

32. **A.** Due to her many hours of volunteering with the veterans' charity last year, Sandy was named the honorary marshal of the 4th of July parade.
   B. Although Mr. Martin yelled loudly, it was inaffective because the classroom was too unruly.
   C. In his horseback riding lessons, John learned how to cantor, gallop, and trot on a horse.
   D. *No mistakes*

33. **A.** In physics class last week, we studied velocity and acceleration.
   B. Carrie was allowed to redecorate her room however she wanted, so she revamped it with different paint and a new bedspread.
   C. The hike was ardjuous in the 80-degree heat, but we persevered and reached the top of the mountain.
   D. *No mistakes*

34. **A.** He has impeccable taste in clothes; I consult with him on all important occasions where I need to look fashionable.
   B. The lunar eclipse can only be seen from distant parts of the country, so we won't be able to observe it from here.
   C. With her storytelling skills, I don't doubt that she will become a great righter in the future.
   D. *No mistakes*

35. **A.** With the glass placed so near to the edge of the counter, it's likely that the cat will come along and knock it right off the edge.
   B. There's an old platitude that says "absince makes the heart grow fonder."
   C. Erika was worried that the ride would be bumpy the whole way, but the road soon leveled out.
   D. *No mistakes*

36. **A.** During the test, all ellectronic devices should be stowed out of sight.
   B. Joan and Barry were only acquaintances, but both hoped they would become friends in due time.
   C. I accidentally put powdered sugar in the recipe instead of cornstarch, and I had to dispose of the whole thing.
   D. *No mistakes*

37. A. Due to a generous gift from a local busines, the fundraising initiative was a huge success.

B. Mario felt so drowsy during the lecture that he could barely stay conscious while the teacher talked.

C. In the climax of the movie, the hero clung precariously to the side of a tall building, threatening to fall.

D. *No mistakes*

Directions: For questions 38–53, look for the word that is spelled incorrectly and mark the corresponding letter on your answer sheet. If there are no errors, mark choice E as your answer.

38. A. demolition
B. cordial
C. occupasional
D. pleasant
E. *No mistakes*

39. A. forfit
B. vital
C. avalanche
D. comfortable
E. *No mistakes*

40. A. peasant
B. ancient
C. marriage
D. problematic
E. *No mistakes*

41. A. forcible
B. irascible
C. tyrannical
D. absence
E. *No mistakes*

42. **A.** driest
 B. dryly
 C. driness
 D. dryer
 E. *No mistakes*

43. **A.** embargos
 B. topazes
 C. sheaves
 D. photos
 E. *No mistakes*

44. **A.** heinous
 B. arrainment
 C. bureau
 D. repetitious
 E. *No mistakes*

45. **A.** corrugated
 B. regrettable
 C. deliberasion
 D. yacht
 E. *No mistakes*

46. **A.** posession
 B. blamable
 C. bookkeeping
 D. whether
 E. *No mistakes*

47. **A.** mediocrity
 B. dilapidated
 C. derogatory
 D. irelevant
 E. *No mistakes*

48. **A.** soverein
 B. mischievous
 C. harassment
 D. masquerade
 E. *No mistakes*

49. **A.** anemia
 B. equilibrium
 C. presumptious
 D. baccalaureate
 E. *No mistakes*

50. **A.** vengence
 B. punctilious
 C. vacillation
 D. resilience
 E. *No mistakes*

51. **A.** beatitude
 B. aggravation
 C. description
 D. beleagered
 E. *No mistakes*

52. **A.** inimitable
 B. iminent
 C. eminent
 D. impartial
 E. *No mistakes*

53. **A.** recognizeable
 B. incongruity
 C. temperamentally
 D. complacency
 E. *No mistakes*

Directions: For questions 54–75, find the line that has an error in spelling and mark the corresponding letter on your answer sheet. If you find no mistake, mark choice D as your answer.

54. **A.** If you set your mind
B. to the task at hand,
C. you can acheive anything.
D. *No mistakes*

55. **A.** I do not value material things
B. excessively, so I do not really
C. have a prized posession.
D. *No mistakes*

56. **A.** I am definitly planning to come
B. to your birthday celebration,
C. but I cannot guarantee that I'll be there on time.
D. *No mistakes*

57. **A.** I'm on our neigborhood's
B. clean up committee, and we're
C. organizing a big event for this coming Wednesday.
D. *No mistakes*

58. **A.** I am very hard to embarrass,
B. so I'd be happy to take the role
C. of a clown in the holiday pageant.
D. *No mistakes*

59. **A.** I have a real dilemma:
B. I don't know what my schedule is going to be
C. for the forseeable future.
D. *No mistakes*

60. **A.** It is extremely important
B. that we protect our natural environment,
C. so do your best to reduce polution.
D. *No mistakes*

61. **A.** I know Kyle will be disapointed if
B. you do not assist him with his
C. project as you promised you would.
D. *No mistakes*

62. **A.** I will study as much as necessery
B. to ensure I get a high grade
C. on the mathematics examination.
D. *No mistakes*

63. **A.** I truley love going to the movies,
B. but unfortunately, this one
C. is a little too weird for my tastes.
D. *No mistakes*

64. **A.** My colleague is accompanying
B. me to the board meeting after
C. we have lunch at a restaurant.
D. *No mistakes*

65. **A.** My little sister told me a bizarre story about
B. a girl who has the power to disapear and was
C. born with all of the knowledge in a set of encyclopedias!
D. *No mistakes*

66. **A.** I am trying to lose a really bad habit;
B. I have a tendancy to interrupt people
C. before they are through speaking.
D. *No mistakes*

67. **A.** My friend Juliana always tells very humorus stories;
B. I think she could have a career as a
C. comedienne when she grows up.
D. *No mistakes*

68. **A.** You may need to consult your
B. calender to find out what
C. chores you are performing next weekend.
D. *No mistakes*

69. **A.** If you are too agressive,
B. you may find that meditation
C. is an effective way to soothe yourself.
D. *No mistakes*

70. **A.** I am not familiar with
B. this particular song.
C. How did you discover it?
D. *No mistakes*

71. **A.** Trevor is extremely
B. jealous of Liara's ability to
C. ilustrate beautiful landscapes.
D. *No mistakes*

72. **A.** I am just an amateur singer
B. but I have dreams of becoming a legitimet
C. professional someday.
D. *No mistakes*

73. **A.** The ability to take constructive
B. criticism is a positive
C. personality traite.
D. *No mistakes*

74. **A.** The very idea that I am entitled to pay
B. less money on rent than my roommate
C. is utterly ludicrous.
D. *No mistakes*

75. **A.** You should be a percussionist;
B. you have an impeccible
C. sense of rhythm!
D. *No mistakes*

Answer Key and Explanations

1. B	**16.** D	**31.** B	**46.** A	**61.** A
2. D	**17.** A	**32.** B	**47.** D	**62.** A
3. C	**18.** C	**33.** C	**48.** A	**63.** A
4. B	**19.** A	**34.** C	**49.** C	**64.** D
5. A	**20.** B	**35.** B	**50.** A	**65.** B
6. D	**21.** A	**36.** A	**51.** D	**66.** B
7. A	**22.** A	**37.** A	**52.** B	**67.** A
8. A	**23.** C	**38.** C	**53.** A	**68.** B
9. C	**24.** B	**39.** A	**54.** C	**69.** A
10. C	**25.** B	**40.** E	**55.** C	**70.** D
11. B	**26.** A	**41.** E	**56.** A	**71.** C
12. D	**27.** D	**42.** C	**57.** A	**72.** B
13. C	**28.** C	**43.** A	**58.** D	**73.** C
14. A	**29.** A	**44.** B	**59.** C	**74.** D
15. D	**30.** A	**45.** C	**60.** C	**75.** B

1. **The correct answer is B.** The correct spelling of *accross* is *across.*
2. **The correct answer is D.** There are no spelling errors.
3. **The correct answer is C.** The correct spelling of *admited* is *admitted.*
4. **The correct answer is B.** The correct spelling of *succeded* is *succeeded.*
5. **The correct answer is A.** The correct spelling of *cirkumference* is *circumference.*
6. **The correct answer is D.** There are no spelling errors.
7. **The correct answer is A.** The correct spelling of *recieved* is *received.*
8. **The correct answer is A.** The correct spelling of *nuisanse* is *nuisance.*
9. **The correct answer is C.** The correct spelling of *marsial* is *martial.*

10. **The correct answer is C.** The correct spelling of *Wendsday* is *Wednesday.*

11. **The correct answer is B.** The correct spelling of *aroussing* is *arousing.*

12. **The correct answer is D.** There are no spelling errors.

13. **The correct answer is C.** The correct spelling of *liesure* is *leisure.*

14. **The correct answer is A.** The correct spelling of *libary* is *library.*

15. **The correct answer is D.** There are no spelling errors.

16. **The correct answer is D.** There are no spelling errors.

17. **The correct answer is A.** The correct spelling of *ocassionaly* is *occasionally.*

18. **The correct answer is C.** The correct spelling of *muetiny* is *mutiny.*

19. **The correct answer is A.** The correct spelling of *donkies* is *donkeys.*

20. **The correct answer is B.** The correct spelling of more than one shelf is *shelves.*

21. **The correct answer is A.** The correct spelling of *blamless* is *blameless.*

22. **The correct answer is A.** The correct spelling of *concurence* is *concurrence.*

23. **The correct answer is C.** The correct spelling of *steadyly* is *steadily.*

24. **The correct answer is B.** The correct spelling of *wierd* is *weird.*

25. **The correct answer is B.** The correct spelling of *auditoreum* is *auditorium.*

26. **The correct answer is A.** Although *except* can be a correctly spelled word in the right context, the word in the sentence should be *accept.*

27. **The correct answer is D.** There are no spelling errors.

28. **The correct answer is C.** *Bean* should be *been*, to fit the context of the sentence. The correct past tense form of the verb *to be* is *has been.* A *bean* is an edible seed.

29. **The correct answer is A.** The correct spelling of *commplex* is *complex.*

30. **The correct answer is A.** *Fair* is the correct spelling and usage when talking about a science competition.

31. **The correct answer is B.** The correct spelling of *beleived* is *believed.*

32. **The correct answer is B.** The correct spelling of *inaffective* is *ineffective.*

33. **The correct answer is C.** The correct spelling of *ardjuous* is *arduous.*

34. **The correct answer is C.** The correct spelling of *righter* is *writer.*

35. **The correct answer is B.** The correct spelling of *absince* is *absence.*

36. **The correct answer is A.** The correct spelling of *ellectronic* is *electronic.*

37. **The correct answer is A.** The correct spelling of *busines* is *business.*

38. **The correct answer is C.** The correct spelling of *occupasional* is *occupational.*

39. **The correct answer is A.** The correct spelling of *forfit* is *forfeit.*

40. **The correct answer is E.** There are no spelling errors.

41. **The correct answer is E.** There are no spelling errors.

42. **The correct answer is C.** The correct spelling of *driness* is *dryness.*

43. **The correct answer is A.** The correct spelling of *embargos* is *embargoes.*

44. **The correct answer is B.** The correct spelling of *arrainment* is *arraignment.*

45. **The correct answer is C.** The correct spelling of *deliberasion* is *deliberation.*

46. **The correct answer is A.** The correct spelling of *posession* is *possession.*

47. **The correct answer is D.** The correct spelling of *irelevant* is *irrelevant.*

48. **The correct answer is A.** The correct spelling of *soverein* is *sovereign.*

49. **The correct answer is C.** The correct spelling of *presumptious* is *presumptuous.*

50. **The correct answer is A.** The correct spelling of *vengence* is *vengeance.*

51. **The correct answer is D.** The correct spelling of *beleagered* is *beleaguered.*

52. **The correct answer is B.** The correct spelling of *iminent* is *imminent.*

53. **The correct answer is A.** The correct spelling of *recognizeable* is *recognizable.*

54. **The correct answer is C.** The correct spelling of *acheive* is *achieve.*

55. **The correct answer is C.** The correct spelling of *posession* is *possession.*

56. **The correct answer is A.** The correct spelling of *definitly* is *definitely.*

57. **The correct answer is A.** The correct spelling of *neigborhood's* is *neighborhood's.*

58. **The correct answer is D.** There are no spelling errors.

59. **The correct answer is C.** The correct spelling of *forseeable* is *foreseeable.*

60. **The correct answer is C.** The correct spelling of *polution* is *pollution.*

61. **The correct answer is A.** The correct spelling of *disapointed* is *disappointed.*

62. **The correct answer is A.** The correct spelling of *necessery* is *necessary.*

63. **The correct answer is A.** The correct spelling of *truley* is *truly.*

64. **The correct answer is D.** There are no spelling errors.

65. **The correct answer is B.** The correct spelling of *disapear* is *disappear.*

66. **The correct answer is B.** The correct spelling of *tendancy* is *tendency.*

67. **The correct answer is A.** The correct spelling of *humorus* is *humorous.*

68. **The correct answer is B.** The correct spelling of *calender* is *calendar.*

69. **The correct answer is A.** The correct spelling of *agressive* is *aggressive.*

70. **The correct answer is D.** There are no spelling errors.

71. **The correct answer is C.** The correct spelling of *ilustrate* is *illustrate.*

72. **The correct answer is B.** The correct spelling of *legitimet* is *legitimate.*

73. **The correct answer is C.** The correct spelling of *trate* is *trait.*

74. **The correct answer is D.** There are no spelling errors.

75. **The correct answer is B.** The correct spelling of *impeccible* is *impeccable.*

Capitalization and Punctuation Drill

75 questions

Directions: For questions 1–37, find the line that has an error in punctuation or capitalization and mark the corresponding letter on your answer sheet. If you find no mistake, mark choice D as your answer.

1. A. "What time are you
B. going to be at school
C. tomorrow," David asked.
D. *No mistakes*

2. A. Mr. McGivers was my neighbor
B. back when my family used to
C. live on Humbolt street.
D. *No mistakes*

3. A. My family lives so far out in the country
B. that aunt Janice has to walk three miles
C. just to visit Mr. McDonald, her closest neighbor.
D. *No mistakes*

4. A. Here's what I'm bringing to the
B. picnic, sandwiches, apples,
C. a thermos full of water, and three cupcakes.
D. *No mistakes*

5. A. I am reading a spooky story
B. called *The Strange Case Of Dr. Jekyll*
C. *and Mr. Hyde* in my English class.
D. No mistakes

6. **A.** The gardener is working
   B. in the backyard; the landscaper
   C. is mowing the front lawn.
   D. *No mistakes*

7. **A.** Queen Mary ordered her daughter,
   B. the Princess, to marry the son of
   C. one of the country's richest dukes.
   D. *No mistakes*

8. **A.** That man in the kitchen is my Uncle Charlie,
   B. and he is my father's brother,
   C. but my Aunt is my mother's sister.
   D. *No mistakes*

9. **A.** My best friend Roalo
   B. and I, are thinking about
   C. trying out for the baseball team.
   D. *No mistakes*

10. **A.** Teresa is english.
    B. She and her parents just moved here
    C. from the United Kingdom.
    D. *No mistakes*

11. **A.** Salvatore was planning to
    B. come to my party but he
    C. has to work that day.
    D. *No mistakes*

12. **A.** The New York Yankees and the
    B. Boston Red Sox are playing in the
    C. world series this year.
    D. *No mistakes*

13. A. Stop running before you fall
B. on the wet floors!
C. They were just mopped!!
D. *No mistakes*

14. A. My sister is majoring in science at college,
B. and the first course she will take is
C. called Biology 101.
D. *No mistakes*

15. A. That house is our's;
B. Tamara lives in
C. the house across the street.
D. *No mistakes*

16. A. Every Winter my family
B. takes a trip to Florida to escape from
C. the cold weather of January and February.
D. *No mistakes*

17. A. "We're going to the
B. cafeteria for lunch
C. today", Zara said.
D. *No mistakes*

18. A. The map indicates that we should
B. head South in order to get to
C. Castle Clinton National Park.
D. *No mistakes*

19. A. Ever since the weather cooled off
B. in late October, the tree
C. has been losing it's leaves.
D. *No mistakes*

20. **A.** Have you ever visited
    B. the Eiffel Tower
    C. in Paris, France?
    D. *No mistakes*

21. **A.** I always make my sauce
    B. with high quality tomatoes
    C. I grow in my very own garden.
    D. *No mistakes*

22. **A.** The city council met last night
    B. and decided to lower taxes.
    C. in the Brooksmith neighborhood.
    D. *No mistakes*

23. **A.** If you look in the medicine chest, you
    B. will find the following items; a toothbrush,
    C. a tube of toothpaste, a bottle of aspirin, and a shaving razor.
    D. *No mistakes*

24. **A.** "Do you happen
    B. to know what time
    C. it is?" Emma asked.
    D. *No mistakes*

25. **A.** The services for easter
    B. will be held at St. John's
    C. located at 123 Main Street.
    D. *No mistakes*

26. **A.** I love vanilla ice cream;
    B. Luiza however prefers
    C. strawberry fudge swirl.
    D. *No mistakes*

27. **A.** The boat, that my mother is sailing,
B. once belonged to her own mother
C. many years ago.
D. *No mistakes*

28. **A.** The titanic was a famous ship that was considered
B. to be unsinkable, but it did indeed sink
C. after hitting an iceberg in the Atlantic Ocean.
D. *No mistakes*

29. **A.** I was wondering if you've ever been
B. to Spain. I'm thinking about
C. taking a trip there next spring.
D. *No mistakes*

30. **A.** I love this novel,
B. I really relate to the
C. character named Scout.
D. *No mistakes*

31. **A.** During our next summer vacation,
B. we plan to go to New York
C. and visit the Empire State building.
D. *No mistakes*

32. **A.** Hello, Janelle. How
B. have you been since the
C. last time we ran into each other?
D. *No mistakes*

33. **A.** Without thinking—I grabbed my
B. little brother's arm and steadied him
C. just as I saw him slipping on the ice.
D. *No mistakes*

34. **A.** Last Saturday night,
B. we went to a restaurant
C. and enjoyed a meal of Mexican food.
D. *No mistakes*

35. **A.** I'm extremely tired I'm
B. staying in tonight instead
C. of going out with my friends.
D. *No mistakes*

36. **A.** The new math teacher
B. was looking forward to introducing
C. his students to the pythagorean theorem.
D. *No mistakes*

37. **A.** Hannahs dream was to be an oceanographer,
B. but she found little encouragement
C. because she lived in the desert.
D. *No mistakes*

Directions: For questions 38–75, look for errors in capitalization and punctuation. If there are no errors, choose choice D.

38. **A.** We spent our vacation at Lake Winnipesauke in New Hampshire.
B. I went to the Doctor's Office to get my cast removed.
C. Have you read the book *Pride and Prejudice*?
D. *No mistakes*

39. **A.** Jane's giving a report on *Born Free.*
B. She fell down and broke her glasses.
C. Ted asked: "Did you see George's chess set?"
D. *No mistakes*

40. A. If you meet me at 5:00, that will give us enough time to do research at the library for our project.

B. Can you please hand me that book the one over on the table?

C. Jared's schedule for next semester is a very busy one.

D. *No mistakes*

41. A. The fortune that came with my Chinese food said I would have a very lucky day tomorrow.

B. Aunt Becky's recipe for cherry pie won the town bake-off last year.

C. After the rain stopped, I found four Earthworms on the sidewalk in front of our house.

D. *No mistakes*

42. A. The Boy Scouts are meeting at Jim's tomorrow.

B. Dr. Bell spoke at Northwestern University last night.

C. Jack exclaimed, "Where is my present"?

D. *No mistakes*

43. A. Have you caught the new marvel movie yet?

B. Brett's favorite things to read are comic books and science magazines.

C. Marjorie went to the Main Street School before her family moved to the town next door.

D. *No mistakes*

44. A. Antonio's favorite book as a child was: *A Tree Grows in Brooklyn.*

B. The farmers' market had a good selection of fruit, vegetables, and farm fresh eggs.

C. How many waffles would you like: one, two, or three?

D. *No mistakes*

45. A. The new neighbor is from South Africa but lived in several other countries before she moved here.

B. Marco was anxious for warm weather so he could take his new Kozy Kamper tent out camping.

C. Gene will likely get a basketball scholarship to Arizona State if he can keep his grades up.

D. *No mistakes*

46. **A.** The Fourth of July is also known as Independence day.
B. Many Americans enjoy swimming.
C. Abby left Jen's house after dinner.
D. *No mistakes*

47. **A.** The government, announcing a bill of rights for its citizens, promised them equal rights under the law.
B. Martin Luther King's birthday was recently designated a federal holiday.
C. Remember that our Constitution is not self-executing; it must be interpreted and applied by the Supreme Court.
D. *No mistakes*

48. **A.** Jennifer's favorite cousin, David, is scheduled to visit over Memorial Day weekend.
B. Ron won the first round of the spelling bee by correctly spelling the word "disenfranchisement," but ended up losing in the second round.
C. We don't have any of those books left in stock; they'll have to be reordered.
D. *No mistakes*

49. **A.** Sally asked, "What time will you be home?"
B. Doug hopes to enter John F. Kennedy High School next Fall.
C. The letter arrived on Saturday, January 15.
D. *No mistakes*

50. **A.** After he had paid the fee and had seen the pictures he was quite satisfied.
B. If I weren't dressed in this uniform, I wouldn't feel so conspicuous.
C. I am depending on the medicine's being delivered without delay.
D. *No mistakes*

51. **A.** Jeremy spent two weeks working on a model of the ship *Titanic*.
B. What time will we be meeting at the Leaf & Bean Café?
C. There's a sale on the sneakers I want, so I'm going to The Mall this afternoon to shop at Sneaker World.
D. *No mistakes*

52. **A.** Georgie taught herself how to knit by watching videos posted on youtube.
  B. As a souvenir, Mira brought back from Belgian chocolate from her trip to Europe.
  C. The second baseman for the Austin Bulls, Jackie Johnson, is my favorite player in Major League Baseball.
  D. *No mistakes*

53. **A.** The new teacher aides were given their assignments and, they were asked to begin work immediately.
  B. Jim's sister, Carol, will begin college in the fall.
  C. My favorite subjects are English, science, and American history.
  D. *No mistakes*

54. **A.** Mary Anne broke her school's scoring record last night, having scored 38 points in the basketball game.
  B. Taking a trip to Canada this summer (would be fine), but I was really hoping to visit Florida instead.
  C. The assembly instructions for my new desk were confusing—so much so that we weren't sure if we were missing any parts.
  D. *No mistakes*

55. **A.** For his Cooking Skills class final, Chris was required to make a three-course dinner and a dessert.
  B. That is my favorite show, but given that its ratings are so low, I'm afraid it will get cancelled.
  C. I went to the store, they were out of the soy milk I like, then I came home.
  D. *No mistakes*

56. **A.** Paige and Ethan were invited to join the principal, Mr. Wright, for lunch.
  B. Lets begin the meeting at 2:15 p.m. today.
  C. My brother is so self-conscious of the braces on his teeth.
  D. *No mistakes*

57. **A.** We will be vacationing in sunny Italy.
  B. Dave will arrive at Kennedy international airport.
  C. We decided to have Charlie read the report.
  D. *No mistakes*

58. **A.** Are you coming to my birthday party?

B. The first snow fell on Sunday October 27.

C. Jack's father drove us to the movies.

D. *No mistakes*

59. **A.** I find that the *Los Angeles Times* has an easier crossword puzzle than the *Chicago Tribune.*

B. Paul's summer internship at *font magazine* starts in June and lasts until August.

C. After we read the *Lord of the Rings* book series, we spent the weekend watching the movie versions.

D. *No mistakes*

60. **A.** Last month, I wrote an editorial about Animal Rights for the School Newspaper.

B. Ariel camped out and waited in line for three days just to buy tickets for a concert by her favorite band, The Boys.

C. Because Shawna took college math courses over the summer, she qualified to get credit for Calculus I in her first semester of college.

D. *No mistakes*

61. **A.** How long has the train been gone?

B. "Well," Jay said, let's get going."

C. Jack's uncle is a fireman.

D. *No mistakes*

62. **A.** I still have the following things to do: mow the lawn before Dad gets home; walk the dog; and drop my books off at the library.

B. Please see the following chapters for more information one, two, and four.

C. Attention, baseball fans: discounted tickets for tomorrow's game are now available.

D. *No mistakes*

63. **A.** She said I should meet her at the library. At 4:00.

B. Mrs. Rodriguez stayed after school to help me prepare for the algebra test, which was very nice of her.

C. The other team beat us by a final score of 50–35; we really had a terrible game.

D. *No mistakes*

64. **A.** A portion of the rental cost of the building, is based on the office space used by the agency.
    B. It is in everyone's interest for the poor to be assisted with heating costs.
    C. Do you understand the meaning of the expression, "full faith and credit"?
    D. *No mistakes*

65. **A.** According to Alvin, he will be "too busy" to help me move the bookshelf.
    B. I called her to share the big news: we won the championship!
    C. "Do you know what you're supposed to be doing? she asked."
    D. *No mistakes*

66. **A.** Anne said, "we really should go now."
    B. You can always say Sam eats well—and often!
    C. I told them my study hall was second period.
    D. *No mistakes*

67. **A.** The childrens' boots got mixed up in the coatroom.
    B. Sheila is trying out for the marching band today.
    C. My sisters and I all went to camp last summer.
    D. *No mistakes*

68. **A.** July is a spectacular month for an exotic beach vacation.
    B. Harold visited his Grandmother in Paramus, New Jersey
    C. Randy needs to go to the Morningvale Mall on Tuesday.
    D. *No mistakes*

69. **A.** What time are we supposed to meet Glenda at the movies?
    B. The pool was supposed to open at 10 a.m., but now it's 10:15 and the pool is still closed.
    C. Mr. Sherman assigned three chapters on the American Revolution for tonight's homework.
    D. *No mistakes*

70. **A.** In the Bennington household, Claudia's Graduation Day was a big event.
    B. The Niborg Aquarium, which is in Sweden, has an amazing stingray exhibit.
    C. Lars's favorite book is *The Catcher in the Rye*.
    D. *No mistakes*

71. **A.** In his tales of adventure and romance, he predicted many scientific achievements of the twentieth century.

B. Today's *Times* has headlines about another woman who has just swum the English Channel.

C. Some Third World Countries have suggested that they be given the right to regularly censor what foreign journalists report about their countries.

D. *No mistakes*

72. **A.** "To eat sparingly is advisable," said the doctor.

B. "Which is the way to the science building?" asked the new student.

C. She inquired, "Are you going to hand in your report before lunch?"

D. *No mistakes*

73. **A.** On a clear evening, you can see Venus.

B. I hope to visit Italy one day soon.

C. This Store has the best prices in town.

D. *No mistakes*

74. **A.** I enjoyed a cup of starbucks coffee with my breakfast.

B. Their house is just half a mile north of the park.

C. *The Grapes of Wrath* is one of my favorite novels.

D. *No mistakes*

75. **A.** My parents love to go on vacations with my sister and me.

B. Last year, we went to Honolulu, Hawaii.

C. We went to a luau and watched fire eaters.

D. *No mistakes*

Answer Key and Explanations

1. C	16. A	31. C	46. A	61. B
2. C	17. C	32. D	47. D	62. B
3. B	18. B	33. A	48. D	63. A
4. B	19. C	34. D	49. B	64. A
5. B	20. D	35. A	50. A	65. C
6. D	21. B	36. C	51. C	66. A
7. B	22. B	37. A	52. A	67. A
8. C	23. B	38. B	53. A	68. B
9. B	24. D	39. C	54. B	69. D
10. A	25. A	40. B	55. C	70. A
11. B	26. B	41. C	56. B	71. C
12. C	27. A	42. C	57. B	72. D
13. C	28. A	43. A	58. B	73. C
14. D	29. D	44. A	59. B	74. A
15. A	30. A	45. D	60. A	75. D

1. **The correct answer is C.** This quotation is a question, so it should end with a question mark, not a comma.

2. **The correct answer is C.** In this context, *street* is part of a proper name for a place, so it should be capitalized.

3. **The correct answer is B.** Words such as *aunt* and *uncle* should be capitalized when they are part of a person's name, such as *Aunt Bea* or *Uncle Buck*.

4. **The correct answer is B.** A colon is used to introduce a list of items, such as this sentence's list of items the speaker is bringing to a picnic. A comma should not be used to introduce a list of items.

5. **The correct answer is B.** Prepositions such as *of* should not be capitalized in titles of books.

6. **The correct answer is D.** This sentence uses a semicolon to connect its two complete clauses correctly.

7. **The correct answer is B.** The words *prince*, *princess*, *king*, and the like are common nouns and do not need to be capitalized unless included in someone's title. A proper noun such as *Prince William* would be capitalized.

8. **The correct answer is C.** A family relationship such as *aunt* should only be capitalized when it is a title followed by a proper name, such as *Aunt Shirley*.

9. **The correct answer is B.** The comma between *I* and *are* is unnecessary.

10. **The correct answer is A.** Names of nationalities, such as *English*, should be capitalized.

11. **The correct answer is B.** When two clauses are joined with a conjunction, such as *but*, there should be a comma before the conjunction.

12. **The correct answer is C.** Titles of special events, such as the *World Series*, should be capitalized.

13. **The correct answer is C.** One exclamation point is sufficient. More than one is not used in a properly punctuated sentence.

14. **The correct answer is D.** The names of subjects, such as *science* or *biology*, should not be capitalized unless they are used in the proper title of a specific course, such as *Biology 101*.

15. **The correct answer is A.** The word *ours* is naturally possessive; it does not need an apostrophe to show possession.

16. **The correct answer is A.** Names of seasons, such as *winter*, should not be capitalized.

17. **The correct answer is C.** At the end of a quotation, the comma should be placed before the closing quotation marks.

18. **The correct answer is B.** A direction, such as *south*, should not be capitalized unless it is used to name a specific geographic region, such as *South Carolina*.

19. **The correct answer is C.** *It's* is a contraction of *it is*. This sentence needs the possessive form of "it," which is *its*.

20. **The correct answer is D.** The names of specific structures, such as *the Eiffel Tower*, and specific places, such as *Paris* and *France*, should be capitalized.

21. **The correct answer is B.** *High-quality* is a compound adjective, so it needs a hyphen to join its two parts.

22. **The correct answer is B.** There should be no period after the word *taxes* because it ends the sentence, being formed by the combined answer choices, too soon.

23. **The correct answer is B.** A colon, not a semicolon, is used to introduce a list of items.

24. **The correct answer is D.** This quotation is punctuated properly.

25. **The correct answer is A.** *Easter* should be capitalized.

26. **The correct answer is B.** The adverb *however* should be offset with commas.

27. **The correct answer is A.** The phrase "that my mother is sailing" does not need to be offset with commas.

28. **The correct answer is A.** The names of specific ships, such as the *Titanic*, should be capitalized.

29. **The correct answer is D.** There are no punctuation mistakes in these sentences.

30. **The correct answer is A.** "I love this novel" and "I really relate to the character named Scout" are both complete clauses, and complete clauses should be separated with a semicolon, not a comma. Separating them with a comma creates a comma splice.

31. **The correct answer is C.** The word *building* is included in the proper noun *Empire State Building.*

32. **The correct answer is D.** There are no punctuation mistakes in these sentences.

33. **The correct answer is A.** *Without thinking* is a fragment. It should be joined to the sentence that follows it with a comma.

34. **The correct answer is D.** There are no mistakes in punctuation or capitalization.

35. **The correct answer is A.** This sentence is a run on. The clauses "I'm extremely tired" and "I'm staying in tonight instead of going out with my friends" should be joined with a conjunction such as *so* or a semicolon.

36. **The correct answer is C.** The proper adjective *Pythagorean* is taken from the proper noun Pythagoras, the inventor of the math formula, and should be capitalized.

37. **The correct answer is A.** There should be a possessive apostrophe before the *s* in *Hannahs*. (The dream belonged to Hannah.)

38. **The correct answer is B.** There is no specific doctor mentioned, so "doctor's office" should be a common noun.

39. **The correct answer is C.** There should be a comma after *asked*, not a colon.

40. **The correct answer is B.** Choice A correctly uses a comma to divide the sentence. Choice B is an incomplete sentence without separated clauses. A correct sentence would put "the one over on the table" in parentheses or set it off with an em dash. Choice C correctly uses the possessive apostrophe and a period to end the sentence.

41. **The correct answer is C.** Although *Earth* is a proper noun when it describes the planet, it is a common noun when the word is used to describe soil or worms, so no capitalization is needed.

42. **The correct answer is C.** The question mark should be placed before the final quotation marks.

43. **The correct answer is A.** *Marvel* is a specific brand name, so it should be capitalized.

44. **The correct answer is A.** In choice A, no colon is needed between *was* and the book title. Choice B correctly uses a possessive apostrophe and commas to separate the list items. Choice B uses a colon and commas correctly to create a list, and a question mark to show that the speaker is asking a question.

45. **The correct answer is D.** In choices A, B, and C, all the capitalized words are correct.

46. **The correct answer is A.** The letter *d* should be capitalized in *Day*, because Independence Day is a proper noun.

47. **The correct answer is D.** There are no mistakes in punctuation or capitalization.

48. **The correct answer is D.** Each of these sentences is punctuated correctly. In choice A, the commas set off *David* because the name modifies the phrase *favorite cousin*. In choice B, the comma correctly separates an independent clause from a dependent clause. In choice C, the semicolon is used to separate two independent (but thematically connected) clauses.

49. **The correct answer is B.** This sentence has an error in capitalization. The word *fall* should not be capitalized.

50. The correct answer is A. The long introductory phrase must be separated from the independent clause by a comma: After he had paid the fee and had seen the pictures, he was quite satisfied.

51. The correct answer is C. The mall is not named, so it should not be capitalized like a proper noun. *Sneaker World* is a specific store, so it is correctly capitalized.

52. The correct answer is A. YouTube is the name of a website and company, so it needs to be capitalized.

53. The correct answer is A. The comma is misplaced. The comma must be placed before the conjunction (in this case *and*) that joins two independent clauses.

54. The correct answer is B. Choice A correctly uses a comma to separate the clauses. Choice C uses a dash to create a break in the sentence but does so by separating clauses correctly. However, choice B uses parentheses to incorrectly set off a necessary part of the sentence. Parentheses should be used to set off information that is not essential to understanding the sentence.

55. The correct answer is C. Choice A correctly uses a comma to separate a dependent clause (*for his Cooking Skills class final*) from an independent clause (*Chris was required to make a three-course dinner and a dessert*). Choice B is a complex sentence, but the commas are placed correctly, and the coordinating conjunction *but* makes it a complete sentence. Choice C is a series of comma splices. The sentence should either be broken up into separate sentences or have coordinating conjunctions added to create balanced clauses.

56. The correct answer is B. An apostrophe is needed in the first word, *Let's*, since it is a contraction for *let us*.

57. The correct answer is B. *International* and *Airport* should both be capitalized.

58. The correct answer is B. There should be a comma after *Sunday*.

59. The correct answer is B. *Font Magazine* is the proper name of a magazine, so it should be capitalized.

60. The correct answer is A. Neither *animal rights* nor *school newspaper* are proper names or titles, so neither noun phrase should be capitalized.

61. The correct answer is B. There should be quotation marks before *let's* because it is a continuation of a direct quote.

62. **The correct answer is B.** Choice A correctly uses a colon and semicolons to create a list of complex items. Choice B is missing any kind of punctuation that tells you that *one, two, and four* is a list. Choice C correctly uses a colon to separate the second clause, which illustrates the first clause in the sentence.

63. **The correct answer is A.** In choice A, the period after *library* is unnecessary, and creates a sentence fragment (*at 4:00*). Choice B correctly uses a comma to create a pause between clauses. Choice C correctly uses a semicolon to divide two independent clauses that are related.

64. **The correct answer is A.** The comma that separates the subject from the predicate does not belong there. The entire sentence in choice C is a question, so the question mark is correctly placed outside the quotation marks.

65. **The correct answer is C.** Choice A uses quotation marks correctly for the partial quote from Alvin. Choice B uses a colon to separate a sentence where the second part explains the first. The sentence's upbeat tone works well with an exclamation point. In choice C, the quotation marks should match exactly what's being said. *She asked* is an extra note, not part of the quote itself, so it should not be inside the quotation marks

66. **The correct answer is A.** The word *we* should be capitalized.

67. **The correct answer is A.** The apostrophe should be placed before the *s* in *children's* since *children* is a plural word.

68. **The correct answer is B.** The word *grandmother* is not a proper noun, so it shouldn't be capitalized.

69. **The correct answer is D.** In choice A, the speaker is asking a simple, complete question, so the question mark is correct and there is no extra punctuation needed. In choice B, the periods in *a.m.* (an abbreviation), the comma (which separates two clauses), and the apostrophe (which shows that this is a possessive pronoun) are correct.

70. **The correct answer is A.** *Graduation day* is not an official holiday and shouldn't be capitalized unless it's at the beginning of a sentence.

71. **The correct answer is C.** There is no reason for the word *countries* to begin with a capital letter.

72. **The correct answer is D.** There are no mistakes in punctuation or capitalization.

73. The correct answer is C. The word *store* should not be capitalized because it is not part of a proper noun.

74. The correct answer is A. *Starbucks* is the name of a company. Therefore, it is a proper noun and should be capitalized.

75. The correct answer is D. There are no mistakes in punctuation or capitalization.

Usage Drill

75 Questions

Directions: For questions 1–30, look for errors in usage. Choose the letter of the sentence containing the error. If you find no mistake, choose answer choice D.

1. **A.** Please wait for me after school.
   B. Mother, can I go to the movies?
   C. Bob and his brother will meet the train.
   D. *No mistakes*

2. **A.** The loud noise of the cars and trucks aggravates those who live near the road.
   B. Joe seems slow on the track, but you will find few players quicker than he on the basketball court.
   C. Admirers of American ballet have made the claim that its stars can dance as well as or better than the best of the Russian artists.
   D. *No mistakes*

3. **A.** Your telling the truth in the face of such dire consequences required great moral courage.
   B. No one among the students was more disgruntled than she when the assignments were handed out.
   C. A full hour before the party was to begin, the room was clean like it had never been before.
   D. *No mistakes*

4. **A.** Never before have I seen anyone who has the skill John has when he repairs engines.
   B. There goes the last piece of cake and the last spoonful of ice cream.
   C. Every one of the campers but John and me is going on the hike.
   D. *No mistakes*

5. **A.** Chicago is larger than any other city in Illinois.
   B. The reason the new leader was so unsuccessful was that she had fewer responsibilities.
   C. Honor as well as profit are to be gained by these studies.
   D. *No mistakes*

6. **A.** The student couldn't complete the task because it was to difficult for him.
   B. We watched the kite soar high in the sky.
   C. Whom did you ask to go to the dance?
   D. *No mistakes*

7. **A.** The teacher asked the child to bring the book home.
   B. Spring will begin at noon today.
   C. Let's share the candy with the whole group.
   D. *No mistakes*

8. **A.** For conscience's sake he gave himself up, though no suspicion had been directed toward him.
   B. Because they were unaware of his interest in the building, they did not understand why he felt so bad about it's being condemned.
   C. "I truly think," he said, "that we are entitled to have the day off in this snowstorm."
   D. *No mistakes*

9. **A.** Dallas is one of the most populous cities in Texas.
   B. Michigan Avenue is a main tourist attraction in Chicago.
   C. New York is the larger city in the United States.
   D. *No mistakes*

10. **A.** The town of Springsburgh held its annual pie eating contest on Tuesday afternoon.
    B. The science museum held an impressive collection of meteorites.
    C. Are you going to vote in the next Presidential Election?
    D. *No mistakes*

11. **A.** It was the most beautiful sight I've ever saw.
    B. Ed's aunt and uncle lived in the South for many years.
    C. Mattie is the older of the two.
    D. *No mistakes*

12. **A.** Have you seen Marie's new coat?
    B. Sue said, "I'm taking dancing lessons this year."
    C. People lay down when they are tired.
    D. *No mistakes*

13. A. The boy threw his shoe in anger.
    B. I laid in bed all night without sleeping.
    C. Keep this as a secret between you and me.
    D. *No mistakes*

14. A. Yesterday, Valerie came to visit me.
    B. The package arrived hear around 5 p.m.
    C. Arnold and I went to dinner at the Panda Palace, which has great egg rolls.
    D. *No mistakes*

15. A. Dad's going fishing in Canada next week.
    B. Barb didn't know whether to laugh or to cry.
    C. Mom put to much baking powder in the cake.
    D. *No mistakes*

16. A. The tiny kitten sat licking it's wounds.
    B. If you wish, we will have chicken for dinner.
    C. It is so cloudy that we cannot see the Milky Way tonight.
    D. *No mistakes*

17. A. When he said that, everyone applauded.
    B. He was much more interesting than I thought he'd be.
    C. Helen asked Molly and I to come to her party.
    D. *No mistakes*

18. A. This kind of movie may frighten small children.
    B. I'm glad to hear that you're planning to go to college.
    C. Myself has bought a new dress for the party.
    D. *No mistakes*

19. A. How many eggs did you use in this cake?
    B. I can't go nowhere until my chores are done.
    C. Neither Shawna nor Sylvia has to work for her spending money.
    D. *No mistakes*

20. **A.** Because a man understands a woman does not mean they are necessarily compatible.

B. After much talk and haranguing, the workers received an increase in wages.

C. If I am chosen, I will try and attend every meeting that is called.

D. *No mistakes*

21. **A.** John and I are meeting friends on Sunday afternoon to shop for prom wear.

B. We are going to Milner Farms on Saturday.

C. He hadn't seen none of the movies the others talked about.

D. *No mistakes*

22. **A.** Was it really she whom you saw last night?

B. The distraught traveler asked Tom and I to give her directions to the nearest bus stop.

C. Making friends is more rewarding than being antisocial.

D. *No mistakes*

23. **A.** Even if history does not repeat itself, knowledge of history can give current problems a familiar look.

B. He proved to his own satisfaction that he was as clever as, if not more so, than she.

C. The citizens of Washington, like Los Angeles, prefer to commute by automobile.

D. *No mistakes*

24. **A.** While we were waiting for the local train, the express roared past.

B. The woman applied for a new job because she wanted to earn more money.

C. The wind blows, the thunder rolled, lightning will fill the sky, and it rains.

D. *No mistakes*

25. **A.** I have found one of those books that teaches how to build a model airplane.

B. There are less derelicts in the downtown area since the crumbling building was razed.

C. The ceremonies were opened by a colorful drum and bugle corps.

D. *No mistakes*

26. **A.** That business is good appears to be true.

B. The school secretary was pleased that the courses she had taken were relevant to her work.

C. Strict accuracy is a necessary requisite in record keeping.

D. *No mistakes*

27. **A.** I'll let you know if my parents can pick us up.
    B. Our whole class sent get-well cards to Hilda.
    C. Harry said he hadn't done nothing wrong.
    D. *No mistakes*

28. **A.** Between you and me, I must say that I find this whole situation to be ridiculous.
    B. The dimensions of the envelope determine the quantity of material that can be enclosed.
    C. The reason why the train was so late today was because the previous train had been derailed.
    D. *No mistakes*

29. **A.** That unfortunate family faces the problem of adjusting itself to a new way of life.
    B. The teacher promptly notified the principal of the fire for which he was highly praised.
    C. All questions regarding procedure should be referred to a disinterested expert.
    D. *No mistakes*

30. **A.** The sky darkened ominously, and rain began to fall.
    B. I wish I had known who will be backing into my car.
    C. After waiting for three hours for Tim, Brianne contacted a Lyft driver to pick her up.
    D. *No mistakes*

Directions: For questions 31–49, choose the best word or words to join the thoughts together.

31. I would bring Aunt Maisie to visit you, _______ I have no car.
    A. while
    B. because
    C. but
    D. therefore

32. Marla has a photographic memory; _______, she usually forgets my birthday.
    A. nevertheless
    B. unless
    C. even though
    D. so

33. We decided not to go skating on Tuesday; _______, we went to the movies.

A. also

B. however

C. instead

D. whereas

34. I left my key at school; _______ I had to ring the bell to get in the house.

A. however

B. nevertheless

C. therefore

D. but

35. The pilot navigated the storm with ease, _______ he landed the jet haphazardly.

A. unless

B. although

C. because

D. after

36. _______ his passionate nature, he often acts purely on impulse.

A. After

B. Because of

C. Despite

D. Until

37. The fame of the author does not assure the quality of his or her works; _______, we must avoid equating success with infallibility.

A. although

B. therefore

C. only if

D. in case

38. Mining is often called the robber industry _______ it neither creates nor replenishes what it takes.

A. because

B. provided that

C. in order that

D. even though

39. His admirers were not numerous, _______ his essays were not widely known.

A. unless

B. for

C. once

D. so that

40. The society was not self-sufficient; _______, it required much outside aid.

A. yet

B. only if

C. unless

D. thus

41. The final end for a nonadapting society is the same _______ a nonadapting animal: extinction.

A. as

B. as for

C. as with

D. of

42. The penalty for violating the law would _______ for multiple offenses.

A. accede

B. nullify

C. diminish

D. escalate

43. Some colleges, _______ enticing students to take arts courses, simply force them.

A. in addition to

B. rather than

C. after

D. before

44. Ciara always shops at the boutiques on Rodeo Drive _______ she is in Beverly Hills.

A. unless

B. until

C. whenever

D. after

45. The custodian had the daunting task of cleaning the cafeteria _______ the students' food fight was broken up.

A. since

B. after

C. while

D. until

46. Margo not only writes television scripts _______ acts in movies.

A. and

B. but she also

C. but also

D. but

47. _______ the politician's overwhelming loss, he maintained his popularity with a small core of followers.

A. Because of

B. In spite of

C. Since

D. In addition to

48. The decision to seek therapeutic treatment is often provoked by a crisis, _______ an arrest or a domestic dispute.

A. before

B. such as

C. rather than

D. just as

49. We had just finished washing the car _______ it began to rain.

A. if

B. until

C. than

D. when

Directions: For questions 50–52, choose which of the four sentences is constructed best.

50. **A.** A police officer's primary job is to prevent crime.

B. A police officer's job is to prevent primary crime.

C. A police officer's job is to prevent crime primarily.

D. A police officer's job is primary crime prevention.

51. **A.** Politicians are not the only ones who have made errors; we have all blundered at being human some time in our lives.

B. Politicians are not the only ones who have made errors; being human, we have all blundered in our lives for some time.

C. Politicians are not the only ones who have made errors; being human, we have all blundered at some time in our lives.

D. Politicians are not the only ones who have made errors; being blundered, we have all been human at some time in our lives.

52. Caliana avoided my look of surprise by _______

A. staring at the ceiling steadily.

B. staring up at the steady ceiling.

C. staring up steadily at the ceiling.

D. staring steadily at the ceiling.

Directions: For questions 53–75, look for errors in usage. If you find no mistake, choose answer choice D.

53. Jerry and Javon usually don't like to ride roller coasters. (2) Since, they might make an exception if they get to spend spring break at Disney World.

A. Because

B. However

C. On account of

D. *No mistakes*

54. **A.** The sky became darker as the storm rolled in.

B. I thought I heard thunder in the distance.

C. Me and Brooke ran as fast as we could.

D. *No mistakes*

55. **A.** We just got a new ferret,

B. and my older sister gave him an

C. adorable name Phineas.

D. *No mistakes*

56. **A.** Last year I attended John H. Bingham

B. High School, but next year I will be

C. going to Westport Community College.

D. *No mistakes*

57. **A.** I asked my cousin Todd if

B. he has ever read the poem "Annabelle Lee"

C. by Edgar Allan Poe.

D. *No mistakes*

58. **A.** Did you know that Sarah's novel

B. is being published in cereal format

C. in *Modern Times* magazine?

D. *No mistakes*

59. **A.** One of the chapters in Victor Hugo's
B. novel *Les Misérables*
C. is called *The Immortal Liver.*
D. *No mistakes*

60. **A.** "Love Song for Selena" is one of my favorite
B. tunes by Carey McReady, but the artist
C. will not reveal who selena is.
D. *No mistakes*

61. **A.** For almost 80 years, Pluto was considered
B. the ninth planet in our solar system, but in 2006
C. it was reclassified as a Dwarf Planet.
D. *No mistakes*

62. **A.** Mr Fitzgerald is going to
B. be my physics teacher
C. next semester.
D. *No mistakes*

63. **A.** There are no tables available
B. at this restaurant, so we shall have to
C. dine someplace else?
D. *No mistakes*

64. **A.** My cousin works in a clock factory
B. on menlo Avenue called
C. It's About Time, LTD.
D. *No mistakes*

65. **A.** I don't know any Stephen Boyd,
B. Jessica said as she held a photo
C. of herself holding his hand.
D. *No mistakes*

66. **A.** Jaime is running for class
B. treasurer; Celine is the editor of
C. the school paper.
D. *No mistakes*

67. **A.** When you pack for your journey,
B. be sure to include, a sweatshirt,
C. a pair of thick socks, and a compass.
D. *No mistakes*

68. **A.** In the 1998 movie *Godzilla*,
B. the giant reptile lays hundreds of eggs
C. inside Madison Square garden.
D. *No mistakes*

69. **A.** Jehani and Lesley are going
B. to the concert in the park on Saturday,
C. and Monica really wants to go with her.
D. *No mistakes*

70. **A.** If Sergei had joined
B. the rugby team this season
C. he would of been the star.
D. *No mistakes*

71. **A.** Next February I will
B. embarked on a new career as a secretary
C. for an advertising executive.
D. *No mistakes*

72. **A.** I found a gold woman's watch
B. while walking down
C. my block last week.
D. *No mistakes*

73. **A.** When Jeremiah saw
    B. Solomon coming through the door,
    C. he was so happy.
    D. *No mistakes*

74. **A.** I except your invitation
    B. to accompany you to
    C. the theater next week.
    D. *No mistakes*

75. **A.** My exercise routine
    B. consists of running, weightlifting,
    C. doing sit-ups, and swims.
    D. *No mistakes*

Answer Key and Explanations

1. B	16. A	31. C	46. C	61. C
2. A	17. C	32. A	47. B	62. A
3. C	18. C	33. C	48. B	63. C
4. B	19. B	34. C	49. D	64. B
5. C	20. C	35. B	50. A	65. A
6. A	21. C	36. B	51. C	66. M
7. A	22. B	37. B	52. D	67. B
8. B	23. C	38. A	53. B	68. C
9. C	24. C	39. B	54. C	69. C
10. C	25. B	40. D	55. C	70. C
11. A	26. C	41. B	56. D	71. B
12. C	27. C	42. D	57. D	72. A
13. B	28. C	43. B	58. B	73. C
14. B	29. B	44. C	59. C	74. A
15. C	30. B	45. B	60. C	75. C

1. **The correct answer is B.** *Can* refers to ability; *may* is used to request permission.

2. **The correct answer is A.** To *aggravate* is to "make worse." The correct word to use is *annoys*.

3. **The correct answer is C.** The clause beginning with "the room was clean…" requires the conjunction *as*, not the preposition *like*, to complete it properly: "the room was clean *as* it had never been before." (One way to remember proper usage of *as* and *like* is to use *like* when no verb follows and *as* when a verb does follow.)

4. **The correct answer is B.** The compound subject— piece of cake *and* spoonful of ice cream—requires a plural verb, *go*.

5. **The correct answer is C.** The subject of the sentence is the singular *honor*. The fact that profit is to be gained as well is additional information, not part of the subject. A singular subject requires a verb that agrees in number; therefore, the correct verb is *is*.

6. **The correct answer is A.** In this sentence, *too* (an adverb meaning "to an excessive degree") should have been used instead of *to* (a preposition expressing motion in a particular direction): "... it was too difficult for him."

7. **The correct answer is A.** Because the action is away from the teacher toward another place, the correct word is *take.*

8. **The correct answer is B.** The possessive form of *it* is *its*. *It's* is the contraction for *it is.*

9. **The correct answer is C.** The use of the word *larger* is incorrect since New York is being compared with more than one city in the United States. The correct word is *largest.*

10. **The correct answer is C.** There's no reason to capitalize a nonspecific event such as a presidential election.

11. **The correct answer is A.** The tense is incorrect. The last part of the sentence should read *I've ever seen.*

12. **The correct answer is C.** The word *lay* is incorrect in this context. The word should be *lie.*

13. **The correct answer is B.** The past tense of the verb *to lie* is *lay.*

14. **The correct answer is B.** This sentence contains a misspelled word. The word *hear*, which means "the act of hearing," should be replaced with the word *here*, which means "a place."

15. **The correct answer is C.** The preposition *to* is incorrect in this context. The word should be *too*, meaning "excessive."

16. **The correct answer is A.** The possessive of *it* is *its*. *It's* is the contraction for *it is.*

17. **The correct answer is C.** The subjective *I* is incorrect in this context. The correct word is *me*, the object of the verb *asked.*

18. **The correct answer is C.** The correct subject pronoun is *I*; the correct verb to pair with the past participle *bought* is *have.*

19. **The correct answer is B.** The double negative (*can't...nowhere*) is incorrect. The correct sentence would be "I can't go anywhere until my chores are done," or "I can go nowhere until my chores are done."

20. **The correct answer is C.** The proper idiomatic form is *try to*: I will *try to* attend.

21. **The correct answer is C.** The use of double negatives, *hadn't* and *none*, makes this sentence incorrect. It should read *hadn't seen any.*

22. **The correct answer is B.** *Tom* and *me* are the objects of the verb *asked.*

23. **The correct answer is C.** You cannot compare people with a city. The sentence should say "The citizens of Washington, like *those* of Los Angeles . . . ."

24. **The correct answer is C.** This sentence contains a list that lacks parallel structure because the verb tenses shift throughout. A correct version using present-tense verbs would read "The wind blows, the thunder rolls, lightning fills the sky, and it rains."

25. **The correct answer is B.** *Less* is a measure of bulk amount. *Fewer* gives the count of individuals.

26. **The correct answer is C.** A requisite is a necessity. "Necessary requisite" is redundant.

27. **The correct answer is C.** The word *nothing* is incorrect in this context because it creates a double negative. The correct word to use is *anything.*

28. **The correct answer is C.** The *reason why* is not *because*; The *reason why is* that . . . . Or the *reason that* is *because* . . . . In choice A, *you and me* are correctly the objects of the preposition *between.*

29. **The correct answer is B.** As written, the sentence is unclear in identifying the object of the praise. Was the teacher highly praised for the fire? Was the principal highly praised for the fire? If the sentence is intended to say that the teacher was highly praised for promptly notifying the principal about the fire, then that is what the sentence should say.

30. **The correct answer is B.** There is a shift in verb tenses in this sentence. *Had known* is in the past tense verb form and *will be backing* is a future tense verb form.

31. **The correct answer is C.** The conjunction *but* is the only choice that makes any sense in the context of the sentence.

32. **The correct answer is A.** The word *nevertheless* generally means "despite the fact that was just stated." It is correct in this instance because it indicates that Marla forgets the author's birthday despite the fact that she has a photographic memory. *Nevertheless* is also the only choice that requires a semicolon before it and a comma after it.

33. **The correct answer is C.** The word *instead* generally means "as an alternative." It is correct in this instance because it indicates that the authors decided to go to the movies as an alternative to skating.

34. **The correct answer is C.** *Nevertheless, however,* and *but* are used to express a contrast. *Therefore* is used to express a result. The second half of this sentence is clearly a result of the first half.

35. **The correct answer is B.** The word *although* indicates a contrast between the first thought and the second thought, as it does in this instance. *Unless* (choice A) introduces a conditional situation, and *because* (choice C) indicates an illogical cause and effect. *After* (choice D) introduces a problem with the order of events.

36. **The correct answer is B.** The sentence hints at a cause-and-effect relationship between clauses. One who acts purely on impulse is most likely to do so *because of* his passionate nature. *Despite* (choice C) signals a contrast, which does not work in this sentence. *After* (choice A) and *until* (choice D) deal with time and do not fit into the sentence.

37. **The correct answer is B.** *Therefore* is used to express a result or conclusion. The second half of this sentence is a conclusion drawn from the first half. It is also the only choice that would properly be followed by a comma.

38. **The correct answer is A.** The word *because* signals that the reason for the first half of the sentence will follow in in the second half. *Provided that* (choice B) and *in case that* (choice C) both introduce a conditional relationship that does not exist between the two parts of the sentence. Even though (choice D) presents a contrast that does not exist.

39. **The correct answer is B.** *For,* like *because,* can be used to signal a situation-and-reason relationship between parts of a sentence, as it does here. The other answer choices do not set up the proper relationship.

40. **The correct answer is D.** *Thus* can be used to signal a reason-and-situation relationship between parts of a sentence, as it does here. The other answer choices do not set up the proper relationship.

41. **The correct answer is B.** The correct idiom to use, and the one that keeps the sentence parallel in structure, is *as for.* Keep in mind that the comparison is being made to *end,* so *as* (choice A) sets up an improper comparison (*end…animal*).

42. **The correct answer is D.** Multiple offenses would require an increased penalty; therefore, *escalate* is the only correct choice.

43. **The correct answer is B.** The opposite of forcing students to take courses is enticing them to do so. *Rather than* is the only choice that signals an opposite connection between the two parts of the sentence.

44. **The correct answer is C.** The word *whenever* joins the thoughts together in a timeframe that is logical. Choices A, B, and C represent impossibilities.

45. **The correct answer is B.** The best word choice to complete this thought will link the two activities in in the sentence in terms of their relationship in time. If the custodian had to clean a mess made during a food fight, the cleaning would have to come *after* the fight occurred.

46. **The correct answer is C.** The correct choice for this sentence will establish parallel structure. *Not only...but also* is the correlative conjunction pair that does this correctly.

47. **The correct answer is B.** Although the politician lost the election, he maintained his popularity with some followers, so the sentence needs a word or phrase to indicate the contrast in situations. *In spite of* sets up the contrast properly.

48. **The correct answer is B.** An arrest or domestic dispute would both be considered examples of a serious crisis, so the correct answer would need to indicate that examples follow the word *crisis*. *Such as* is the phrase that best introduces the examples.

49. **The correct answer is D.** The sentence describes two activities in terms of their relationship in time. Only choice D connects the sentence correctly.

50. **The correct answer is A.** This sentence demonstrates correct usage. The other answer choices suffer from modifier misplacement.

51. **The correct answer is C.** This sentence demonstrates correct usage. The other answer choices suffer from incorrect and confusing syntax.

52. **The correct answer is D.** The ceiling is "up," so choices B and C can be eliminated for redundancy. *Steadily* describes the manner in which Caliana stared and should be placed next to the word it describes (*staring*).

53. **The correct answer is B.** *Since*, *because*, and *on account of* all indicate a result. *However* is used to express a contrast. Seeing the word *exception* should provide a clue that what is stated in the second sentence provides a contrast to the information in the first sentence.

54. **The correct answer is C.** The sentence should read: Brooke and I ran as fast as we could.

55. **The correct answer is C.** The clarifying information—the ferret's name—needs to be introduced with a colon in this sentence.

56. **The correct answer is D.** *No mistakes.*

57. **The correct answer is D.** *No mistakes.*

58. **The correct answer is B.** There is a spelling error in this sentence. *Cereal* means "a breakfast food made from grains"; *serial* means "occurring in a series."

59. **The correct answer is C.** While the title of a novel should be italicized, a chapter title should be placed within quotation marks.

60. **The correct answer is C.** *Selena* is someone's name, so it should be capitalized.

61. **The correct answer is C.** The term *dwarf planet* is not a proper name, so it should not be capitalized.

62. **The correct answer is A.** An abbreviated title such as *Mrs.* needs to end with a period.

63. **The correct answer is C.** This sentence is a declarative statement, so it should end with a period, not a question mark.

64. **The correct answer is B.** Since Menlo Avenue is the proper name of a specific road, it should be capitalized.

65. **The correct answer is A.** "I don't know any Stephen Boyd" is something Jessica said, and quotes belong within quotation marks.

66. **The correct answer is M.** *No mistakes.*

67. **The correct answer is B.** There should not be a comma at the beginning of the list. Therefore, the comma after *include* is misplaced.

68. **The correct answer is C.** *Garden* is part of the name of the structure, so it should be capitalized.

69. **The correct answer is C.** There is a pronoun/antecedent error in this sentence. *Jehani* and *Lesley* are two people, yet *her* is a singular pronoun. It should be replaced with *them.*

70. **The correct answer is C.** *Of* is not an auxiliary verb; the correct verb to use here is *would have.*

71. The correct answer is B. The auxiliary verb *will* indicates that the sentence is referring to the future, and it should be paired with the present tense *embark* to form *will embark*; *embarked* is in the past tense.

72. The correct answer is A. This sentence has a misplaced modifier because the adjective *gold* should modify *watch*, yet it is placed next to *woman*, which makes it sound as though a woman is made of gold. *Gold* should be moved between *woman's* and *watch.*

73. The correct answer is C. This sentence has a vague pronoun reference because it is unclear if *he* refers to Jeremiah or Solomon. The pronoun *he* should be replaced with either *Jeremiah* or *Solomon.*

74. The correct answer is A. This sentence uses a wrong word. *Except* means "excluding," so it does not make sense in this context. The correct word would be *accept*, which means "say 'yes' to."

75. The correct answer is C. This sentence lacks parallel structure because *running*, *weightlifting*, and *doing* (sit-ups) are all written in the progressive tense, but *swims* is in the present tense. *Swims* should be replaced with *swimming.*

Composition and Written Expression Drill

Directions: For questions 1–37, you will be given pieces of writing followed by one or more questions about changing the writing. Four answers will be given for each question. Choose the best answer.

Questions 1 and 2 refer to the following paragraph.

(1) Last year I <u>start</u> playing violin in the school orchestra. (2) Although I did not play it well at first, I'd improved a lot by the end of the year.

1. What is the best way to write the underlined part of sentence 1?

A. starting

B. started

C. starts

D. *No change*

2. Choose the best last sentence to add to this story.

A. This year I'm good enough to play a solo in the spring concert!

B. My friend Angelo just started playing flute in the orchestra.

C. Sarah Chang is considered to be one of the best violinists in the world.

D. When I first started studying it, I found the violin very difficult to play.

Question 3 refers to the following paragraph.

(1) The *Apollo 11* mission was affected by many technical difficulties before the lunar module finally landed on the moon. (2) <u>Also,</u> the moonwalk proceeded effortlessly.

3. What is the best way to write the underlined part of sentence 2?

A. Consequently,

B. Nevertheless,

C. As a matter of fact,

D. *No change*

Questions 4 and 5 refer to the following paragraph.

(1) Every Saturday I go of the library. (2) I love reading through the non-fiction books.

4. What is the best way to write the underlined part of sentence 1?

A. at

B. to

C. on

D. *No change*

5. Choose the best last sentence to add to this story.

A. My favorite is a biography of the poet Maya Angelou.

B. The best novel I ever read is *Little Women*.

C. The librarian's name is Mr. Beasley.

D. I have to complete my book report by Thursday.

Question 6 refers to the following paragraph.

(1) I purchased the bicycle last week and the skateboard less than a month ago. (2) Unfortunately, neither one of them are functioning properly.

6. What is the best way to write the underlined part of sentence 2?

A. neither one of them is

B. both of them isn't

C. neither the bicycle nor the skateboard are

D. *No change*

Questions 7 and 8 refer to the following paragraph.

(1) Sarah comes to my house for dinner next Tuesday. (2) My dad is going to cook ravioli and garlic bread for the occasion.

7. What is the best way to write the underlined part of sentence 1?

A. came

B. is coming

C. come

D. *No change*

8. Choose the best last sentence to add to this story.

A. Tonight we are having tacos for dinner.

B. My mom cooks dinner on Monday nights.

C. I've been friends with Sarah since kindergarten.

D. I'm sure it will be delicious!

Question 9 refers to the following paragraph.

(1) Athletes who hope to compete in the Olympics undergo grueling training, give up all their hobbies, and forego most social activities. (2) Nevertheless, so few of them won medals or even made the team.

9. What is the best way to write the underlined part of sentence 2?

A. had won medals or had even made the team

B. win medals or even made the team

C. win medals or even make the team

D. *No change*

Questions 10 and 11 refer to the following paragraph.

(1) Archie Zambroski was one of America's premier inventors. (2) In addition few Americans have ever heard of Archie. (3) Archie invented many gizmos and gadgets found in most households in America: including the under-the-cabinet paper towel roll holder and the lint catcher for dryers. (4) Unfortunately, Zambroski never made the fortune of which he dreamed.

10. What is the best way to write the underlined part of sentence 2?

A. However,

B. In spite of,

C. Once,

D. *No change*

11. What is the best way to write the underlined part of sentence 3?

A. America; including

B. America: For example

C. America, including

D. *No change*

Questions 12 and 13 refer to the following paragraph.

(1) Researchers have done numerous studies in recent years to determine the effects of video games on the motor skills of preschoolers. (2) In other words. Scientists want to see what, if any, effect video games have on preschoolers' coordination. (3) Researchers once thought that video games slowed the development of physical abilities of preschoolers. (4) Now, however, researchers tend to agree that preschoolers can develop hand-eye coordination by playing video games.

12. What is the best way to write the underlined part of sentence 2?

A. words: scientists

B. words, scientists

C. words—Scientists

D. *No change*

13. What is the best way to write the underlined part of sentence 4?

A. miraculously

B. simultaneously

C. but

D. *No change*

Question 14 refers to the following paragraph.

(1) These people lose sight of an important fact: many of the founding fathers of our country were comparatively young men. (2) Today more than ever, our country needs young, idealistic politicians.

14. Choose the topic sentence that best fits the paragraph.

A. Young people don't like politics.

B. Many people think that only older men and women who have had a great deal of experience should hold public office.

C. The holding of public office should be restricted to highly idealistic people.

D. Our Constitution prescribes certain minimum ages for certain elected federal officeholders.

Questions 15 and 16 refer to the following paragraph.

(1) At the end of each year, the city's Lost and Found department is required by law to catalog any unclaimed items and then donate them to Charitable Organizations. (2) According to the catalog of items, the most frequently unclaimed items are shoes mittens lunchboxes and purses.

15. What is the best way to write the underlined part of sentence 1?

A. to: charitable organizations

B. to, Charitable Organizations

C. to charitable organizations

D. *No change*

16. What is the best way to write the underlined part of sentence 2?

A. are shoes, mittens, lunchboxes, and purses

B. are shoes; mittens; lunchboxes; purses

C. are: shoes and mittens and lunchboxes and purses

D. *No change*

Question 17 refers to the following paragraph.

(1) Jacob is highly allergic to peanuts and must avoid eating this food. (2) Instead, he must be careful not to consume any products made with peanuts or peanut oil.

17. What is the best way to write the underlined part of sentence 2?

A. In addition

B. Because

C. However

D. *No change*

Questions 18 and 19 refer to the following paragraph.

(1) When an average person looks at a mailbox or a dead tree, he or she sees just a mailbox or a dead tree. (2) Likewise, a photographer can look at the same items and envision beautiful and interesting photographs. (3) The World might be a more delightful place if all people viewed the world around them through the eyes of a photographer.

18. What is the best way to write the underlined part of sentence 2?

A. Furthermore,

B. Additionally,

C. On the other hand,

D. *No change*

19. What is the best way to write the underlined part of sentence 3?

A. world

B. planet

C. worldwide

D. *No change*

Questions 20 and 21 refer to the following paragraph.

(1) Professor Johnson and dr. Tannebaum spent years working together on a novel. (2) Johnson contributed his knowledge of science, and Tannebaum contributed his knowledge of medicine. (3) The novel that they was writing slowly took shape and finally reached completion ten years after they typed the first words.

20. What is the best way to write the underlined part of sentence 1?

A. doctor Tannebaum

B. Dr. Tannebaum

C. doc Tannebaum

D. *No change*

21. What is the best way to write the underlined part of sentence 3?

A. wrote

B. had wrote

C. had been written

D. *No change*

Questions 22 and 23 refer to the following paragraph.

(1) Most successful chefs, especially those working in expensive restaurants, attend College to learn to cook. (2) Many of the world's greatest cities boast a number of culinary schools, or schools for aspiring chefs. (3) Athens, Paris, New York, San Francisco, Tokyo. Are home to such culinary institutes.

22. What is the best way to write the underlined part of sentence 1?

A. a College

B. college

C. College,

D. *No change*

23. What is the best way to write the underlined part of sentence 3?

A. San Francisco, and Tokyo are home

B. San Francisco, Tokyo—Are home

C. San Francisco and Tokyo is home

D. *No change*

Question 24 refers to the following paragraph.

(1) Abraham Lincoln delivered his Second Inaugural Address only days before the Union won the Civil War. (2) Furthermore, he never gloated about his imminent victory anywhere in the speech.

24. What is the best way to write the underlined part of sentence 2?

A. Indeed,

B. Even so,

C. In addition,

D. *No change*

Questions 25 and 26 refer to the following paragraph.

(1) One of the fastest growing industries of the last twenty-five years is the baby food manufacturing industry. (2) Because each baby food company wants to outsell the other baby food companies, new flavors and food combinations are created each month. (3) Company baby food "tasters" have to try such new flavors as pears, zucchini, and peas or sweet potato, mango, and kale. (4) Without the taste buds of these loyal employees—millions of American babies would be forced to eat old-fashioned baby foods like green beans or strained carrots.

25. What is the best way to write the underlined part of sentence 1?

A. twenty five

B. Twenty Five

C. twentyfive

D. *No change*

26. What is the best way to write the underlined part of sentence 4?

A. employees: millions

B. employees and millions

C. employees, millions

D. *No change*

Questions 27 and 28 refer to the following paragraph.

(1) Although small schools usually have good teacher-to-student ratios and small classes, large schools have advantages, two. (2) For example, large schools often have more course offerings than small schools. (3) Large schools can offer advanced courses instead of just History, Science, and Math.

27. What is the best way to write the underlined part of sentence 1?

A. in addition to

B. too

C. besides

D. *No change*

28. What is the best way to write the underlined part of sentence 3?

A. history, science, and math

B. History; Science; Math

C. history, and science, and math

D. *No change*

Questions 29 and 30 refer to the following paragraph.

(1) Valerie knows more about fashion than anyone else in her class. (2) She watched all the fashion shows on television, reads all the fashion magazines, and attends all the city's fashion premiers. (3) Valerie has said many times that she wants to go to school to become a fashion designer. (4) Than, when the time is right, she'll design new, cutting-edge fashion lines using vintage items she finds at thrift stores.

29. What is the best way to write the underlined part of sentence 2?

A. had watched

B. had been watching

C. watches

D. *No change*

30. What is the best way to write the underlined part of sentence 4?

A. Then

B. Regardless

C. Before

D. *No change*

Questions 31 and 32 refer to the following paragraph.

(1) Mr. and Mrs. Johannson were a retired couple who had lived in Wisconsin all their lives. (2) For sixty years, they had put up with the bitterly cold Winters in Wisconsin, and they had had enough. (3) The Johannsons sold their house and their cars, bought an RV, and decided to spend the rest of their days on the road.

31. What is the best way to write the underlined part of sentence 2?

A. winters

B. Weather

C. Winter Weathers

D. *No change*

32. What is the best way to write the underlined part of sentence 3?

A. there

B. they're

C. Their

D. *No change*

Questions 33–35 refer to the following paragraph.

(1) In the 1940s, record albums were the best-selling way to produce recorded music, so a great many companies went into the business of producing them. (2) When companies started to introduce compact disc (CD) recordings in the 1980s. These recordings were such great sellers that they rapidly became the *new* best-selling form of recorded music in the industry. (3) By 1988, CDs were selling more copies than record albums, showing that consumers preferred the CD format. (4) As a result, music companies that once produced record albums could no longer succeed by selling albums.

33. What is the best way to write the underlined part of sentence 2?

A. 1980s, these

B. 1980s these

C. 1980s and these

D. *No change*

34. What is the best way to write the underlined part of sentence 4?

A. Nevertheless

B. Alternatively

C. On the other hand

D. *No change*

35. Choose the best last sentence to add to this story.

A. However, some album covers are still considered to be valuable works of art.

B. By 1989, record albums began to disappear from stores.

C. Albums are made of vinyl.

D. Do you own any albums?

Questions 36–37 refer to the following paragraph.

(1) As opposed too low-fat diets, the Mediterranean diet does not prohibit fats but focuses on healthier fat choices. (2) In addition, the Mediterranean diet promotes the importance of physical activity and the enjoyment of sharing meals with Family, Co-workers, and Friends.

36. What is the best way to write the underlined part of sentence 1?

A. two

B. also

C. to

D. *No change*

37. What is the best way to write the underlined part of sentence 2?

A. family, and coworkers, and friends

B. family, coworkers, and friends

C. Family; Coworkers; Friends

D. *No change*

Directions: For questions 38–75, follow the instructions and select the best answer.

38. Choose the topic sentence that best fits the paragraph.

The first thing to do is gather several apples—a few good choices include Goldrush, Harrison, and Grimes Golden apples. Put your apples, and spices to taste, in a large pot and fill it with water until the apples are completely submerged. Bring it to a boil, stir for about an hour, strain it until you're left with the juice, refrigerate it, and serve your delicious beverage any time of day.

A. If you're eager to make apple cider, here's an easy recipe for doing so.

B. Did you know that most people don't drink enough fluids during the day?

C. Apples are one of the most popular and versatile fruits in the United States.

D. Do you know how to make a delicious homemade apple pie?

39. Choose the topic sentence that best fits the paragraph.

First, your ability to secure a position might depend on your English. Your prospective employer will notice how well you write the answers to the questions on your application. And when you are interviewed, he will notice how well you speak.

A. As you move up the success ladder, what you write and what you say will determine in part your rate of climb.

B. If you wish to enter business, there are three good reasons why you should study English.

C. You will need to write reports accurately and interestingly.

D. You will need to talk effectively with your fellow workers, with your superiors, and perhaps with the public.

40. Choose the sentence that expresses the idea most clearly.

A. Kim liked the skateboard with the nylon wheels that his father had built.

B. Kim liked the new skateboard his father had built with the nylon wheels.

C. The skateboard with the nylon wheels which his father had built new Kim liked.

D. His father had built a new skateboard which Kim liked with nylon wheels.

41. Identify where the sentence, "Its shell, called a *cowrie*, is white or light yellow and is about one inch long," should be placed in the paragraph below.

(1) Along the shores of the Indian Ocean is found a pretty little shellfish that is noted for furnishing what may have been the first money ever used. (2) Millions of people around the ocean were using these cowries for money long before furs or cattle or other kinds of money were used anywhere, as far as is known. (3) Cowries have been found in Assyria, many miles inland.

A. Before sentence 1

B. Between sentence 1 and 2

C. Between sentence 2 and 3

D. Between sentence 3 and 4

42. Choose the sentence that is complete and correctly written.

A. Cold-blooded reptiles with no mechanism for controlling body temperature.

B. Reptiles, which have no mechanism for controlling body temperature, are described as cold-blooded animals.

C. Reptiles are described as cold-blooded animals, this means that they have no mechanism for controlling body temperature.

D. Reptiles are described as cold-blooded animals and they have no mechanism for controlling body temperature.

43. Choose the topic sentence that best fits the paragraph.

Today, more people spend time on their mobile phones than reading books or newspapers. People can pay bills and keep in touch with friends and family online. Now, we can purchase virtually anything we need from the comfort of our home computers.

A. Technology is changing the way we live.

B. Everyone has a mobile phone these days.

C. Advances in technology are more trouble than they're worth.

D. People love shopping online.

44. Choose the topic sentence that best fits the paragraph.

There are important areas in our lives in which opinions play a major role. Every time we look into the future, we depend on opinions. Every time we attempt to judge facts, we depend on opinions. And every time we attempt to advance into the "not yet known area," we depend on opinions.

A. Opinions should not be taken lightly.

B. Newspaper editorials are based upon opinion rather than upon facts.

C. In some ways, they actually go beyond facts.

D. Scientific inquiry leaves no room for opinions.

45. Identify where the sentence, "Geodes commonly house an internal lining of quartz crystals," should be placed in the paragraph below.

(1) Geodes are geological structures that naturally occur in sedimentary and volcanic rocks. (2) They are typically hollow and spherical in shape and can vary greatly in size. (3) These crystals can come in a variety of colors, based on the chemicals and impurities involved in their formation. (4) The colors inside of each geode, which remains a mystery until it is opened, and the dazzling crystalline world that waits within, is part of the reason why these objects are so prized and sought after.

A. Between sentence 1 and 2

B. Between sentence 2 and 3

C. Between sentence 3 and 4

D. After sentence 4

46. Choose the sentence that does not belong in the paragraph.

(1) If something becomes suddenly popular, it is called a *fad.* (2) Parents are often dismayed by teenage fads. (3) If something's popularity endures, it is called a *trend.* (4) If something's popularity affects other things, it is called a *style.*

A. Sentence 1

B. Sentence 2

C. Sentence 3

D. Sentence 4

47. Choose the sentence that does not belong in the paragraph.

(1) Human forms of cultural behavior are found among the Japanese monkey. (2) Members of the Japan Monkey Center have found among local monkey groups a wide variety of customs based on social learning. (3) The males of certain groups, for instance, take turns looking after the infants while the mothers are eating. (4) The scientists have also been able to observe the process by which behavioral innovations, such as swimming and sweet potato washing, developed and spread from individual to individual in the monkey group. (5) Japanese scientists found that female tigers swam more than male monkeys.

A. Sentence 1

B. Sentence 2

C. Sentence 3

D. Sentence 5

48. Choose the sentence that does not belong in the paragraph.

(1) The island countries of the Caribbean area produce large quantities of oil, tropical fruits, and vegetables. (2) They are also rich in minerals. (3) The Caribbean Sea is to the American continent a central sea, just as the Mediterranean is to the European continent. (4) This region is capable of supplying the United States with many goods formerly imported from Africa and Asia. (5) In exchange, the countries of this region need the manufactured goods that can be provided only by an industrial nation.

A. Sentence 1

B. Sentence 2

C. Sentence 3

D. Sentence 4

49. Identify where the sentence, "Drivers who use alcohol tend to disregard their usual safety practices," should be placed in the paragraph below.

(1) Many experiments on the effects of alcohol consumption show that alcohol decreases alertness and efficiency. (2) It decreases self-consciousness and at the same time increases confidence and feelings of ease and relaxation. (3) It impairs attention and judgment. (4) It destroys fear of consequences. (5) Usual cautions are thrown to the wind. (6) Their reaction time slows down; normally quick reactions are not possible for them.

A. Between sentences 1 and 2

B. Between sentences 2 and 3

C. Between sentences 4 and 5

D. Between sentences 5 and 6

50. Choose the word that best completes this sentence.

When the teacher announced a pop quiz, an ________ groan went around the classroom.

A. ecstatic

B. agonized

C. erroneous

D. inattentive

51. Which of the following sentences offers the *least* support for the topic of "Why cities should build bike lanes"?

A. Bike lanes are expensive to create and difficult to enforce.

B. Commuting by bike is a healthy and environmentally sustainable way to get around.

C. Bike lanes have shown to be highly effective in other towns.

D. Having bike lanes has been known to reduce auto accidents significantly.

52. Which sentence does *not* belong in the paragraph?

(1) Solar energy is considered a major potential energy source for the future. (2) With no toxic byproducts, it is one of the cleaner energy sources available to us today. (3) Wind energy is also a "clean" energy source. (4) Solar energy can also be implemented on a household or community level.

A. Sentence 1

B. Sentence 2

C. Sentence 3

D. Sentence 4

53. Choose the best word to join the following thoughts together.

The route to the beach is easy, ______ you may have to wait in traffic during summer months.

A. so

B. because

C. and

D. but

54. Which of these choices expresses the idea most clearly?

A. Robin's recipe for making a chocolate soufflé involves combining the ingredients gently, then letting them rise in the oven without opening the door.

B. Chocolate souffles need ingredients according to Robin. Combine them. Then you should shut the oven door. When you're baking, don't open the door.

C. Into the oven and don't open the door, Robin's recipe for chocolate soufflé calls for gently combining ingredients.

D. Robin's recipe for chocolate soufflé: stir ingredients, bake in the oven.

55. Which sentence does *not* belong in the paragraph?

(1) Mt. Everest has become a surprising tourist destination in recent years. (2) Once viewed as a dangerous and near-impossible climb for even the most experienced mountain climbers, it has now become a popular destination for people who can afford extensive equipment and training. (3) I would love to take a selfie on top of Mt. Everest in order to ramp up my Instagram engagement. (4) However, the trek has become no less dangerous over the years, with dozens of people dying on the treacherous climb. (5) Anyone who wants to climb Mt. Everest should be fully aware of the risks and challenges of climbing the tallest mountain in the world.

A. Sentence 2

B. Sentence 3

C. Sentence 4

D. Sentence 5

56. Choose the word that best completes this sentence.

Simon couldn't find the remote control until he checked the couch and found it wedged _____ two cushions.

A. around

B. on

C. inside

D. between

57. Which of the following sentences would *best* fit at the end of this paragraph?

(1) To attract hummingbirds, start by hanging a feeder outside. (2) You can find feeders online or at your local garden store. (3) Fill your feeder with hummingbird food, which can be purchased, or you can make your own by making a simple syrup of water and sugar.

A. If you hang your feeder near flowers, you're more likely to see hummingbirds soon.

B. Hummingbird feeders come in a variety of shapes and colors.

C. The most common hummingbird type of hummingbird is the ruby-throated hummingbird.

D. Hummingbird feeders usually cost about twenty dollars.

58. Which of the following sentences provides the *most* support for the topic "Why the town of Smithville should have a recycling program"?

A. A recycling program would take three years to get up and running.

B. The neighboring town of North Haverbrook has saved thousands of dollars of landfill costs due to their own recycling program.

C. Recycling programs typically include paper, some kinds of plastics, and glass.

D. A recycling program would cost a lot of money to start and maintain.

59. Choose the word that *best* completes this sentence.

Neither Sandy _____ Fred had ever been to Nebraska before.

A. and

B. or

C. nor

D. that

60. Choose the pair of sentences that best develops this topic sentence.

Drinking 64 ounces of water per day is ideal.

A. Feeling dehydrated? Drinking more water during the day will help.

B. Doctors recommend drinking eight glasses of water every day to stay hydrated. Staying hydrated can help improve mental and physical performance.

C. Losing water through sweat is a leading cause of dehydration. Dehydration can also slow down weight loss.

D. Eating a healthy diet and getting 30 minutes of exercise per day are essential for good health as well. A well-balanced life is necessary for a healthy body.

61. Which of these expresses the idea most clearly?

A. The internet, local newspapers are failing. As a reader, newspapers are not screens, which is where most people get their news nowadays.

B. With most people consuming news online, the internet is failing newspapers, readers are fleeing to digital sources of information.

C. As more readers get their news digitally on computers, tablets, and phones, local newspapers are failing.

D. The digital revolution is killing newspapers (that are less common than they used to be).

62. Choose the word that *best* completes this sentence.

______ she had a dentist appointment scheduled for that afternoon, Gina did not eat any sugary snacks.

A. Although

B. So

C. For

D. Because

63. Which sentence does *not* belong in the paragraph?

(1) Right now in Jones Park, there is no space where dogs are allowed to run off-leash. (2) The park is 25 acres large. (3) Local dog owners are hoping to have part of the park designated as a dog park. (4) They're organizing a phone and email campaign to the city council to get the necessary funding.

A. Sentence 1

B. Sentence 2

C. Sentence 3

D. Sentence 4

64. Choose the *best* word to join the following thoughts together.

The weather is supposed to get much colder this evening, _____ you should bring a jacket with you.

A. so

B. because

C. or

D. if

65. Choose the pair of sentences that best develops this topic sentence.

Students should not be allowed to bring cell phones into the classroom.

A. Cell phones are a distraction. Students are more likely to text each other than use the phones for classroom activities.

B. Students can be trusted not to use their phones while classes are happening. They also need to have phones in case of an emergency where they need to contact parents.

C. Test scores are higher in classrooms where cell phones are banned. Teachers have the power to make the decision for their own classrooms.

D. Schools that allow cell phones tend to have higher rates of cyberbullying. But phones can be a useful tool in the classroom.

66. Choose the sentence that would *best* introduce the following paragraph.

(1) Studies show that limiting screen time at least an hour before bedtime can help. (2) The "blue light" from phone and tablet screens interferes with the brain's natural sleep cycles. (3) Experts recommend sticking to a set bedtime routine to help restore those cycles and improve sleep quality.

A. Blue light is a health hazard.

B. Let's review the brain's natural sleep cycles.

C. Who wants to talk about sleep?

D. Are you looking for better sleep?

67. Choose the word that *best* completes this sentence.

Because the light bulb had burned out, Dan had to _____ through the dark room to find the flashlight.

A. glide

B. run

C. stumble

D. look

68. Choose the *best* title for the following paragraph.

(1) Although having exotic animals as pets is illegal in many cities, some people do this anyway. (2) Having a tiger cub as a pet may seem like a fun idea, but the reality is often very different. (3) The animals are still considered wild animals and are not equipped to live in residential areas. (4) They might also not be getting the proper care that they would get in the wild or from qualified professionals. (5) There is also a risk that people may get hurt by these wild animals.

A. Choosing the Right Pet for You

B. The Dangers of Exotic Pets

C. Exotic Pet Laws

D. Do Tigers Make Good Pets?

69. Choose the word that *best* completes this sentence.

The music festival was only half over when the rain started; Kevin was ______ that he hadn't remembered to bring his umbrella.

A. thrilled

B. astonished

C. annoyed

D. forgetful

70. Which of the following sentences offers the *least* support for the topic of "Why the United States should no longer follow Daylight Saving Time"?

A. Daylight Saving Time is known as "summer time" in other parts of the world.

B. Arizona already does not follow Daylight Saving Time, so there is a precedent.

C. The changes in time affect US international business and relations.

D. Sudden changes in time and schedule can have a negative effect on health.

71. Which of the following sentences would *best* fit at the end of this paragraph?

(1) Studies have shown that having a longer school year benefits students. (2) During summer break, many students lose skills that were learned over the previous year. (3) Lengthening the school year helps decrease those gaps for students.

A. Longer school years are not popular with teachers.

B. Extending the school year is expensive to the school district as well.

C. Students tend to forget math and reading skills over the summer.

D. These gains also help increase student test scores.

72. Choose the word that *best* completes this sentence.

At the end of the movie, most of the crowd stayed to watch the secret scene _____ the credits.

A. before

B. after

C. while

D. since

73. Which sentence does *not* belong in the paragraph?

(1) Single-use plastic (like straws and plastic shopping bags) are an increasingly difficult problem for the environment. (2) Tons of plastic are found every year in the ocean, negatively affecting plant and animal life. (3) Some communities are hoping to eliminate some of this waste by banning plastic bags and encouraging shoppers to use reusable shopping bags. (4) Oil spills are another form of pollution responsible for damaging the environment.

A. Sentence 1

B. Sentence 2

C. Sentence 3

D. Sentence 4

74. Which sentence offers the *least* support for the topic of "Why students should be required to learn a second language"?

A. In a world economy, bilingual people will have an advantage.

B. Strong language skills often translate into other academic areas.

C. Students can choose any language they want to learn.

D. Learning another language helps build cultural understanding.

75. Choose the word that *best* joins the thoughts together.

I was planning to go to Gregory's party this weekend, ______ I have a family dinner scheduled at the same time.

A. nor

B. and

C. but

D. so

Answer Key and Explanations

1. B	16. A	31. A	46. B	61. C
2. A	17. A	32. D	47. D	62. D
3. B	18. C	33. A	48. C	63. B
4. B	19. A	34. D	49. D	64. A
5. A	20. B	35. B	50. B	65. A
6. A	21. A	36. C	51. A	66. D
7. B	22. B	37. B	52. C	67. C
8. D	23. A	38. A	53. D	68. B
9. C	24. B	39. B	54. A	69. C
10. A	25. D	40. A	55. B	70. A
11. C	26. C	41. C	56. D	71. D
12. B	27. B	42. B	57. A	72. B
13. D	28. A	43. A	58. B	73. D
14. B	29. C	44. A	59. C	74. C
15. C	30. A	45. B	60. B	75. C

1. **The correct answer is B.** The phrase *last year* indicates that this sentence is written in the past tense, but *start* is in the present tense. Choice B correctly uses the past tense. Choice A is in the present progressive tense, and choice C is in the present tense.

2. **The correct answer is A.** This story tracks the violinist's progress beginning in the past. Therefore, it would make sense to end it with information about the present. Choice B shifts the focus to the speaker's friend, so it does not resolve the story well. Choice C also shifts focus to someone who is not part of the story. Choice D would have been a fine second sentence for this story, but it is about the past, so it fails to continue the progression in the other sentences.

3. **The correct answer is B.** The word *nevertheless* generally means "despite the fact that was just stated." It is correct in this instance because it indicates that the moonwalk proceeded effortlessly despite the fact that the mission was affected by many technical difficulties.

4. **The correct answer is B.** There is a word choice error in this sentence. *Of* is not the right preposition to use when indicating progress toward a place such as a library. The best preposition is *to.*

5. **The correct answer is A.** This story is about how the speaker likes reading non-fiction books at the library. This sentence resolves the story by specifying the speaker's favorite non-fiction book. Choice B shifts the focus to fiction books, so it is not the best conclusion to the story. Choice C shifts the focus to the librarian. Choice D shifts the focus to a book report.

6. **The correct answer is A.** The words *neither one* indicate that the subject is singular. *Is* agrees with a singular subject. Choices B and C have faulty subject-verb agreement.

7. **The correct answer is B.** The phrase *next Tuesday* shows that this sentence is in the future tense, but *comes* is in the present tense. Choice B corrects that error because *is coming* is the future progressive tense of *come.* Choice A is in the past tense. Choice C is in the present tense.

8. **The correct answer is D.** The topic of this story is how the speaker's friend is coming to dinner next Tuesday to eat ravioli that the speaker's dad will cook. This sentence resolves that story with a comment about the dinner. Choice A shifts the focus to tonight's dinner. Choice B shifts the focus to yet another night's dinner. Choice C shifts the focus to when the speaker and Sarah became friends.

9. **The correct answer is C.** Sentence 2 incorrectly shifts to the past tense, so both verbs should be switched from past to present tense. It is important to read all the answer choices before selecting one. On a quick glance, you might have picked choice B, which would have been incorrect because only the first verb was changed to the present tense.

10. **The correct answer is A.** The word *however* generally means "nevertheless," "yet," or "even though." It is correct in this instance because the sentences indicate Zambroski was one of America's premier inventors even though few have heard of him.

11. **The correct answer is C.** A colon is used before a list of items that illustrate or amplify what is stated before the colon. The word *including* indicates there are examples following America and would not be used in addition to a colon.

12. **The correct answer is B.** The phrase "in other words" is a sentence fragment and should be used as an introductory phrase for the rest of the sentence that follows. The only punctuation needed after the phrase is a comma, and *Scientists* would be rewritten as *scientists.*

13. **The correct answer is D.** No change

14. **The correct answer is B.** The first development sentence begins with "these people." The topic sentence must tell us who these people are, so you can immediately eliminate choices C and D. Choice B then becomes clearly the best answer because it offers an opinion that contrasts with the bulk of the paragraph.

15. **The correct answer is C.** The words "charitable organizations" are not the name of a specific organization that needs to be capitalized the way that "Red Cross" or "Catholic Youth Organization" would be.

16. **The correct answer is A.** Commas are needed to separate the listed items in this sentence.

17. **The correct answer is A.** *Instead* means "as an alternative to," but sentence 2 continues the ideas presented in sentence 1—that Jacob needs to avoid peanuts—and it lists other items to avoid in addition to just the peanuts themselves. *Furthermore* is the closest in meaning to "in addition to."

18. **The correct answer is C.** The phrase "on the other hand" is used to link two ideas that are dissimilar or opposite.

19. **The correct answer is A.** The word *world* is a common noun and would need capitalization only if used as part of a name like World Health Organization.

20. **The correct answer is B.** The word *doctor* by itself is a common noun, but both *Doctor* and its abbreviation, *Dr.*, require capitalization when used as part of a title or a name.

21. **The correct answer is A.** The passage is written in past tense, and the past tense form of the verb *write* is *wrote.*

22. **The correct answer is B.** The word *college* is capitalized only when it is included in a proper noun, such as Austin College or Mississippi College.

23. **The correct answer is A.** A list of cities by itself is a sentence fragment, as is a sentence beginning with a verb and having no subject.

24. **The correct answer is B.** The words *even so* generally mean "despite the fact that was just stated." It is correct in this instance because it indicates that Lincoln didn't gloat about his victory despite the fact that the Union was about to win the war.

25. **The correct answer is D.** No change

26. **The correct answer is C.** An introductory prepositional phrase such as "without the taste buds of these loyal employees" should be set apart from the rest of the sentence by a comma.

27. **The correct answer is B.** Meaning "also," the correct word *too* is often mistakenly replaced by its homonym, *two*.

28. **The correct answer is A.** These subjects are common nouns and would need capitalization only if they were included in a proper noun, for example the name of a college course such as "The History of Science and Math in Western Civilization."

29. **The correct answer is C.** The passage is written in present tense, and the verb *watch* must agree with the rest of the passage, hence the use of the word *watches*.

30. **The correct answer is A.** The word *then* indicates a sequence of events. Many people mistakenly use the word *than* in its place.

31. **The correct answer is A.** The names of the four seasons are common nouns and do not need capitalization unless they are included in a title such as "the Winter Olympics."

32. **The correct answer is D.** No change.

33. **The correct answer is A.** The phrase "When companies started to introduce compact disc (CD) recordings in the 1980s" is a dependent clause used as an introductory phrase, so it must be followed by a comma. Using the period instead of a comma creates a sentence fragment. The sentence should read "When companies started to introduce compact disc (CD) recordings in the 1980s, these recordings were such great sellers that they rapidly became the *new* best-selling form of recorded music in the industry."

34. **The correct answer is D.** No change. The phrase "As a result" indicates a consequential relationship between the popularity of CDs and the resulting drop in album sales. Choices A, B, and C would be used to show a relationship of opposites instead of cause and effect.

35. **The correct answer is B.** Sentence 1 mentions the date 1988, which begins a timeline of events marking the decline in popularity of the record album that continues in sentence 2. Choice B provides an ending to the timeline and draws the fate of records albums to a logical conclusion—that by 1989, they began to disappear from stores. Choice A introduces information that is not related to the topic being discussed here. While choice C provides an interesting contrast to the paragraph topic, it does so before the timeline established in sentence 1 has been completed. Choice D asks a question that has no tie-in with the rest of the paragraph and introduces a shift in point of view from third person to second person.

36. **The correct answer is C.** In this sentence, the preposition *to* should be used in the introductory phrase. Although they sound the same, the words *two* and *too* are homonyms for the preposition *to* with different meanings, so choices A and D are incorrect. *Also* is a synonym for the incorrect *too* used here, so choice B is incorrect as well.

37. **The correct answer is B.** In this underlined part of this sentence, common nouns are used that do not require capitalization. If specific people were named, capitalization would be needed for proper nouns.

38. **The correct answer is A.** The subordinate sentences in the paragraph are steps in a recipe. We are told that a "beverage" is being made, one that uses apples; therefore, choice A would be an appropriate topic sentence here. The paragraph isn't about getting enough fluids (choice B), the popularity of apples (choice C), or how to make an apple pie (choice D).

39. **The correct answer is B.** Because the second sentence begins with the word *first*, it is obvious that the sentence that is about to offer "three good reasons" should be the topic sentence. If choice B were not offered, choice A might well have served as a topic sentence, but choice B is clearly better. Choices C and D are quite obviously development sentences.

40. **The correct answer is A.** The clause "with the nylon wheels" modifies *skateboard.*

41. **The correct answer is C.** In a paragraph about the use of cowries as money, an explanation of exactly what a cowrie is should be offered as early as possible.

42. **The correct answer is B.** Choice A is a sentence fragment. Choice C is a comma splice of two independent clauses. Choice D is a run-on sentence.

43. **The correct answer is A.** The subordinate sentences in the paragraph support the notion that technology is changing the way we live. Choices B and D would better serve as supporting details than topic sentences. Choice C runs counter to the argument in the paragraph.

44. **The correct answer is A.** The first development sentence is practically a restatement of the topic sentence. If opinions play a major role in important areas in our lives, obviously they should not be taken lightly. Choice B is clearly a development sentence; choice C could not possibly serve as a topic sentence because its subject is the pronoun *they*, which has no reference; and choice D contradicts the paragraph.

45. **The correct answer is B.** Sentence 3 contains a key context clue for determining the correct sentence placement. The phrase "these crystals" indicates that this subject is brought up earlier in the paragraph. Since there's no mention of the crystals in the previous sentences, this sentence must introduce them; therefore, choice B is correct.

46. **The correct answer is B.** This paragraph serves to define the terms *fad*, *trend*, and *style*. While the reaction of parents to teenage fads is certainly a related topic, it belongs in another paragraph.

47. **The correct answer is D.** The paragraph is about Japanese monkeys and their human behaviors. Tigers have no place in this paragraph.

48. **The correct answer is C.** The paragraph concerns the economies of the Caribbean islands and their resources, produce, and trade. The Mediterranean Sea might make an interesting topic for comparison with the Caribbean, but it has no place in this paragraph.

49. **The correct answer is D.** The topic sentence introduces the subject of the deleterious effects of alcohol. Sentences 2, 3, and 4 clearly follow with their use of *it* to refer to alcohol. Placing the sentence after sentence 4 might flow logically, but doing so would leave the possessive pronoun *their* in sentence 6 without a reference noun. Sentence 6 obviously refers to *drivers*, so the sentence about the drivers must appear between sentences 5 and 6.

50. **The correct answer is B.** From the word *groan*, you can infer that the tone is not a positive or happy one, which helps rule out choice A. *Erroneous* (choice C) doesn't work because neither the groan nor the students is a mistake. *Inattentive* (choice D) also doesn't fit because there is no indication that the people in the classroom are not paying attention. *Agonized* (choice B) works the best here, because it conveys an unhappy tone by the students.

51. **The correct answer is A.** Choices B, C, and D all provide positive reasons why bike lanes are a good thing, but choice A uses examples that could turn a listener against the idea.

52. **The correct answer is C.** The main topic of the paragraph is solar energy, so the sentence about wind energy is out of place.

53. **The correct answer is D.** You need a coordinating conjunction here that shows you how the sentences are related. Choice A is incorrect because *so* suggests that the first part of the sentence causes the second part of the sentence. Choice B is incorrect; *because* suggests that the second part of the sentence explains the first, but waiting in traffic would likely not make it easier to get to the beach. Choice C is incorrect because *and* suggests that the two parts of the sentence mean equal things, but you're trying to show a contrasting relationship.

54. **The correct answer is A.** Choice A clearly lays out Robin's process for making a soufflé. Choice B is choppy, and the short sentences are a combination of fragments and unclear directions. Choice C is confusingly constructed, with unclear modifiers and a process that doesn't make much sense. Choice D is constructed correctly but has less information.

55. **The correct answer is B.** The paragraph is mainly a third-person informational paragraph, so the writer's personal opinion is out of place. The rest of the sentences support the main idea of the paragraph and match the informational tone.

56. **The correct answer is D.** This question is a matter of finding the correct preposition. Choice A doesn't fit, because one object can't be located around two objects. From the context, you know that the remote wasn't in an obvious place, so it is very unlikely that the remote was on top of the couch cushions (choice B). Although option C is closer, the remote is not likely *inside* the couch cushions themselves, but rather, between them.

57. **The correct answer is A.** The sentence at the end of the paragraph should follow the flow of the paragraph. Choices B and D talk about the feeder itself, although the paragraph has already moved on to talk about filling the feeder. Choice C talks about hummingbirds directly, even though the paragraph is about how to set up a feeder, not the birds themselves, so the sentence is out of place. Choice A logically follows the rest of the paragraph: how to attract the birds, where to get a feeder, what to put in the feeder, and then where to hang the feeder.

58. **The correct answer is B.** The supporting information should be information that would encourage people to support Smithville's recycling program. Choices A and D would likely not convince a reader to support the program. Choice C simply describes what the recycling program would include, not why it should exist. Choice B provides an incentive to recycle (another town has saved money by doing it), so this is the best option.

59. **The correct answer is C.** The word *neither* tells you that it should be *nor. And* (choice A) conflicts with *neither. Or* (choice B) would work if the sentence had started with *either. That* (choice D) does not fit the sentence.

60. **The correct answer is B.** The sentences should provide information that supports the idea that drinking 64 ounces of water is ideal. Choice A is more of an introduction and does not provide any extra or supporting information. Choice B explains that doctors recommend drinking the water and lists some of the benefits of drinking water, so this supports the topic sentence. Choice C describes drawbacks of dehydration but does not directly support the topic sentence (how to stay hydrated). Choice D moves the focus to diet and overall health, not drinking water, so it does not support the topic sentence very well.

61. **The correct answer is C.** In choice A, the first sentence is confusing: what's failing—the internet or newspapers? The second sentence also has a dangling modifier (*as a reader*) that is not connected to anything else in the sentence. The sentence is also a run-on. Choice B is a comma splice, and the different parts of the sentence are not clearly related. Choice C organizes a complete idea (why digital reading is causing local newspapers to fail) and states it clearly. Choice D is lacking detail and is also a run-on sentence with incorrect parentheses.

62. **The correct answer is D.** The given sentence has two parts that are cause and effect: Gina did not eat sugary snacks due to her dentist appointment, not in spite of it. Choices A and C set up an incorrect relationship for the two clauses in the sentence. Choice B creates a sentence that does not include a complete thought. Choice D fully explains that the first part of the sentence illustrates the second part.

63. **The correct answer is B.** The paragraph is about the potential dog park, not Jones Park in general, so this sentence does not match the rest of the paragraph.

64. **The correct answer is A.** The word in the blank should be a coordinating conjunction to link the two ideas. Choice A does this by setting up the first part of the sentence as a reason for the second part (#1 is true, *so* #2 should happen). Choices B and D get the meaning of the sentence backwards, suggesting that the weather is getting colder because you should wear a jacket. Choice C incorrectly sets up the sentence as an either/or.

65. **The correct answer is A.** Both sentences in choice A support the topic sentence. In choice B, the information presented is the opposite of the writer's main point. In choice C, one sentence supports the topic sentence, but the second sentence does not. In choice D, the first sentence supports the topic sentence, but the second sentence does not.

66. **The correct answer is D.** The paragraph is about how to improve sleep, so choice D fits the best. Choice A is too narrow—blue light is only one aspect of the paragraph. Choice B is inaccurate because although the paragraph mentions sleep cycles; they are not the focus of the paragraph. Choice C is too broad, leaving choice D as the better option.

67. **The correct answer is C.** Because the sentence tells you that the room is dark, it is unlikely that Dan is able to glide (choice A) or run (choice B) through the room. It is also unlikely that he is able to look (choice D) around the dark room without light. That leaves *stumble* (choice C) as the best verb out of the given choices.

68. **The correct answer is B.** "The Dangers of Exotic Pets" summarizes the theme of all the sentences in the paragraph: the drawbacks of having exotic pets in general. "Choosing the Right Pet for You" (choice A) is incorrect because the paragraph is not about how to choose a pet. "Exotic Pet Laws" (choice C) is incorrect because although the paragraph mentions that having exotic pets is often illegal, there is no discussion of specific laws. "Do Tigers Make Good Pets?" (choice D) is too specific; the paragraph is about exotic pets in general, not just tigers.

69. **The correct answer is C.** From the tone of the sentence, it's likely that the word that belongs in the blank is negative, so *thrilled* (choice A) doesn't work. *Astonished* (choice B) doesn't work because there's no indication that he was surprised that he hadn't brought his umbrella. *Forgetful* (choice D) is redundant because the sentence already says Kevin forgot his umbrella. *Annoyed* works best in the context of the sentence.

70. **The correct answer is A.** Choice A offers a generic statement about the name of Daylight Saving Time but does not offer supporting information about whether or not it should be followed. Choice B gives a positive example of how the United States doesn't need Daylight Saving Time. Choices C and D offer reasons why Daylight Saving Time is a problem.

71. **The correct answer is D.** Choices A and B are arguments against having a longer school year, so they don't really fit with the rest of the paragraph. Choice C repeats the idea in sentence 2, so it's redundant. Choice D offers information supporting the rest of the paragraph without redundancy.

72. **The correct answer is B.** The sentence states that the crowd stayed *after* (choice B) the movie ended. The secret scene could not take place *before* (choice A) the movie or *while* (choice C) the movie was going on. *Since* (choice D) implies something that happened in the past.

73. **The correct answer is D.** The main topic of the paragraph is the problem of plastic pollution and the steps some are taking to fix it. Sentence 4 is about oil spills, which is off-topic.

74. **The correct answer is C.** Choices A, B, and D all give reasons why learning a language is a benefit. Choice C is a statement of what students can do but does not do anything to suggest *why* they should learn a second language.

75. **The correct answer is C.** The two parts of the sentence conflict: the writer has two events scheduled at the same time. *But* (choice C) is the coordinating conjunction that contrasts the two parts of the sentence.

Chapter 4

Math

Introduction to Math Questions

Math questions on the TACHS and HSPT exams assess basic mathematical knowledge and its real-world applications. There are five main content areas in which the questions fall. Here, we will give you a brief overview of each area and then walk through a sample question for each content area.

The most prevalent content area deals with **number systems** and **numeration**. This is your run-of-the-mill basic arithmetic knowledge—everyday math. The test will assess everything from your knowledge of place value terms, arithmetic of decimals and fractions, exponent rules, and order of operations for simplifying arithmetic expressions, to divisibility rules and properties of integers and rational numbers. You will also see questions about counting, ratios and proportions, and percentages. A related content area is focused on **measurement** and includes problems involving the conversion of units within a given system (e.g., centimeters to kilometers) and between systems (e.g., yards to meters). Another commonly assessed problem type involves time measurement.

Basic high school **algebra** and **geometry** are two other math content areas. They are not exhaustive, but rather they hit the main ideas in each subject. For instance, regarding algebra, you can expect to encounter problems asking you to evaluate an algebraic expression for specific values of the variables, solve elementary linear and quadratic equations, factor trinomials, and set up an algebraic expression or equation used to solve a real-world problem. For the geometry content area, you should be familiar with computing perimeter and area of basic shapes as well as volume and surface area of basic solids; you should be able to do so within and outside the context of a word problem. Basic coordinate geometry is also assessed, so problems that ask you to identify the equation of a line or the location of a point in the xy-plane are often found on the exam.

Lastly, you will see questions focused on **basic data/graphical analysis**, **elementary probability**, and **elementary statistics**. Basic data analysis problems involve interpreting graphs (bar graphs, pie charts, line graphs, etc.) and using the information provided by them to answer questions about the context they are describing. Probability problems tend to focus on computing likelihood of basic events occurring, given either a frequency table or a situation in which all outcomes are equally likely. Statistics problems tend to focus on mean, median, and mode; inferential statistics skills are not tested in these exams.

The best way to prepare yourself for these questions is to first refresh your memory on the basic terminology, rules, and methods of the topics mentioned above. You will not be able to reason your way to a correct answer unless you are familiar with these tools.

Math Question Preview

Let's look at some sample questions.

1. If a number is divisible by 16, it must also be divisible by which of the following?

A. 8

B. 12

C. 24

D. 32

The correct answer is A. Since 16 is divisible by 8, the number must also be divisible by 8. A common error here is to select choice D because it is a multiple of 16. However, only factors of 16 are guaranteed to divide evenly into a number into which 16 divides.

2. Compute:

3 hours	01 minutes	02 seconds
– 2 hours	54 minutes	58 seconds

A. 1 hour, 53 minutes, 56 seconds

B. 6 minutes, 4 seconds

C. 1 hour, 6 minutes, 4 seconds

D. 7 minutes, 4 seconds

The correct answer is B. Borrow 1 minute to perform the subtraction in the seconds column, and then borrow 1 hour to perform the subtraction in the minutes column:

$^{2}\not{3}$ hours	$^{60}\not{0}\not{1}$ minutes	$^{62}\not{0}\not{2}$ seconds
– 2 hours	54 minutes	58 seconds
0 hours	6 minutes	4 seconds

Be especially careful when borrowing units from a higher unit to make sure the conversion factor is correct.

3. What is the circumference of a circle with an area of 121π square inches?

A. 11π inches

B. 11 inches

C. 44π inches

D. 22π inches

The correct answer is D. You need the radius to determine the circumference. The area of a circle with radius r is πr^2. Set this equal to 121π and solve for r:

$$\pi r^2 = 121\pi$$

$$\frac{\pi r^2}{\pi} = \frac{121\pi}{\pi}$$

$$r^2 = 121$$

$$r = 11$$

The radius, $r = 11$ inches. The formula for the circumference of a circle is $2\pi r$, so, the circumference is $2\pi(11) = 22\pi$ inches. Typical errors with this type of problem are getting the formula wrong or using the diameter ($2r$) instead of the radius (r).

4. Jack can fly his single-engine airplane at a maximum speed of 150 miles per hour in still air. If he flies against a wind with speed s miles per hour, what would be his speed?

A. $150 + s$ miles per hour

B. $150s$ miles per hour

C. $150 - s$ miles per hour

D. $s - 150$ miles per hour

The correct answer is C. Since Jack is flying against the wind, his speed is decreased by the speed of the wind, namely by s miles per hour. So, his speed would be $150 - s$ miles per hour.

5. Suppose a box contains 12 birthday candles of different colors: 2 red, 3 white, 1 green, 1 yellow, 3 blue, and 2 purple. If you select one candle from the box without looking, what is the probability that the candle you choose is neither white nor purple?

A. $\frac{5}{12}$

B. $\frac{1}{12}$

C. $\frac{1}{2}$

D. $\frac{7}{12}$

The correct answer is D. There are 5 candles that are white or purple, leaving 7 that are neither of these colors. Since each of the 12 candles is equally likely to be chosen, the probability of selecting a candle that is neither white nor purple is $\frac{7}{12}$.

Math can be one of the most challenging sections on the TACHS and HSPT exams, so we've included two practice sets in this workbook. These practice sets include question types like the sample questions above and that vary in level of difficulty. As with the other sections of this book, there's no time limit on these questions, so focus on the questions—what they are asking you to solve, and what skills you've learned in school that you can use to solve them.

Appendix Alert

Before diving into the math drills, you might want to review the math study guide (page 507) in Appendix C. You will find a list of formulas and rules and conversions that you will need to put into practice when solving the problems presented in the drills. Try to memorize as many of the formulas as you can before test day with this valuable take-along resource.

You will also find answer sheets for these drills in Appendix C, starting on page 519.

Math Drill 1

75 Questions

Directions: The following questions cover the math concepts you will encounter on the TACHS and HSPT exams. Choose the answer you think is best for each item and mark the corresponding letter on your answer sheet.

SHOW YOUR WORK HERE

1. What is the difference between 97 and 10?

A. 87

B. 107

C. 970

D. 9.7

2. Jared has $5 in his savings account now. He just took a job earning $20 per week. How many weeks will it take Jared to have enough money to buy a bicycle that costs $65?

A. 2 weeks

B. 3 weeks

C. 4 weeks

D. 6 weeks

3. Maxine types 70 words per minute. Dorian types 10 percent faster than Maxine. How many words can Dorian type in 15 minutes?

A. 1,045

B. 1,050

C. 1,155

D. 1,375

SHOW YOUR WORK HERE

4. 45,110 ÷ 9,022 =
   A. 5,000
   B. 500
   C. 50
   D. 5

5. What will a 9 ft. by 15 ft. rectangular rug cost at $5 a square yard?
   A. $75
   B. $60
   C. $675
   D. $225

6. 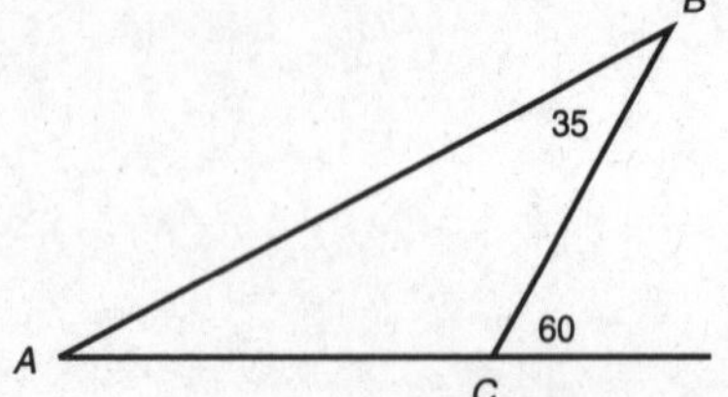

   The measure of angle A is
   A. 15°
   B. 20°
   C. 25°
   D. 35°

7. If $4(3x - 2) = 16$, $x =$
   A. 1.5
   B. –2
   C. 2
   D. –1.5

SHOW YOUR WORK HERE

8. While trying to achieve a new high score on a video game, Eric recorded scores of 6,776; 6,892; 6,990; 7,010; and 7,012. What was his average score for those five games?

   A. 6,890

   B. 6,936

   C. 6,956

   D. 6,990

9. $\frac{3}{5} + 1.25 + 0.004 =$

   A. 1.750

   B. 1.854

   C. 1.9

   D. 2.25

10. Solve: $\frac{10^6}{10^3}$

    A. 1 billion

    B. 1 million

    C. 1,000

    D. 100

    E. 1^3

11. $71.4 \times 98.2 =$

    A. 4,011.38

    B. 5,321.48

    C. 6,921.38

    D. 7,011.48

    E. 8,231.48

Math Drill 1

SHOW YOUR WORK HERE

12. $\dfrac{4\frac{2}{3}+\frac{1}{6}}{\frac{1}{3}} =$

A. 9

B. $10\frac{1}{3}$

C. $12\frac{3}{24}$

D. $14\frac{1}{2}$

E. 23

13. $(0.25)^2$

A. 0.00625

B. 0.0625

C. 0.625

D. 1.625

14. (3 + 1) + [(2 – 3) – (4 – 1)] =

A. 6

B. 2

C. 0

D. –2

E. –4

15. 10,001 – 8,093 =

A. 1,908

B. 1,918

C. 2,007

D. 18,094

E. 20,007

SHOW YOUR WORK HERE

16. 10% of $\frac{1}{5}$ of \$50 is

A. \$100

B. \$5

C. \$1

D. 103

E. $\frac{3}{5}$

17.

$$\begin{array}{r} \text{4 hours 12 minutes 10 seconds} \\ -\ \text{2 hours 48 minutes 35 seconds} \\ \hline \end{array}$$

A. 2 hr. 23 min. 25 sec.

B. 2 hr. 12 min. 40 sec.

C. 1 hr. 23 min. 35 sec.

D. 1 hr. 23 min. 25 sec.

18. How many square inches are there in R rooms, each having S square feet?

A. RS

B. $144RS$

C. $9 \div RS$

D. $S + R$

19. A rectangle has a length twice as long as its width. If its width is x, its perimeter is

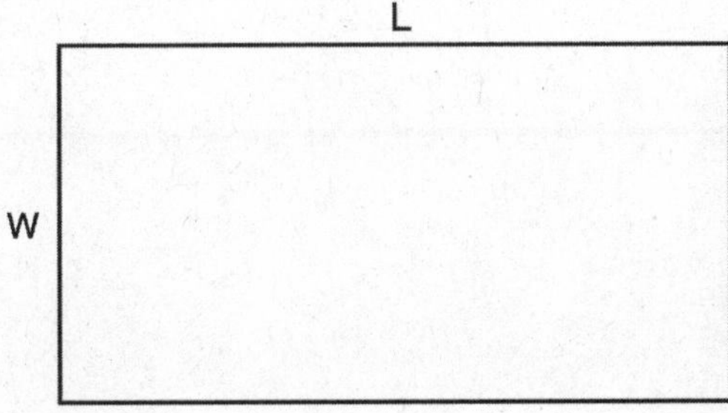

A. 6

B. $2x^2$

C. $4x$

D. $6x$

Math Drill 1

SHOW YOUR WORK HERE

20. If $a = 1$, $b = 2$, $c = 3$, and $d = 5$, find the value of $\sqrt{b(d+a)-b(c+a)}$.

A. 2

B. 3.5

C. 4

D. $\sqrt{20}$

E. 50

21. If we double the value of a and c in the fraction $\frac{ab}{c}$, the value of the fraction is

A. doubled.

B. multiplied by 4.

C. halved.

D. unchanged.

22. One runner can run M miles in H hours. Another faster runner can run N miles in L hours. The difference in their rates can be expressed as which of the following?

A. $\frac{M-N}{H}$

B. $MH - HL$

C. $\frac{HN}{M-L}$

D. $\frac{N}{L} - \frac{M}{H}$

23. Four games drew an average of 36,500 people per game. If the attendance at the first three games was 32,000, 35,500, and 38,000, how many people attended the fourth game?

A. 36,500

B. 37,000

C. 39,000

D. 40,500

SHOW YOUR WORK HERE

Math Drill 1

24. Which of the following is *not* a multiple of 4?

A. 24
B. 34
C. 44
D. 64

25. What is the difference between $(4 \times 10^3) + 6$ and $(2 \times 10^3) + (3 \times 10) + 8$?

A. 168
B. 55,968
C. 3,765
D. 1,968

26. Simplify: $-2\,[-4\,(2-1) + (3+2)]$

A. 18
B. 2
C. -18
D. -2

27. Which of the following has the same value as 0.5%?

A. 0.005%
B. $\frac{1}{2}\%$
C. $\frac{1}{50}\%$
D. $\frac{1}{500}\%$

28. If $a = 9$, $b = 2$, and $c = 1$, what is the value of $\sqrt{a+3b+c}$?

A. 7
B. 16
C. 6
D. 4

9 + 3(2) + 1

29. If $14x - 2y = 32$ and $x + 2y = 13$, then $x =$

SHOW YOUR WORK HERE

A. 5

B. 8

C. 3

D. 4

30. The surface area of a brick with the dimensions 6" × 3" × 2" is

A. 36 sq. in.

B. 72 sq. in.

C. 128 sq. in.

D. 72 cu. in.

31. Solve for n: $7(3 \times n) + 4 = 2{,}104$

A. 10^0

B. 10

C. 10^2

D. 10^3

32. A new restaurant, The Pizza Parlor, boasts the widest variety of toppings in the city. The owners claim that their 72 topping choices are 50 percent more than the next closest competitor, Patty's Pizzas. If The Pizza Parlor's claim is true, how many topping choices does Patty's Pizzas offer?

A. 24

B. 36

C. 48

D. 144

SHOW YOUR WORK HERE

33. What percentage of 220 is 24.2?

A. 909%

B. 99%

C. 40%

D. 11%

34. 98 reduced by $\frac{5}{7}$ is equivalent to

A. 28.

B. 33.

C. 66.

D. 70.

35. $12\frac{1}{2} \div \frac{1}{2} + \frac{3}{2} \times 4 - 3 =$

A. 1

B. $4\frac{3}{4}$

C. 20

D. 28

36. The shadow of a man 6 feet tall is 12 feet long. He is standing next to a tree that casts a 50-foot shadow. How tall is the tree?

A. 100'

B. 50'

C. 25'

D. 15'

37. $0.0515 \times 100 =$

A. $5{,}150 \div 100$

B. 5.15×10

C. $0.00515 \times 1{,}000$

D. $510{,}000 \div 10$

SHOW YOUR WORK HERE

38. 45 is to ____ as 90 is to 0.45.

A. 0.225

B. 0.900

C. 4.50

D. 9.00

39. Which of the following groups is arranged in order from smallest to largest?

A. $\frac{3}{7}, \frac{11}{23}, \frac{15}{32}, \frac{1}{2}, \frac{9}{16}$

B. $\frac{3}{7}, \frac{15}{32}, \frac{11}{23}, \frac{1}{2}, \frac{9}{16}$

C. $\frac{11}{23}, \frac{3}{7}, \frac{15}{32}, \frac{1}{2}, \frac{9}{16}$

D. $\frac{15}{32}, \frac{1}{2}, \frac{3}{7}, \frac{11}{23}, \frac{9}{16}$

40. An airplane on a 3,000-mile transatlantic flight took 4 hours and 20 minutes to get from New York to its destination. To avoid a storm, however, the pilot went off his course, adding 200 miles to the distance of the flight. Approximately how fast did the plane travel?

A. 710 mph

B. 738 mph

C. 744 mph

D. 772 mph

SHOW YOUR WORK HERE

41. How long should an object $6\frac{1}{2}$ feet long be drawn if, according to the scale, $\frac{1}{4}$ inch in the drawing equals 1 foot?

A. $1\frac{3}{4}$ inches

B. $1\frac{5}{8}$ inches

C. $\frac{7}{8}$ inches

D. $\frac{5}{8}$ inches

42. This square has a side of 1". What is its diagonal distance from one corner to another?

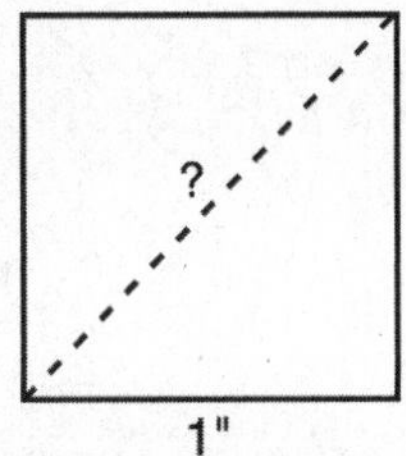

A. 1 inch

B. $\sqrt{2}$ inches

C. $\sqrt{3}$ inches

D. 2 inches

Math Drill 1

Math Drill 1

SHOW YOUR WORK HERE

43. If 9 million barrels of oil are consumed daily in the United States, how many barrels are required to meet commercial and industrial needs?

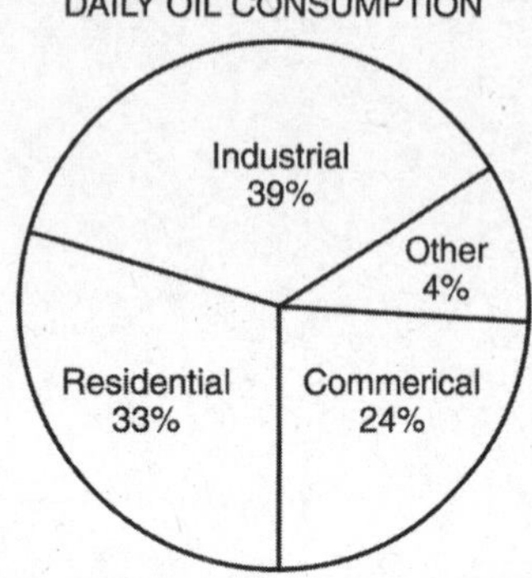

A. 2,840,000
B. 3,420,000
C. 4,750,000
D. 5,670,000

44. Simplify: $-6 - [2 - (3a - b) + b] + a$

A. $4 - 3a + 2b$
B. $-6 + 3a + b$
C. $-8 + 4a - 2b$
D. $-8 + 3a - b$

45. Solve for x: $\left(\frac{2}{3} + \frac{1}{5}\right) - \left(\frac{1}{4} + \frac{1}{2}\right) = x$

A. $\frac{13}{30}$
B. $\frac{7}{60}$
C. $\frac{51}{60}$
D. $\frac{37}{60}$

SHOW YOUR WORK HERE

46. If $ab + 4 = 52$, and $a = 6$, $b =$

A. 42

B. 8

C. 21

D. 4

47. On a blueprint, 3 inches represent 24 feet. How long must a line be to represent 96 feet?

A. 36 inches

B. 12 inches

C. 6 inches

D. 4 inches

48.

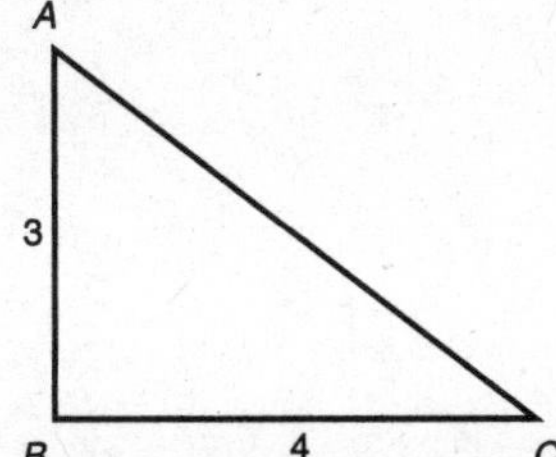

What is the length of $\overline{AC}$ in the right triangle above?

A. 4.5

B. 3.5

C. 5

D. 4

49. On a trip to his grandmother's house, Skippy averaged 15 miles per hour on his bicycle. If his grandmother's house is 78 miles away, about how long did it take Skippy to get to his grandmother's house?

A. $3\frac{1}{2}$ hours

B. 5 hours

C. 6 hours

D. $13\frac{1}{2}$ hours

SHOW YOUR WORK HERE

50. A train left Albany for Buffalo, a distance of 290 miles, at 10:10 a.m. The train was scheduled to reach Buffalo at 3:45 p.m. If the average rate of the train on this trip was 50 mph, it arrived in Buffalo

A. about 5 minutes early.

B. on time.

C. about 5 minutes late.

D. about 13 minutes late.

51. A bakery shop sold three kinds of cake. The prices of these were 25¢, 30¢, and 35¢ per pound. The income from these sales was $36. If the number of pounds of each kind of cake sold was the same, how many pounds were sold?

A. 120 pounds

B. 90 pounds

C. 60 pounds

D. 45 pounds

52. A plumber needs eight sections of pipe, each 3' 2" long. If pipe is sold only by the 10' section, how many sections must the plumber buy?

A. 1

B. 2

C. 3

D. 4

SHOW YOUR WORK HERE

Math Drill 1

53. What is the total area of the shaded part of the figure?

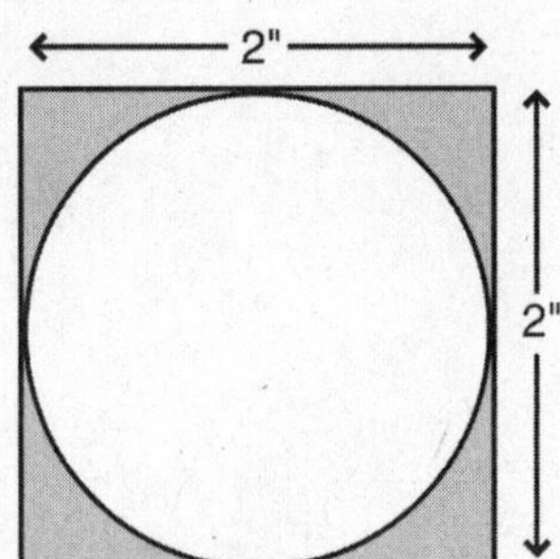

A. $\frac{2}{7}$ in.^{2}

B. $\frac{1}{2}$ in.^{2}

C. $\frac{6}{7}$ in.^{2}

D. $1\frac{3}{7}$ in.^{2}

54. Which of the following is a pair of reciprocals?

A. (12, –12)

B. (0, 0)

C. $\left(3\frac{3}{4}, \frac{4}{15}\right)$

D. $(5^2, 2^5)$

55. $\frac{100^4}{10^8} =$

A. 10^4

B. 1000

C. 1

D. 10^{12}

56. 6 + (–12) + 7 + (–3) =

A. –2

B. 2

C. 28

D. –8

SHOW YOUR WORK HERE

57. The piece of property shown below is to be divided into uniform building lots of 100 × 100 sq. ft. Twenty percent of the property must be left undeveloped. How many houses may be built on this property?

1,000 ft.

500 ft. 500 ft.

1,000 ft.

A. 20

B. 40

C. 50

D. 100

58. Find the area of a triangle with dimensions $b = 16$ centimeters and $h = 13$ centimeters.

A. 104 sq. centimeters

B. 140 sq. centimeters

C. 144 sq. centimeters

D. 208 sq. centimeters

59. Simplify: $\dfrac{5\frac{2}{3}}{2\frac{5}{6}}$

A. $2\frac{1}{2}$

B. $\frac{1}{2}$

C. 2

D. $1\frac{1}{3}$

SHOW YOUR WORK HERE

60. $5^3 \times 3^4$

A. $5 \times 3 \times 3 \times 4$

B. $5 \times 5 \times 5 \times 3 \times 3 \times 3$

C. $5 \times 5 \times 5 \times 3 \times 3 \times 3 \times 3$

D. $5 \times 5 \times 5 \times 5 \times 3 \times 3 \times 3$

61. If $x - 3 < 12$, x is

A. less than 15.

B. greater than 16.

C. equal to 15.

D. less than 18.

62. If $n = 2$, solve for r:

$$r = 35 - (3 + 6)(-n)$$

A. 53

B. 17

C. –53

D. –17

63. How many sixths are there in $\frac{4}{5}$?

A. $4\frac{4}{5}$

B. $5\frac{1}{5}$

C. 6

D. $2\frac{2}{5}$

64. Solve: $-3 - [(2 - 1) - (3 + 4)] =$

A. 3

B. 12

C. –6

D. –9

Math Drill 1

65. Solve for x: $\frac{x}{2} + 36 = 37.25$

SHOW YOUR WORK HERE

A. 18.5
B. 3.5
C. 2.5
D. 12.5

66. If $17x - 3y = 1$ and $2y - 17x = 5$, solve for y.

A. 6
B. 1
C. –1
D. –6

67. If 5 pints of water are needed to water each square foot of lawn, what is the minimum number of gallons of water needed for a lawn 8' by 12'?

A. 60
B. 56
C. 80
D. 30

68. A baseball team has won 50 games out of 75 played. It has 45 games still to play. How many of these must the team win to have a 60% winning percentage for the season?

A. 20
B. 22
C. 25
D. 30

SHOW YOUR WORK HERE

69. Clarissa priced seven tennis rackets. The prices are shown below.

$24, $46, $23, $47, $33, $36, $50

What is the median price?

A. $24

B. $36

C. $37

D. $47

70. What is the least common denominator for $\frac{2}{3}$, $\frac{1}{2}$, $\frac{5}{6}$, and $\frac{7}{9}$?

A. 36

B. 32

C. 24

D. 18

71. The fraction $\frac{9}{10}$ can also be expressed as which of the following decimals?

A. 0.9

B. 0.09

C. 0.009

D. 9.0

SHOW YOUR WORK HERE

72. The chart below shows the annual production of DVDs in various countries as measured in millions.

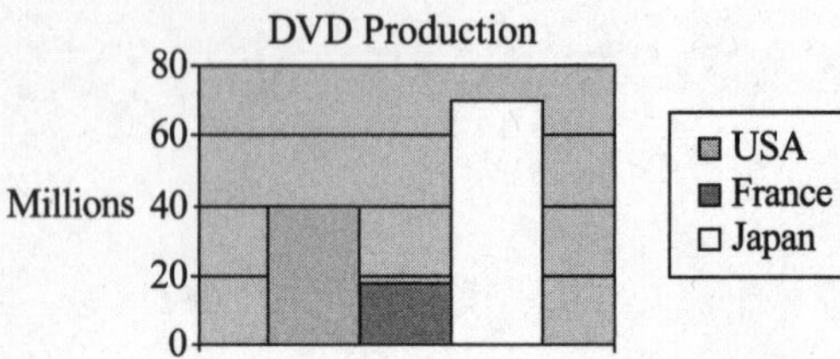

Based on the information in the chart, about how many DVDs does Japan produce each year?

A. 70

B. 70,000,000

C. 60

D. 60,000,000

73. 350 students are taking an exam; $\frac{4}{7}$ of these students are girls. How many boys are taking the exam?

A. 150

B. 200

C. 500

D. 550

SHOW YOUR WORK HERE

74. Mrs. Breen came home from the store and put two half-gallon containers of milk into the refrigerator. Jim came home from school with a few friends, and they all had milk and cookies. When they had finished, only $\frac{1}{2}$ of one container of milk remained. How much milk did the boys drink?

A. $1\frac{1}{2}$ pints

B. $1\frac{1}{2}$ quarts

C. 3 quarts

D. $1\frac{1}{2}$ gallons

75. Round 52.693 to the nearest tenth.

A. 52.7

B. 53

C. 52.69

D. 52.6

Answers Math Drill 1

Answer Key and Explanations

1. A	**16.** C	**31.** C	**46.** B	**61.** A
2. B	**17.** C	**32.** C	**47.** B	**62.** A
3. C	**18.** B	**33.** D	**48.** C	**63.** A
4. D	**19.** D	**34.** A	**49.** B	**64.** A
5. A	**20.** A	**35.** D	**50.** D	**65.** C
6. C	**21.** D	**36.** C	**51.** A	**66.** D
7. C	**22.** D	**37.** C	**52.** C	**67.** A
8. B	**23.** D	**38.** A	**53.** C	**68.** B
9. B	**24.** B	**39.** B	**54.** C	**69.** B
10. C	**25.** D	**40.** B	**55.** C	**70.** D
11. D	**26.** D	**41.** B	**56.** A	**71.** A
12. D	**27.** B	**42.** B	**57.** B	**72.** B
13. B	**28.** D	**43.** D	**58.** A	**73.** A
14. C	**29.** C	**44.** C	**59.** C	**74.** C
15. A	**30.** B	**45.** B	**60.** C	**75.** A

1. **The correct answer is A.** The term *difference* is a clue to subtract; 97 – 10 = 87. The sum of 97 and 10 is 107 (choice B), the product of 97 and 10 is 970 (choice C), and the quotient of dividing 97 by 10 is 9.7 (choice D).

2. **The correct answer is B.** The key to solving the problem is to determine how many weeks of earning $20 will give Jared the money he needs to add to his savings to equal $65. Divide 60 by 20: 60 ÷ 20 = 3. Jared will earn $60 in three weeks; add that to the $5 he has in savings, and Jared will have the $65 total that he needs to buy the bicycle.

3. **The correct answer is C.** Dorian types 110 percent of Maxine's speed, or 1.10 × 70 = 77. In 15 minutes, Dorian types 77 × 15 = 1,155 words.

4. **The correct answer is D.**

$$\begin{array}{r} 5 \\ 9{,}022\overline{)45{,}110} \\ \underline{45{,}110} \\ 0 \end{array}$$

5. **The correct answer is A.** First convert the dimensions of the rug to yards (3 ft. = 1 yd.). Multiply these new numbers to obtain the area. Multiply the area by $5 to determine the total cost.

$$\begin{aligned} A &= 9 \text{ ft.} \times 15 \text{ ft.} \\ &= 3 \text{ yd.} \times 5 \text{ yd.} = 15 \text{ sq. yards} \end{aligned}$$

$$15 \text{ sq. yds.} \times \$5 = \$75$$

6. **The correct answer is C.** A straight line represents a "straight angle" of 180°. An angle of 60° is given, so $m\angle C$ must be 120° to complete the line. Knowing that all the angles in a triangle added together equal 180°,

$$\begin{aligned} m\angle A + m\angle B + m\angle C &= 180 \\ m\angle A + 35 \ + 120 &= 180 \\ m\angle A &= 180 \ - 155 \\ m\angle A &= 25 \end{aligned}$$

7. **The correct answer is C.** Solve for x:

$$\begin{aligned} 4(3x-2) &= 16 \\ 12x - 8 &= 16 \\ 12x &= 24 \\ x &= \frac{24}{12} \\ x &= 2 \end{aligned}$$

8. **The correct answer is B.** To find the average, divide the sum of the scores by the number of scores:

$$6{,}776 + 6{,}892 + 6{,}990 + 7{,}010 + 7{,}012 = 34{,}680$$

There are five scores, so

$$34{,}680 \div 5 = 6{,}936$$

9. **The correct answer is B.** Convert $\frac{3}{5}$ to a decimal and then add the numbers:

$$\frac{3}{5} = 0.6$$

$$0.6 + 1.25 + 0.004 = 1.854$$

10. **The correct answer is C.** Remember: to divide exponents with the same base, subtract the exponents.

$$\frac{10^6}{10^3} = 10^{6-3} = 10^3 = 1{,}000$$

11. **The correct answer is D.**

$$\begin{array}{r l} 71.4 & \\ \times\ 98.2 & \\ \hline 1428 & \\ 57120 & \text{Mulitply without the decimal points. Use trailing zeros to help with alignment.} \\ 642600 & \\ \hline 7{,}011.48 & \text{Reinsert the decimal point.} \end{array}$$

12. **The correct answer is D.** Simplify the numerator by finding the least common multiple of the fractions and adding the fractions, as shown:

$$\frac{4\frac{2}{3}+\frac{1}{6}}{\frac{1}{3}} = \frac{4\frac{4}{6}+\frac{1}{6}}{\frac{1}{3}} = \frac{4\frac{5}{6}}{\frac{1}{3}}$$

Proceed as you would to divide any fraction:

$$4\frac{5}{6} \div \frac{1}{3} = \frac{29}{\cancel{6}} \bullet \frac{\cancel{3}^{1}}{1} = 14\frac{1}{2}$$

13. **The correct answer is B.** $(0.25)^2 = 0.25 \times 0.25 = 0.0625$

14. The correct answer is C. Begin with the innermost group and work outward:

$$(3 + 1) + [(2 - 3) - (4 - 1)]$$
$$= (3 + 1) + [(-1) - (3)]$$
$$= (3 + 1) + [-1 -3]$$
$$= (3 + 1) + [-4]$$
$$= 4 + [-4]$$
$$= 0$$

15. The correct answer is A. Try to estimate the answer rather than calculate:

$$\begin{array}{r} 10,001 \\ -\ 8,093 \\ \hline 1,908 \end{array}$$

16. The correct answer is C. One fifth of \$50 is \$10. Ten percent, or $\frac{1}{10}$ of \$10, is \$1.

17. The correct answer is C. Borrow 1 minute from the minutes column, and 1 hour from the hours column. Then subtract:

$$\begin{array}{r} 3 \text{ hr. } 71 \text{ min. } 70 \text{ sec.} \\ -\ 2 \text{ hr. } 48 \text{ min. } 35 \text{ sec.} \\ \hline 1 \text{ hr. } 23 \text{ min. } 35 \text{ sec.} \end{array}$$

18. The correct answer is B. *R* rooms each with *S* square feet contain a total of *RS* square feet. Because there are 144 square inches in each square foot, the rooms contain 144*RS* square inches.

19. The correct answer is D. If the width is x, the length, which is twice as long, is $2x$. The perimeter is equal to the sum of the four sides: $2x + 2x + x + x = 6x$.

20. The correct answer is A. This is a problem that must be done carefully. $a = 1$, $b = 2$, $c = 3$, $d = 5$

$$\sqrt{b(d+a)-b(c+a)}$$
$$= \sqrt{2(5+1)-2(3+1)}$$
$$= \sqrt{2(6)-2(4)}$$
$$= \sqrt{12-8}$$
$$= \sqrt{4}$$
$$= 2$$

21. **The correct answer is D.** Doubling the value of one of the factors of the numerator and the value of the denominator does not change the value of the fraction. It actually creates an equivalent fraction. Test this rule with fractions having numerical values for the numerator and denominator.

22. **The correct answer is D.** The rate of the first runner is $\frac{M}{H}$ miles per hour. The rate of the second is $\frac{N}{L}$ miles per hour. The second runner is faster, so the difference in their rates is written $\frac{N}{L}-\frac{M}{H}$.

23. **The correct answer is D.** To find the average, you divide the sum of the game attendance by the number of games, but you already have the average (36,500), so you first need to identify the total attendance of all four games. Multiply the given average by 4:

$$\begin{array}{r} 36,000 \\ \times \quad 4 \\ \hline 146,000 \end{array}$$

Add the attendance for the first three games together and subtract the total from 146,000:

$$32,000 + 35,500 + 38,000 = 105,500$$
$$146,000 - 105,500 = 40,500$$

The fourth game attracted 40,500 people.

24. **The correct answer is B.** No whole number multiplied by 4 equals 34.

25. **The correct answer is D.**

$$\begin{array}{r} (4\times 10^3)+6=4,006 \\ -(2\times 10^3)+(3\times 10)+8=2,038 \\ \hline \text{The difference is 1,968.} \end{array}$$

26. **The correct answer is D.** Begin with the innermost parentheses and work your way outward. Note that a negative sign in front of a grouping symbol reverses the signs of all numbers within.

Step 1. –2 [–4 (2 – 1) + (3 + 2)]
Step 2. –2 [–4 (1) + (5)]
Step 3. –2 [–4 + 5]
Step 4. –2 [+1] = –2

27. The correct answer is B. $0.5 = \frac{1}{2}$. Therefore, 0.5% must equal $\frac{1}{2}\%$.

28. The correct answer is D. Substitute the values into the expression.

$$\begin{aligned}&\sqrt{9+3(2)+1}\\&=\sqrt{9+6+1}\\&=\sqrt{16}\\&=4\end{aligned}$$

29. The correct answer is C. Write down both equations and add them together.

$$\begin{aligned}14x - 2y &= 32\\+\quad x + 2y &= 13\\\hline 15x &= 45\\x &= 3\end{aligned}$$

30. The correct answer is B. The surface of a rectangular solid such as a brick is found by calculating the area of each face of the brick and finding the sum of the areas of the faces. The brick has 6 faces:

Two faces 6" × 3"; total 36 sq. in.

Two faces 6" × 2"; total 24 sq. in.

Two faces 3" × 2"; total 12 sq. in.

Total 72 sq. in.

The surface area of a solid figure is expressed in square measure. Only volume is expressed in cubic measure.

31. The correct answer is C.

$$\begin{aligned}7(3\times n)+4 &= 2{,}104\\7(3n)+4 &= 2{,}104\\21n+4 &= 2{,}104\\21n &= 2{,}100\\n &= 100,\ \text{or } 10^2\end{aligned}$$

Answers Math Drill 1

32. **The correct answer is C.** If The Pizza Parlor's 72 toppings are 50% more, then they are 150% of Patty's Pizzas' toppings. Let Patty's Pizzas' toppings = x:

$$150\% \text{ of } x = 72$$
$$1.5x = 72$$
$$x = \frac{72}{1.5}$$
$$x = 48$$

33. **The correct answer is D.** $\frac{24.2}{220} = 0.11 = 11\%$

34. **The correct answer is A.** Be careful. This problem asks you to reduce 98 by $\frac{5}{7}$. In other words, find $\frac{2}{7}$ of 98.

$$98 \bullet \frac{2}{7} = \frac{\cancel{98}^{14}}{1} \bullet \frac{2}{\cancel{7}_1} = 28$$

35. **The correct answer is D.** Bracket the multiplication and division operations from left to right. Then calculate.

$$\left(12\frac{1}{2} \div \frac{1}{2}\right) + \left(\frac{3}{2} \times 4\right) - 3$$
$$= \left(\frac{25}{2} \div \frac{1}{2}\right) + \left(\frac{3}{2} \times \frac{4}{1}\right) - 3$$
$$= \left(\frac{25}{2} \times \frac{2}{1}\right) + \left(\frac{12}{2}\right) - 3$$
$$= 25 + 6 - 3$$
$$= 28$$

36. **The correct answer is C.** This is a simple proportion. A man casts a shadow twice as long as his height. Therefore, so does the tree. Therefore, a tree that casts a shadow 50′ long is 25′ high.

37. **The correct answer is C.** 0.0515 × 100 = 5.15, and so does 0.00515 × 1,000. You should be able to do this problem by moving decimal points and not by multiplying out. To divide by 10, move the decimal point one place to the left. Move it two places to the left to divide by 100, three places to divide by 1,000, and so forth. To multiply by 10, 100, 1,000, and so forth, move the decimal point the corresponding number of places to the right. This is an important skill to review.

38. **The correct answer is A.** This is a simple proportion.

$$\frac{45}{x} = \frac{90}{.45}$$

Since 90 ÷ 2 = 45, .45 ÷ 2 = .225

39. **The correct answer is B.** $\frac{3}{7}, \frac{15}{32}$, and $\frac{11}{23}$ are all less than $\frac{1}{2}$, and $\frac{9}{16}$ is larger than $\frac{1}{2}$.

Compare the size of fractions this way:

$$\frac{3}{7} \times \frac{15}{32}$$

Because the product of 7 and 15 is larger than the product of 32 and 3, $\frac{15}{32}$ is the larger fraction. Using the same method, $\frac{15}{32} < \frac{11}{23}$.

40. **The correct answer is B.** Since distance = rate × time, rate = distance ÷ time. Total distance traveled is 3,200 miles. Total time is 4 hours 20 minutes. Convert the minutes into a decimal and plug it into the formula:

$$t = 4 \text{ hours, } 20 \text{ minutes} = 4\tfrac{1}{3} \text{ hours}$$

$$r = 3,200 \div 4\tfrac{1}{3} \text{ hours}$$

$$r \approx 738 \text{ mph}$$

41. **The correct answer is B.** Since one foot corresponds to $\frac{1}{4}$ inch in the drawing, the drawing should be $6\frac{1}{2} \bullet \frac{1}{4}$ inches long.

$$6\tfrac{1}{2} \bullet \tfrac{1}{4}$$
$$= \tfrac{13}{2} \bullet \tfrac{1}{4}$$
$$= \tfrac{13}{8}$$
$$= 1\tfrac{5}{8} \text{ inches}$$

42. **The correct answer is B.** Use the Pythagorean theorem $c^2 = a^2 + b^2$ to find the length of the diagonal:

$$c^2 = 1^2 + 1^2$$
$$c^2 = 2$$
$$c = \sqrt{2}$$

Answers Math Drill 1

43. **The correct answer is D.** Commercial and industrial needs total 63% of daily oil consumption. Since consumption is 9 million barrels, 63% of 9 million is 5,670,000 barrels.

44. **The correct answer is C.** When simplifying, begin with the innermost grouping symbols first, and work your way outward.

Step 1. $-6 - [2 - (3a - b) + b] + a$
Step 2. $-6 - [2 - 3a + b + b] + a$
Step 3. $-6 - [2 - 3a + 2b] + a$
Step 4. $-6 - 2 + 3a - 2b + a$
Step 5. $-8 + 4a - 2b$

45. **The correct answer is B.** Start by finding the least common denominator for the fractions. Then do the operations in parentheses and solve for x.

$$\left(\frac{2}{3}+\frac{1}{5}\right)-\left(\frac{1}{4}+\frac{1}{2}\right)=x$$
$$\left(\frac{10}{15}+\frac{3}{15}\right)-\left(\frac{1}{4}+\frac{2}{4}\right)=x$$
$$\frac{13}{15}-\frac{3}{4}=x$$
$$\frac{52}{60}-\frac{45}{60}=\frac{7}{60}$$

46. **The correct answer is B.** If $a = 6$, $ab + 4 = 52$ becomes $6b + 4 = 52$. If $6b + 4 = 52$,

$$6b = 52 - 4$$
$$6b = 48$$
$$b = 8$$

47. **The correct answer is B.** If 3 inches equal 24 feet, then 1 inch equals 8 feet. A line representing 96 feet, therefore, must be 12 inches long ($96 \div 8 = 12$).

48. **The correct answer is C.** The Pythagorean theorem is used to find the length of the sides of right triangles. The square of the length of the longest side (the hypotenuse) is equal to the sum of the squares of the other two sides. Once we know the square of the length of the longest side, it is easy to find the length.

$$(AC)^2 = (AB)^2 + (BC)^2$$
$$(AC)^2 = 3^2 + 4^2$$
$$(AC)^2 = 25$$
$$AC = \sqrt{25} = 5$$

49. The correct answer is B. $78 \div 15 = 5.2$, which is approximately 5.

50. The correct answer is D. Use the formula $D = R \times T$ to find the time it took to get to Buffalo: time = distance ÷ rate. The travel time of the trip was equal to 290 miles ÷ 50 mph. Travel time = $\frac{1}{50}$% hours, or 5 hours, 48 minutes. The scheduled travel time was between 10:10 a.m. and 3:45 p.m., an interval of 5 hours, 35 minutes. Therefore, the train took about 13 minutes longer than scheduled.

51. The correct answer is A. Since the number of pounds of each kind of cake sold was the same, we can say that a pound of cake sold for an average price of 30¢ per pound:

25¢ + 30¢ + 35¢ = 90¢ ÷ 3 = 30¢ per lb.

Divide the total sales income of $36 by 30¢ to find how many pounds were sold.

$36 ÷ 0.30 = 120 pounds

52. The correct answer is C. Eight sections, each 3' 2" long, is equivalent to 8 × 38" = 304". 304" = $25\frac{1}{3}$ feet; therefore the plumber will need to buy three of the 10-foot sections.

53. The correct answer is C. Subtract the area of the circle from the area of the square to find the area of only the shaded part. Note that the diameter of the circle equals the width of the square.

Area of square = $s^2 = 4$ sq. in.
Area of circle = $\pi r^2 = \pi(1)^2 = \pi$ sq. in.
Area of square – Area of circle

$$4 \text{ sq. in.} - \frac{22}{7} \text{ sq. in.}$$

$$= \frac{6}{7} \text{ sq. in., or } \frac{6}{7} \text{ in.}^2$$

54. The correct answer is C. The reciprocal of a fraction is the fraction inverted. To find the answer, you would have to convert $3\frac{3}{4}$ into an improper fraction, $\frac{15}{4}$. The fraction $\frac{15}{4}$ is the reciprocal of $\frac{4}{15}$.

55. The correct answer is C. The long way to solve this problem is to multiply both the numerator and denominator out, and then divide. If you notice that 100^4 can also be written as 10^8, the answer becomes more apparent:

$$100 = 10^2$$
$$100^4 = 10^2 \times 10^2 \times 10^2 \times 10^2 = 10^8$$
$$\frac{100^4}{10^8} = \frac{10^8}{10^8} = 1$$

56. The correct answer is A. When expressed without the parentheses, this equation is 6 – 12 + 7 – 3. Solve by completing one part at a time:

$$\begin{aligned} 6 - 12 + 7 - 3 &= -6 + 7 - 3 \\ &= 1 - 3 \\ &= -2 \end{aligned}$$

57. The correct answer is B. The entire property is 1,000 ft. × 500 ft., which equals 500,000 sq. ft. Twenty percent must be left undeveloped. 500,000 × 20% = 100,000. 500,000 – 100,000 = 400,000 sq. ft. to be developed. Each building lot is 100 × 100 = 10,000 sq. ft. 400,000 divided by 10,000 = 40 houses.

58. The correct answer is A. The area of a triangle is found using the formula $A = \frac{1}{2}bh$. Since the base measures 16 centimeters and the height measures 13 centimeters, the area equals $\frac{1}{2} \times (16) \times (13)$, or 104 square centimeters.

59. The correct answer is C. Convert the mixed numbers into improper fractions. Then divide.

$$\begin{aligned} \frac{5\frac{2}{3}}{2\frac{5}{6}} &= \frac{\frac{17}{3}}{\frac{17}{6}} \\ &= \frac{17}{3} \div \frac{17}{6} \\ &= \frac{17}{3} \times \frac{6}{17} = \frac{6}{3} = 2 \end{aligned}$$

60. The correct answer is C. Exponents signify how many times a number is multiplied by itself. Count the 5s and 3s carefully.

61. The correct answer is A. Because $x - 3 < 12$, x can be any number less than 15.

62. **The correct answer is A.** To subtract signed numbers, change the sign of the number being subtracted (the subtrahend) and proceed as in algebraic addition.

$$r = 35 - (9)(-n)$$
$$r = 35 - (9)(-2)$$
$$r = 35 - (-18)$$
$$r = 35 + 18 = 53$$

63. **The correct answer is A.** Simply divide $\frac{4}{5}$ by $\frac{1}{6}$ to find the answer.

$$\frac{4}{5} \div \frac{1}{6} = \frac{4}{5} \times \frac{6}{1} = \frac{24}{5} = 4\frac{4}{5}$$

64. **The correct answer is A.** Begin working with the innermost parentheses and work your way out.

$$\begin{aligned} -3 - [(2-1) - (3+4)] &= -3 - [(1) - (7)] \\ &= -3 - [1-7] \\ &= -3 - [-6] \\ &= -3 + 6 \\ &= 3 \end{aligned}$$

65. **The correct answer is C.**

$$\frac{x}{2} + 36 = 37.25$$
$$\frac{x}{2} = 37.25 - 36$$
$$\frac{x}{2} = 1.25$$
$$x = 2.50$$

66. **The correct answer is D.** Add the equations to eliminate x: $-y = 6$, so that $y = -6$.

$$\begin{array}{r} 17x - 3y = 1 \\ +\ 2y - 17x = 5 \\ \hline \end{array}$$ Set up the addition problem.

$$\begin{array}{r} -3y + 17x = 1 \\ +\ 2y - 17x = 5 \\ \hline -y = 6 \\ y = -6 \end{array}$$ Align the x and y components and solve.

67. The correct answer is A. The lawn is 8' × 12' = 96 sq. ft.; 96 × 5 = 480 pints of water needed. There are 8 pints in 1 gallon, so 480 ÷ 8 = 60 gallons are needed.

68. The correct answer is B. The whole season consists of 120 games. For a season record with 60% wins, the team must win 72 games. Since it has already won 50, it must win 22 more games out of those left.

$$\frac{50+x}{75+45} = 60\%$$
$$\frac{50+x}{120} = 0.6$$
$$50 + x = 72$$
$$x = 22$$

69. The correct answer is B. To find the median, put the set of prices in ascending numerical order and select the middle value:

$23.00

$24.00

$33.00

$36.00← median

$46.00

$47.00

$50.00

In this set of numbers, $37 (choice C) is the mean, or average price of the rackets; $47 (choice D) was the middle value in the original list, but the values must be listed in increasing order to identify the median. The value of $24 (choice A) is nothing more than one of the tennis racket prices in the set.

70. The correct answer is D. As a multiple of 3, 2, 6, and 9, 18 is the least common denominator (LCM) of the given fractions. While 36 (choice A) is also a common denominator, it is not the *least* common denominator.

71. The correct answer is A. Fractions are converted into decimals by dividing the numerator by the denominator; 9 divided by 10 is 0.9.

72. The correct answer is B. Japan is represented by the white bar that places yearly DVD production at 70 million, or 70,000,000.

73. The correct answer is A. If $\frac{4}{7}$ of the students taking the test are girls, $\frac{3}{7}$ of the students are boys.

$$\frac{3}{7} \text{ of } 350 = \frac{3}{7} \times \frac{350}{1} = 150$$

There are 150 boys taking the exam. Choice B (200) is the number of girls taking the exam. Choice C (500) is the sum of the number of boys taking the exam and the number of all students taking the exam. Choice D (550) is the sum of the number of girls taking the exam and the number of all students taking the exam.

74. The correct answer is C. There are 4 quarts in a gallon, so there are 2 quarts in each half-gallon container. If only $\frac{1}{2}$ of one of the containers remained, then the boys drank 3 quarts.

75. The correct answer is A. To round to the nearest tenth means to limit the number to one digit to the right of the decimal point. The digit to the right of the decimal point is 6. However, the next digit is 9, which means you must round up to 52.7. Choice B (53) is rounded to the nearest whole number, or the ones place. Choice C (52.69) is rounded to the nearest hundredth, and Choice D (52.6) is incorrectly rounded down instead of up.

Math Drill 2

75 Questions

Directions: The following questions cover the math concepts you will encounter on the TACHS and HSPT exams. Choose the answer you think is best for each item and and mark the corresponding letter on your answer sheet.

SHOW YOUR WORK HERE

1. The difference between 1,001,000 and 999,999 is

A. 101,001.

B. 1,999.

C. 10,001.

D. 1,001.

2. Simplify: $-3 - [-2 + (5 - 6) - 3]$

A. +3

B. –1

C. +1

D. –3

3. Simplify: $0.6 + 1\frac{1}{2} + \frac{3}{4}$

A. 2.31

B. 2.52

C. 2.85

D. $2\frac{13}{20}$

4. 5:6 as 15:?

A. 25

B. 16

C. 18

D. 12

SHOW YOUR WORK HERE

5. A photograph measuring 5" wide × 7" long must be reduced in size to fit a space 4 inches long in an advertising brochure. How wide must the space be so that the picture remains in proportion?

   A. $1\frac{4}{7}$"

   B. $2\frac{6}{7}$"

   C. $4\frac{3}{5}$"

   D. $5\frac{3}{5}$"

6. 217 – 109 + 99 – 111 + 202 – 104 =

   A. 104

   B. 184

   C. 194

   D. 294

7. The prime factorization of 12 is

   A. 2 • 2 • 3

   B. 4 + 8

   C. 6 • 2

   D. 4 • 3

8. The least common multiple of 2 and 6 is

   A. 6

   B. 12

   C. 3

   D. 2

SHOW YOUR WORK HERE

9. Which of the following illustrates the commutative property of multiplication?

A. $3 \cdot (0.2 + 9.8) = 3 \cdot (0.2) + 3 \cdot (9.8)$

B. $\frac{3}{8}\left(5+\frac{1}{2}\right)=\left(5+\frac{1}{2}\right)\frac{3}{8}$

C. $\frac{1}{6}(4 \cdot 8)=\left(\frac{1}{6} \cdot 4\right)8$

D. $\frac{4}{3} \cdot 1 = \frac{4}{3}$

10. 0.12% is equal to which of the following?

A. 1.2

B. 0.12

C. 0.012

D. 0.0012

11. Mr. Adams has a circular flower bed with a diameter of 4 feet. He wishes to increase the size of this bed so that it will have four times as much planting area. What must be the diameter of the new bed?

A. 6 feet

B. 8 feet

C. 12 feet

D. 16 feet

12. If $3x - 2 = 13$, what is the value of $12x + 20$?

A. 5

B. 20

C. 30

D. 80

SHOW YOUR WORK HERE

13. If p pencils cost c cents, how much will n pencils at the same rate cost?

A. $\frac{pc}{n}$ cents

B. $\frac{cn}{p}$ cents

C. npc cents

D. $\frac{np}{c}$ cents

14. An ordinary die is thrown. What are the odds that a 1 will come up?

A. $\frac{1}{4}$

B. $\frac{1}{6}$

C. $\frac{1}{8}$

D. $\frac{1}{12}$

15. In the figure below, the largest possible circle is cut out of a square piece of tin. What is the area of the remaining piece of tin (in square inches)?

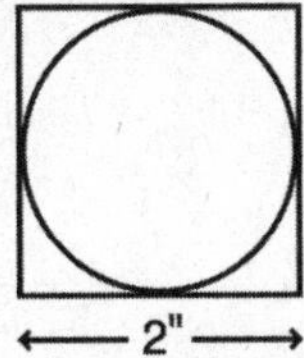

A. 0.14

B. 0.75

C. 0.86

D. 3.14

Math Drill 2

16. A store puts a pair of pants originally priced at $17 on sale at a 20% discount. What is the new selling price?

A. $16.80

B. $13.60

C. $3.40

D. $16.75

SHOW YOUR WORK HERE

17. 56,152 ÷ 7,019 =

A. 8

B. 80

C. 800

D. 8,000

18. 0.17% =

A. 1.7

B. 0.17

C. 0.017

D. 0.0017

19. $\dfrac{\frac{2}{3}+\frac{3}{8}}{\frac{1}{4}-\frac{3}{16}} =$

A. $15\frac{2}{3}$

B. $\frac{25}{16}$

C. $\frac{13}{32}$

D. $\frac{50}{3}$

SHOW YOUR WORK HERE

20. Increased by 175%, the number 24 becomes

A. 38.

B. 42.

C. 48.

D. 66.

21. Look at the graph below. Then read the question and choose the correct answer.

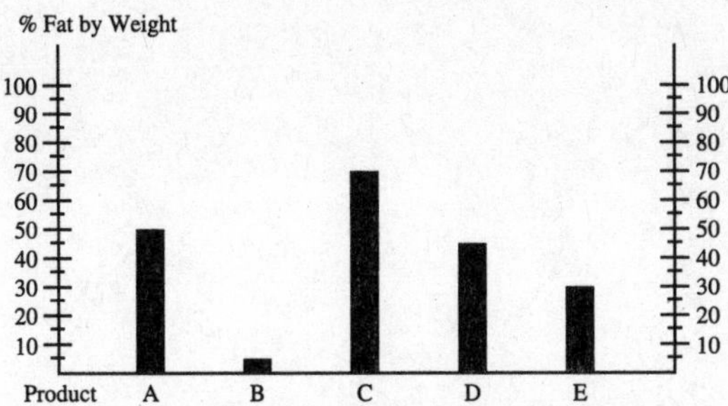

According to FDA regulations, in order to print the designation "light" on its labels, a product must contain no more than 45% fat by weight. Which of these products may be labeled "light"?

A. D only

B. B and E only

C. B, D, and E only

D. A and C only

SHOW YOUR WORK HERE

22. Two years ago a company purchased 500 dozen pencils at 40 cents per dozen. This year only 75% as many pencils were purchased as were purchased two years ago, but the price was 20% higher than the old price. What was the total cost of pencils purchased by the company this year?

A. \$180

B. \$187.50

C. \$240

D. \$257.40

23. With an 18% discount, John was able to save \$13.23 on a coat. What was the original price of the coat?

A. \$69.75

B. \$71.50

C. \$73.50

D. \$74.75

24. If $n = \sqrt{20}$, then

A. $\sqrt{5} > n > \sqrt{3}$.

B. $3 > n > 2$.

C. $n = 4.5$.

D. $4 < n < 5$.

E. $n > 5$.

25. If a certain job can be performed by 18 clerks in 26 days, the number of clerks needed to perform the job in 12 days is

A. 24.

B. 30.

C. 39.

D. 52.

SHOW YOUR WORK HERE

Math Drill 2

26. 7 days, 3 hours, 20 minutes – 4 days, 9 hours, 31 minutes =
   A. 2 days, 17 hours, 49 minutes
   B. 2 days, 17 hours, 69 minutes
   C. 3 days, 10 hours, 49 minutes
   D. 3 days, 10 hours, 69 minutes

27. If 10 workers earn $5,400 in 12 days, how much will 6 workers earn in 15 days?
   A. $10,500
   B. $5,400
   C. $4,050
   D. $2,025

28. How many more 9" × 9" linoleum tiles than 1' × 1' tiles will it take to cover a 12' × 12' floor?
   A. 63
   B. 98
   C. 112
   D. 144

29. Find the area of a circle with a diameter of 6".
   A. 29.26 square inches
   B. 28.26 square inches
   C. 27.96 square inches
   D. 27.26 square inches

SHOW YOUR WORK HERE

30. Colleen is 14 years old. She babysits for \$8.50 an hour. Yesterday she babysat for $3\frac{1}{2}$ hours. Which expression shows how much she earned?

A. $14 \times \$8.50$

B. $2 \times 3\frac{1}{2}$

C. $3\frac{1}{2} \times \$8.50$

D. $\left(3\frac{1}{2} \times 2\right) \times \$8.50$

31. Solve for x: $x^2 + 5 = 41$

A. ±6

B. ±7

C. ±8

D. ±9

32. If $\frac{2}{3}$ of a jar is filled with water in 1 minute, how long will it take to fill the remainder of the jar?

A. 15 seconds

B. 20 seconds

C. 30 seconds

D. 40 seconds

33. $\frac{1}{4}$% of 1,500 =

A. 60

B. 15

C. 7.50

D. 3.75

E. 1.50

SHOW YOUR WORK HERE

34. Find the area of a triangle with dimensions $b = 12'$, $h = 14'$.

A. 168 sq. ft.

B. 84 sq. ft.

C. 42 sq. ft.

D. 24 sq. ft.

35. If $A^2 + B^2 = A^2 + X^2$, then B equals

A. $\pm X$.

B. $X^2 - 2A^2$.

C. $\pm A$.

D. $A^2 + X^2$.

36. If $7 \times 6 = Y$, which is true?

A. $Y \div 7 = 6$

B. $Y \times 7 = 6$

C. $7 \div Y = 6$

D. $Y + 6 = 7$

37. 75% of 4 is the same as what percent of 9?

A. $22\frac{1}{2}$

B. $33\frac{1}{3}$

C. 36

D. 40

Math Drill 2

SHOW YOUR WORK HERE

38. If $\frac{1}{2}$ cup of spinach contains 80 calories, and the same amount of peas contains 300 calories, how many cups of spinach have the same caloric content as $\frac{2}{3}$ cup of peas?

A. $\frac{2}{5}$

B. $1\frac{1}{3}$

C. 2

D. $2\frac{1}{2}$

39. If 2 packages of cookies are enough for 10 children, how many packages will be needed for 15 children?

A. 6

B. 5

C. 4

D. 3

40. 759 – 215 =

A. 353

B. 454

C. 508

D. 544

41. Edna bought 4 packages of balloons with 6 in each package, and 2 packages with 3 large balloons in each. How many balloons did Edna buy?

A. 10

B. 15

C. 26

D. 30

SHOW YOUR WORK HERE

42. $7 + n = 15$

Which expression is equal to n?

A. $(15 \div 7)$

B. $(15 - 7)$

C. (15×7)

D. $(15 + 7)$

43. A real estate investor buys a house and lot for $44,000. He pays $1,250 to have it painted, $1,750 to fix the plumbing, and $1,000 for grading a driveway. At what price must he sell the property in order to make a 12% profit?

A. $53,760

B. $52,800

C. $52,000

D. $49,760

44. The scale on a map is $\frac{1}{8}''$ = 25 miles. If two cities are $3\frac{7}{8}''$ apart on the map, what is the actual distance between them?

A. 31 miles

B. 56 miles

C. 675 miles

D. 775 miles

45. What is 28,973 rounded to the nearest thousand?

A. 30,000

B. 29,000

C. 28,900

D. 28,000

Math Drill 2

46. A bakery received a shipment of 170 cupcakes that will be sold by the box. If each box holds 12 cupcakes, approximately how many boxes will be needed?

A. 8

B. 14

C. 20

D. 25

47. In order to make $\frac{7}{8}$ cup of salad dressing, add $\frac{1}{4}$ cup of vinegar to the oil. How much oil will you use?

A. $\frac{3}{8}$ cup

B. $\frac{5}{8}$ cup

C. $\frac{6}{8}$ cup

D. $\frac{3}{4}$ cup

48. The scale of a map is $\frac{3}{8}''$ = 5 miles. If the distance between points A and B is $4\frac{1}{2}''$ on the map, what is the distance in actuality?

A. 12 miles

B. 36 miles

C. 48 miles

D. 60 miles

SHOW YOUR WORK HERE

SHOW YOUR WORK HERE

49. Find the diameter of a circle with an area of 78.5 sq. in.

A. 25 feet

B. 10 feet

C. 25 inches

D. 10 inches

50. Solve for x: $5 \times (2 + x) = 15$

A. 1

B. 2

C. 4

D. 5

51.

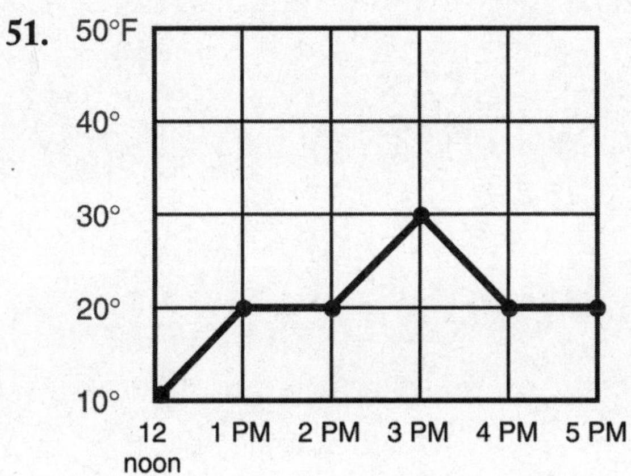

Which of the following is shown by the graph?

A. There was no change in temperature between 1 and 2 p.m.

B. There was no change in temperature between 3 and 4 p.m.

C. The highest temperature occurred at 12 noon.

D. The lowest temperature occurred at 5 p.m.

Math Drill 2

SHOW YOUR WORK HERE

52. $6 \div 0.0006 =$
A. 0.0036
B. 10,000
C. 60,000
D. 100,000

53. What is the value of x^5, if $x = 3$?
A. 81
B. 243
C. 15
D. 35

54. If $x = 0.25$, $\frac{1}{x} =$
A. $\frac{1}{25}$
B. 4
C. $\frac{1}{4}$
D. 1

55. $\frac{5^5}{5^3} =$
A. 0.04
B. $1\frac{2}{3}$
C. 25
D. 3,000

56. $X^3 \cdot X^2$
A. X^6
B. X^5
C. $2X^5$
D. $2X^6$

SHOW YOUR WORK HERE

57.

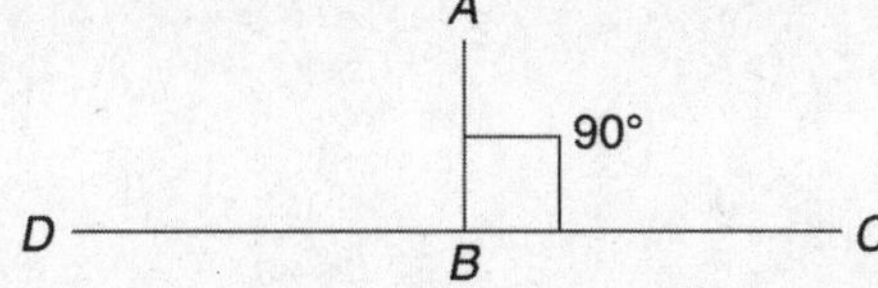

In the figure above, Angle *ABD* is a(n)

A. straight angle and measures 180°.

B. acute angle and measures 35°.

C. obtuse angle and measures 360°.

D. right angle and measures 90°.

58. Which of the following has a quotient that is NOT smaller than the dividend?

A. $0 \div 8$

B. $1 \div 8$

C. $2 \div 8$

D. $8 \div 8$

59. Simplify: $1 - [5 + (3 - 2)]$

A. –3

B. –5

C. 6

D. 0

60. Simplify: $-3 - [-2 + (5 - 6) - 3]$

A. +3

B. –1

C. +1

D. –3

61. What is the value of $x^2 + 2xy + y^2$ when $x = 4$ and $y = -7$?

A. –121

B. –89

C. 9

D. 121

Math Drill 2

62. $\frac{2}{3} \cdot \frac{3}{2} + \frac{1}{4} \div \frac{1}{3} - \frac{7}{12} =$

SHOW YOUR WORK HERE

A. $\frac{2}{3}$

B. $\frac{7}{6}$

C. $2\frac{2}{3}$

D. $\frac{19}{6}$

63. A piece of wood 35 feet, 6 inches long was used to make 4 shelves of equal length. The length of each shelf was

A. 9 feet, $1\frac{1}{2}$ inches.

B. 8 feet, $10\frac{1}{2}$ inches.

C. 8 feet, $1\frac{1}{2}$ inches.

D. 7 feet, $10\frac{1}{2}$ inches.

64.

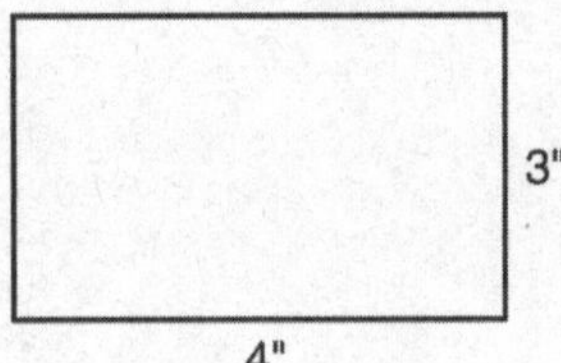

What is the area of this figure?

A. 1 sq. inch

B. 7 sq. inches

C. 12 sq. inches

D. 14 sq. inches

65. Solve for x: $2x^2 + 3 = 21$

A. ±3

B. ±5

C. ±9

D. ±10

SHOW YOUR WORK HERE

66. If $3x - 6 = 2$, find x.

A. $\frac{8}{3}$

B. 8

C. $\frac{4}{3}$

D. $\frac{2}{3}$

67. If $-3(y + 2) = 9$, find y.

A. –3

B. 15

C. –5

D. 3

68. If an odd number is subtracted from an odd number, which of the following could be the answer?

A. 1

B. 2

C. 7

D. 9

69. A fence is being installed around the 156-meter perimeter of a swimming pool. How many posts will be used if they are spaced 12 meters apart?

A. 11

B. 12

C. 13

D. 14

Math Drill 2

SHOW YOUR WORK HERE

70. 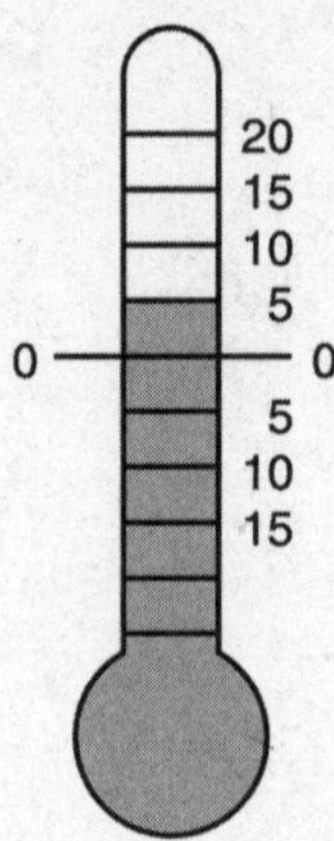

If the temperature decreases by 15 degrees below that shown on the thermometer, what will the new temperature be?

A. 20°

B. 10°

C. –10°

D. –20°

71. A car dealer sold three different makes of cars. The price of the first make was \$4,200, the second \$4,800, and the third \$5,400. The total sales were \$360,000. If three times as many of the third car was sold as the first, and twice as many of the second make were sold than the first, how many cars of the third make were sold?

A. 15

B. 24

C. 36

D. 42

72. Which sequence of fractions is arranged in order of least to greatest?

SHOW YOUR WORK HERE

A. $\frac{1}{3}, \frac{1}{18}, \frac{1}{11}, \frac{1}{7}$

B. $\frac{1}{18}, \frac{1}{11}, \frac{1}{7}, \frac{1}{3}$

C. $\frac{1}{3}, \frac{1}{7}, \frac{1}{11}, \frac{1}{18}$

D. $\frac{1}{8}, \frac{1}{7}, \frac{1}{11}, \frac{1}{3}$

73. Population figures for a certain area show there are $1\frac{1}{2}$ times as many single men as single women in the area. The total population is 18,000. There are 1,122 married couples, with 756 children. How many single men are there in the area?

A. 3,000

B. 4,500

C. 6,000

D. 9,000

74. If it takes three men 56 minutes to fill a trench 4' × 6' × 5', and two of the men work twice as rapidly as the third, how many minutes will it take the two faster men alone to fill this trench?

A. 70 minutes

B. 60 minutes

C. 50 minutes

D. 40 minutes

75. The length of a rectangular family room is 10 feet more than twice the width of the room. The area of the room is 300 square feet. What is the length of the room?

A. 5 feet

B. 10 feet

C. 15 feet

D. 30 feet

SHOW YOUR WORK HERE

Answer Key and Explanations

1. D	**16.** B	**31.** A	**46.** B	**61.** C
2. A	**17.** A	**32.** C	**47.** B	**62.** B
3. C	**18.** D	**33.** D	**48.** D	**63.** B
4. C	**19.** D	**34.** B	**49.** D	**64.** C
5. B	**20.** D	**35.** A	**50.** A	**65.** A
6. C	**21.** C	**36.** A	**51.** A	**66.** A
7. A	**22.** A	**37.** B	**52.** B	**67.** C
8. A	**23.** C	**38.** D	**53.** B	**68.** B
9. B	**24.** D	**39.** D	**54.** B	**69.** C
10. D	**25.** C	**40.** D	**55.** C	**70.** C
11. B	**26.** A	**41.** D	**56.** B	**71.** C
12. D	**27.** C	**42.** B	**57.** D	**72.** B
13. B	**28.** C	**43.** A	**58.** A	**73.** D
14. B	**29.** B	**44.** D	**59.** B	**74.** A
15. C	**30.** C	**45.** B	**60.** A	**75.** D

1. **The correct answer is D.** This is a simple subtraction problem designed to test how carefully you can subtract. It is possible to calculate the correct answer without pencil and paper. 999,999 is only 1 less than a million, and 1,001,000 is 1,000 greater than a million. The difference, then, is 1,000 + 1, or 1,001. Or, you may figure the problem in the following way:

$$\begin{array}{r} 1,001,000 \\ -\ \ 999,999 \\ \hline 1,001 \end{array}$$

2. **The correct answer is A.** Remember the order of operations as you solve the problem.

Step 1: $-3 - [-2 + (5 - 6) - 3]$
Step 2: $-3 - [-2 + (-1) - 3]$
Step 3: $-3 - [-2 - 1 - 3]$
Step 4: $-3 - [-6]$
Step 5: $-3 + 6 = +3$

3. **The correct answer is C.** By far the easiest way to solve this problem is to convert the fractions into decimals: 0.6 + 1.5 + 0.75 = 2.85. If you were to convert the answer to a fraction, the correct answer would be $2\frac{17}{20}$.

4. **The correct answer is C.** This proportion asks you to find the missing element. A proportion is a statement of equality between two ratios, so we know that 5 bears the same relationship to 15 as 6 does to the unknown number. Since 3 × 5 equals 15, we know 3 × 6 equals the unknown number. The number, thus, is 18. The completed proportion should read: 5:6 as 15:18. Proportions may also be written with a set of two colons replacing the word "as." In this case, the proportion would read: 5:6::15:18.

5. **The correct answer is B.** This is a simple proportion: $\frac{7}{4} = \frac{5}{x}$. x is the unknown width. Cross-multiply:

$$7x = 20$$

$$x = \frac{20}{7}, \text{ or } 2\frac{6}{7}"$$

6. **The correct answer is C.** 207 – 109 + 99 – 111 + 202 – 104 = 194

7. **The correct answer is A.** Prime factorization is factoring a number to the point where all factors are prime.

$$12 =$$
$$3 \times 4 =$$
$$3 \times 2 \times 2$$

8. **The correct answer is A.** The least common multiple is the smallest number divisible by both given numbers. The number 6 is both a multiple of 2 and the least common multiple of 2 and 6.

9. **The correct answer is B.** The commutative property of multiplication states that you may move the numbers around to be multiplied in different ways and achieve the same product. Choices A and C demonstrate the associative property of multiplication, which states you can regroup factors without affecting the final product. Choice D illustrates the multiplicative identity property.

10. **The correct answer is D.** To convert a percentage to a decimal number, move the decimal point to the left two places. The percentage 0.12% can be written in decimal form as 0.0012.

11. The correct answer is B. The area of the flower bed is 4π sq. ft. ($A = \pi r^2$). The area of the new bed is to be four times as great, or 16π sq. ft. A bed with an area of 16π sq. ft. must have a diameter of 8 feet and a radius of 4 feet, since $A = \pi r^2$.

12. The correct answer is D. Solve the equation for x:

$$3x - 2 = 13$$
$$3x = 15$$
$$x = 5$$

If $x = 5$, then $12x + 20 = 12(5) + 20 = 80$.

13. The correct answer is B. If p pencils cost c cents, the cost of each pencil is $\frac{c}{p}$ cents. To find the cost of n pencils, we multiply the cost of each times n:

$$\frac{c}{p} \bullet n = \frac{cn}{p}$$

14. The correct answer is B. An ordinary die has six sides, each having a different number of dots. The chance of any face coming up is the same is $\frac{1}{6}$.

15. The correct answer is C. The area of a square = s^2
The area of this square = $2^2 = 4$
The area of a circle = $\pi \bullet r^2$

$$\left(r = \frac{1}{2}d\right)(\pi = 3.14)$$

The area of this circle = $\pi \bullet 1^2 = \pi \bullet 1 = \pi$
The difference between the area of this square and the area of this circle is $4 - 3.14 = 0.86$.

16. The correct answer is B. Reduce the $17 price by 20%.

20% of 17 = $17 × 0.20 = $3.40

$17 – 3.40 = $13.60 (new price)

Choice A indicates a reduction of only 20 cents. Choice C represents a reduction *to* 20% of the original price, or an 80% decrease in price.

17. The correct answer is A. 56,152 ÷ 7,019 = 8.

Answers Math Drill 2

18. **The correct answer is D.** To convert a percentage to a decimal number, move the decimal point to the left two places. The percentage 0.17% can be written in decimal form as 0.0017.

19. **The correct answer is D.** This is a complex fraction requiring all your skills in working with fractions. First, find common denominators to add the numerators and subtract the denominators.

$$\frac{\frac{16}{24}+\frac{9}{24}}{\frac{4}{16}-\frac{3}{16}}=\frac{\frac{25}{24}}{\frac{1}{16}}$$

Then, divide the numerator by the denominator and solve.

$$\frac{25}{24}\div\frac{1}{16}=\frac{25}{\cancel{24}_{3}}\bullet\frac{\cancel{16}^{2}}{1}=\frac{50}{3}$$

20. **The correct answer is D.** This question doesn't ask you to determine 175% of 24; instead, it asks you to *increase* 24 by 175%. First, calculate 175% of 24 using multiplication: 24 × 1.75 = 42. Next, add 42 to 24.

$$24\times1.75=42$$
$$42+24=66$$

21. **The correct answer is C.** The regulations state that a "light" product contains *no more than 45% fat.* Product D, which contains exactly 45% fat, may be labeled "light" along with B and E.

22. **The correct answer is A.** 500 dozen @ \$0.40 per dozen = purchase of two years ago
75% of 500 dozen = 375 dozen pencils purchased this year
20% of \$0.40 = \$0.08 increase in cost per dozen
375 dozen × \$0.48 = \$180 spent on pencils this year

23. **The correct answer is C.** The problem asks, "What number is \$13.23 18% of?"

$$\$13.23\div0.18=\$73.50$$

24. **The correct answer is D.** The square root of 20 is less than the square root of 25, which is 5, and greater than the square root of 16, which is 4. Therefore, *n* is between 4 and 5.

25. **The correct answer is C.** The size of the job can be thought of this way: 18 clerks working for 26 days do 18 × 26 or 468 clerk-days of work. To do 468 clerk-days of work in only 12 days would require 468 ÷ 12 = 39 clerks.

26. **The correct answer is A.** You must borrow one day's worth of hours and one hour's worth of minutes and rewrite the problem as:

$$\begin{array}{r} \text{6 days 26 hr. 80 min.} \\ -\text{ 4 days 9 hr. 31 min.} \\ \hline \text{2 days 17 hr. 49 min.} \end{array}$$

27. **The correct answer is C.** If 10 men earn \$5,400 in 12 days, each man earns \$540 in 12 days, or \$45 per day. Therefore, 6 men working for 15 days at \$45 per day will earn \$4,050.

28. **The correct answer is C.** A floor 12' × 12' is 144 sq. ft. in area and would require 144 tiles that are each 1' × 1'. Twelve tiles would be placed along the width and length of the room. If 9" tiles are used, it requires 16 of them placed end to end to cover the length of the room. Therefore, it requires 16 × 16 tiles to cover the floor, or 256 tiles. It requires 112 more 9" tiles than 12" tiles to cover the floor.

29. **The correct answer is B.** The area of a circle is $A = \pi r^2$; the radius equals $\frac{1}{2}$, the diameter. $r = 3$, and $\pi = \frac{22}{7}$, or 3.14.

$A = \pi r^2$
$A = \pi\,(3)^2$
$A = 9\pi$
$A = 9(3.14) = 28.26$ sq. in.

30. **The correct answer is C.** Three numbers are given in this problem, but only two are necessary to solve the problem: the charge per hour and the number of hours Colleen babysat.

$$\$8.50 \text{ per hour} \times 3\tfrac{1}{2} \text{ hours} = \$8.50 \times 3\tfrac{1}{2}$$

31. **The correct answer is A.** If $x^2 + 5 = 41$

$$x^2 = 41 - 5$$
$$x^2 = 36$$
$$x = \pm 6$$

32. **The correct answer is C.** If $\frac{2}{3}$ of the jar is filled in 1 minute, then $\frac{1}{3}$ of the jar is filled in $\frac{1}{2}$ minute. Since the jar is $\frac{2}{3}$ full, $\frac{1}{3}$ remains to be filled. The jar will be full in another $\frac{1}{2}$ minute, or 30 seconds.

33. **The correct answer is D.** $\frac{1}{4}\%$ written as a decimal is 0.0025. (1,500)(0.0025) = 3.75. You could have done this problem in your head by thinking: 10% of 1,500 is 150; 1% of 1,500 is 15; $\frac{1}{4}$ of 1% = 15 ÷ 4 = 3.75.

34. **The correct answer is B.** The formula for the area of a triangle is $A = \frac{1}{2}bh$. Plug in the numbers:

$$A = \frac{1}{2} \cdot 12 \cdot 14$$
$$A = 84 \text{ sq. ft.}$$

35. **The correct answer is A.** Subtract A^2 from both sides of the equation: $B^2 = X^2$, therefore $B = \pm X$.

36. **The correct answer is A.** Since $7 \times 6 = Y$, $Y = 42$.

$$42 \div 7 = 6$$

37. **The correct answer is B.**

$$75\% \text{ of } 4 = 3$$
$$3 = 33\frac{1}{8}\% \text{ of } 9$$

38. **The correct answer is D.** $\frac{1}{2}$ cup spinach = 80 calories

$$\frac{1}{2} \text{ cup of peas} = 300 \text{ calories}$$
$$1 \text{ cup of peas} = 600 \text{ calories}$$
$$\frac{2}{3} \text{ cup of peas} = 400 \text{ calories}$$
$$400 \div 80 = 5 \text{ half cups of spinach}$$
$$= 2\frac{1}{2} \text{ cups of spinach}$$

39. **The correct answer is D.** If 2 packages of cookies will serve 10 children, you may assume that 1 package will serve 5 children. Therefore, 3 packages will serve 15 children.

40. **The correct answer is D.** 759 –215 = 544

41. **The correct answer is D.** 4 × 6 = 24 and 2 × 3 = 6; 24 + 6 = 30.

42. **The correct answer is B.** 15 – 7 = 8; 7 + 8 = 15

43. **The correct answer is A.** Add the cost of the house, driveway, painting, and plumbing: \$44,000 + \$1,250 + \$1,750 + 1,000 = \$48,000. If he wants to make a 12% profit when reselling the house, he should increase the total cost by 12% to find the new selling price:

$$12\% \text{ of } \$48,000 = \$5,760$$

$$\$48,000 + \$5,760 = \$53,760$$

44. **The correct answer is D.** The scale is $\frac{1}{8}$" = 25 miles. In $3\frac{7}{8}$", there are 31 units measuring $\frac{1}{8}$". The distance is 31 • 25 = 775 miles.

45. **The correct answer is B.** In the number 28,973, the digit 8 is in the thousands place. The hundreds digit is greater than 5, so the next nearest thousand is 9; therefore, 29,000 is the answer.

46. **The correct answer is B.** 170 ÷ 12 = 14 with a remainder of 2. The closest number given is 14.

47. **The correct answer is B.** $\frac{1}{4} = \frac{2}{8}$, and $\frac{7}{8} - \frac{2}{8} = \frac{5}{8}$.

48. **The correct answer is D.** The map distance is $4\frac{1}{2}$" or $\frac{9}{2}$" or $\frac{36}{8}$". Each $\frac{3}{8}$" = 5 miles, and we know there are twelve $\frac{3}{8}$" units in $\frac{36}{8}$". Therefore, the twelve $\frac{3}{8}$" units correspond to 60 miles in actuality.

49. **The correct answer is D.** The area of a circle is found by $A = \pi r^2$. The radius is half the diameter. To find the diameter when the area is known, divide the area by π to find the square of the radius:

$$78.5 \div 3.14 = 25$$

Since the square of the radius is 25, we know the radius is 5, and the diameter is twice the radius, or 10 inches.

50. **The correct answer is A.** 5 × (2 + 1) = 5 × 3 = 15

51. **The correct answer is A.** According to the graph, the temperature at 1 p.m. was 20°, and at 2 p.m. it was *still* 20°.

52. The correct answer is B. Be careful in counting places and in positioning the decimal point.

$$.0006 \times 10{,}000 = 6$$

53. The correct answer is B. Substitute 3 for x. The problem, then, is to compute 3^5.

$$3^5 = 3 \cdot 3 \cdot 3 \cdot 3 \cdot 3$$
$$= 243$$

Choice C would have resulted if you had multiplied 5 × 3, instead of 3 times itself 5 times.

54. The correct answer is B. This is a simple division problem. Divide 1.0 by 0.25. Here is another way to solve this problem. Since $0.25 = \frac{1}{4}$, the reciprocal of $\frac{1}{4}$ is 4.

55. The correct answer is C. In this problem, the bases are the same, so you must subtract the exponent of the divisor from that of the dividend to find the answer:

$$5^5 \div 5^3 = 5^{5-3} = 5^2 = 25$$

Therefore, choice C is the correct answer. Note that the bases must be identical, and the exponents must be subtracted. You can check this answer by multiplying each number out and dividing.

$$\frac{5^5}{5^3} = \frac{3{,}125}{125} = 25$$

56. The correct answer is B. When multiplying, if the bases are identical, add the exponents:

$$X^3 \cdot X^2 = X^5$$

Note that because we are multiplying, the coefficient remains 1.

57. The correct answer is D. Angle *ABC* and angle *ABD* are supplementary angles. Since angle *ABC* = 90°, angle *ABD* must also equal 90° (180° – 90° = 90°). A right angle contains 90°.

58. The correct answer is A. 0 ÷ 8 = 0. Choice B is $1 \div 8 = \frac{1}{8}$; choice C is $2 \div 8 = \frac{2}{8}$; and choice D is 8 ÷ 8 = 1. In 0 ÷ 8, 0 is the dividend and 8 is the divisor. The quotient is the result obtained when the dividend is divided by the divisor.

59. **The correct answer is B.** Begin removing the innermost grouping symbols, rewriting each time a set of symbols is removed:

Step 1: $1 - [5 + (3 - 2)]$
Step 2: $1 - [5 + 1]$
Step 3: $1 - [6]$
Step 4: $1 - 6 = -5$

A minus sign in front of a bracket or parenthesis reverses the sign of the number inside. A positive sign does not.

60. **The correct answer is A.**

Step 1: $-3 - [-2 + (5 - 6) - 3]$
Step 2: $-3 - [-2 + (-1) - 3]$
Step 3: $-3 - [-2 - 1 - 3]$
Step 4: $-3 - [-6]$
Step 5: $-3 + 6 = +3$

A minus sign in front of a bracket or parenthesis reverses the sign of the number inside. A positive sign does not.

61. **The correct answer is C.** Plug in the values for x and y:

$$x^2 + 2xy + y^2 = 4^2 + 2(4)(\ 7) + (\ 7)^2$$
$$= 16 \quad 56 + 49$$
$$= 9$$

62. **The correct answer is B.** Be careful to use the correct process. First use multiplication, division, addition, and finally subtraction.

$$\frac{2}{3}\bullet\frac{3}{2}+\frac{1}{4}\div\frac{1}{3}-\frac{7}{12}$$
$$\left(\frac{2}{3}\bullet\frac{3}{2}\right)+\left(\frac{1}{4}\div\frac{1}{3}\right)-\frac{7}{12}$$
$$1+\frac{3}{4}-\frac{7}{12}$$
$$\frac{12}{12}+\frac{9}{12}-\frac{7}{12}=\frac{4}{12}=\frac{7}{6}$$

63. **The correct answer is B.** First convert the feet to inches.
35 feet, 6 inches = 420 inches + 6 inches = 426 inches

$426 \div 4 = 106.5$ inches per shelf = 8 feet, $10\frac{1}{2}$ inches per shelf.

64. The correct answer is C. The area of a rectangle is found by multiplying the length by the width.

$$4" \times 3" = 12 \text{ square inches}$$

65. The correct answer is A.

$$2x^2 + 3 = 21$$
$$2x^2 = 21 - 3$$
$$2x^2 = 18$$
$$x^2 = 9$$
$$x = \pm 3$$

You should have been able to predict that x would be a small number, since, according to the equation, twice its square is no larger than 21.

66. The correct answer is A. This equation can be solved in two steps:

Step 1: Move –6 to the right side and change the sign.

$$3x = 2 + 6$$
$$3x = 8$$

Step 2: Divide by the coefficient of the variable.

$$\frac{3x}{3} = \frac{8}{3}$$
$$x = \frac{8}{3}$$

67. The correct answer is C.

Step 1: First, remove the grouping parentheses:

$$-3(y + 2) = 9$$
$$-3y - 6 = 9$$

Step 2: Then move –6 to the right side, change its sign, and combine:

$$-3y = 9 + 6$$
$$-3y = 15$$

Step 3: Divide through by the coefficient of the variable:

$$\frac{-3y}{-3} = \frac{15}{-3}$$
$$y = -5$$

68. **The correct answer is B.** An odd number subtracted from an odd number will always result in an even number. The only even number given is 2.

69. **The correct answer is C.** 156 meters ÷ 12 meters = 13; there will be 13 posts used.

70. **The correct answer is C.** $5^\circ - 15^\circ = -10^\circ$

71. **The correct answer is C.** Solve this problem as you would any mixture value problem. The numbers of cars sold are all related to the number of those sold for $4,200. Call the number of $4,200 cars sold x. Then, the number of $5,400 cars sold is $3x$, and the number of $4,800 cars is $2x$.

The value of $4,200 cars sold is $4,200 • x.
The value of $4,800 cars sold is $4,800 • $2x$.
The value of $5,400 cars sold is $5,400 • $3x$.
The sum of these values equals the total sales.

$$\begin{aligned}(\$4,200 \cdot x) + (\$4,800 \cdot 2x) + (\$5,400 \cdot 3x) &= \$360,000 \\ \$4,200x + \$9,600x + \$16,200x &= \$360,000 \\ \$30,000x &= \$360,000 \\ x &= \$360,000 \div \$30,000 \\ x &= 12\end{aligned}$$

Since $x = 12$ of the $4,200 cars, $3x$, or 36, of the third make (at $5,400) were sold.

72. **The correct answer is B.** The denominator of a fraction shows how many parts the whole has been divided into. Therefore, $\frac{1}{18} < \frac{1}{11} < \frac{1}{7} < \frac{1}{3}$.

73. **The correct answer is D.** Subtract from the total population of 18,000 the 756 children and the 2,244 married people:

18,000 – 756 – 2,244 = 15,000 single men and women

Because there are $1\frac{1}{2}$ times as many men as women, we know that 60% of the 15,000 single people are men, and 40% are women:

60% of 15,000 = 9,000

74. **The correct answer is A.** Each fast worker is equivalent to two slow workers; therefore, the three men are the equivalent of five slow workers. The whole job, then, requires 5 × 56 = 280 minutes for one slow worker. It also requires half that time, or 140 minutes, for one fast worker, and half as much again, or 70 minutes, for two fast workers.

75. The correct answer is D. Let w represent the width of the room. Then, the length is $2w + 10$. The area of a rectangular room is length times width. Using this fact yields the following equation:

$$w(2w + 10) = 300$$

Solving this equation for w yields:

$$\begin{aligned} w(2w + 10) &= 300 \\ 2w^2 + 10w &= 300 \\ 2w^2 + 10w - 300 &= 0 \\ (2w + 30)(w - 10) &= 0 \\ w &= \cancel{-15},\ 10 \end{aligned}$$

The width of the room is 10 feet. Thus, the length is 30 feet.

Chapter 5

HSPT® Verbal Skills

Introduction to HSPT® Verbal Skills Questions

Words are the most essential elements of communication, so it is important to be able to understand them in ways beyond the mere understanding of their definitions. The Verbal Skills section of the HSPT exam will measure your ability to do just that by testing your mastery of analogies, verbal logic, synonyms and antonyms, and verbal classifications.

Analogy questions measure how well you can comprehend the relationships between word sets. These questions consist of two sets of words. The first set is provided for you, and the two words in the set share a specific relationship. You must then complete the second set by choosing a word that helps that set express the same relationship as the first set.

Relationship types include the following:

- Association (**Example:** *spoon* is to *fork*)
- Cause and effect (**Example:** *cold* is to *frostbite*)
- Characteristic (**Example:** *powerful* is to *gorilla*)
- Degree (**Example:** *warm* is to *sweltering*)
- Part to whole (**Example:** *page* is to *book*)
- Purpose (**Example:** *saw* is to *cut*)
- Sequence (**Example:** *first* is to *second*)
- Antonym (**Example:** *big* is to *small*)
- Synonym (**Example:** *smart* is to *intelligent*)

Verbal logic questions measure your ability to reach a conclusion based on the information in three statements. These questions require you to use the first two statements to decide if a third statement is true, false, or uncertain. You will choose "uncertain" if the first two statements do not provide enough information to reach a firm conclusion about the third statement.

Synonym and antonym questions measure your ability to identify different words that share the same meanings (synonyms) and words that have opposite meanings (antonyms). These words are presented as short sentences, which you will complete by choosing the appropriate synonym or antonym.

Verbal classification questions require you to examine a selection of words and choose the one that does not belong with the others. The words may share the same kinds of relationships you will encounter when answering analogy questions. The correct answer may share some relationship with the other words, but it will still be unlike in some significant way.

HSPT Verbal Skills Questions Preview

Now we'll walk you through examples of each type of verbal skills question.

1. Newspaper is to inform as comic strip is to

A. educate.

B. entertain.

C. funny.

D. read.

The correct answer is B. This is a typical analogy question, and when answering analogy questions, the first question you should ask yourself is "what is the relationship?" In this case, you are trying to identify the relationship between *newspaper* and *inform*. A newspaper informs readers about current events. Informing is a newspaper's purpose. Therefore, this is a purpose analogy, so you need to identify the purpose of a comic strip. Does a comic strip educate you about anything? Well, this is not beyond the realm of possibility, but not very usual for comic strips, so choice A may not be the best answer. Let's move on to *entertain* (choice B). Do comic strips entertain people? Entertainment is certainly the intended purpose of most comic strips, so choice B is looking like a strong answer. *Funny* (choice C) is not a purpose; it is a characteristic. Eliminate it. *Read* (choice D) is not a purpose either. It is an action. Eliminate that one as well and choose choice B.

2. a *deceptive* plan is

A. clever

B. honorable

C. misleading

D. foolish

The correct answer is C. For this synonym question, start by defining the meaning of the provided word. Notice the similarity of the word *deceptive* to the word *deceive*, which means "to mislead." *Deceptive* means "misleading." *Honorable* is a near antonym of *deceptive*. It may be foolish (choice D) to devise a deceptive plan, but the two words are not synonyms. Those who devise a deceptive plan may consider themselves clever (choice A), but these words are not synonyms either.

3. Elise is taller than Desmond. Desmond is taller than Boris. Boris is taller than Elise. If the first two statements are true, the third is

A. true.

B. false.

C. uncertain.

The correct answer is B. When you see a question that ends with the statement "If the first two statements are true, the third is," and the answer choices are A. true; B. false; and C. uncertain, you know you're looking at a verbal logic question. What do we learn from the first two statements? We learn that Elise is the tallest person. She is taller than Desmond and Boris, who is not as tall as Desmond. So can Boris be taller than Elise? Nope. Therefore, the correct answer is B. false.

4. Concise means the *opposite* of

A. rambling.

B. brief.

C. finish.

D. busy.

The correct answer is A. We're dealing with opposites here, which means that this is an antonym question. Just as you would with a synonym question, you must first define the provided word. In the case of this particular question, that word is *concise,* which means "to the point." Another way to say "to the point" is *brief.* That means choice B would be the correct answer if this were a synonym question, but since it isn't, you must eliminate choice B. What is the opposite of "to the point"? The opposite is *rambling* (choice A). Choice C seems to confuse the word *concise* with *continue,* which is the opposite of *finish. Busy* (choice D) just seems to be a random distracter. It certainly does not mean the opposite of *concise.*

5. Which word does *not* belong with the others?

   A. heart
   B. lung
   C. toenail
   D. liver

The correct answer is C. This is a verbal classification question, and as you would with an analogy question, you should first identify a relationship. In this case, you are looking for the unifying relationship among the majority of answer choices. What does a heart, a lung, a toenail, and a liver have in common? There are all body parts. Yet that can't be the intended relationship, because one of these things must be set aside to take its rightful place as the correct answer. Can you think of a different relationship? Well, a heart, a lung, and a liver are not just body parts; they are internal organs. A toenail, however, is not an internal organ. It does not belong with the others, and choice C is our correct answer.

Appendix Alert

Remember, Appendix B (page 473) is a robust list of antonyms and synonyms. You might want to revisit them before working through the synonym and antonym drills. Look to the analogy study guide (page 509) for some tips on how to navigate these sometime tricky word relationship questions.

You will find the answer sheet for the drills in this chapter in Appendix C, starting on page 521.

Analogies Drill

75 Questions

Directions: In the following questions, the first two words are related to each other in a certain way. The third and fourth words must be related to each other in the same way. Choose from among the four choices the word that is related to the third word in the same way that the second word is related to the first. Mark the corresponding letter on your answer sheet.

1. Prostrate is to flat as vertical is to

A. circular.

B. horizontal.

C. geometric.

D. erect.

2. Educated is to know as rich is to

A. poor.

B. wise.

C. own.

D. money.

3. France is to America as meter is to

A. gallon.

B. degree.

C. yard.

D. pound.

4. Square is to circle as rectangle is to

A. round.

B. triangle.

C. oval.

D. cube.

5. Light is to lamp as heat is to
   A. furnace.
   B. light.
   C. sun.
   D. room.

6. Skillful is to clumsy as deft is to
   A. alert.
   B. awkward.
   C. dumb.
   D. agile.

7. Pit is to peach as sun is to
   A. planet.
   B. moon.
   C. orbit.
   D. solar system.

8. Up is to down as left is to
   A. diagonal.
   B. right.
   C. above.
   D. around.

9. Ice cream is to dairy as hamburger is to
   A. vegetables.
   B. bun.
   C. meat.
   D. grain.

10. Tadpole is to frog as caterpillar is to
   A. butterfly.
   B. bee.
   C. bird.
   D. tadpole.

11. Fur is to rabbit as scales are to

A. human.

B. elephant.

C. fish.

D. reptile.

12. Pencil is to writing as voice is to

A. texting.

B. speaking.

C. moving.

D. hearing.

13. Piece is to cake as easy is to

A. simple.

B. pie.

C. snap.

D. cinch.

14. Muzzle is to dog as trunk is to

A. tree.

B. car.

C. suitcase.

D. elephant.

15. Teacher is to classroom as lawyer is to

A. trial.

B. courtroom.

C. boardroom.

D. judge.

16. Firecracker is to fireworks as trickle is to

A. waterfall.

B. drip.

C. puddle.

D. explosion.

17. Painter is to brush as sculptor is to

A. clay.

B. brick.

C. chisel.

D. palette.

18. Peony is to flower as pomegranate is to

A. vegetable.

B. tree.

C. bloom.

D. fruit.

19. Lid is to box as cork is to

A. float.

B. bottle.

C. wine.

D. stopper.

20. None is to little as never is to

A. nothing.

B. infrequently.

C. negative.

D. much.

21. Receive is to admit as settle is to

A. resist.

B. anger.

C. remain.

D. adjust.

22. Beaker is to chemist as hammer is to

A. nails.

B. geologist.

C. construction.

D. architect.

23. Follow is to lead as dependent is to

A. subservient.

B. supportive.

C. child.

D. autonomous.

24. State is to country as country is to

A. island.

B. capitol.

C. continent.

D. planet.

25. Obstruct is to impede as impenetrable is to

A. impervious.

B. hidden.

C. merciful.

D. porous.

26. Include is to omit as acknowledge is to

A. notice.

B. ignore.

C. recognize.

D. greet.

27. Youth is to young as maturity is to

A. people.

B. parents.

C. grandmother.

D. old.

28. Week is to month as season is to

A. holiday.

B. spring.

C. year.

D. planting.

29. Thanksgiving is to November as Christmas is to

A. Santa Claus.

B. holiday.

C. snow.

D. December.

30. Remember is to forget as find is to

A. locate.

B. keep.

C. lose.

D. return.

31. Ship is to anchor as automobile is to

A. brake.

B. wheel.

C. stop.

D. accelerator.

32. End is to abolish as begin is to

A. establish.

B. finish.

C. tyranny.

D. crusade.

33. Wood is to decay as iron is to

A. dampness.

B. rust.

C. steel.

D. ore.

34. Year is to decade as decade is to

A. age.

B. era.

C. century.

D. millennium.

35. Flour is to wheat as gravel is to

A. rock.

B. road.

C. dirt.

D. brick.

36. Attack is to protect as offense is to

A. combat.

B. defense.

C. conceal.

D. reconcile.

37. Divide is to multiply as subtract is to

A. plus.

B. reduce.

C. multiply.

D. add.

38. My is to mine as your is to

A. you.

B. ours.

C. yours.

D. you're.

39. Leave is to stay as depart is to

A. home.

B. disembark.

C. run.

D. remain.

40. Car is to mechanic as people is to

A. doctor.

B. lawyer.

C. spouse.

D. butcher.

41. Forest is to tree as crowd is to

A. person.

B. alone.

C. men.

D. many.

42. Fiction is to novelist as fact is to

A. legend.

B. story.

C. historian.

D. research.

43. Sickness is to health as death is to

A. mortician.

B. skull.

C. old.

D. life.

44. Inventor is to machine as author is to

A. book.

B. poet.

C. creator.

D. artist.

45. Weight is to pound as distance is to

A. liter.

B. mile.

C. space.

D. race.

46. Conceal is to reveal as ascend is to

A. embark.

B. descend.

C. mount.

D. leave.

47. Sword is to duel as pen is to

A. book.

B. inkwell.

C. ink.

D. write.

48. Reprimand is to disapproval as compliment is to

A. flatter.

B. approval.

C. affirmation.

D. insult.

49. Gold is to yellow as ruby is to

A. black.

B. purple.

C. red.

D. white.

50. Periodic is to recurring as determined is to

A. cowardly.

B. hopeless.

C. perseverant.

D. lazy.

51. Anarchy is to law as discord is to

A. difference.

B. agreement.

C. adaptation.

D. confusion.

52. Fruit is to apple as vegetable is to

A. carrot.

B. pomegranate.

C. pumpkin.

D. banana.

53. Accident is to carelessness as response is to
    A. answer.
    B. correct.
    C. stimulus.
    D. effect.

54. Correction is to erroneous as clarification is to
    A. criticism.
    B. failure.
    C. amend.
    D. ambiguous.

55. Automobile is to horse as telephone is to
    A. wagon.
    B. telegraph.
    C. communication.
    D. transportation.

56. Intimidate is to bully as dismay is to
    A. unnerve.
    B. destroy.
    C. dismantle.
    D. forego.

57. Spontaneous is to calculated as impromptu is to
    A. ad lib.
    B. scheduled.
    C. verbose.
    D. prolific.

58. Critic is to play as teacher is to
    A. job.
    B. work.
    C. newspaper.
    D. essay.

59. Lion is to pride as fish is to
- **A.** water.
- **B.** fearful.
- **C.** aquatic.
- **D.** school.

60. Referee is to rules as conscience is to
- **A.** regulations.
- **B.** morality.
- **C.** thoughts.
- **D.** behavior.

61. Money is to steal as idea is to
- **A.** lose.
- **B.** manuscript.
- **C.** plagiarize.
- **D.** thief.

62. Book is to paper as scroll is to
- **A.** cloth.
- **B.** binding.
- **C.** roll.
- **D.** parchment.

63. Beg is to borrow as offer is to
- **A.** lender.
- **B.** bank.
- **C.** lend.
- **D.** repay.

64. Lazy is to inert as resist is to
- **A.** refuse.
- **B.** reply.
- **C.** respond.
- **D.** active.

65. Cylinder is to circle as pyramid is to

A. sphere.

B. point.

C. triangle.

D. angle.

66. Crocodile is to reptile as kangaroo is to

A. amphibian.

B. mammal.

C. opossum.

D. canine.

67. Wild is to wolf as domestic is to

A. dog.

B. coyote.

C. pet.

D. cat.

68. Subject is to predicate as senator is to

A. congress.

B. capitol.

C. representative.

D. senate.

69. Spread is to scatter as separate is to

A. integrate.

B. distribute.

C. reap.

D. group.

70. Exuberant is to mood as adroit is to

A. proficient.

B. adept.

C. movement.

D. dexterous.

71. Defiance is to opposition as exertion is to

A. expert.

B. vigor.

C. endeavor.

D. challenge.

72. Perpetuity is to impermanence as interminable is to

A. impertinent.

B. brief.

C. incessant.

D. eternal.

73. Erratic is to predictable as exorbitant is to

A. reasonable.

B. productive.

C. absorbent.

D. implicit.

74. Tailor is to pattern as builder is to

A. architect.

B. contractor.

C. blueprint.

D. foundation.

75. Weeping is to tears as breathing is to

A. air.

B. carbon dioxide.

C. nose.

D. mouth.

Answer Key and Explanations

1. D	16. A	31. A	46. B	61. C
2. C	17. C	32. A	47. D	62. D
3. C	18. D	33. B	48. B	63. C
4. C	19. B	34. C	49. C	64. A
5. A	20. B	35. A	50. C	65. C
6. B	21. C	36. B	51. B	66. B
7. D	22. B	37. D	52. A	67. A
8. B	23. D	38. C	53. C	68. D
9. C	24. C	39. D	54. D	69. B
10. A	25. A	40. D	55. B	70. C
11. C	26. B	41. A	56. A	71. D
12. B	27. D	42. C	57. B	72. B
13. B	28. C	43. D	58. D	73. A
14. D	29. D	44. A	59. D	74. C
15. B	30. C	45. B	60. B	75. B

1. **The correct answer is D.** The relationship is that of synonyms. *Prostrate* means "flat"; *vertical* means "erect."

2. **The correct answer is C.** The relationship is that of cause and effect. When you are *educated*, you *know*; when you are *rich*, you *own*. When you are rich, you also have money. An analogy must maintain parallelism in parts of speech. For *money* to have been the correct answer, the second term would have had to have been a noun such as *knowledge*.

3. **The correct answer is C.** The relationship cannot be defined by looking at the first two words alone. After you look at the third word and see that it is a European measure of length (metric), you might then look for another measure of length. Because the only choice offered is *yard*, you might state the relationship as *European* is to *American* as it applies to countries and measures of length.

4. **The correct answer is C.** The relationship is that of cause and effect. Rounding the corners of a square produces a circle; rounding the corners of a rectangle produces an oval.

5. **The correct answer is A.** The relationship is that of object-purpose. The purpose of a lamp is to give light; the purpose of a furnace is to give heat.

6. **The correct answer is B.** The relationship is that of opposites or antonyms. *Clumsy* is the opposite of *skillful*; *awkward* is the opposite of *deft*.

7. **The correct answer is D.** The relationship is that of part to whole or, more specifically, that of a center to its surroundings. The *pit* is at the center of the *peach*; the *sun* is at the center of the *solar system*.

8. **The correct answer is B.** The relationship is that of antonyms. Each of the given words is a direction, and *up* and *down* are opposite to each other; *right* is the only option that fits this pattern.

9. **The correct answer is C.** The relationship is that of classification. *Ice cream* is a *dairy* product, and *hamburger* is a *meat* product.

10. **The correct answer is A.** The relationship is that of degree. A *tadpole* is an early developmental stage of a *frog*, and a *caterpillar* is an early developmental stage of a *butterfly*.

11. **The correct answer is C.** The relationship is that of whole to part. *Rabbits* are covered in *fur*, and *fish* are covered in *scales*.

12. **The correct answer is B.** The relationship is that of purpose. A *pencil* is a tool used to express written language (*writing*), and a *voice* is a tool used to express spoken language (*speaking*).

13. **The correct answer is B.** The relationship is that of association. "*Piece of cake*" is a common expression to say something is easy to do. "*Easy as pie*" is a similar common expression to suggest that something is easy to do.

14. **The correct answer is D.** The relationship is that of part to whole. A *muzzle* is a name for a *dog's* nose, and a *trunk* is the name for an *elephant's* nose.

15. **The correct answer is B.** The relationship is that of function. A *teacher* works in a *classroom*, and a *lawyer* practices in a *courtroom*.

16. **The correct answer is A.** The relationship is that of degree. A *firecracker* is a very small explosion compared to *fireworks*. Similarly, a *trickle* is a very small amount of water compared to a *waterfall*.

17. **The correct answer is C.** The relationship is that of worker to tool. A *brush* is a *painter's* tool, and a *chisel* is a *sculptor's* tool.

18. **The correct answer is D.** The relationship is that of classification. A *peony* is a specific type of *flower*, and a *pomegranate* is a specific type of *fruit*.

19. **The correct answer is B.** The relationship is that of purpose. The purpose of a *lid* is to close a *box*; the purpose of a *cork* is to close a *bottle*. *Cork* is easily associated with all the choices, so you must recognize the purposeful relationship of the initial pair to choose the correct answer.

20. **The correct answer is B.** The relationship of the terms is that of degree. *None* is the ultimate, the empty set, of *little*; *never* bears the same relationship to *infrequently*.

21. **The correct answer is C.** If you think in terms of a house, you can see that the terms on each side of the relationship are synonymous. You can *receive* a person into your home or *admit* the person. Once the person decides to *remain*, that person *settles* in.

22. **The correct answer is B.** The relationship is that of worker to tool. A *chemist* uses a *beaker* in the laboratory; a *geologist* uses a *hammer* to chip at rocks in the field or laboratory. Avoid the "trap" of choice C. A hammer is certainly used in construction, but the relationship of the first two terms requires that a person be involved to complete the analogy.

23. **The correct answer is D.** The relationship is that of antonyms. *Follow* is the opposite of *lead*, just as *dependent* is the opposite of *autonomous*.

24. **The correct answer is C.** This is a part-to-whole analogy. A *state* is part of a *country*; a *country* is part of a *continent*.

25. **The correct answer is A.** The relationship is one of true synonyms. *Obstruct* and *impede* are synonyms, as are *impenetrable* and *impervious*.

26. **The correct answer is B.** This analogy involves true antonyms. *Include* is the opposite of *omit*, and *acknowledge* is the opposite of *ignore*.

27. **The correct answer is D.** The relationship is that of characteristics, but you should be aware of the grammar component as well. *Youth* is a noun form; *young* is an adjective. Both refer to the early years. *Maturity* is a noun form, and *old* an adjective. *Maturity* and *old* refer to the later years of existence.

28. **The correct answer is C.** The relationship is part to whole. A *week* is part of a *month*; a *season* is part of a *year*.

29. The correct answer is D. The relationship is that of association. *Thanksgiving* is in *November*; *Christmas* is in *December.*

30. The correct answer is C. This is an antonym relationship. *Remember* and *forget* are opposites; *find* and *lose* are opposites.

31. The correct answer is A. The relationship is that of purpose. *Anchors* stop *ships*; *brakes* stop *automobiles*. The second word in each pair is the part used to stop the first word.

32. The correct answer is A. The relationship is that of synonyms. *End* and *abolish* are synonyms, and *begin* and *establish* are synonyms.

33. The correct answer is B. The relationship is that of object to action. Wood *decays*; iron *rusts.*

34. The correct answer is C. The relationship is that of part to whole. A *year* is one-tenth of a *decade*; a *decade* is one-tenth of a *century.*

35. The correct answer is A. The relationship is that of smaller to larger. *Flour* is ground *wheat*; *gravel* is broken *rock.*

36. The correct answer is B. The words in each pair are antonyms. *Attack* and *protect* are opposites, and *offense* and *defense* are opposites.

37. The correct answer is D. The words in each pair are antonyms. To *divide* and *multiply* are opposite actions, and to *subtract* and *add* are opposite actions.

38. The correct answer is C. Each pair matches the possessive adjective and possessive pronoun forms, the first for *I* (*my* and *mine*), and the second for *you* (*your* and *yours*).

39. The correct answer is D. The words in each pair are antonyms. *Leave* is the opposite of *stay* and *depart* is the opposite of *remain.*

40. The correct answer is D. The relationship is that of task to worker. Repairing a *car* is what a *mechanic* does; "repairing" people is what *doctors* do.

41. The correct answer is A. The relationship is that of part to whole. A *tree* is one part of a *forest*; a *person* is one part of a *crowd.*

42. The correct answer is C. The relationship is that of function. A *novelist* writes *fiction*; a *historian* writes about *facts.*

43. **The correct answer is D.** The words in each pair are antonyms. *Sickness* and *health* are opposites, and *death* and *life* are opposites.

44. **The correct answer is A.** The relationship is that of purpose. *Inventors* create new *machines*; *authors* create new *books*.

45. **The correct answer is B.** The relationship is that of classification. A *pound* is a unit of weight; a *mile* is a unit of *distance*.

46. **The correct answer is B.** The words in each pair are antonyms. *Conceal* and reveal are opposites, and *ascend* and *descend* are opposites.

47. **The correct answer is D.** The relationship is that of function. A *sword* is a tool used for *dueling*; a *pen* is a tool used for *writing*.

48. **The correct answer is B.** The relationship is that of definition. A *reprimand* is a verbal show of *disapproval*; a *compliment* is a verbal show of *approval*.

49. **The correct answer is C.** *Gold* is a deep shade of *yellow*; *ruby* is a deep shade of *red*.

50. **The correct answer is C.** Something that is *periodic* is *recurring*; someone (or something) who is *determined* is *perseverant*.

51. **The correct answer is B.** *Anarchy* occurs in the absence of *law*; *discord* is the result of a lack of *agreement*.

52. **The correct answer is A.** The relationship is that of classification. An *apple* is type of *fruit*; *carrot* is the only *vegetable* listed.

53. **The correct answer is C.** An *accident* may be the result of *carelessness*; a *response* may be the result of a *stimulus*.

54. **The correct answer is D.** Something *erroneous* is in error and subject to *correction*; something *ambiguous* is confusing and subject to *clarification*.

55. **The correct answer is B.** *Horses* were used for transportation before *automobiles*; *telegraphs* were used for communication before *telephones*.

56. **The correct answer is A.** The words in each pair are synonyms. To *intimidate* is to *bully*, and to *dismay* is to *unnerve*.

57. **The correct answer is B.** The words in each pair are antonyms. *Spontaneous* is the opposite of *calculated*, and *impromptu* is the opposite of *scheduled.*

58. **The correct answer is D.** *Critics* analyze and evaluate *plays*; *teachers* analyze and evaluate *essays.*

59. **The correct answer is D.** The relationship is that of part to whole. A *lion* is a member of a *pride*; a *fish* is a member of a *school.*

60. **The correct answer is B.** A *referee* enforces *rules*; a *conscience* enforces *morality.*

61. **The correct answer is C.** The second word in each pair refers to the theft of something represented by the first word in the pair.

62. **The correct answer is D.** *Books* consist of *paper* pages; *scrolls* are pieces of *parchment.*

63. **The correct answer is C.** The relationship is not of precise synonyms, but it is close. Both *beg* and *borrow* have to do with *ask for* and *take.* Both *offer* and *lend* have to do with *give. Repay* also has to do with *give*, but it implies a previous activity not implied in the relationship of *beg* and *borrow.*

64. **The correct answer is A.** One who is *lazy* is *inert.* One who *resists*, *refuses.* The relationship is one of characteristics or even synonyms.

65. **The correct answer is C.** A *circle* is the base of a *cylinder*; a *triangle* is the base of a *pyramid.* We have explained this as a part-to-whole relationship. The actual statement of the analogy is whole-to-part.

66. **The correct answer is B.** This is a true part-to-whole analogy. A *crocodile* is part of a larger group, *reptiles.* A *kangaroo* is part of a larger group, *mammals.*

67. **The correct answer is A.** *Wild* is a characteristic of *wolf* as *domestic* is a characteristic of both *dog* and *cat.* You must narrow further to choose the best answer. *Dog* is the domestic counterpart of *wolf*, so *dog* creates the best analogy.

68. **The correct answer is D.** This is a part-to-part relationship. Both *subject* and *predicate* are parts of a sentence; both *senator* and *representative* are parts of the congress. Choice A is an incorrect answer because a senator's relationship to congress is that of part-to-whole.

69. **The correct answer is B.** All four terms—*spread*, *scatter*, *separate*, and *distribute*—are synonyms.

70. **The correct answer is C.** The relationship is one of association or characteristic. *Exuberant* is an adjective used to describe *mood*; *adroit* is an adjective used to describe *movement*.

71. **The correct answer is D.** *Opposition* leads to *defiance*; *challenge* leads to *exertion*. The actual statement of the analogy is effect and its cause.

72. **The correct answer is B.** The relationship is that of true antonyms. The false choices are synonyms or partial antonyms, making this a very difficult analogy question.

73. **The correct answer is A.** This is an antonym relationship. *Erratic* and *predictable* are opposites, and *exorbitant* and *reasonable* are opposites.

74. **The correct answer is C.** This is a purpose relationship. A *tailor* follows a *pattern* to construct a piece of clothing; a *builder* follows a *blueprint* to construct a building.

75. **The correct answer is B.** This is a cause-and-effect relationship. When one *weeps*, one expels *tears*; when one *breathes*, one expels *carbon dioxide*.

Antonyms Drill

75 Questions

Directions: In the following questions, choose the word that means the opposite of the given word. Mark the corresponding letter on your answer sheet.

1. Grant means the *opposite* of

A. confiscate.
B. money.
C. land.
D. give.

2. Assent means the *opposite* of

A. agree.
B. disagree.
C. climb.
D. fall.

3. Smother means the *opposite* of

A. cuddle.
B. expel.
C. aerate.
D. rescue.

4. Loyal means the *opposite* of

A. lovely.
B. unfaithful.
C. unlucky.
D. usual.

5. Frigid is the *opposite* of
   - **A.** freezing.
   - **B.** arid.
   - **C.** scorching.
   - **D.** lukewarm.

6. Factual means the *opposite* of
   - **A.** untrue.
   - **B.** correct.
   - **C.** real.
   - **D.** instinctive.

7. Enormous means the *opposite* of
   - **A.** massive.
   - **B.** miniscule.
   - **C.** annoying.
   - **D.** sad.

8. Artificial means the *opposite* of
   - **A.** authentic.
   - **B.** man-made.
   - **C.** crafted.
   - **D.** surreal.

9. Stale means the *opposite* of
   - **A.** flat.
   - **B.** furious.
   - **C.** feverish.
   - **D.** fresh.

10. Unblemished means the *opposite* of
    - **A.** happy.
    - **B.** marked.
    - **C.** experienced.
    - **D.** curious.

11. Fanciful means the *opposite* of

A. bizarre.

B. realistic.

C. plain.

D. complicated.

12. Concealed means the *opposite* of

A. obvious.

B. guarded.

C. covered.

D. simple.

13. Disenchanted means the *opposite* of

A. overwhelmed.

B. lonely.

C. critical.

D. enthralled.

14. Exhausted is the *opposite* of

A. relieved.

B. drained.

C. refreshed.

D. amused.

15. Regretful means the *opposite* of

A. unapologetic.

B. reformed.

C. simple.

D. unimaginative.

16. Uninspired means the *opposite* of

A. bored.

B. motivated.

C. agitated.

D. prepared.

17. Agony means the *opposite* of

A. comfort.

B. dislike.

C. knowledge.

D. amusing.

18. Manual means the *opposite* of

A. spectacular.

B. illegal.

C. automated.

D. slowly.

19. Injustice means the *opposite* of

A. freedom.

B. fairness.

C. loyalty.

D. captivity.

20. Cynical means the *opposite* of

A. optimistic.

B. joyous.

C. cranky.

D. insecure.

21. Repentant means the *opposite* of

A. boring.

B. inattentive.

C. unapologetic.

D. artistic.

22. Frank means the *opposite* of

A. imaginary.

B. deceitful.

C. easy.

D. beautiful.

23. Grasp means the *opposite* of

- **A.** pull.
- **B.** underestimate.
- **C.** misunderstand.
- **D.** donate.

24. Neglect means the *opposite* of

- **A.** analyze.
- **B.** hinder.
- **C.** create.
- **D.** support.

25. Multiply means the *opposite* of

- **A.** add.
- **B.** reduce.
- **C.** reject.
- **D.** enlarge.

26. Attract means the *opposite* of

- **A.** find.
- **B.** divide.
- **C.** forget.
- **D.** repel.

27. Enhanced means the *opposite* of

- **A.** plain.
- **B.** extraordinary.
- **C.** alone.
- **D.** fortified.

28. Carnivore means the *opposite* of

- **A.** eater.
- **B.** animal.
- **C.** vegetarian.
- **D.** plant.

29. Unstable means the *opposite* of
    A. mean.
    B. aware.
    C. firm.
    D. content.

30. Disengaged means the *opposite* of
    A. attached.
    B. bored.
    C. optimistic.
    D. farfetched.

31. Fetching means the *opposite* of
    A. dizzying.
    B. endearing.
    C. unappealing.
    D. romantic.

32. Rage means the *opposite* of
    A. discomfort.
    B. serenity.
    C. lethargy.
    D. sensibility.

33. Agile means the *opposite* of
    A. temperamental.
    B. smart.
    C. complicated.
    D. sluggish.

34. Profit means the *opposite* of
    A. success.
    B. loss.
    C. equality.
    D. disaster.

35. Swear means the *opposite* of

A. proclaim.

B. injure.

C. deny.

D. affirm.

36. Remote means the *opposite* of

A. immediate.

B. distant.

C. ambitious.

D. repetitive.

37. Oblivious means the *opposite* of

A. light.

B. wise.

C. aware.

D. indignant.

38. Demanding means the *opposite* of

A. chaotic.

B. easy.

C. humiliating.

D. fiery.

39. Retreat means the *opposite* of

A. bring.

B. exist.

C. wander.

D. advance.

40. Meandering means the *opposite* of

A. general.

B. practical.

C. funny.

D. straightforward.

41. Crabby means the *opposite* of

A. animalistic.

B. pleasant.

C. humorous.

D. grouchy.

42. Anonymous means the *opposite* of

A. known.

B. adept.

C. wealthy.

D. shy.

43. Demolish means the *opposite* of

A. tarnish.

B. love.

C. create.

D. injure.

44. Anxious means the *opposite* of

A. neurotic.

B. confident.

C. difficult.

D. permanent.

45. Bankrupt means the *opposite* of

A. corrupt.

B. artistic.

C. virtuous.

D. wealthy.

46. Jeopardy means the *opposite* of

A. safety.

B. knowledge.

C. fairness.

D. loyalty.

47. Sympathetic means the *opposite* of

A. receptive.

B. intuitive.

C. ruthless.

D. patriotic.

48. Literal means the *opposite* of

A. immediate.

B. floral.

C. imprecise.

D. symbolic.

49. Consecutive means the *opposite* of

A. complicated.

B. interrupted.

C. frequent.

D. basic.

50. State means the *opposite* of

A. imply.

B. demand.

C. discover.

D. remember.

51. Dishonesty means the *opposite* of

A. deception.

B. integrity.

C. phoniness.

D. friendliness.

52. Mysterious means the *opposite* of

A. impressive.

B. fortuitous.

C. ambitious.

D. visible.

53. Farfetched means the *opposite* of

A. immediate.

B. ornate.

C. believable.

D. enviable.

54. Sedate means the *opposite* of

A. boisterous.

B. lackluster.

C. placid.

D. generous.

55. Inconsiderate means the *opposite* of

A. irresponsible.

B. underhanded.

C. arrogant.

D. selfless.

56. Harmonious means the *opposite* of

A. warlike.

B. cooperative.

C. interesting.

D. determined.

57. Obscure means the *opposite* of

A. misunderstood.

B. incoherent.

C. famous.

D. distant.

58. Appealing means the *opposite* of

A. inviting.

B. defensive.

C. unclean.

D. repulsive.

59. Modern means the *opposite* of
   - **A.** influential.
   - **B.** outdated.
   - **C.** controversial.
   - **D.** recent.

60. Neutral means the *opposite* of
   - **A.** compassionate.
   - **B.** passionate.
   - **C.** emboldened.
   - **D.** empty.

61. Remarkable means the *opposite* of
   - **A.** impatient.
   - **B.** rate.
   - **C.** ordinary.
   - **D.** sparkling.

62. Unfortunate means the *opposite* of
   - **A.** lucky.
   - **B.** excited.
   - **C.** reverent.
   - **D.** angry.

63. Sincere means the *opposite* of
   - **A.** combative.
   - **B.** enraged.
   - **C.** phony.
   - **D.** amused.

64. Thrifty means the *opposite* of
   - **A.** calm.
   - **B.** frugal.
   - **C.** agitated.
   - **D.** wasteful.

65. Retired means the *opposite* of

A. exhausted.

B. active.

C. regretful.

D. original.

66. Cramped means the *opposite* of

A. spacious.

B. blissful.

C. artistic.

D. distant.

67. Rigid means the *opposite* of

A. wistful.

B. optimistic.

C. flexible.

D. edible.

68. Tardy means the *opposite* of

A. functional.

B. punctual.

C. emotional.

D. rational.

69. Improvised means the *opposite* of

A. prepared.

B. fictional.

C. unplanned.

D. celebrated.

70. Steady means the *opposite* of

A. doomed.

B. elated.

C. unflappable.

D. unreliable.

71. Optional means the *opposite* of
   - A. mandatory.
   - B. considerate.
   - C. fateful.
   - D. sectional.

72. Creative means the *opposite* of
   - A. inventive.
   - B. unimaginative.
   - C. active.
   - D. reactive.

73. Refuse means the *opposite* of
   - A. operate.
   - B. generate.
   - C. pander.
   - D. accept.

74. Appalling means the *opposite* of
   - A. nauseating.
   - B. heartbreaking.
   - C. provoking.
   - D. satisfying.

75. Erode means the *opposite* of
   - A. eliminate.
   - B. build.
   - C. display.
   - D. find.

Answer Key and Explanations

1. A	16. B	31. C	46. A	61. C
2. B	17. A	32. B	47. C	62. A
3. C	18. C	33. D	48. D	63. C
4. B	19. B	34. B	49. B	64. D
5. C	20. A	35. C	50. A	65. B
6. A	21. C	36. A	51. B	66. A
7. B	22. B	37. C	52. D	67. C
8. A	23. C	38. B	53. C	68. B
9. D	24. D	39. D	54. A	69. A
10. B	25. B	40. D	55. D	70. D
11. B	26. D	41. B	56. A	71. A
12. A	27. A	42. A	57. C	72. B
13. D	28. C	43. C	58. D	73. D
14. C	29. C	44. B	59. B	74. D
15. A	30. A	45. D	60. B	75. B

1. **The correct answer is A.** In this case, the word *grant* means "to give," so its opposite is to *confiscate.* Remember that you are looking for the antonym, not the synonym. Also, don't be tricked by the other meanings for *grant*—a sum of money (choice B) or a tract of land (choice C).

2. **The correct answer is B.** To *assent* is to agree; its opposite is to *disagree. Assent* is in no way related to *ascend* (to rise) or *ascent* (the act of rising or going upward).

3. **The correct answer is C.** To *smother* is to shut out all air; to *aerate* is to supply with air. Although the act of *smothering* might be reversed by rescuing, *aerate* is the more direct antonym.

4. **The correct answer is B.** *Loyal* means "faithful." The best antonym is *unfaithful.*

5. **The correct answer is C.** *Frigid* means "cold," so *scorching*, or "hot," is the opposite.

6. **The correct answer is A.** Something that is *factual* is true, so *untrue* is the opposite.

7. **The correct answer is B.** *Enormous* means "large," so *miniscule*, or "small," is the opposite.

8. **The correct answer is A.** *Artificial* means "fake," so *authentic*, or "real," is the opposite.

9. **The correct answer is D.** *Stale* means "old or outdated," so *fresh* is the opposite.

10. **The correct answer is B.** *Unblemished* means "pure or unmarked," so *marked* is the opposite.

11. **The correct answer is B.** *Fanciful* means "imaginary or unreal," so *realistic* is the opposite.

12. **The correct answer is A.** *Concealed* means "hidden or disguised," so *obvious* is the opposite.

13. **The correct answer is D.** *Disenchanted* means "disillusioned or disappointed," so *enthralled* (which means "fascinated") is the opposite.

14. **The correct answer is C.** *Exhausted* means "tired," so *refreshed* is the opposite.

15. **The correct answer is A.** *Regretful* means "apologetic or full of regrets," so *unapologetic* is the opposite.

16. **The correct answer is B.** *Uninspired* means "lacking enthusiasm or purpose," so *motivated* is the opposite.

17. **The correct answer is A.** *Agony* means "extreme discomfort or unhappiness," so *comfort* is the opposite.

18. **The correct answer is C.** Something that's done *manually* is done by hand, so *automated* (or performed automatically) is the opposite.

19. **The correct answer is B.** *Injustice* means "unfairness," so *fairness* is the opposite.

20. **The correct answer is A.** *Cynical* means "pessimistic," so *optimistic* is the opposite.

21. **The correct answer is C.** *Repentant* means "apologetic or regretful," so *unapologetic* is the opposite.

22. **The correct answer is B.** *Frank* means "honest," so *deceitful* (or "dishonest") is the opposite.

23. **The correct answer is C.** To *grasp* something is to understand it, so *misunderstand* is the opposite.

24. **The correct answer is D.** *Neglect* means "to abandon or treat something with a lack of care," so *support* is the opposite.

25. **The correct answer is B.** To *multiply* is to expand the number of things, so *reduce* is the opposite.

26. **The correct answer is D.** To *attract* means "to draw something in," so *repel*, or push away, is the opposite.

27. **The correct answer is A.** *Enhanced* means "heightened or improved," so *plain* is the opposite.

28. **The correct answer is C.** A *carnivore* eats meat, so *vegetarian* is the opposite.

29. **The correct answer is C.** Something that is *unstable* is unsupported or insecure, so *firm* is the opposite.

30. **The correct answer is A.** *Disengaged* means "disconnected," so *attached*, or "connected," is the opposite.

31. **The correct answer is C.** *Fetching* means "attractive or appealing," so *unappealing* is the opposite.

32. **The correct answer is B.** *Rage* is strong, emotional anger, so *serenity*, or peace, is the opposite.

33. **The correct answer is D.** *Agile* means "nimble or lively," so *sluggish*, or "slow and listless," is the opposite.

34. **The correct answer is B.** *Profit* is income or gain, so *loss* is the opposite.

35. **The correct answer is C.** One of the meanings of *swear* is to declare or affirm something, so among these options, *deny* is the opposite.

36. **The correct answer is A.** *Remote* means "distant," so *immediate*, or "close," is the opposite.

37. **The correct answer is C.** To be *oblivious* is to not understand what's happening, so *aware* is the opposite.

38. **The correct answer is B.** Something that is *demanding* is difficult, so *easy* is the opposite.

39. **The correct answer is D.** *Retreat* means "to pull back," so *advance*, or "move forward," is the opposite.

40. The correct answer is D. *Meandering* means "winding or complicated," so *straightforward* is the opposite.

41. The correct answer is B. *Crabby* is a synonym for *cranky* or *grouchy*, so *pleasant*, or "good-natured," is the opposite.

42. The correct answer is A. *Anonymous* means "unnamed or unknown," so *known* is the opposite.

43. The correct answer is C. To *demolish* is to destroy, so *create* is the opposite.

44. The correct answer is B. *Anxious* means "nervous," so *confident* is the opposite.

45. The correct answer is D. To be *bankrupt* is to be without wealth, so *wealthy* is the opposite.

46. The correct answer is A. *Jeopardy* means "danger," so *safety* is the opposite.

47. The correct answer is C. *Sympathetic* means "understanding or kind, so *ruthless*, which means "cruel or unfeeling," is the opposite.

48. The correct answer is D. *Literal* means "a strict or faithful representation," so *symbolic*, or "figurative," is the opposite.

49. The correct answer is B. *Consecutive* means "in a sequence or in a row," so *interrupted* is the opposite.

50. The correct answer is A. To *state* is to say something directly, so *imply*, or "make an indirect inference," is the opposite.

51. The correct answer is B. *Dishonesty* means "lying or deceit," so *integrity*, which means "honesty," is the opposite.

52. The correct answer is D. When something is *mysterious*, it is difficult to see the truth, so *visible* is the opposite.

53. The correct answer is C. *Farfetched* means "unlikely or implausible," so *believable* is the opposite.

54. The correct answer is A. *Sedate* means "calm or placid," so *boisterous*, which means "noisy or excitable," is the opposite.

55. The correct answer is D. *Inconsiderate* means "not thinking of others," so *selfless* is the opposite.

56. **The correct answer is A.** *Harmonious* means "free from disagreement," so *warlike*, or "full of conflict", would be the opposite.

57. **The correct answer is C.** As an adjective, *obscure* means "not well known," so *famous* would be the opposite.

58. **The correct answer is D.** *Appealing* means "attractive or tempting," so *repulsive*, or "unattractive," is the opposite.

59. **The correct answer is B.** *Modern* means "current or contemporary," which is the opposite of *outdated*.

60. **The correct answer is B.** *Neutral* means "in the middle," or" impartial," so *passionate*, having strong feelings, is the opposite.

61. **The correct answer is C.** If something is *remarkable*, it is extraordinary or noteworthy, so *ordinary* is the opposite.

62. **The correct answer is A.** *Unfortunate* means "unlucky or disastrous," so *lucky* is the opposite.

63. **The correct answer is C.** *Sincere* means "genuine or honest," so *phony* is the opposite.

64. **The correct answer is D.** *Thrifty* means" careful with money," or "frugal," so *wasteful* is the opposite.

65. **The correct answer is B.** *Retired* means "no longer working," so *active* is the opposite.

66. **The correct answer is A.** A *cramped* space is crowded or small, so *spacious* is the opposite.

67. **The correct answer is C.** *Rigid* means "stiff or unbending," so *flexible*, or changeable, is the opposite.

68. **The correct answer is B.** *Tardy* means "late," so *punctual*, which means "on time," is the opposite.

69. **The correct answer is A.** If something is *improvised*, it's created or done on the fly. *Prepared*, or planned, is the opposite.

70. **The correct answer is D.** *Steady* means "stable or grounded," so *unreliable*, or "unstable," is the opposite.

71. The correct answer is A. *Optional* means "voluntary" or "not required," so *mandatory* (required) is the opposite.

72. The correct answer is B. *Creative* means "inventive or imaginative," so *unimaginative* is the opposite.

73. The correct answer is D. To *refuse* is to reject, so *accept* (or take) is the opposite.

74. The correct answer is D. *Appalling* means "awful or inexcusable," so *satisfying*, or "fulfilling and nourishing," is the opposite.

75. The correct answer is B. To *erode* is to wear away, so the opposite of that would be to build something up.

Synonyms Drill

75 Questions

Directions: In the following questions, choose the word that means the same as or about the same as the italicized word. Mark the corresponding letter on your answer sheet.

1. A *precocious* child is

A. precious.
B. proper.
C. tall.
D. quick.

2. A *sallow* face is

A. ruddy.
B. sickly.
C. healthy.
D. young.

3. A *stench* is a

A. puddle of slimy water.
B. pile of debris.
C. foul odor.
D. dead animal.

4. A *sullen* child is

A. grayish yellow.
B. soaking wet.
C. very dirty.
D. angrily silent.

5. *Meager* most nearly means
   A. well received.
   B. long overdue.
   C. scanty.
   D. valuable.

6. A *novice* is
   A. competitive.
   B. frightened.
   C. inexperienced.
   D. skilled.

7. A *tenant* is a(n)
   A. occupant.
   B. landlord.
   C. owner.
   D. farmer.

8. *Calculated* most nearly means
   A. multiplied.
   B. compared.
   C. answered.
   D. figured out.

9. Critical *acclaim* is
   A. amazement.
   B. praise.
   C. booing.
   D. laughter.

10. *Erect* most nearly means
    A. paint.
    B. design.
    C. destroy.
    D. construct.

11. *Relish* most nearly means

A. care.

B. enjoy.

C. amusement.

D. speed.

12. *Impose* most nearly means

A. disguise.

B. escape.

C. require.

D. tax.

13. An *alias* is a(n)

A. enemy.

B. sidekick.

C. hero.

D. assumed name.

14. *Itinerant* most nearly means

A. traveling.

B. shrewd.

C. insurance.

D. aggressive.

15. *Ample* most nearly means

A. overweight.

B. enthusiastic.

C. well-shaped.

D. plentiful.

16. A *terse* response is

A. pointed.

B. trivial.

C. nervous.

D. lengthy.

17. *Increment* most nearly means
   - A. an improvisation.
   - B. an increase.
   - C. feces.
   - D. specification.

18. A *misconstrued* message is
   - A. ignored.
   - B. clearly understood.
   - C. confidential.
   - D. interpreted erroneously.

19. *Vestige* most nearly means
   - A. design.
   - B. trace.
   - C. strap.
   - D. robe.

20. *Capitulate* most nearly means
   - A. surrender.
   - B. execute.
   - C. finance.
   - D. retreat.

21. An *extenuating* circumstance is
   - A. mitigating.
   - B. opposing.
   - C. incriminating.
   - D. distressing.

22. A *subservient* employee is
   - A. underestimated.
   - B. underhanded.
   - C. subordinate.
   - D. evasive.

23. *Image* most nearly means

A. newspaper.

B. picture.

C. fantasy.

D. oldest.

24. A *garrulous* salesperson is

A. complaining.

B. overly friendly.

C. careless.

D. overly talkative.

25. *Stimulate* most nearly means

A. reward.

B. give an incentive to.

C. antagonize.

D. lower the efficiency of.

26. *Instill* most nearly means

A. measure exactly.

B. predict accurately.

C. impart gradually.

D. restrain effectively.

27. *Irrelevant* testimony is

A. unproven.

B. hard to understand.

C. not pertinent.

D. insincere.

28. A *prior* appointment is

A. private.

B. definite.

C. later.

D. previous.

29. *Deplete* most nearly means

A. exhaust.

B. include.

C. deliver.

D. reject.

30. A *candid* opinion is

A. biased.

B. written.

C. honest.

D. confidential.

31. *Ailment* most nearly means

A. illness.

B. food allergy.

C. operation.

D. problem.

32. *Nonchalance* most nearly means

A. interest.

B. poverty.

C. care.

D. indifference.

33. A *fundamental* skill is

A. adequate.

B. detailed.

C. basic.

D. truthful.

34. *Reluctance* most nearly means

A. eagerness.

B. ability.

C. unreliability.

D. unwillingness.

35. A *diligent* worker is

A. incompetent.

B. careless.

C. cheerful.

D. industrious.

36. *Intact* most nearly means

A. undamaged.

B. unattended.

C. a total loss.

D. repaired.

37. *Resolved* most nearly means

A. offered.

B. refused.

C. hesitated.

D. determined.

38. *Rigorously* most nearly means

A. usually.

B. never.

C. strictly.

D. leniently.

39. An *amicable* relationship is

A. friendly.

B. tender.

C. accessible.

D. inimical.

40. *Clamor* most nearly means

A. murmur.

B. noise.

C. questions.

D. singing.

41. A *declined* invitation is
  A. suspected.
  B. misunderstood.
  C. consented.
  D. refused.

42. A *noxious* odor is
  A. concentrated.
  B. harmful.
  C. gaseous.
  D. heavy.

43. A *trivial* matter is
  A. of a personal nature.
  B. very significant.
  C. interesting and educational.
  D. of little importance.

44. An *obsolete* machine is
  A. complicated.
  B. out of date.
  C. highly suitable.
  D. reliable.

45. *Dexterity* most nearly means
  A. skill.
  B. punctuality.
  C. courtesy.
  D. cooperation.

46. *Placate* most nearly means
  A. escort.
  B. appease.
  C. interview.
  D. detain.

47. An *expedient* solution is

A. inconvenient.

B. expensive.

C. advantageous.

D. time-consuming.

48. *Prerogatives* most nearly means

A. ideals.

B. privileges.

C. demands.

D. weapons.

49. A *prolific* tree is

A. talented.

B. popular.

C. forward looking.

D. productive.

50. A *frugal* person is

A. friendly.

B. hostile.

C. thoughtful.

D. economical.

51. *Imperative* most nearly means

A. impending.

B. impossible.

C. compulsory.

D. flawless.

52. *Access* most nearly means

A. too much.

B. admittance.

C. extra.

D. arrival.

53. A *subsequent* event is
   A. preceding.
   B. early.
   C. following.
   D. winning.

54. *Heritage* most nearly means
   A. will.
   B. believer.
   C. legend.
   D. inheritance.

55. A *cultured* pearl is
   A. malformed.
   B. decomposed.
   C. exiled.
   D. cultivated.

56. *Atone* most nearly means
   A. repent.
   B. rebel.
   C. sound.
   D. impotent.

57. A *predatory* animal is
   A. introductory.
   B. intellectual.
   C. preaching.
   D. carnivorous.

58. A coat of *mail* is
   A. armor.
   B. seaside.
   C. rapid travel.
   D. wool.

59. A *florid* complexion is

A. seedy.

B. ruddy.

C. hot.

D. overflowing.

60. *Feasible* most nearly means

A. simple.

B. practical.

C. visible.

D. lenient.

61. *Supplant* most nearly means

A. approve.

B. displace.

C. widespread.

D. appease.

62. A *prevalent* opinion is

A. current.

B. permanent.

C. widespread.

D. temporary.

63. *Contend* most nearly means

A. assert.

B. agree.

C. temper.

D. appease.

64. *Enthrall* most nearly means

A. throw in.

B. captivate.

C. support.

D. deceive.

65. *Desecrate* most nearly means

A. to improve upon.

B. to occupy.

C. to profane.

D. to hide.

66. *Ostracize* most nearly means

A. delight.

B. exclude.

C. include.

D. hide.

67. An *exorbitant* rent is

A. priceless.

B. worthless.

C. extensive.

D. excessive.

68. *Obliterate* most nearly means

A. annihilate.

B. review.

C. demonstrate.

D. detect.

69. *Austerity* most nearly means

A. priority.

B. anxiety.

C. self-discipline.

D. solitude.

70. *Salutary* most nearly means

A. popular.

B. beneficial.

C. urgent.

D. forceful.

71. *Acquiesce* most nearly means

A. endeavor.

B. discharge.

C. comply.

D. inquire.

72. *Diffidence* most nearly means

A. shyness.

B. distinction.

C. interval.

D. conflict.

73. *Reprisal* most nearly means

A. retaliation.

B. advantage.

C. warning.

D. denial.

74. *Capitulate* most nearly means

A. repeat.

B. surrender.

C. finance.

D. retreat.

75. A *reputable* source is

A. infamous.

B. capable.

C. significant.

D. respected.

Answer Key and Explanations

1. D	16. A	31. A	46. B	61. B
2. B	17. B	32. D	47. C	62. C
3. C	18. D	33. C	48. B	63. A
4. D	19. B	34. D	49. D	64. B
5. C	20. A	35. D	50. D	65. C
6. D	21. A	36. A	51. C	66. B
7. A	22. C	37. D	52. B	67. D
8. D	23. B	38. C	53. C	68. A
9. B	24. D	39. A	54. D	69. C
10. D	25. B	40. B	55. D	70. B
11. B	26. C	41. D	56. A	71. C
12. C	27. C	42. B	57. D	72. A
13. D	28. D	43. D	58. A	73. A
14. A	29. A	44. B	59. B	74. B
15. D	30. C	45. A	60. B	75. D

1. **The correct answer is D.** *Precocious* refers to is one who is quick or advanced in development: *Precocious* kids were a constant feature in '80s family sitcoms.

2. **The correct answer is B.** A sallow complexion is of a sickly, yellowish hue: After a prolonged illness, he reappeared, thin and *sallow*, but happy to be alive.

3. **The correct answer is C.** A stench is an offensive smell or foul odor: "Let me shower and remove the *stench* of work from my being!" he declared dramatically.

4. **The correct answer is D.** *Sullen* means "morose" or "angrily silent": The *sullen* teenager slumped in the corner after being grounded by his parents.

5. **The correct answer is C.** *Meager* means "lacking in quality or quantity": His *meager* belongings did not affect his positive outlook.

6. **The correct answer is D.** *Novice* means "inexperienced": The *novice* chef presented burnt offerings for the first course.

7. **The correct answer is A.** A tenant is an occupant: The landlord handed the keys to the new *tenant.*

8. **The correct answer is D.** *Calculated* means "worked or figured out": The couple *calculated* the cost of buying a new car.

9. **The correct answer is B.** Acclaim is praise and approval: The actor's performance earned him much critical *acclaim.*

10. **The correct answer is D.** *Erect* means "to raise, construct, set up, or assemble": The construction team began to *erect* the new City Hall.

11. **The correct answer is B.** To relish something is to enjoy it: I *relish* the idea of a long and relaxing vacation.

12. **The correct answer is C.** To impose is to establish or require by authority: The state will *impose* a new sales tax on candy purchases.

13. **The correct answer is D.** An alias is an assumed name: In the novel *Les Misérables*, Monsieur Madeleine was one *alias* used by the escaped convict Jean Valjean.

14. **The correct answer is A.** *Itinerant* means "traveling from place to place": The *itinerant* sales rep's route covers the Pacific Northwest.

15. **The correct answer is D.** That which is ample is large, spacious, abundant, or plentiful: We had an *ample* supply of baked goods for the carnival cake walk.

16. **The correct answer is A.** *Terse* means "concise" and "succinct": Elle's *terse* reply made it obvious that he had upset her.

17. **The correct answer is B.** An increment is a specified increase, usually a small one: He was denied the salary *increment* given to the other employees.

18. **The correct answer is D.** To misconstrue is to misinterpret: The background noise caused her to *misconstrue* the phone message, and she missed her ride.

19. **The correct answer is B.** A vestige is a trace of something lost or vanished: His perfect manners are a *vestige* of a society long gone.
    Vestige is a difficult word, one that is picked up in the course of wide reading.

20. **The correct answer is A.** To capitulate is to give in, give up, or surrender: The protesters were not ready to *capitulate* although they knew theirs was a lost cause.

21. **The correct answer is A.** *Extenuating* can mean "mitigating," or "providing a partial excuse or justification for something": Airlines will sometime defer fines when passengers change their flights due to *extenuating* circumstances.
    If you missed this question, do not be upset. Both the word and its definition are very high-level words.

22. **The correct answer is C.** *Subservient* means "inferior," "subordinate," or "submissive": The apprentice became frustrated with his *subservient* role in the business.

23. **The correct answer is B.** An image is a picture: The entire wall was decorated with the same *image* of her dog customized with 50 filter effects.

24. **The correct answer is D.** To be garrulous is to be overly talkative: Miss Payne was a *garrulous* old gossip.

25. **The correct answer is B.** *Stimulate* means "to quicken" or "to provide an incentive to": The new bonus program was intended to *stimulate* productivity.

26. **The correct answer is C.** To instill is to impart gradually or set permanently in one's mindset: The teacher tried to *instill* a love for reading in her students.

27. **The correct answer is C.** Something *irrelevant* is not pertinent or has nothing to do with the matter at hand": His lengthy reports contained many *irrelevant* statements.

28. **The correct answer is D.** *Prior* means "earlier in time or order," or "previous to": He had a *prior* appointment with the manager.

29. **The correct answer is A.** Something depleted has been emptied, exhausted, or reduced to a great amount: The supply of pamphlets has been *depleted.*

30. **The correct answer is C.** *Candid* means "honest" and "fair": Mr. Dorman asked for a *candid* opinion about his performance.

31. **The correct answer is A.** An ailment is a sickness or illness: The patient was being treated for a serious *ailment.*

32. **The correct answer is D.** *Nonchalance* means "indifference" or "apathy": The defendant's *nonchalance* was disturbing to the courtroom observers.

33. **The correct answer is C.** *Fundamental* means "basic": Our argument was based on *fundamental* economic principles.

34. **The correct answer is D.** Reluctance is an unwillingness to act: Miss Fulton showed her *reluctance* to serve as a relief operator.

35. **The correct answer is D.** *Diligent* means "industrious" or "hard-working": His assistant was a *diligent* worker.

36. **The correct answer is A.** *Intact* means "undamaged" or "in one piece": The vehicle was left *intact* after the accident.

37. **The correct answer is D.** *Resolved* means "made a firm decision about" or "determined to do": He *resolved* to act at once.

38. **The correct answer is C.** Something done rigorously is done "rigidly" or "strictly": The departmental rules were *rigorously* enforced.

39. **The correct answer is A.** *Amicable* means "friendly" or "agreeable": Relations between England and the United States are *amicable.*

40. **The correct answer is B.** A clamor is violent shouting: I could plainly hear the *clamor* of the crowd.

41. **The correct answer is D.** Something declined is turned down or refused: He *declined* our offers to help him.

42. **The correct answer is B.** *Noxious* means "unhealthy" or "bad for the body": It was reported that *noxious* fumes were escaping from the tanks.

43. **The correct answer is D.** Something trivial is of little importance: The girls spent their evening discussing *trivial* matters.

44. **The correct answer is B.** *Obsolete* means "past its time of usefulness": This equipment is *obsolete.*

45. **The correct answer is A.** Dexterity is mental skill or quickness: The dispatcher was commended for her *dexterity.*

46. **The correct answer is B.** To placate is to appease or to lessen one's anger: He was asked to *placate* the irate customer.

47. **The correct answer is C.** *Expedient* means "advantageous" or "suitable to bring about a desired result given the circumstances": This is the most *expedient* method for achieving the desired results.

48. The correct answer is B. Prerogatives are rights or privileges: The men refused to give up their *prerogatives* without a struggle.

49. The correct answer is D. *Prolific* means "producing fruit in abundance": The *prolific* apple trees kept our barrels filled.

50. The correct answer is D. *Frugal* means "thrifty" or economical": By living a *frugal* life as a young woman, the retired teacher could now travel around the world.

51. The correct answer is C. *Imperative* means "compulsory or necessary": It is *imperative* that you see a doctor before the rash spreads.

52. The correct answer is B. Access is admittance: Jim is the only person who has *access* to the safe.

53. The correct answer is C. *Subsequent* means "following": In *subsequent* meetings we will be discussing the progress of this project.

54. The correct answer is D. *Heritage* means "inheritance" or "legacy": Americans were left a wonderful *heritage* by their ancestors.

55. The correct answer is D. *Cultured* means "cultivated," or produced by artificial means": *Cultured* pearls are less expensive than natural ones.

56. The correct answer is A. *Atone* means "to repent": The prisoner wanted to *atone* for his past crimes.

57. The correct answer is D. *Predatory* means "living by feeding on other animals," or "carnivorous": Lions are *predatory* animals.

58. The correct answer is A. Mail is armor composed of metal links or plates: Swords could not pierce a knight's suit of *mail.*

59. The correct answer is B. *Florid* means "having a ruddy reddish skin tone": The salesman had a *florid* complexion.

60. The correct answer is B. *Feasible* means "possible or achievable": The engineers thought the bridge would be economically *feasible.*

61. The correct answer is B. *Supplant* means "to displace or replace.": In industry today, new ideas constantly *supplant* older ones.

62. **The correct answer is C.** *Prevalent* means "widespread": A belief in the existence of witches was *prevalent* during the seventeenth century.

63. **The correct answer is A.** *Contend* means "assert or argue." The defense attorney plans to *contend* that his client was out of town when the crime was committed.

64. **The correct answer is B.** To enthrall is to captivate or charm: The storyteller was able to *enthrall* his young audience with his tales of his pet iguana.

65. **The correct answer is C.** *Desecrate* means "to profane or treat abusively": Vandals attempted to *desecrate* the flag by burning it.

66. **The correct answer is B.** *Ostracize* means "to exclude": Children often *ostracize* classmates who seem different in any way.

67. **The correct answer is D.** *Exorbitant* means "excessive": Some tenants are charged *exorbitant* rents by greedy landlords.

68. **The correct answer is A.** To obliterate is to annihilate: Humankind could *obliterate* itself in an atomic war.

69. **The correct answer is C.** Austerity is self-discipline: Crude oil shortages make *austerity* a necessity.

70. **The correct answer is B.** *Salutary* means "beneficial": A decrease in contagious diseases shows the *salutary* effects of preventive medicine.

71. **The correct answer is C.** To acquiesce is to comply: The police were forced to *acquiesce* to the kidnapper's demands.

72. **The correct answer is A.** Diffidence is shyness: Janet's *diffidence* kept her from participating in class discussions.

73. **The correct answer is A.** Reprisal is retaliation: She refused to testify against her boss to avoid *reprisal.*

74. **The correct answer is B.** To capitulate is to surrender: Mr. Jones was forced to *capitulate* to his students' demands.

75. **The correct answer is D.** *Reputable* means "respected": I knew the history book was a *reputable* source because its author is renowned for accurately reporting events.

Verbal Logic and Verbal Classification Drill

75 Questions

Directions: For questions 1–40, mark one answer—the answer you think is best—for each problem.

1. Which word does not belong with the others?
   - **A.** Hurricane
   - **B.** Tornado
   - **C.** Typhoon
   - **D.** Earthquake

2. Which word does not belong with the others?
   - **A.** Sundial
   - **B.** Watch
   - **C.** Time
   - **D.** Clock

3. Which word does not belong with the others?
   - **A.** Light
   - **B.** Elated
   - **C.** Gleeful
   - **D.** Joyous

4. Which word does not belong with the others?
   - **A.** Robbery
   - **B.** Murder
   - **C.** Death
   - **D.** Burglary

5. Which word does not belong with the others?
   - A. Tuberculosis
   - B. Measles
   - C. Fever
   - D. Flu

6. Which word does not belong with the others?
   - A. Stag
   - B. Monkey
   - C. Bull
   - D. Ram

7. Which word does not belong with the others?
   - A. Car
   - B. Plane
   - C. Van
   - D. Truck

8. Which word does not belong with the others?
   - A. Ostrich
   - B. Elephant
   - C. Whale
   - D. Zebra

9. Which word does not belong with the others?
   - A. Stripes
   - B. Dots
   - C. Plaid
   - D. Fabric

10. Which word does not belong with the others?
    - A. Centimeter
    - B. Inch
    - C. Pound
    - D. Foot

11. Which word does not belong with the others?
   A. Atlantic
   B. Pacific
   C. Australia
   D. Indian

12. Which word does not belong with the others?
   A. Baseball
   B. Hockey
   C. Soccer
   D. Football

13. Which word does not belong with the others?
   A. Saxophone
   B. Viola
   C. Harp
   D. Guitar

14. Which word does not belong with the others?
   A. Email
   B. Letter
   C. Text message
   D. Phone call

15. Which word does not belong with the others?
   A. Stop
   B. Yield
   C. Road
   D. Caution

16. Which word does not belong with the others?
   A. Soap opera
   B. Jazz
   C. Country
   D. Rock

17. Which word does not belong with the others?

A. Frigid

B. Glacial

C. Blistering

D. Frosty

18. Which word does not belong with the others?

A. Spring

B. Halt

C. Leap

D. Vault

19. Which word does not belong with the others?

A. Florist

B. Grocery store

C. Bakery

D. Ice cream parlor

20. Which word does not belong with the others?

A. Over

B. Under

C. Around

D. Floor

21. Which word does not belong with the others?

A. Forked

B. Whole

C. Split

D. Diverged

22. Which word does not belong with the others?

A. Noun

B. Adjective

C. Verb

D. Parentheses

23. Which word does not belong with the others?

A. Book

B. Chapter

C. Index

D. Glossary

24. Which word does not belong with the others?

A. Calico

B. Chihuahua

C. Terrier

D. Border collie

25. Which word does not belong with the others?

A. Swing

B. Slide

C. Bars

D. Bench

26. Which word does not belong with the others?

A. Shrimp

B. Lobster

C. Tuna

D. Clams

27. Which word does not belong with the others?

A. Eggplant

B. Plum

C. Violet

D. Scarlet

28. Which word does not belong with the others?

A. Dejected

B. Despondent

C. Delighted

D. Devastated

29. Which word does not belong with the others?
    A. Snorkel
    B. Shark
    C. Mask
    D. Flippers

30. Which word does not belong with the others?
    A. Theater
    B. Drama
    C. Comedy
    D. Musical

31. Which word does not belong with the others?
    A. Verse
    B. Stanza
    C. Chapter
    D. Line

32. Which word does not belong with the others?
    A. Accepting
    B. Choosy
    C. Finicky
    D. Particular

33. Which word does not belong with the others?
    A. Jupiter
    B. The moon
    C. Venus
    D. Earth

34. Which word does not belong with the others?
    A. Sweater
    B. Jeans
    C. Vest
    D. Blouse

35. Which word does not belong with the others?

A. Faint

B. Faded

C. Dim

D. Vivid

36. Which word does not belong with the others?

A. Cottage

B. School

C. Mansion

D. Cabin

37. Which word does not belong with the others?

A. Garbage truck

B. Crane

C. Bulldozer

D. Forklift

38. Which word does not belong with the others?

A. Hands

B. Face

C. Time

D. Numbers

39. Which word does not belong with the others?

A. Ballet

B. Shoes

C. Hip-hop

D. Tap

40. Which word does not belong with the others?

A. Corn

B. Peas

C. Asparagus

D. Broccoli

Directions: For questions 41–75, choose the best answer based on the information given.

41. All tumps are winged boscs. No blue boscs have wings. No tumps are blue. If the first two statements are true, the third is

A. true.

B. false.

C. uncertain.

42. Bagels are less expensive than muffins. Rolls are less expensive than bagels. Muffins are less expensive than rolls. If the first two statements are true, the third is

A. true.

B. false.

C. uncertain.

43. Aiden read fewer books than Terry. Terry read fewer books than Genevieve. Genevieve read more books than Aiden. If the first two statements are true, the third is

A. true.

B. false.

C. uncertain.

44. Bill runs faster than Mike. Jeff runs faster than Bill. Jeff is not as fast as Mike. If the first two statements are true, the third is

A. true.

B. false.

C. uncertain.

45. Jim lives on Maple Street. Angela lives on Evergreen Avenue. They live in the same town. If the first two statements are true, the third is

A. true.

B. false.

C. uncertain.

46. A platypus lays eggs. A goose lays eggs. A platypus is a bird. If the first two statements are true, the third is

A. true.

B. false.

C. uncertain.

47. Every human has a heart. Sally is a human. Sally has a heart. If the first two statements are true, the third is

A. true.

B. false.

C. uncertain.

48. A leap year happens every four years. This year is a leap year. The next leap year will be in two years. If the first two statements are true, the third is

A. true.

B. false.

C. uncertain.

49. My mother said I had to get a B or higher on the history test to stay on the baseball team. I got an A on the test. I will have to stop being on the baseball team. If the first two statements are true, the third is

A. true.

B. false.

C. uncertain.

50. Oahu is a Hawaiian island. George was born on Oahu. George is a native of Hawaii. If the first two statements are true, the third is

A. true.

B. false.

C. uncertain.

51. Maria was one of ten entrants in the science fair. Her project won second place. Maria placed higher than more than half of the people in the science fair. If the first two statements are true, the third is

A. true.

B. false.

C. uncertain.

52. A haiku is a poem with three lines. A sonnet is a poem with fourteen lines. Both haiku and sonnets must rhyme. If the first two statements are true, the third is

    A. true.

    B. false.

    C. uncertain.

53. Bennett is allergic to dogs. Bennett is not allergic to rodents. Having a hamster as a pet would not trigger Bennett's allergies. If the first two statements are true, the third is

    A. true.

    B. false.

    C. uncertain.

54. Janie is scheduled to take her swim test on Saturday. Phillip is scheduled to take his swim test next month. Both Janie and Phillip will be taking their test at the same pool. If the first two statements are true, the third is

    A. true.

    B. false.

    C. uncertain.

55. Li's birthday party is on the first Saturday of July. Jeremiah's birthday is on the second Sunday of July. Both Li's and Jeremiah's birthday parties are taking place on the same weekend. If the first two statements are true, the third is

    A. true.

    B. false.

    C. uncertain.

56. Most fish have scales. A dolphin does not have scales. A dolphin is not a fish. If the first two statements are true, the third is

    A. true.

    B. false.

    C. uncertain.

57. Billy finished the race in 22 minutes. Armando finished the race in 20 minutes. Billy is a faster runner than Armando. If the first two statements are true, the third is

    A. true.

    B. false.

    C. uncertain.

58. The school board in my district has decided to extend the school year by one week. All four schools in the district will be affected. My school will soon have a longer year. If the first two statements are true, the third is

A. true.

B. false.

C. uncertain.

59. Georgia's family has dogs. Milton's family has cats. Both families like animals. If the first two statements are true, the third is

A. true.

B. false.

C. uncertain.

60. Archie works more hours than Fiona. Brandon works fewer hours than Fiona. Brandon works more hours than Archie. If the first two statements are true, the third is

A. true.

B. false.

C. uncertain.

61. Alma is sitting in the middle of a three-person back seat. Glenn is sitting next to Alma. Jerry is not sitting next to Glenn. If the first two statements are true, the third is

A. true.

B. false.

C. uncertain.

62. Sierra is at the front of the line. Tisha is third in line. Melanie is behind both of them in line. If the first two statements are true, the third is

A. true.

B. false.

C. uncertain.

63. Farmer Jim grows more peaches than Farmer Dan. Farmer Dan grows more peaches than Farmer Sue. Farmer Sue grows fewer peaches than Farmer Jim. If the first two statements are true, the third is

A. true.

B. false.

C. uncertain.

64. Marina is taller than Kaitlyn. Kaitlyn is shorter than Bianca. Bianca is taller than Marina. If the first two statements are true, the third is

A. true.

B. false.

C. uncertain.

65. All members of the Tigers soccer team last year are staying on the team this year. Joey is on the Tigers this year. Joey was a member of the Tigers last year. If the first two statements are true, the third is

A. true.

B. false.

C. uncertain.

66. The green fish swims faster than the yellow fish. The green fish swims slower than the striped fish. The striped fish swims faster than the yellow fish. If the first two statements are true, the third is

A. true.

B. false.

C. uncertain.

67. Frankie delivers newspapers to his entire neighborhood every morning. Ginny lives on Frankie's street. Ginny receives a newspaper every day. If the first two statements are true, the third is

A. true.

B. false.

C. uncertain.

68. Patrick's cat Patches has a bell on her collar. His cat Sparky has no bell. When Patrick hears a bell outside his door, he knows Sparky is coming. If the first two statements are true, the third is

A. true.

B. false.

C. uncertain.

69. Quentin sent out party invitations only to members of his class. Serena received an invitation yesterday. Serena is in the same class as Quentin. If the first two statements are true, the third is

A. true.

B. false.

C. uncertain.

70. Charlotte was the starting pitcher in yesterday's softball game. Mireille pitches right after Charlotte. Mireille is not pitching in today's game. If the first two statements are true, the third is

A. true.

B. false.

C. uncertain.

71. Jason arrived before Stephanie. Allie arrived before Jason. Stephanie arrived before Allie. If the first two statements are true, the third is

A. true.

B. false.

C. uncertain.

72. The market has tomatoes for sale today. The market is out of avocados. Sam bought avocadoes at the market today. If the first two statements are true, the third is

A. true.

B. false.

C. uncertain.

73. Drivers are required to stop at a red light. Drivers are not required to stop at yellow lights. Mina received a traffic ticket for driving through a yellow light. If the first two statements are true, the third is

A. true.

B. false.

C. uncertain.

74. Tony is lower than Rosemary on the rock-climbing wall. Candice has climbed higher than Tony. Candice is higher on the wall than Rosemary. If the first two statements are true, the third is

A. true.

B. false.

C. uncertain.

75. All of the suitcases in the luggage rack are black. Etta's suitcase is gray. Etta's suitcase is on the luggage rack. If the first two statements are true, the third is

A. true.

B. false.

C. uncertain.

Answer Key and Explanations

1. D	16. A	31. C	46. C	61. A
2. C	17. C	32. A	47. A	62. C
3. A	18. B	33. B	48. B	63. A
4. C	19. A	34. B	49. B	64. C
5. C	20. D	35. D	50. A	65. C
6. B	21. B	36. B	51. A	66. A
7. B	22. D	37. A	52. C	67. A
8. A	23. A	38. C	53. A	68. B
9. D	24. A	39. B	54. C	69. A
10. C	25. D	40. A	55. B	70. B
11. C	26. C	41. A	56. C	71. B
12. B	27. D	42. B	57. B	72. B
13. A	28. C	43. A	58. A	73. B
14. D	29. B	44. B	59. A	74. C
15. C	30. A	45. C	60. B	75. B

1. **The correct answer is D.** An earthquake is a natural disaster caused by movement of the earth's crust. The other choices (hurricane, tornado, and typhoon) are wind-based natural disasters.

2. **The correct answer is C.** Time is a general classification. The other choices are objects that tell time.

3. **The correct answer is A.** *Elated, gleeful*, and *joyous* are synonyms.

4. **The correct answer is C.** Death is the fact of dying. The other choices are crimes, one of which just happens to cause death.

5. **The correct answer is C.** A *fever* is a symptom. All the other choices are diseases.

6. **The correct answer is B.** *Monkey* is the general term describing a whole class of primates, regardless of gender. All the other choices are specifically male animals.

7. **The correct answer is B.** A plane is the only vehicle that flies; all the others are modes of ground transportation.

8. **The correct answer is A.** An ostrich is a bird, while the other choices are all mammals.

9. **The correct answer is D.** Stripes, dots, and plaid are types of patterns, while fabric is a material.

10. **The correct answer is C.** A pound measures weight, while centimeters, inches, and feet all measure length.

11. **The correct answer is C.** The Atlantic, Pacific, and Indian are all oceans, while Australia is a country and a continent.

12. **The correct answer is B.** Baseball, soccer, and football are all sports that use balls, but hockey uses a puck.

13. **The correct answer is A.** A viola, harp, and guitar are all string instruments, while a saxophone is a wind instrument.

14. **The correct answer is D.** Emails, letters, and text messages are all forms of written communication, while a phone call is a type of verbal communication.

15. **The correct answer is C.** "Stop," "Yield," and "Caution" are all types of road signs, while the road is a surface.

16. **The correct answer is A.** Jazz, country, and rock are all genres of music, while a soap opera is a genre of television show.

17. **The correct answer is C.** *Frigid*, *glacial*, and *frosty* are all synonyms for "cold," while *blistering* is a synonym for "hot."

18. **The correct answer is B.** The verbs *spring*, *leap*, and *vault* are all synonyms for "jump," while *halt* is a synonym for "stop."

19. **The correct answer is A.** Grocery stores, bakeries, and ice cream parlors all sell food, while a florist sells flowers.

20. **The correct answer is D.** *Over*, *under*, and *around* are all prepositions that describe the location of something, while *floor* is a noun that describes a surface.

21. **The correct answer is B.** The adjectives *forked*, *split*, and *diverged* describe something that is divided, which is the antonym of *whole.*

22. **The correct answer is D.** Nouns, adjectives, and verbs are all types of words that make up sentences, while parentheses are a type of punctuation.

23. **The correct answer is A.** Chapters, indexes, and glossaries are all individual parts of a book, while a book itself is the whole thing.

24. **The correct answer is A.** Chihuahuas, terriers, and border collies are all breeds of dogs, while calico is a breed of cat.

25. **The correct answer is D.** Swings, slides, and bars are all types of play equipment specific to playgrounds, while a bench is not a piece of equipment for playing or specific to playgrounds.

26. **The correct answer is C.** Shrimp, lobster, and clams are all types of shellfish, while tuna is a type of fish.

27. **The correct answer is D.** Eggplant, plum, and violet are all varieties of the color purple, while scarlet is a shade of red.

28. **The correct answer is C.** The adjectives *dejected*, *despondent*, and *devastated* are all synonyms for "unhappy," while *delighted* means "happy."

29. **The correct answer is B.** A snorkel, mask, and flippers are all types of scuba gear, while a shark is an underwater animal.

30. **The correct answer is A.** *Drama*, *comedy*, and *musical* all describe genres of a work (like a play or movie), while a theater is a location.

31. **The correct answer is C.** A verse, stanza, and line are all parts of a poem, while a chapter is part of a book.

32. **The correct answer is A.** The adjectives *choosy*, *finicky*, and *particular* are synonyms for "picky," while *accepting* means the opposite of picky.

33. **The correct answer is B.** Jupiter, Venus, and Earth are all planets, while the moon is a satellite of Earth.

34. **The correct answer is B.** A sweater, a vest, and a blouse are all types of shirts, while jeans are a type of pants.

35. **The correct answer is D.** Adjectives *faint*, *faded*, and *dim* all describe something that is not strong (like light or weight), while *vivid* means "bright."

36. **The correct answer is B.** Cottages, mansions, and cabins are all types of houses, while a school is a different kind of building (not housing).

37. **The correct answer is A.** A crane, a bulldozer, and a forklift are all types of construction equipment, while a garbage truck is a kind of vehicle.

38. **The correct answer is C.** Hands, face, and numbers are all parts of a clock, while time is what's measured by a clock.

39. **The correct answer is B.** Ballet, hip-hop, and tap are all types of dancing, while shoes are an item of clothing, as well as a type of equipment used in dance.

40. **The correct answer is A.** Peas, asparagus, and broccoli are all green vegetables, while corn is a yellow vegetable.

41. **The correct answer is A.** Because the first two statements are true, all tumps are a part of a larger set of boscs with wings. Blue boscs have no wings; therefore, they cannot be tumps, nor can tumps be blue.

42. **The correct answer is B.** List the items in order from the least expensive to the most expensive: rolls, bagels, then muffins. Muffins are more expensive than rolls, not less.

43. **The correct answer is A.** The correct order of who read how many books is Genevieve, Terry, and Aiden. Given that Genevieve read the most, the third statement is true.

44. **The correct answer is B.** If the first two statements are true, Jeff runs faster than both Bill and Mike.

45. **The correct answer is C.** Without knowing where Maple Street and Evergreen Avenue are, there is no way to tell if Jim and Angela live in the same town.

46. **The correct answer is C.** A platypus is actually a mammal (one of the only mammals that lays eggs), but you don't need to know that to know that the statements don't give you enough information to decide whether or not a platypus is a bird. There is not enough information given to suggest that *only* birds lay eggs.

47. **The correct answer is A.** Since every human has a heart, Sally must also have a heart because she is human.

48. **The correct answer is B.** If this year is a leap year and leap years happen every four years, then the next leap year will be four years from now, not two.

49. **The correct answer is B.** An "A" grade is higher than a "B" grade, which means the speaker would be allowed to stay on the baseball team, so the third statement is false.

50. **The correct answer is A.** Because Oahu is part of Hawaii, someone born on Oahu would be Hawaiian, so the statement is true.

51. **The correct answer is A.** If Maria came in second place out of ten people, she placed higher than eight other people, which is more than half of the original ten entrants.

52. **The correct answer is C.** The first two statements tell you how many lines each poem has, but there is no information given about whether the poems rhyme or not—so there is not enough information to determine whether the third statement is true or false.

53. **The correct answer is A.** A hamster is a type of rodent, which means Bennett would be able to have one as a pet without being allergic.

54. **The correct answer is C.** The first two statements tell you when Janie and Phillip are taking their tests, but there is not enough information to tell you where they're taking their tests.

55. **The correct answer is B.** Li's birthday party is happening on the first weekend of July, while Jeremiah's birthday party is happening on the second weekend of July, so the third statement is false.

56. **The correct answer is C.** Because the first statement says *most* and not *all*, there is not enough information given to help you determine whether a dolphin is a fish.

57. **The correct answer is B.** Armando took less time to finish the race, so he is the faster runner in this case.

58. **The correct answer is A.** The key phrases are "in my district" and "all the schools in the district." Because the speaker's school is in the district, his or her school will be included in the new schedule.

59. **The correct answer is A.** Given that both families have pets, you can conclude that the third statement is true.

60. **The correct answer is B.** If Archie works more hours than Fiona, and Fiona works more hours than Brandon, then Brandon cannot work more hours than Archie.

61. **The correct answer is A.** From the first statement, you know that there are three people in the back seat. If Alma is sitting in the middle, she is sitting next to the two other people, but the two other people are not sitting next to each other because Alma is sitting between them.

62. **The correct answer is C.** Sierra is first in line and Tisha is third, but there is not enough information to tell you where Melanie is standing. She could be second in line, which would make the statement false; or she could be fourth or more in line, which would make the statement true.

63. **The correct answer is A.** In this scenario, Farmer Jim grows the most peaches, because he grows more than Farmer Dan, who grows more than Farmer Sue.

64. **The correct answer is C.** Based on the first two statements, you know only that Kaitlyn is shorter than both Marina and Bianca. There is not enough information given to tell you if Bianca is taller than Marina.

65. **The correct answer is C.** Although there's a chance that Joey was a member of the Tigers last year, there is not enough information to conclude that he was on the team last year and isn't a new player this year. There is nothing in the first statement that says there are no new players on the team this year in addition to last year's team members.

66. **The correct answer is A.** The green fish is faster than the yellow fish, and the striped fish is faster than the green fish. Therefore, both fishes are faster than the yellow fish.

67. **The correct answer is A.** Assuming the first statement is true, the key word is *entire*, meaning "all." Given that Ginny lives in Frankie's neighborhood, she would be included in that group of people receiving a newspaper every morning.

68. **The correct answer is B.** Patches has a bell, but Sparky does not, so if Patrick is hearing a bell, he's hearing Patches.

69. **The correct answer is A.** The word *only* in the first statement is your key word. Quentin didn't send out any invitations to people who are not in his class, so if Serena received an invitation, she must be in his class.

70. **The correct answer is B.** If Mireille pitches after Charlotte does, and there is a game today, then Mireille would be the pitcher.

71. **The correct answer is B.** Based on the first two (true) statements, the order of arrival is Allie, Jason, then Stephanie, so the third statement is false.

72. **The correct answer is B.** If the market is out of avocados, Sam could not have bought avocados today.

73. **The correct answer is B.** Based on the statements, it is not illegal for drivers to drive through yellow lights, so if you stick to the facts outlined, the third statement is false.

74. **The correct answer is C.** Based on the first two statements, you know that Rosemary is higher than Tony, and Tony is lower than Rosemary, so both Candice and Rosemary are higher than Tony. However, there is not enough information given to determine where Candice and Rosemary are, compared to each other.

75. **The correct answer is B.** Given that all suitcases on the luggage rack are black, and Etta's suitcase is not black, you can conclude that her suitcase is *not* on the luggage rack, making the third statement false.

Chapter 6

Quantitative Skills and Ability

Introduction to Quantitative Skills and Ability Questions

The HSPT exam Quantitative Skills section and the TACHS Ability sections assess basic pattern recognition and quantitative reasoning. The question types you will see on test day depends on which exam you take.

On the HSPT® Exam: Quantitative Skills Questions

The first quantitative skills question type we will discuss concerns **sequences**. You will be given a list of numbers or letters, or both, for which there is a discernible pattern used to get from one to the next; you will be asked to identify certain missing terms of this sequence.

Another question type is categorized as **reasoning**. These questions often describe a scenario that can be transformed into an algebraic equation that can be solved or an arithmetic expression that can be simplified. To successfully solve the reasoning questions, you need to be comfortable translating a sentence into mathematical symbols. Once you can do that, the rest unfolds just like questions you prepared for in the Math test section. Reasoning questions can also present you with a diagram and instruct you to select the correct statement regarding relationships of various quantities (e.g., angles, side lengths) within the diagram. Your geometry preparation will come in handy here!

The third quantitative skills question type deals with **geometric and nongeometric comparisons**. You will be given three quantities and asked to identify the correct relationship among them from a list of four. The quantities used in these questions come from all five content areas assessed in the Math test. In a sense, these questions are just multi-step versions of those included on the Math test; you use the same content knowledge to assess each quantity and then compare them numerically.

Quantitative Skills Questions Preview

Let's walk through some sample quantitative skills questions together.

1. Look at this series. What number should come next?

2, 5, 10, 13, 26, ____, …

A. 29

B. 39

C. 52

D. 55

The correct answer is A. The pattern in the series is: add 3, multiply by 2, add 3, multiply by 2, and so on. At this point in the series, you are to add 3. The next term is 29.

2. The product of 3 and what number, when subtracted from 6, leaves 15?

A. 21

B. –7

C. –3

D. 12

The correct answer is C. Let x be the number. It satisfies the equation $6 - 3x = 15$. Solve for x:

$$6 - 3x = 15$$
$$-3x = 9$$
$$x = \frac{9}{-3}$$
$$x = -3$$

3. Examine A, B, and C. Choose the best answer.

A. 0.4×10^{-3}

B. 0.004×10^{2}

C. 0.04×10^{-2}

A. A = B = C

B. A = C and B > C

C. A < B < C

D. B > C and A > B

The correct answer is B. In each option, the exponent on the 10 determines the number of places to move the decimal point to the right (if positive) or to the left (if negative).

Specifically:

$$0.4 \times 10^{-3} = 0.0004$$
$$0.004 \times 10^{2} = 0.4$$
$$0.04 \times 10^{-2} = 0.0004$$

A = C and B > C.

4. The pie is divided into sixteen equal portions. Study the pie and find the best answer.

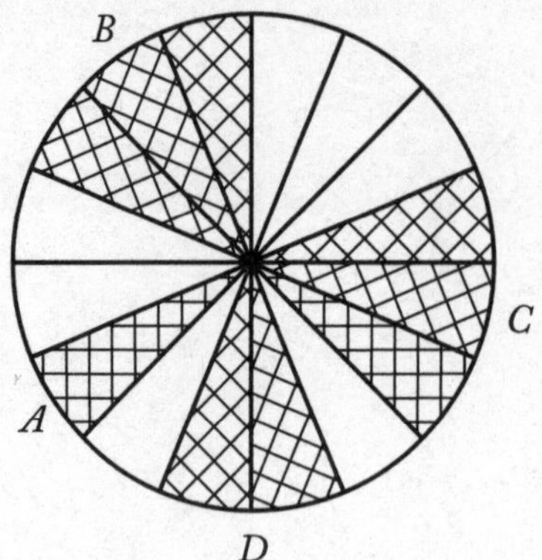

A. $A + D = B + C$

B. $D - A = B - C$

C. $C - D = A$

D. $B = A + C$

The correct answer is C. Begin by counting the pie wedges in each portion; write the number of wedges next to the letter—*A* (1), *B* (3), *C* (3), *D* (2). Now perform the very simple arithmetic for each statement.

Statement A: 1 + 2 = 3 + 3; 3 = 6—false
Statement B: 2 – 1 = 3 – 3; 1 = 0—false
Statement C: 3 – 2 = 1—**true**
Statement D: 3 = 1 + 3; 3 = 4—false

On the TACHS: Ability Questions

The TACHS Ability questions assess your ability to reason spatially and using (sometimes subtle) geometric pattern recognition. One type of these questions is **paper folding**. In these problems, a flat square piece of paper is folded one, two, or three times. Each fold is shown side-by-side in a sequence of folds ending in a hole punch. In each diagram, the paper is always folded on top of the original square. The broken lines indicate the original position of the paper prior to that fold, and the solid lines indicate the position of the folded paper. The folded paper always remains within the edges of the original square.

To find the answer to the question, you must mentally unfold the paper and determine the position of the holes now present on the original square piece of paper. You will choose the pattern that indicates the position of these holes. The best way to acclimate yourself to doing these problems is to have a stack of square papers and a hole punch; literally fold the paper using different sequences of folds, punch holes, and observe where they line up!

The other two question types address geometric pattern recognition: **figure classification** and **figure matrices**. The thought process used to solve these two types of questions is similar; they are simply displayed in different ways. Regarding figure classification, three figures shown together share some type of similarity. You must choose the figure from the answer choices that shares that similarity. With figure matrices, you are presented with a three-by-three matrix of figures. Most often, the figure in the bottom right corner will be missing, and you will need to determine which of the answer choices is the figure that completes the matrix. The figures are related either by row or by column. The same pattern is used to produce the two complete rows or columns. The goal is to determine this pattern and apply it to identify the missing figure.

Ability Questions Preview

Let's walk through some sample ability questions together.

1. Look at the top row to see how a square piece of paper is folded and where holes are punched in it. Then look at the bottom row to decide which answer choice shows how the paper will look when it is completely unfolded.

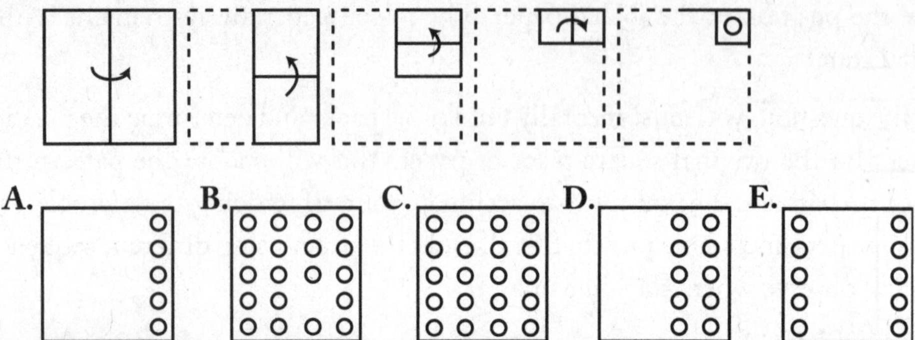

The correct answer is C. The first fold divides the paper square in half from left to right, thereby producing two layers throughout the entire folded construct. Next, the paper is folded in half from bottom to top, producing four layers throughout. Next, the paper is folded in half again from bottom to top, producing eight layers throughout. And finally, the paper is folded in half from left to right. All told, the entire folded construct is comprised of 16 layers.

Now, the hole is punched near the fold, and it goes through all 16 layers. Hence, the final result will consist of 16 holes.

2. The first three figures are alike in certain ways. Choose the answer choice that goes with the first three figures.

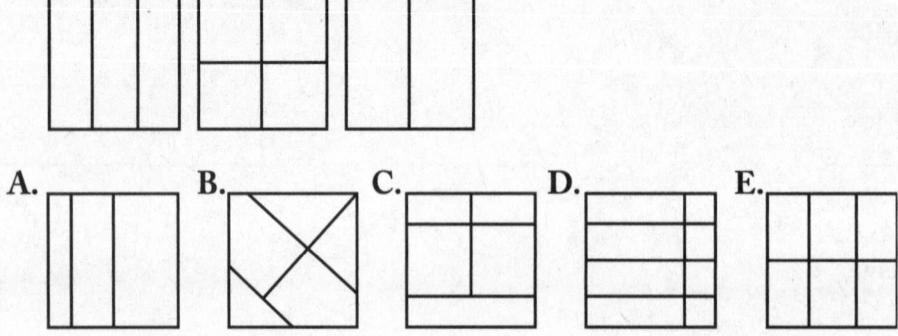

The correct answer is E. The commonality across the three figures is that each figure is a square that has been divided into equal parts—three, four, and two, respectively. Only choice E, divided into six equal parts, follows that pattern.

3. Find the figure that completes the puzzle.

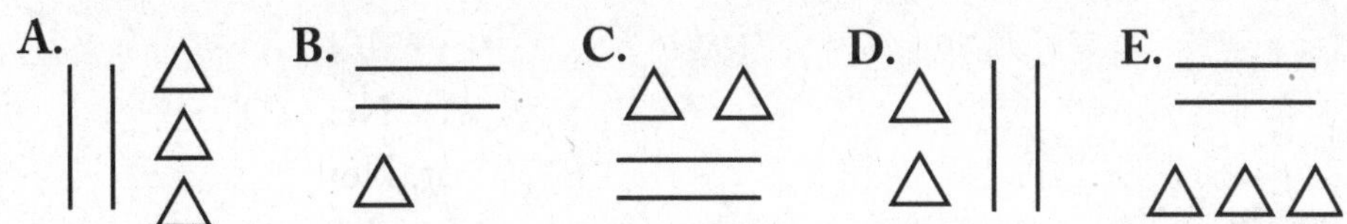

The correct answer is E. The pattern is exhibited across rows in this matrix. For both rows 1 and 2, there are always two parallel line segments positioned along three different edges—no cell in a row has the line segments along the same edge. This observation is particularly important for this problem, as it will enable you to select from two seemingly correct choices. Then, as you move from left to right in a row, the number of triangles increases by one—one in the first cell, two in the second, and three in the third. The only choice that satisfies all of these conditions is choice E.

Although the Quantitative Comparisons and Ability sections are the shortest sections on their respective tests, scoring well on them is an important step toward getting the high entrance exam score that you're aiming for. So, put on your "outside the box" thinking cap and dive in.

> **Appendix Alert**
>
> **You will find the answer sheet for the drills in this chapter in Appendix C, starting on page 525.**

HSPT® Quantitative Skills Drill

Sequence

25 Questions

Directions: Choose the answer you think is best to the following questions. Mark the corresponding letter on your answer sheet.

SHOW YOUR WORK HERE

1. Consider the following series. What is the next term?

10, 9, 8, 9, 8, 7, 8 …

A. 6
B. 7
C. 8
D. 9

2. Consider the following series. What is the missing term?

27, 33, 25, ____, 23, 29, 21, …

A. 31
B. 24
C. 28
D. 30

3. Consider the following series. What number should come next?

10, 14, 18, 22, 26 …

A. 28
B. 29
C. 30
D. 32

4. Consider the following series. What term should come next?

ABC FED GHI LKJ ___

A. ONM

B. NOP

C. MNO

D. MON

5. Consider the following series. What are the next two terms?

$\frac{2}{3}, \frac{9}{4}, \frac{8}{27}, \_\_\_, \_\_\_, \ldots$

A. $\frac{16}{81}, \frac{243}{27}$

B. $\frac{81}{16}, \frac{32}{243}$

C. $\frac{16}{81}, \frac{32}{243}$

D. $\frac{81}{16}, \frac{243}{32}$

6. Consider the following series. What are the next two terms?

16, 11, 8, 8, 4, 5, ___, ___, ...

A. $1, \frac{5}{2}$

B. 0, 2

C. $2, \frac{5}{2}$

D. 2, 2

SHOW YOUR WORK HERE

HSPT® Quantitative Skills Drill

SHOW YOUR WORK HERE

7. Consider the following series. What are the missing two terms?

   3, 8, 6, 11, 9, ____, ____, 17, 15, …

   A. 14, 12
   B. 7, 12
   C. 16, 7
   D. 9, 14

8. Consider the following series. What is the missing term?

   5, 8, 13, ____, 29, 40, …

   A. 16
   B. 18
   C. 20
   D. 22

9. Consider the following series. What is the missing term?

   ABDB ACEB ADFB ____ AFHB

   A. ADGB
   B. AEGB
   C. AFGB
   D. ACGB

10. Consider the following series. What is the missing term?

    0.1, 0.01, ____, 0.0000001, …

    A. 0.001
    B. 0.0001
    C. 0.01
    D. 0.000001

SHOW YOUR WORK HERE

11. Consider the following series. What are the next two terms?

XQ, VR, TS, ____, ____, …

A. RT, PU

B. UU, VW

C. TR, UP

D. VW, UU

12. Consider the following series. What is the next term?

53, 51, 47, 39, ____, …

A. 7

B. 35

C. 31

D. 23

13. Consider the following series. What are the next two terms?

$\frac{5}{8}, \frac{5}{4}, \frac{3}{2}, 3, \frac{13}{4}$, ____, ____, …

A. $\frac{7}{2}, 7$

B. $\frac{13}{2}, \frac{27}{4}$

C. $\frac{7}{4}, \frac{7}{2}$

D. $\frac{13}{2}, \frac{7}{3}$

14. Consider the following series. What is the missing term?

11, 13, 17, ____, 23, 29, …

A. 18

B. 19

C. 20

D. 21

HSPT® Quantitative Skills Drill

SHOW YOUR WORK HERE

15. Consider the following series. What is the missing term?

ABC EFG ___ OPQ ...

A. IJK
B. PQR
C. STU
D. UVW

16. Consider the following series. What is the missing term?

___, 0.30, 0.45, 0.75, 1.20, ...

A. 0.05
B. 0.10
C. 0.15
D. 0.20

17. Consider the following series. What is the missing term?

86, 83, 80, 76, 72, 67, ___, ...

A. 60
B. 62
C. 64
D. 66

18. Consider the following series. What is the next term?

B3, 6F, J3, ___, ...

A. 6N
B. L6
C. 6L
D. 9N

19. Consider the following series. What is the next term?

2.3, 3.44, 4.555, ____, …

A. 5.66
B. 5.666
C. 5.4444
D. 5.6666

SHOW YOUR WORK HERE

20. Consider the following series. What are the next two terms?

$1\frac{1}{2}, 2\frac{1}{6}, 2\frac{5}{6}$, ____, ____, …

A. $3\frac{5}{6}, 4\frac{1}{6}$
B. $3\frac{1}{6}, 4\frac{1}{2}$
C. $3\frac{1}{2}, 4\frac{1}{6}$
D. $2\frac{7}{9}, 3\frac{1}{6}$

21. Consider the following series. What is the missing term?

ZYWX VUST RQOP ___ JIGH

A. MNKL
B. LKMN
C. NMKL
D. NMLK

HSPT® Quantitative Skills Drill

SHOW YOUR WORK HERE

22. Consider the following series. What is the missing term?

$$\frac{C}{3}, \text{\_\_\_}, \frac{M}{75}, \frac{R}{375}, \ldots$$

A. $\frac{H}{15}$

B. $\frac{I}{45}$

C. $\frac{G}{15}$

D. $\frac{G}{45}$

23. Consider the following series. What are the next two terms?

$$5, 7\frac{1}{2}, 6, 9, 7\frac{1}{2} \text{\_\_\_}, \text{\_\_\_}, \ldots$$

A. 6, 9

B. 5, $7\frac{1}{2}$

C. $11\frac{1}{4}$, $9\frac{3}{4}$

D. 9, $13\frac{1}{2}$

24. Consider the following series. What are the missing two terms?

$$W, \frac{2}{3}, T, \frac{4}{9}, \text{\_\_\_}, \text{\_\_\_}, N, \frac{16}{81}, \ldots$$

A. R, $\frac{8}{21}$

B. Q, $\frac{8}{27}$

C. R, $\frac{8}{27}$

D. Q, $\frac{8}{21}$

25. Consider the following series. What is the missing term?

1.1, 2.8, 3.9, ____, 10.6, …

A. 5.6
B. 6.7
C. 7.6
D. 8.7

SHOW YOUR WORK HERE

Quantitative Reasoning

25 Questions

> **Directions:** Choose the best answer to the following questions. Mark the corresponding letter on your answer sheet.

SHOW YOUR WORK HERE

26. What number is 5 more than $\frac{1}{3}$ of 18?

A. 6
B. 11
C. 1
D. 14

27. What number is 7 less than 4 squared?

A. 9
B. 25
C. 16
D. 11

28. What number multiplied by 9 is 3 more than 42?

A. 27
B. 45
C. 7
D. 5

29. The sum of 30% of a number and 50% of the same number is 96. What is the number?

A. 60
B. 120
C. 136
D. 150

SHOW YOUR WORK HERE

30. What number added to 60 is 3 times the product of 4 and 5?

A. 10
B. 0
C. 15
D. 5

31. What number is 5 more than $\frac{2}{3}$ of 27?

A. 14
B. 32
C. 9
D. 23

32. What number is $\frac{1}{2}$ of the average of 7, 18, 5, 39, and 11?

A. 40
B. 5
C. 8
D. 20

33. What number divided by 2 leaves 4 more than 6?

A. 5
B. 10
C. 20
D. 4

34. What number subtracted from 7 leaves $\frac{1}{4}$ of 20?

A. 13
B. 5
C. 12
D. 2

SHOW YOUR WORK HERE

35. What number is 3 more than the cube of 4 divided by 4?

A. 61

B. 39

C. 67

D. 19

36. The product of 25% of a positive number and 40% of the same number is 14.4. What is the number?

A. 1.2

B. 12

C. 14.4

D. 144

37. What number subtracted from 82 leaves 3 more than $\frac{4}{5}$ of 80?

A. 64

B. 5

C. 15

D. 67

38. What number divided by 6 is $\frac{1}{8}$ of 96?

A. 48

B. 72

C. 12

D. 84

39. What number is 15 more than $\frac{5}{9}$ of 99?

A. 45

B. 60

C. 70

D. 81

40. One less than four times this number is 27.

A. 1

B. 7

C. 14

D. 24

SHOW YOUR WORK HERE

41. Thirty percent of the sum of this number and 5 is 18.

A. 0.4

B. 9.4

C. 50

D. 55

42. Two less than six times a number is the same as 10 more than 3 times the same number. What is the number?

A. 4

B. 5

C. 9

D. 12

43. The reciprocal of the sum of this number and 2 is $\frac{3}{8}$.

A. $\frac{3}{2}$

B. 2

C. $\frac{2}{3}$

D. 3

SHOW YOUR WORK HERE

44. The average of a number, twice the same number, and 6 more than 3 times this number is 12.

A. 4

B. 5

C. 9

D. 24

45. If 72 is 120% of a number, what is 80% of this number?

A. 36

B. 48

C. 60

D. 69

46. Which of these figures have shading that is symmetric?

SHOW YOUR WORK HERE

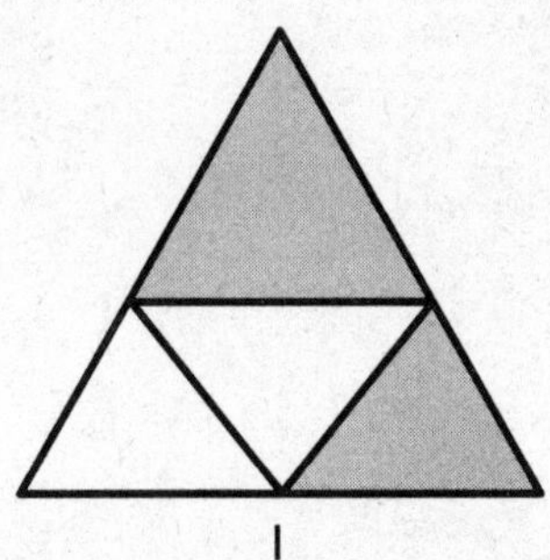

I

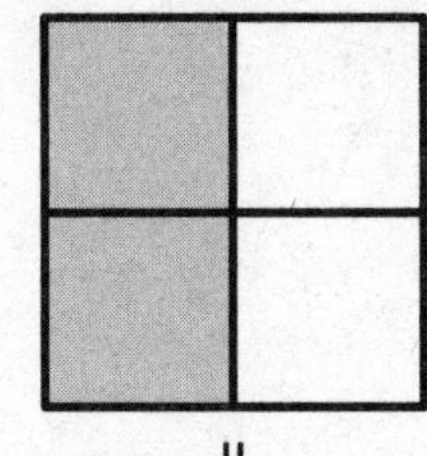

II

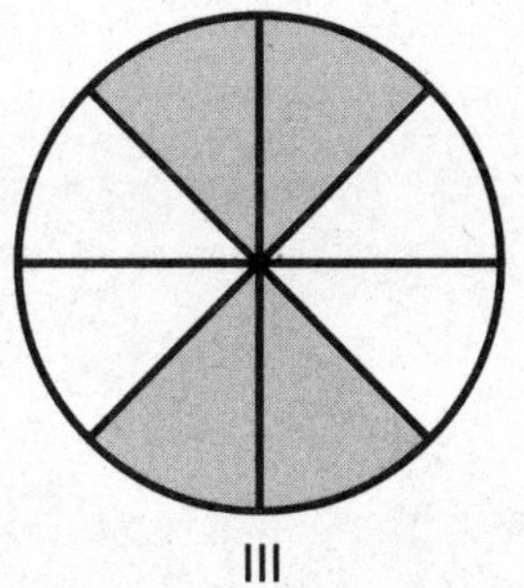

III

A. I and II
B. I and III
C. II and III
D. I, II, and III

SHOW YOUR WORK HERE

47. If $XY = 5$ and $XZ = 13$, then $ZY =$ ____.

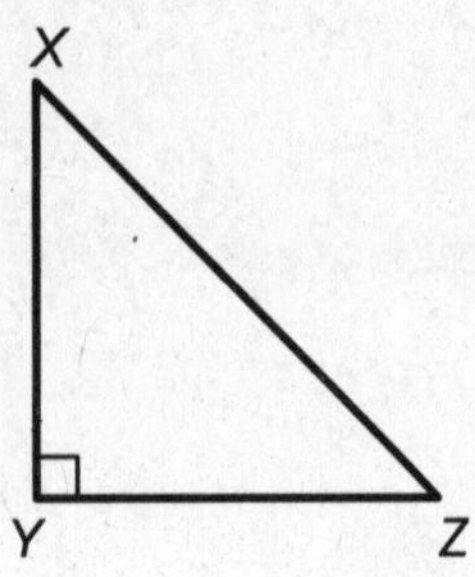

A. 8
B. 10
C. 12
D. 18

48. $\frac{5}{9}$ of this number is the same as $\frac{3}{4}$ of the sum of 15 and 5.

A. 60
B. 54
C. 9
D. 27

49. Which of the following equalities is true?

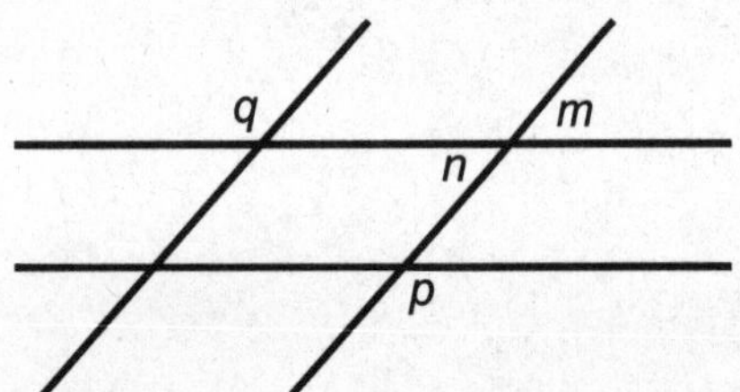

A. $\angle q = \angle m$
B. $\angle n = \angle q$
C. $\angle m = \angle n$
D. $\angle p + \angle m = 90°$

HSPT® Quantitative Skills Drill

50. Which of the following figures are similar?

SHOW YOUR WORK HERE

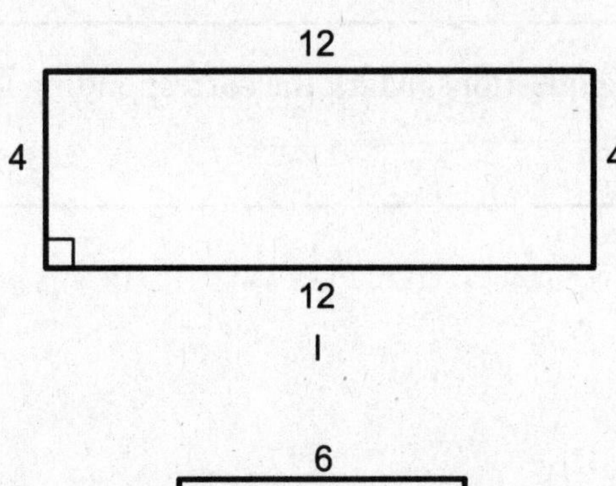

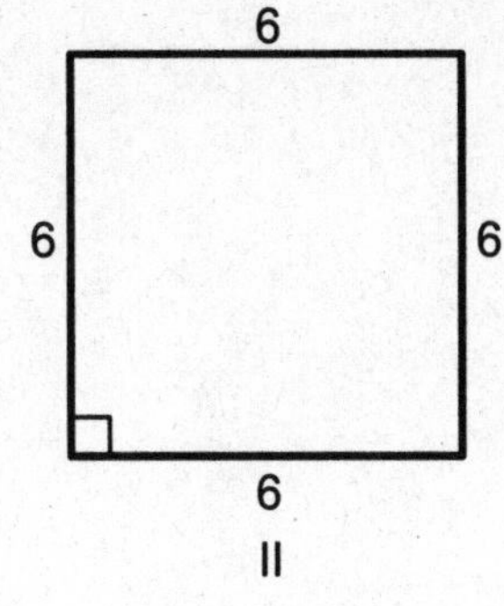

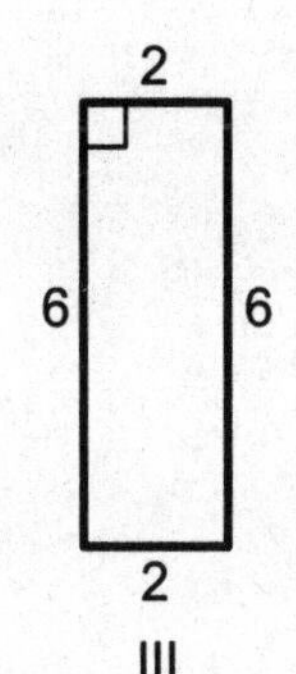

A. I and III

B. I and II

C. II and III

D. None of them

Geometric and Nongeometric Comparisons

25 Questions

Directions: Choose the best answer to the following questions. Mark the corresponding letter on your answer sheet.

SHOW YOUR WORK HERE

51. Examine A, B, and C and determine the best answer.

- **A.** 0.4
- **B.** 4%
- **C.** $\frac{2}{5}$

A. A is greater than C, which is greater than B.

B. A is equal to C and greater than B.

C. A is equal to B and greater than C.

D. A is less than B and equal to C.

52. Examine A, B, and C and determine the best answer if both x and y are greater than zero.

- **A.** $5(x + y)$
- **B.** $5x + y$
- **C.** $5(x + y) + x$

A. A, B, and C are equal.

B. B is less than A, which is less than C.

C. C is greater than A and less than B.

D. A and B are equal.

53. Examine A, B, and C and determine the best answer.

> **A.** 3(2 + 3)
> **B.** (2 + 3)3
> **C.** 3(2) + 3

A. A plus C is greater than B.
B. C is greater than A, which is smaller than B.
C. A and B are equal.
D. B is greater than A and C.

54. Examine A, B, and C and determine the best answer.

> **A.** (4 × 2) – 3
> **B.** (4 × 3) – 2
> **C.** (4 + 3) – 2

A. A is greater than C.
B. A, B, and C are equal.
C. C is greater than B.
D. A and C are equal.

55. Examine A, B, and C and determine the best answer.

> **A.** 0.001×10^4
> **B.** $10.0 \div 10^3$
> **C.** $0.1 \div 10^2$

A. A = B and B < C
B. C > B > A
C. B = C and C > A
D. C < B < A

SHOW YOUR WORK HERE

SHOW YOUR WORK HERE

56. Examine A, B and C and determine the best answer.

- **A.** 200% of 0.5
- **B.** 50% of 2
- **C.** 0.02% of 500

A. A > B > C
B. A = B and C < A
C. B < C < A
D. A = B = C

57. Suppose $0 < x < 1$. Examine A, B, and C and determine the best answer.

- **A.** x^2
- **B.** $2x$
- **C.** x^3

A. C > A > B
B. C > A and A < B
C. A = B and B < C
D. C < A < B

58. Examine A, B, and C and determine the best answer.

- **A.** 5 + 3 × (4 – 2)
- **B.** 5 + 3 × 4 – 2
- **C.** (5 + 3) × (4 – 2)

A. A = B = C
B. A < B < C
C. A = C and B < C
D. B < A < C

59. Suppose $y > 1$. Examine A, B, and C and determine the best answer.

SHOW YOUR WORK HERE

A. y

B. $\frac{1}{y}$

C. y^2

A. C > B > A

B. A < C < B

C. B < A < C

D. C < A < B

60. Examine A, B, and C and determine the best answer.

A. $\frac{2}{3}+\frac{3}{7}$

B. $\frac{2+3}{3+7}$

C. $\frac{14+9}{21}$

A. A = C and B < A

B. A = B and C < A

C. A < B < C

D. A < C < B

61. Examine A, B, and C and determine the best answer.

SHOW YOUR WORK HERE

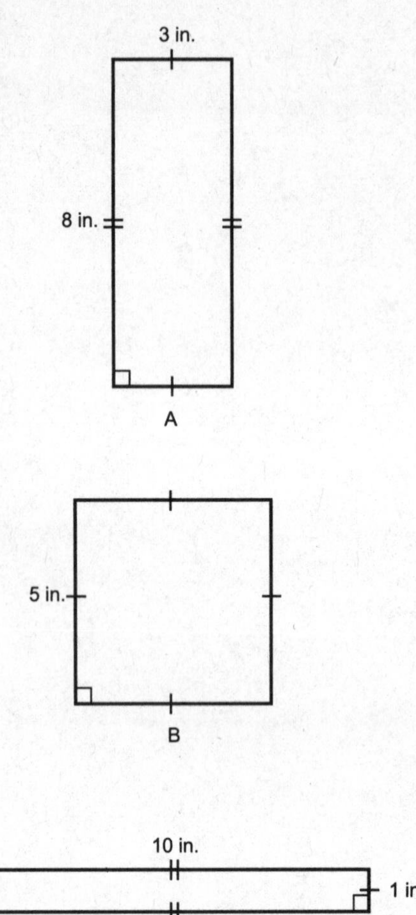

A. All three have the same perimeter.

B. The perimeter of B is less than the perimeter of C, and the perimeter of C is less than the perimeter of A.

C. The perimeter of B is less than the perimeter of A, and the perimeter of A is less than the perimeter of C.

D. The perimeter of A equals the perimeter of C, and the perimeter of B is less than the perimeter of A.

62. Examine A, B, and C and determine the best answer.

SHOW YOUR WORK HERE

A. -5^2

B. $(-5)^2$

C. $-(-5)^2$

A. A = B = C

B. A = B and B > C

C. A = C and C < B

D. A = B and A < C

63. Examine A, B, and C and determine the best answer.

SHOW YOUR WORK HERE

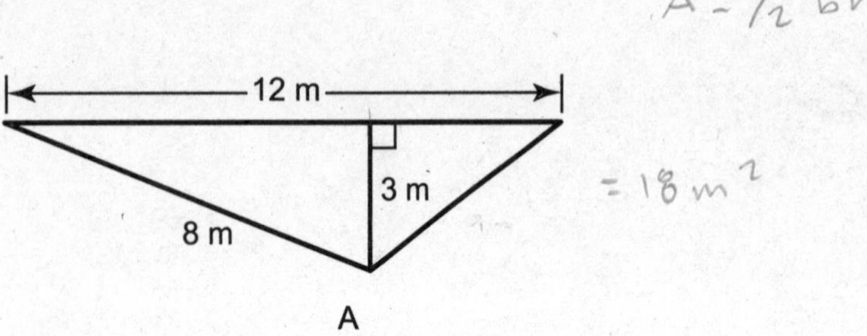

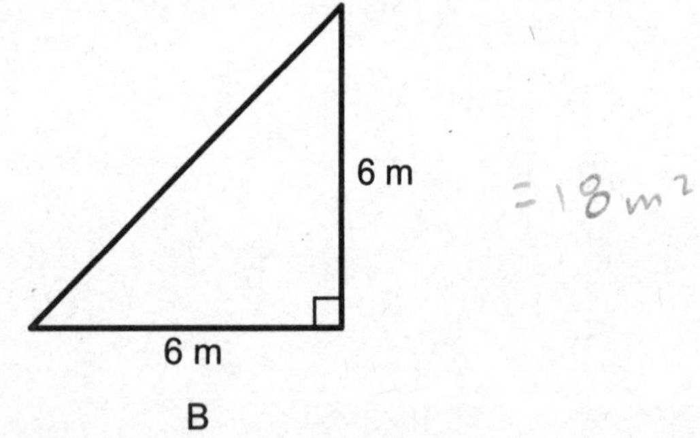

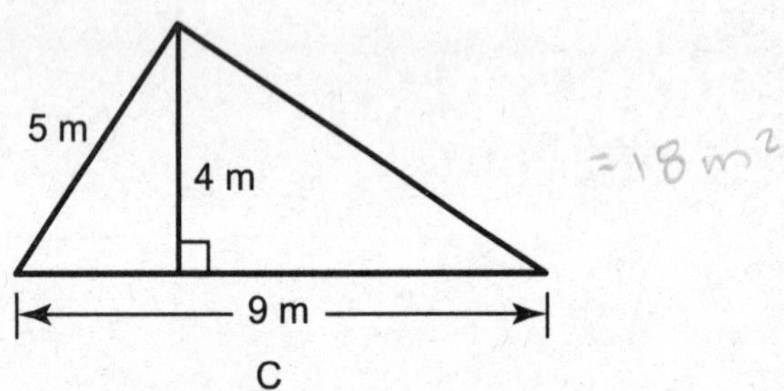

A. The area of A is less than the area of B, and the area of B is less than the area of C.

B. All three have the same area.

C. The area of A equals the area of C, and the area of C is less than the area of B.

D. The area of B equals the area of C, and the area of C is greater than the area of A.

64. Examine A, B, and C and determine the best answer.

    A. $-4(8 - 2)$
    B. $-32 + 8$
    C. $-4(8) - 2$

  A. A = B and B > C
  B. A = C and C < B
  C. A = B and B < C
  D. A = C and C > B

65. Examine A, B, and C and determine the best answer.

    A. $(4 \times 3) \times 2$
    B. $4 \times (3 \times 2)$
    C. $(4 \times 3) \times (4 \times 2)$

  A. A < B and B < C
  B. B < A and A < C
  C. A = B and B < C
  D. A = B = C

66. Examine A, B, and C and determine the best answer.

    A. The reciprocal of the square of 3.
    B. The cube of $\frac{1}{2}$.
    C. Twice two-thirds.

  A. C < A and A = B
  B. B < A and A < C
  C. A < B and B < C
  D. A = B and B < C

SHOW YOUR WORK HERE

67. Assume the lines *l* and *m* are parallel. Select the best answer.

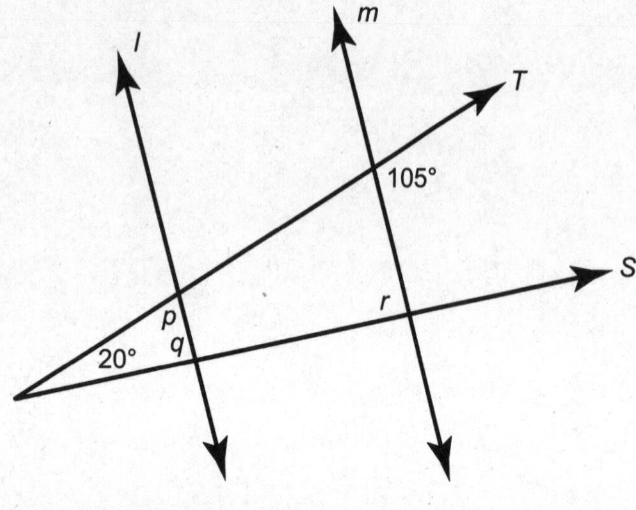

A. $p < r$ and $r = q$

B. $p < r < q$

C. $p < q$ and $p = r$

D. $q < r$ and $p > r$

68. Assume $y < x < 0$. Examine A, B, and C and determine the best answer.

A. xy

B. $2y$

C. $x + y$

A. C < B and B < A

B. B < C and C < A

C. A < B and B < C

D. A < C and C < B

SHOW YOUR WORK HERE

69. Suppose $0 < x < 1$. Examine A, B, and C and determine the best answer.

A. x

B. x^2

C. $\sqrt{x}$

A. A < B and B < C

B. C < B and B < A

C. B < A and A < C

D. C < A and A < B

70. Examine A, B, and C and determine the best answer.

A. $\dfrac{\frac{2}{3}}{\frac{1}{2}}$

B. $\dfrac{\frac{2}{3}}{2}$

C. $\dfrac{\frac{2}{3}}{2}$

A. A = B = C

B. C < B and B < A

C. A < C and C < B

D. C < A and A = B

71. Examine A, B, and C and determine the best answer.

A. $0.2 \div 0.04 \div 2$

B. $0.2 \div (0.04 \div 2)$

C. $(0.2 \div 0.04) \div 2$

A. A < B and B < C

B. A < C and C < B

C. A = B = C

D. A = C and C < B

72. Examine A, B, and C and determine the best answer.

SHOW YOUR WORK HERE

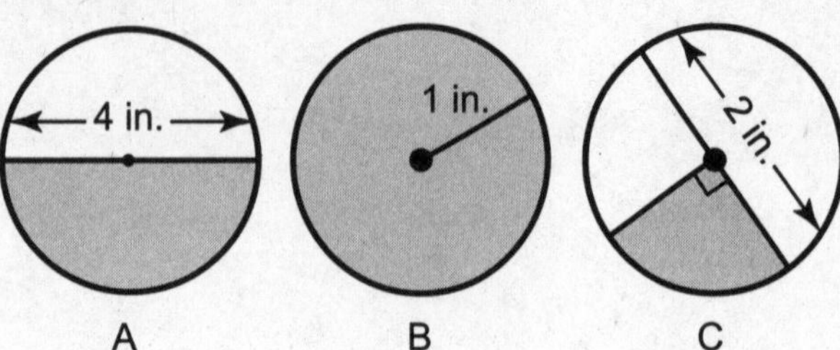

A. Area of the shaded region in A is less than the area of the shaded region in B, and the area of the shaded region in B is less than the area of the shaded region in C.
B. Area of the shaded region in C is less than the area of the shaded region in B, and the area of the shaded region in B is less than the area of the shaded region in A.
C. Area of the shaded region in C is greater than the area of the shaded region in A, and the area of the shaded region in B equals the area of the shaded region in A.
D. All three shaded regions have the same area.

73. Examine A, B, and C and determine the best answer.

A. $4 \times 2 + 3 \times 4$
B. $4 \times (2 + 3)$
C. 44

A. A = B = C
B. A = C and B < C
C. B = C and A < B
D. A = B and B < C

SHOW YOUR WORK HERE

74. Examine A, B, and C and determine the best answer.

  A. $1\frac{2}{5} - 1\frac{1}{3}$

  B. $5\frac{1}{2} \times 2\frac{1}{5}$

  C. $\frac{1}{2} \div 2\frac{1}{2}$

A. A < C and C < B
B. B < C and C < A
C. A < B and B < C
D. A < B and C < B

75. Examine A, B, and C and determine the best answer.

  A. The sum of the squares of 4 and 5.

  B. The square of the sum of 4 and 5.

  C. The product of the squares of 4 and the cube of 2.

A. A = B and B < C
B. B < C and C < A
C. A < B and B < C
D. A = B and C < A

Answer Keys and Explanations

Sequences

1. B	6. D	11. A	16. C	21. C
2. A	7. A	12. D	17. B	22. A
3. C	8. C	13. B	18. A	23. C
4. C	9. B	14. B	19. D	24. B
5. B	10. B	15. A	20. C	25. B

Quantitative Reasoning

26. B	31. D	36. B	41. D	46. C
27. A	32. C	37. C	42. A	47. C
28. D	33. C	38. B	43. C	48. D
29. B	34. D	39. C	44. B	49. C
30. B	35. D	40. B	45. B	50. A

Geometric and Nongeometric Comparisons

51. B	56. B	61. D	66. C	71. D
52. B	57. D	62. C	67. A	72. B
53. D	58. B	63. B	68. B	73. D
54. D	59. C	64. A	69. C	74. A
55. D	60. A	65. C	70. D	75. C

1. **The correct answer is B.** The pattern is "subtract 1, subtract 1, add 1, etc." At this point in the series, subtract 1 from 8 to get 7.

2. **The correct answer is A.** The series on both sides of the blank reads +6, –8. 25 + 6 = 31. Then, to confirm, 31 – 8 = 23.

3. **The correct answer is C.** The pattern in this series is to add 4 to each number. 26 + 4 = 30.

4. **The correct answer is C.** This series is basically the alphabet, but every other set presents the letters in reverse order. As we reach the next set, we are back to alphabetical order again. If you quickly write the alphabet across the page in your workbook (or your test booklet), you will find alphabetic series questions much easier to figure out.

5. **The correct answer is B.** With each term, the power of 2 and the power of 3 are increased by one, and the position of the power of 2 and power of 3 in the fraction change from numerator to denominator. The next term has $2^4 = 16$ in the denominator and $3^4 = 81$ in the numerator. The term after that has $2^5 = 32$ in the numerator and $3^5 = 243$ in the denominator.

6. **The correct answer is D.** The odd terms (the 1st, 3rd, 5th, etc.) are obtained by dividing the previous odd term by 2, and the even terms (the 2nd, 4th, 6th, etc.) are obtained by subtracting 3 from the previous even term. So, the next two terms are $4 \div 2 = 2$ and $5 - 3 = 2$.

7. **The correct answer is A.** The pattern is "alternate between adding 5 and subtracting 2." At this point in the series, add 5 to 9 to get 14, and then subtract 2 from 14 to get 12.

8. **The correct answer is C.** The pattern is "add 3, add 5, add 7, etc." At this point in the series, add 7 to 13 to get 20. Note that then adding 9 to this gives 29, the next term provided.

9. **The correct answer is B.** Each set begins with *A* and ends with *B*. Then we find an alphabetic sequence beginning with *B* at the second position in each set and an alphabetic sequence beginning with *D* in the third position in each set.

10. **The correct answer is B.** The pattern is "multiply by 0.1, multiply by 0.01, multiply by 0.001, etc." At this point in the series, multiply 0.01 by 0.01 to get 0.0001. Note that then multiplying 0.0001 by 0.001 gives 0.0000001, the next term provided.

11. **The correct answer is A.** The pattern is "the first letter in the pair is obtained by going backward in the alphabet by 2 letters, and the second letter in the double is obtained by proceeding forward in the alphabet to the next letter." So, the next two terms of the sequence are RT and PU.

12. **The correct answer is D.** The pattern is "subtract 2, subtract 4, subtract 8, subtract 16, etc." So, the next term of the sequence is $39 - 16 = 23$.

13. **The correct answer is B.** The pattern is "alternate between multiplying by 2 and adding $\frac{1}{4}$." So, the next two terms are $\frac{13}{4} \times 2 = \frac{13}{2}$ and $\frac{13}{2} + \frac{1}{4} = \frac{27}{4}$.

Answers HSPT® Quantitative Skills Drill

14. **The correct answer is B.** These are all consecutive prime numbers. The prime number between 17 and 23 is 19.

15. **The correct answer is A.** Each term starts with a vowel and is followed by the two consecutive consonants that come after it in the alphabet. So, IJK should fill in the blank.

16. **The correct answer is C.** The pattern is "add two consecutive terms to get the next one." So, the number you would add to 0.30 to get 0.45 is 0.15. Therefore, this is the first term.

17. **The correct answer is B.** The pattern is "subtract 3, subtract 3, subtract 4, subtract 4, subtract 5, subtract 5." Subtracting 5 from 67 gives 62 as the next term.

18. **The correct answer is A.** The pattern is to "skip 3 letters to get the next term in the sequence, alternate between using a 3 and 6 as the second part of a term in the sequence, and reverse the order of letter and number with each consecutive term." Here, skipping 3 letters after J gives the letter N; the next term should use a 6, and the number should come first. The next term is 6N.

19. **The correct answer is D.** Each time, the digit in the ones place increases by 1. The number string following the decimal point increases in length by one digit, and the number used to create that string increases by 1. So, the next term in the sequence must be 5.6666.

20. **The correct answer is C.** Each term in the sequence is obtained by adding $\frac{2}{3}$ to the previous one. The next two terms are found as follows:

$$2\frac{5}{6}+\frac{2}{3}=\frac{17}{6}+\frac{2}{3}=\frac{21}{6}=3\frac{3}{6}=3\frac{1}{2}$$

$$3\frac{1}{2}+\frac{2}{3}=\frac{7}{2}+\frac{2}{3}=\frac{25}{6}=4\frac{1}{6}$$

21. **The correct answer is C.** This is a difficult question. You can see immediately that we are dealing with the alphabet in reverse and that no letters have been skipped. But what is the rule that governs? Assign a number to each letter in the first group, basing the number on natural sequence. Thus, figure W-X-Y-Z would be 1-2-3-4; here they appear Z-Y-W-X or 4-3-1-2. Follow through with the remaining groupings, and you will find that all adhere to the same 4-3-1-2 rule. The answer becomes apparent: NMKL.

22. **The correct answer is A.** The pattern is "multiply the denominator of a term by 5 to get the denominator of the next term, and to skip 4 letters to get the letter in the numerator." Skipping four letters after C yields the letter H and multiplying 3 by 5 yields 15. So, the next term in the sequence is $\frac{H}{15}$.

23. **The correct answer is C.** The pattern is "alternate between multiplying by $\frac{3}{2}$ and subtracting $\frac{3}{2}$." The next two terms are as follows:

$$7\frac{1}{2} \times \frac{3}{2} = \frac{15}{2} \times \frac{3}{2} = \frac{45}{4} = 11\frac{1}{4}$$

$$11\frac{1}{4} - \frac{3}{2} = \frac{45}{4} - \frac{3}{2} = \frac{39}{4} = 9\frac{3}{4}$$

24. **The correct answer is B.** The odd terms (the 1st, 3rd, 5th, etc.) are obtained by moving backward through the alphabet and skipping two letters to get the next one. The even terms (the 2nd, 4th, 6th, etc.) are obtained by multiplying by $\frac{2}{3}$. So, the next two terms are Q and $\frac{8}{27}$.

25. **The correct answer is B.** The pattern is "add two consecutive terms to get the next one." So, the missing term is 2.8 + 3.9 = 6.7.

26. **The correct answer is B.** Begin with $\frac{1}{3}$ of 18:

$$\frac{1}{3} \times \frac{18}{1} = 6$$

Then, 6 + 5 = 11.

27. **The correct answer is A.** First figure 4 squared. The number 7 less than 16 is 9:

$$4^2 = 4 \times 4 = 16$$
$$16 - 7 = 9$$

28. **The correct answer is D.** 42 + 3 = 45. 45 ÷ 9 = 5.

29. **The correct answer is B.** Let x equal the number.

$$30\% + 50\% = 80\% = 0.80$$
$$0.80x = 96$$
$$x = 96 \div 0.80$$
$$= 120$$

30. **The correct answer is B.** 4 × 5 = 20 × 3 = 60. We need to add nothing at all (0) to 60 to get 60.

31. **The correct answer is D.** First, find of $\frac{2}{3}$ 27: $\frac{2}{3} \times 27 = 18$. Then add: 18 + 5 = 23.

32. The correct answer is C. The sum of $7 + 18 + 5 + 39 + 11 = 80$.

$$80 \div 5 = 16$$
$$\frac{1}{2} \text{ of } 16 = 8$$

33. The correct answer is C. This problem can be done with algebra. If x is the number you are looking for, solve as follows:

$$x \div 2 = 6 + 4$$
$$2(x \div 2) = (6 + 4)2$$
$$x = 20$$

34. The correct answer is D. To begin, find $\frac{1}{4}$ of 20. This is the same as saying $20 \div 4$, which equals 5. If x is the number you are looking for, solve as follows:

$$7 - x = 5$$
$$x = 2$$

35. The correct answer is D. The cube of 4 divided by 4 is the square of $4 = 16$. $16 + 3 = 19$.

36. The correct answer is B. Let x represent the number. 25% of x is $0.25x$, and 40% of x is $0.40x$. The product is $(0.25x)(0.40x) = 14.4$. Simplifying the equation yields the equivalent equation $0.1x^2 = 14.4$. Divide by 0.1 to get $x^2 = 144$. Taking the square root gives $x = 12$.

37. The correct answer is C. $\frac{4}{5}$ of $80 = 64 + 3 = 67$; $82 - 67 = 15$.

38. The correct answer is B. $\frac{1}{8}$ of $96 = 12 \times 6 = 72$.

39. The correct answer is C. $\frac{5}{9}$ of $99 = 55 + 15 = 70$.

40. The correct answer is B. Let x be the number. The given description translates to the equation $4x - 1 = 27$. Adding 1 to both sides and then dividing by 4 yields $x = 7$.

41. The correct answer is D. Let x be the number. The given description translates to the equation $0.30(x + 5) = 18$. Dividing both sides by 0.30 and the subtracting 5 yields $x = 55$.

42. The correct answer is A. Let x be the number. The given description translates to the equation $6x - 2 = 3x + 10$. Adding 2 to and subtracting $3x$ from both sides yields the equation $3x = 12$. Dividing by 3 yields $x = 4$.

43. **The correct answer is C.** Let x be the number. The given description translates to the equation $\frac{1}{x+2} = \frac{3}{8}$. Cross-multiplying yields the equation $3(x + 2) = 8$, which is equivalent to $3x + 6 = 8$. Subtracting 6 from both sides and then dividing by 3 yields $x = \frac{2}{3}$.

44. **The correct answer is B.** Let x be the number. The given description translates to the equation $\frac{x + 2x + (6 + 3x)}{3} = 12$,, which is equivalent to $\frac{6x + 6}{3} = 12$. Multiplying both sides by 3 yields $6x + 6 = 20$. So, subtracting 6 from both sides and then dividing by 6 yields $x = 5$.

45. **The correct answer is B.** Let x be the number. The given description translates to the equation $1.20x = 72$. So, dividing both sides by 1.2 yields $x = 60$. Then, 80% of 60 is $0.80(60) = 48$.

46. **The correct answer is C.** The shading in II is symmetric about the horizontal edge shared by the two shaded squares, and the shading in III is symmetric about the center of the circle.

47. **The correct answer is C.** Since XYZ is a right triangle, use the Pythagorean theorem to get $5^2 + (ZY)^2 = 13^2$. So, $25 + (ZY)^2 = 169$, which is equivalent to $(ZY)^2 = 144$. Taking the square root of both sides gives $ZY = 12$.

48. **The correct answer is D.** Let x be the number. The given description translates to the equation $\frac{5}{9}x = \frac{3}{4}(15 + 5)$, which is equivalent to $\frac{5}{9}x = 15$. Multiplying both sides by $\frac{9}{5}$ yields $x = 27$.

49. **The correct answer is C.** Vertical angles are always congruent, so $\angle m = \angle n$. Note that corresponding angles obtained by cutting two lines with a transversal are NOT congruent unless the two lines are parallel; this is not assumed here.

50. **The correct answer is A.** Corresponding sides of the rectangles I and III are in the same proportion of $\frac{1}{2}$. So, they are similar.

51. **The correct answer is B.** If we change A, B, and C so that they are all in the same form—in this case, decimals—we see that A = 0.4, B = 0.04, and C = 0.4. Therefore, A is equal to C and greater than B.

52. **The correct answer is B.** Perform the multiplication as indicated to arrive at these values:

$$A = 5x + 5y$$
$$B = 5x + y$$
$$C = 5x + 5y + x = 6x + 5y$$

It can now be seen that choice B has the least value, choice C has the greatest value, and choice A has a value between these. Therefore, B is less than A, which is less than C.

53. **The correct answer is D.** First do the arithmetic. Choice A is 15; choice B is 125; and choice C is 9. B is greater than A and C.

54. **The correct answer is D.** Determine the numerical value of A, B, and C:

A. $(4 \times 2) - 3 = 8 - 3 = 5$
B. $(4 \times 3) - 2 = 12 - 2 = 10$
C. $(4 \times 3) - 2 = 7 - 2 = 5$

Compare the values: B > A, and A = C; thus B > C. Now, test each answer choice to see which one is true. The only true statement is that A and C are equal.

55. **The correct answer is D.** A = 10 because you move the decimal point 4 units to the right; B = 0.01 because you move the decimal point 3 units to the left; and C = 0.001 because you move the decimal point 2 units to the left. So, C < B < A.

56. **The correct answer is B.** A is equal to 2(0.5) = 1.0; B is equal 0.5(2) = 1.0; and C is equal to 0.0002(500) = 0.1. So, A = B and C < A.

57. **The correct answer is D.** This is perhaps easiest to see by using a specific value of x satisfying the condition $0 < x < 1$. Take $x = \frac{1}{2}$. Observe $x^2 = \left(\frac{1}{2}\right)^2 = \frac{1}{4}$, $2x = 2\left(\frac{1}{2}\right) = 1$, and $x^3 = \left(\frac{1}{2}\right)^3 = \frac{1}{8}$. So, C < A and A < B.

58. **The correct answer is B.** Using the order of operations, A is equal to 5 + 3(2) = 5 + 6 = 11; B is equal to 5 + 12 – 2 = 17 – 2 = 15; and C is equal to 8(2) = 16. So, A < B and B < C.

59. **The correct answer is C.** This is perhaps easiest to see by using a specific value of y satisfying the condition $y > 1$. Take $y = 2$. Observe $\frac{1}{y} = \frac{1}{2}$ and $y^2 = 2^2 = 4$. So, B < A and A < C.

60. **The correct answer is A.** A is equal to $\frac{2(7) + 3(3)}{3(7)} = \frac{23}{21}$; B is equal to $\frac{5}{10} = \frac{1}{2}$; and C is equal to $\frac{23}{21}$. So, A = C and B < A.

61. **The correct answer is D.** The perimeter of A is 2(3) + 2(8) = 22 inches; the perimeter of B is 4(5) = 20 inches; and the perimeter of C is 2(10) + 2(1) = 22 inches. So, A = C and B < A.

62. **The correct answer is C.** A is equal to –25; B is equal to 25; and C is equal to –25. So, A = C and C < B.

63. **The correct answer is B.** The area of A is $\frac{1}{2}(3)(12) = 18m^2$; the area of B is $\frac{1}{2}(6)(6) = 18m^2$; and the area of C is $\frac{1}{2}(4)(9) = 18m^2$. So, all three have the same area.

64. **The correct answer is A.** Using the order of operations, A is equal to –4(6) = –24, B is equal to –24, and C is equal to –32 – 2 = –34. So, A = B and B > C.

65. **The correct answer is C.** Both A and B equal 24 since the parentheses are unnecessary when simply multiplying three numbers. However, C equals (12)(8) = 96. So, A = B and B < C.

66. **The correct answer is C.** A is equal to $\frac{1}{3^2} = \frac{1}{9}$, B is equal to $\left(\frac{1}{2}\right)^3 = \frac{1}{8}$, and C is equal to $2 \cdot \frac{2}{3} = \frac{4}{3}$. So, A < B and B < C.

67. **The correct answer is A.** First, note that $p = 75°$ since the angle under the line *T* and adjacent to the angle labeled as having a measure of 105° has a measure of 75°, and this angle and p are corresponding angles; since l and m are parallel lines cut by the transversal *T*, corresponding angles must be congruent. Next, since the sum of the three angles of any triangle must be 180°, it follows that $q = 85°$. Finally, since r and q are corresponding angles, they are congruent; so, $r = 85°$. Hence, $p < r$ and $r = q$.

68. **The correct answer is B.** First, since $y < x < 0$, it follows that xy is positive, while both $2y$ and $y + x$ are negative. So, xy is the largest of the three quantities. Also, $2y = y + y < y + x$ since $y < x$. So, $2y$ is less than $y + x$. Hence, B < C and C < A.

69. **The correct answer is C.** This is perhaps easiest if you plug in a value for x satisfying the condition $0 < x < 1$, say $x = \frac{1}{4}$. Observe that $x^2 = \left(\frac{1}{4}\right)^2 = \frac{1}{16}$ and $\sqrt{x} = \sqrt{\frac{1}{4}} = \frac{1}{2}$. So, B < A and A < C.

70. **The correct answer is D.** A is equal to $\frac{2}{3} \div \frac{1}{2} = \frac{2}{3} \cdot 2 = \frac{4}{3}$; B is equal to $2 \div \frac{3}{2} = 2 \cdot \frac{2}{3} = \frac{4}{3}$; and C is equal to $\frac{2}{3} \div 2 = \frac{2}{3} \cdot \frac{1}{2} = \frac{1}{3}$. So, C < A and A = B.

71. **The correct answer is D.** Using the order of operations, A is equal to $5 \div 2 = 2.5$, B is equal to $0.2 \div 0.02 = 10$, and C is equal to $5 \div 2 = 2.5$. So, A = C and C < B.

Answers HSPT® Quantitative Skills Drill

72. **The correct answer is B.** The area of the shaded portion of A is $\frac{1}{2}\pi(2)^2 = 2\pi$ in^2; the area of the shaded portion of B is $\pi(1)^2 = \pi$ in^2; and the area of the shaded portion of C is $\frac{1}{4}\pi(1)^2 = \frac{1}{4}\pi$ in^2. So, C < B and B < A.

73. **The correct answer is D.** Using the order of operations, A is equal to 8 + 12 = 20 and B is equal to 4(5) = 20. So, A = B and B < C.

74. **The correct answer is A.** Convert all mixed numbers to improper fractions and then perform the indicated operation. Doing so shows that A is equal to $\frac{7}{5} - \frac{4}{3} = \frac{21-20}{15} = \frac{1}{15}$; B is equal to $\frac{11}{2} \cdot \frac{11}{5} = \frac{121}{10} = 12\frac{1}{10}$; and C is equal to $\frac{1}{2} \div \frac{5}{2} = \frac{1}{2} \cdot \frac{2}{5} = \frac{1}{5}$. So, A < C and C < B.

75. **The correct answer is C.** A is equal to $4^2 + 5^2 = 16 + 25 = 41$; B is equal to $(4 + 5)^2 = 9^2 = 81$; and C is equal to $4^2 \cdot 2^3 = 16 \cdot 8 = 128$. So, A < B and B < C.

TACHS Ability Questions Drill

25 Questions

Figure Classification

Directions: In questions 1–9, the first figures are alike in certain ways. Choose the answer choice that goes with the first three figures. Mark the corresponding letter on your answer sheet.

1.

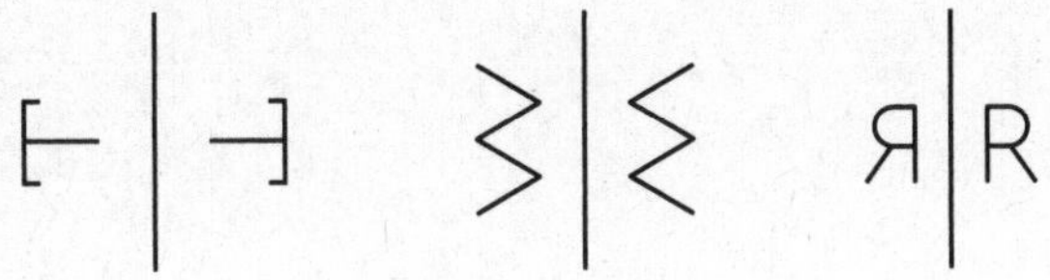

A.

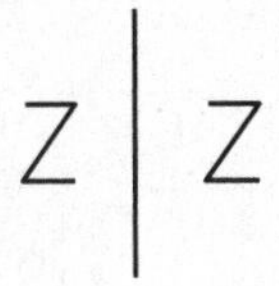

B.

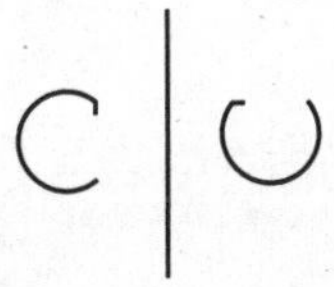

C.

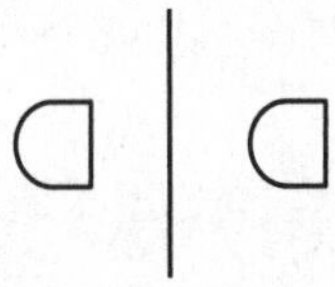

D.

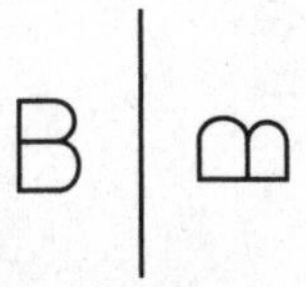

E.

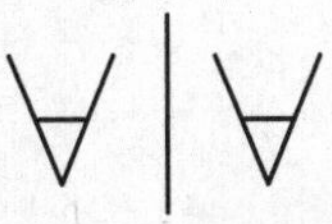

2.

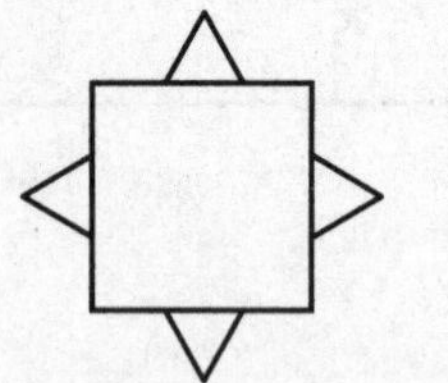

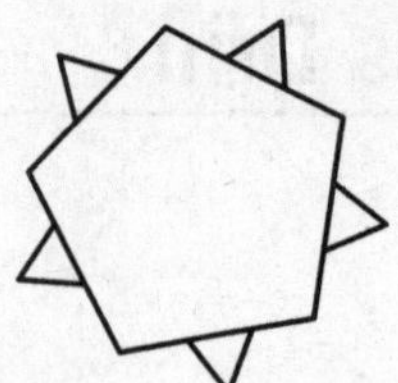

A.

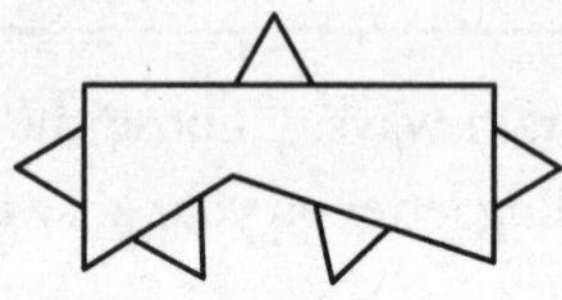

B.

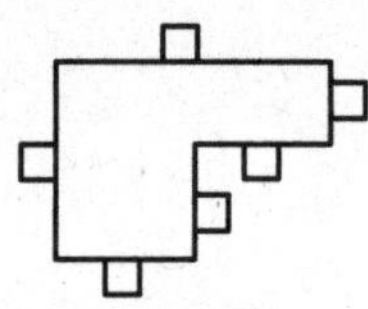

C.

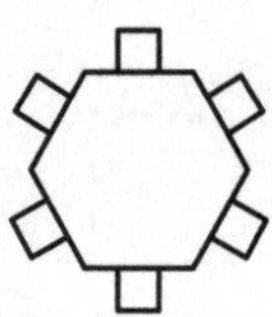

D.

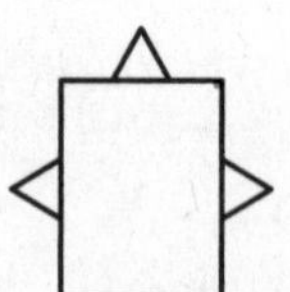

E.

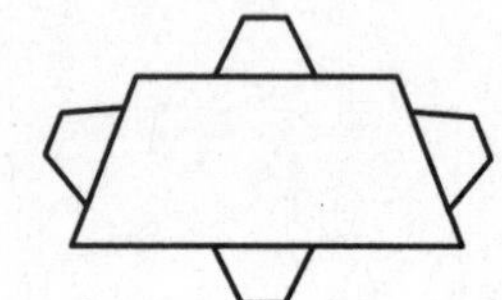

3. 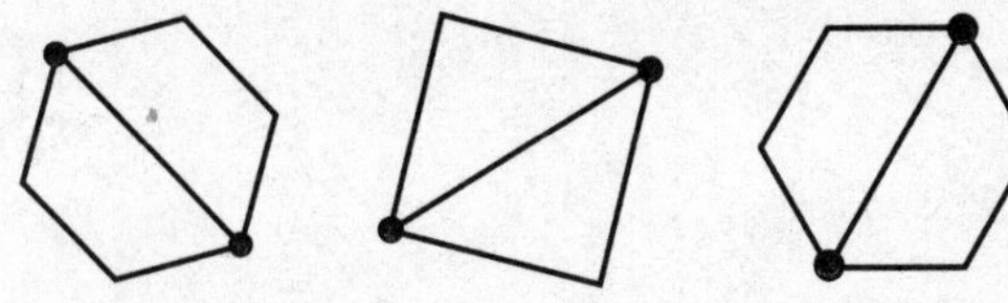

A. 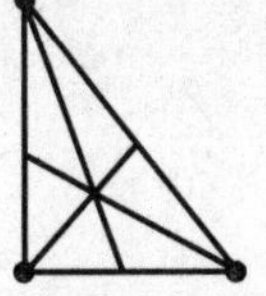

B. 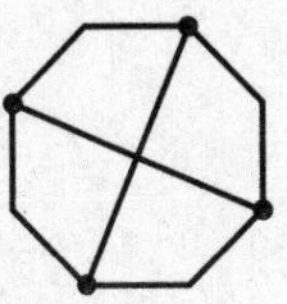

C. 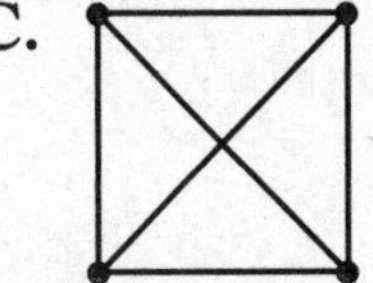

D. 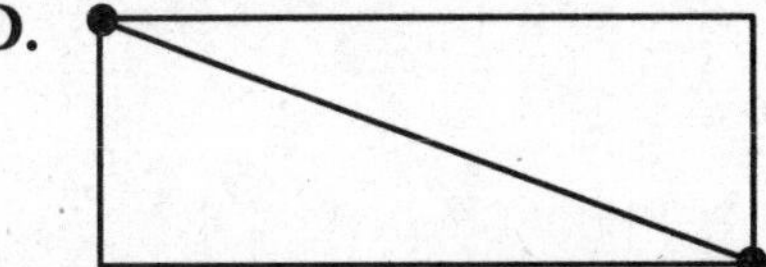

E. 

4. 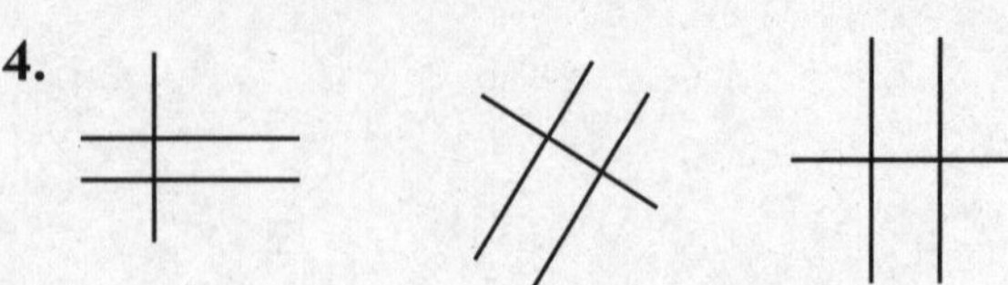

A. 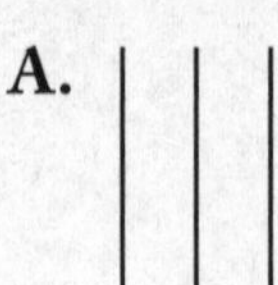

B.

C. 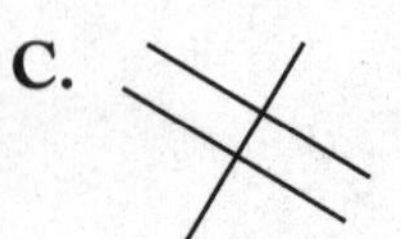

D.

E.

5. 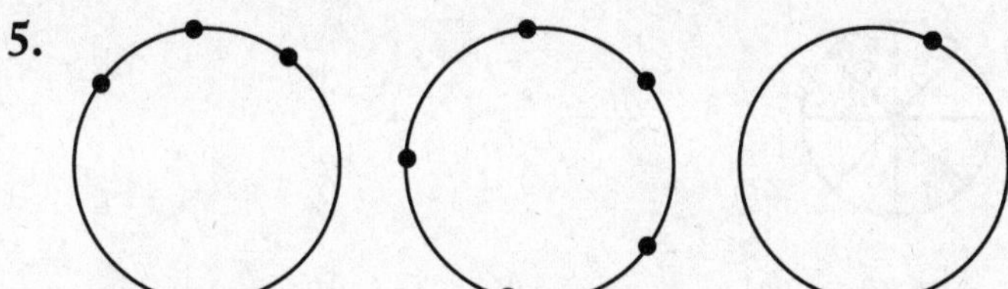

A. 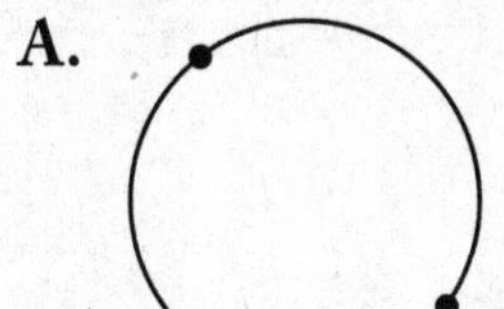

B. 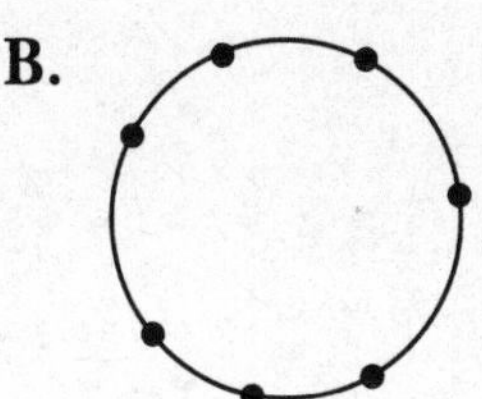

C. 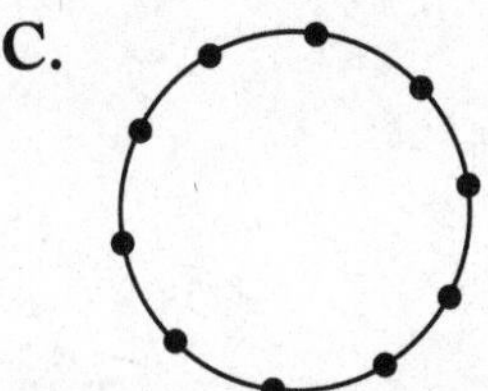

D. 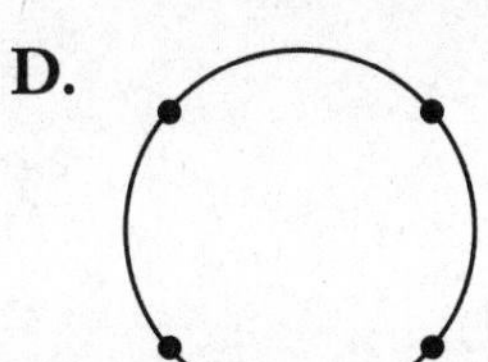

E. 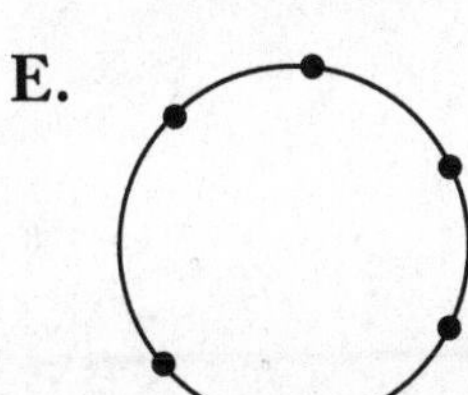

6. 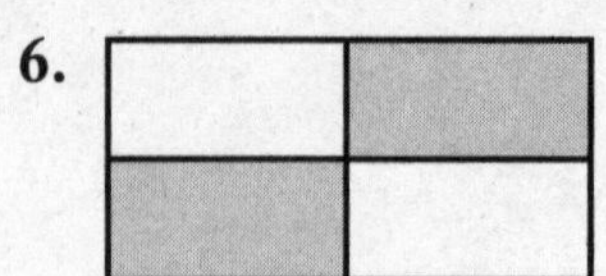  

A. 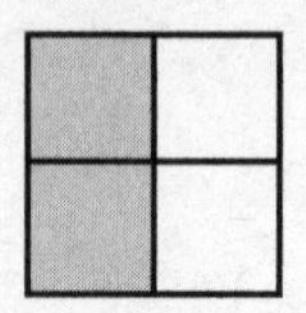

B. 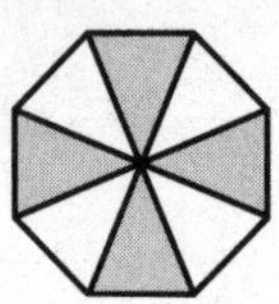

C. 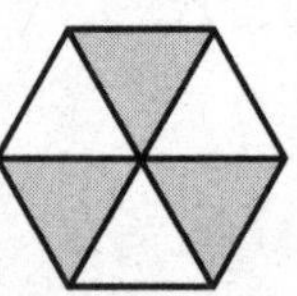

D. 

E. 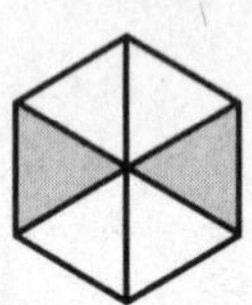

7. 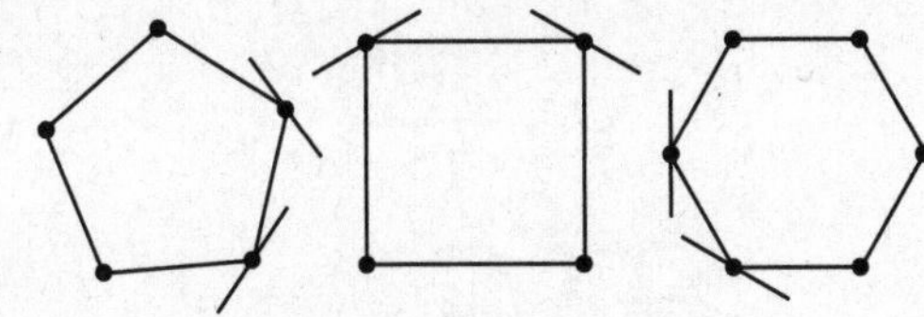

A. 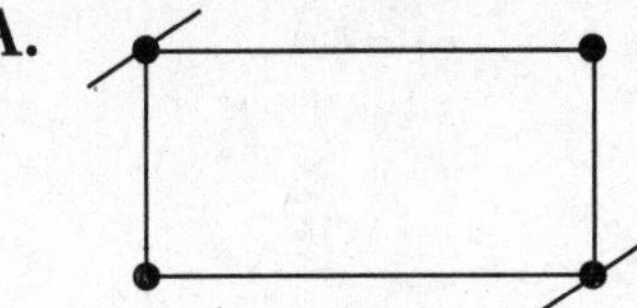

B. 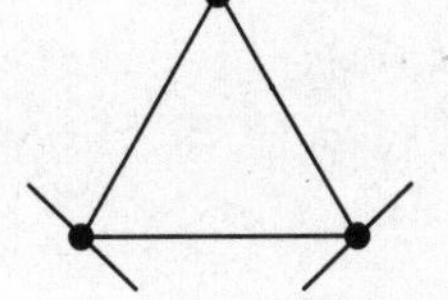

C. 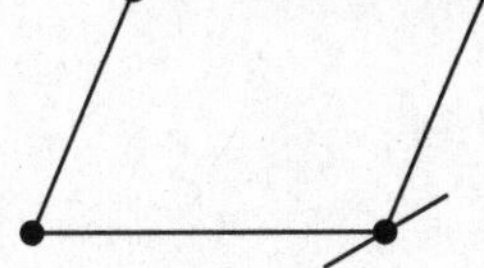

D. 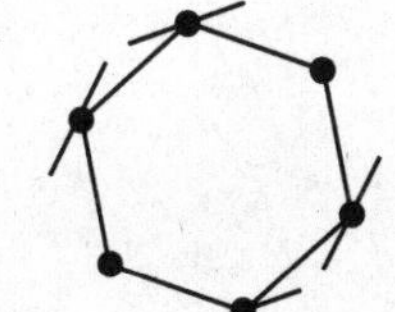

E. 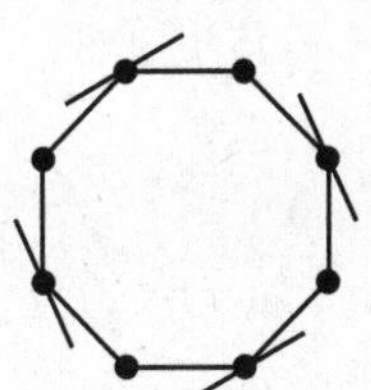

8. 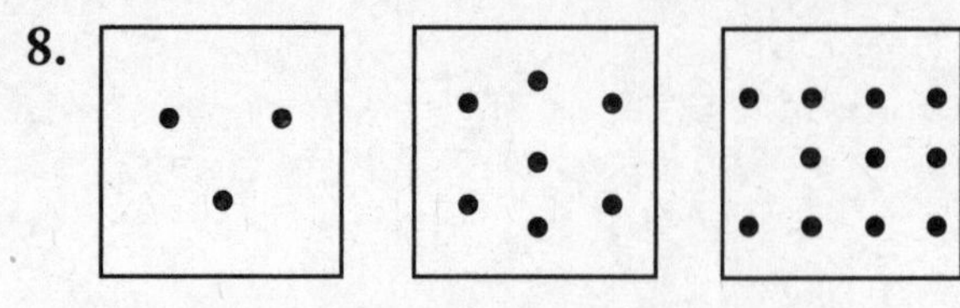

A. 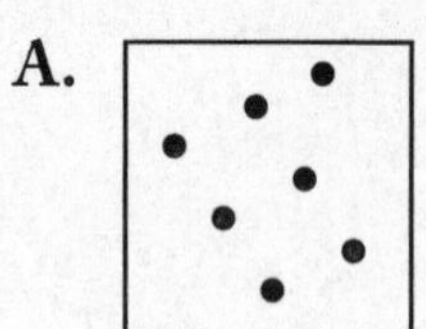

B. 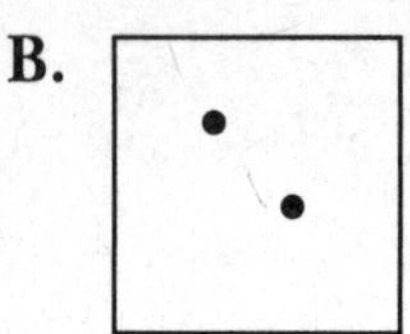

C. 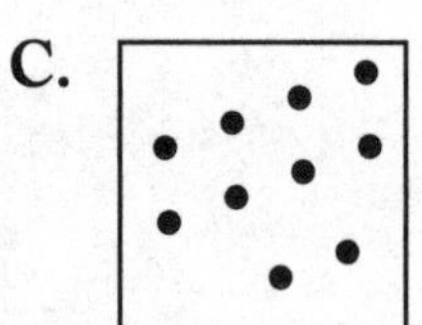

D. 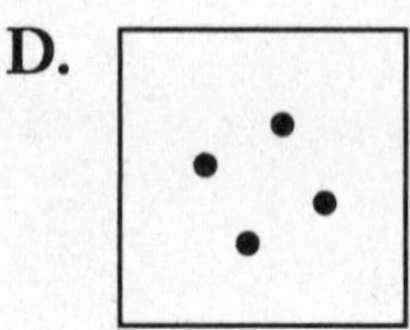

E. 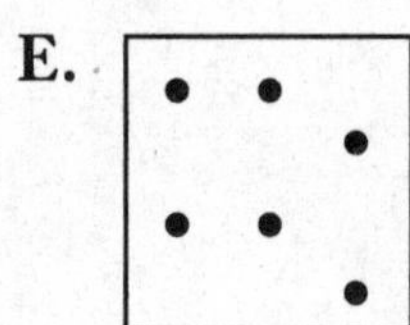

9. 

A. 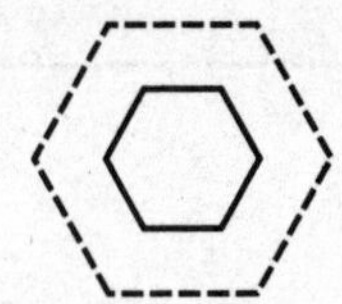

B. 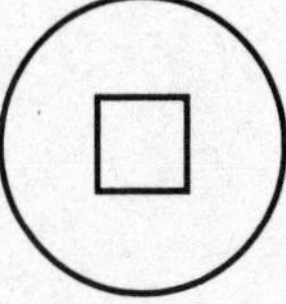

C. 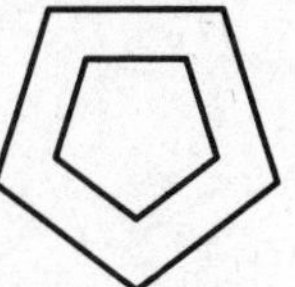

D. 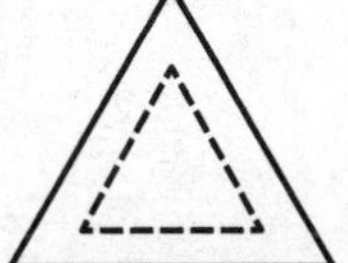

E. 

Figure Matrices

Directions: For questions 10–17, find the figure that completes the puzzle. Mark the corresponding letter on your answer sheet.

10. 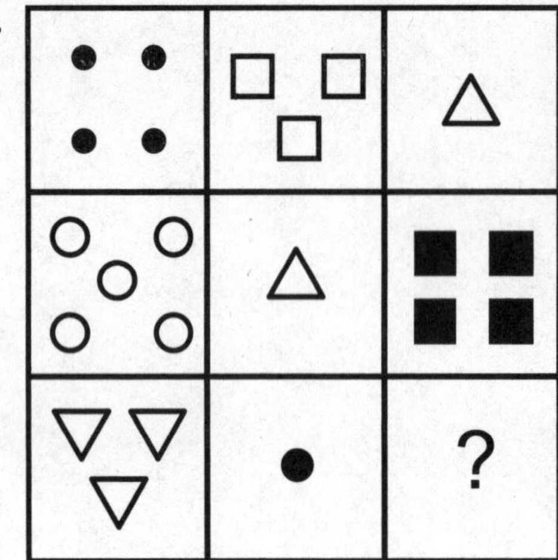

A.

B.

C.

D.

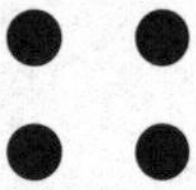

E.

11. 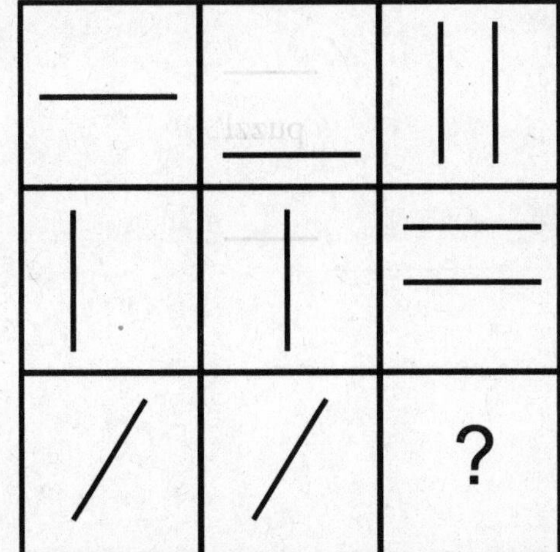

A. 

B. 

C. 

D.

E. 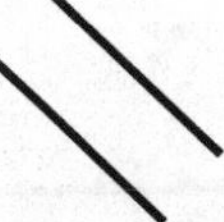

12.

?

A. 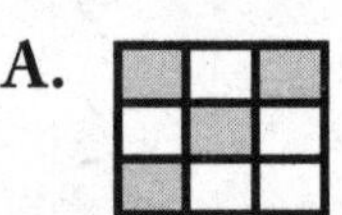

B. 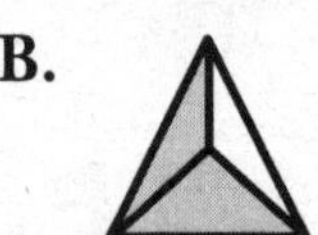

C. 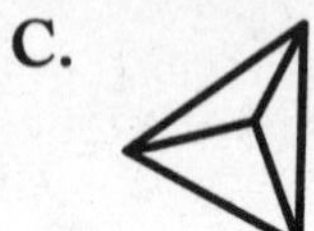

D. 

E. 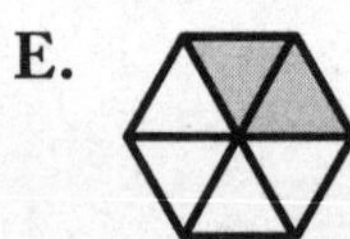

13. 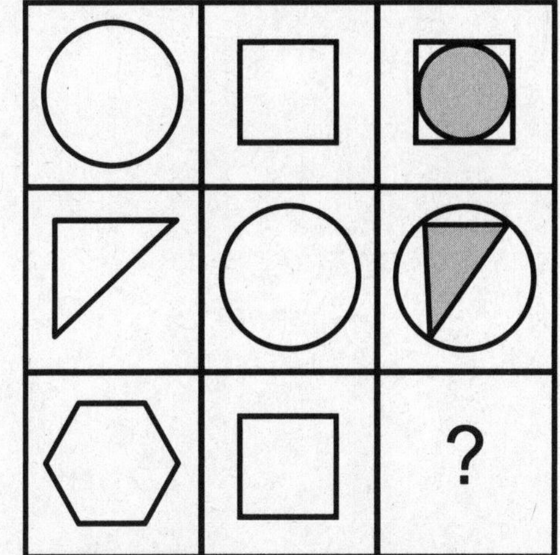

A. 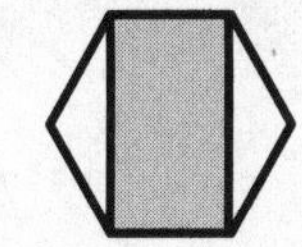

B. 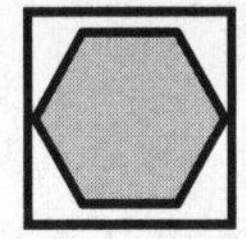

C. 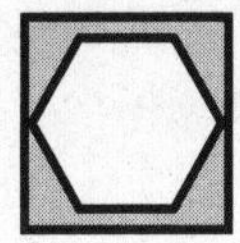

D. 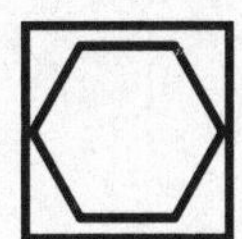

E. 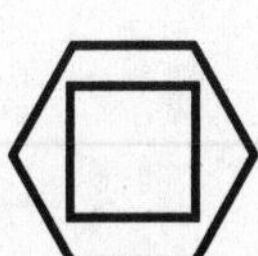

14. ?

A.

B.

C.

D.

E.

15. 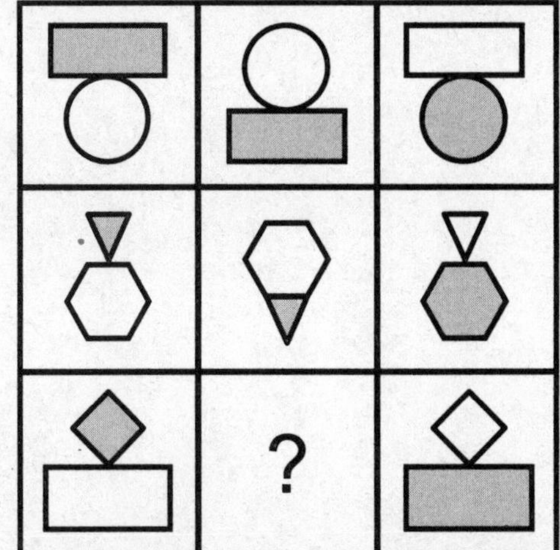

A. 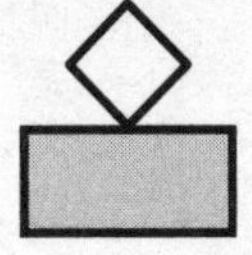

B. 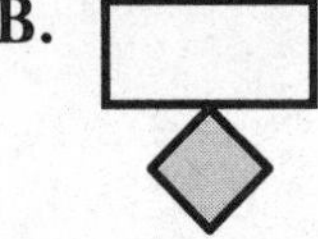

C. 

D. 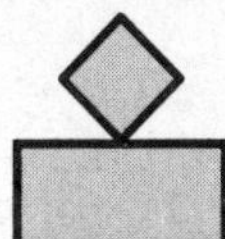

E. 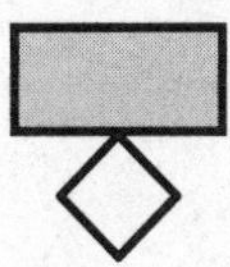

16. 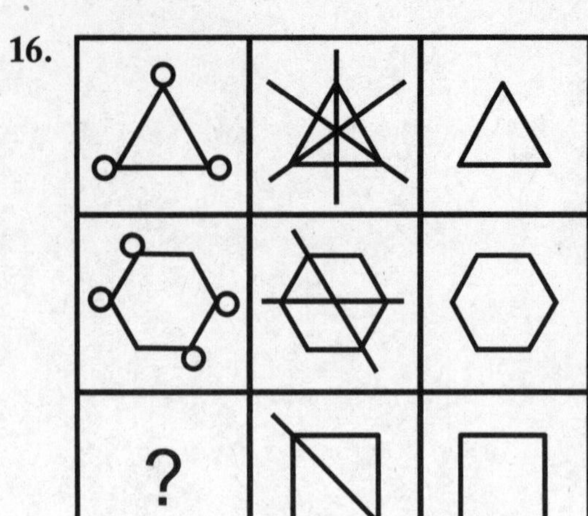

A. 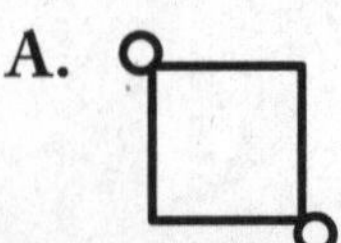

B. 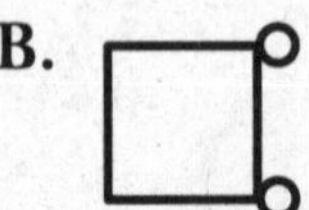

C. 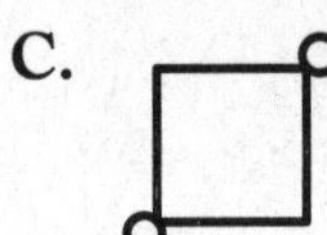

D.

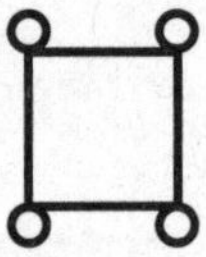

E.

17. 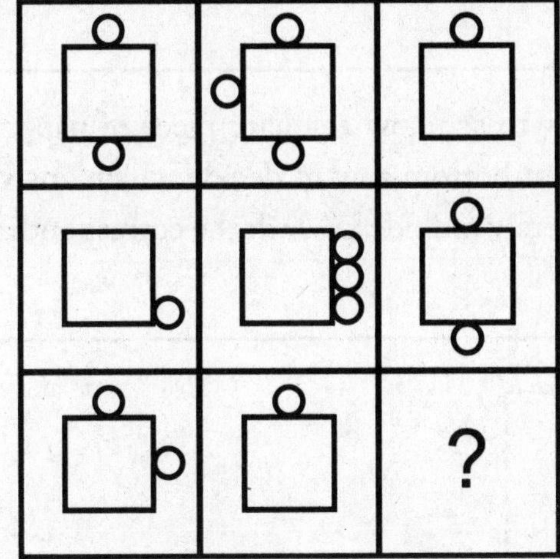

A.

B.

C.

D.

E.

Paper Folding

Directions: For questions 18–25, look at the top row to see how a square piece of paper is folded and where holes are punched in it. Then look at bottom row to decide which answer choice shows how the paper will look when it is completely unfolded. Mark the corresponding letter on your answer sheet.

18. 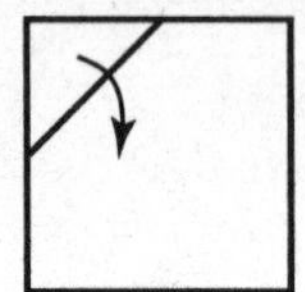 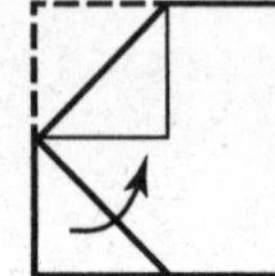 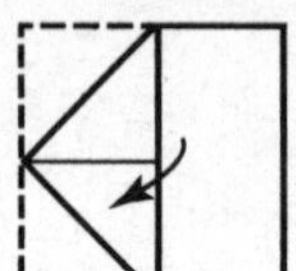 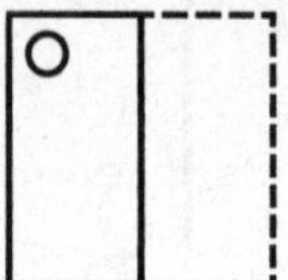

A. 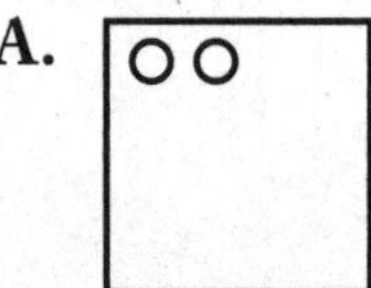

B. 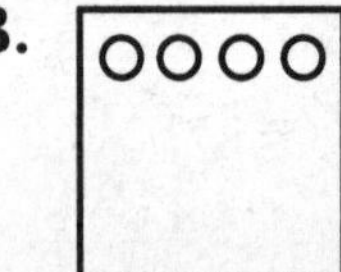

C. 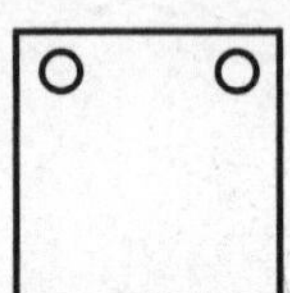

D. 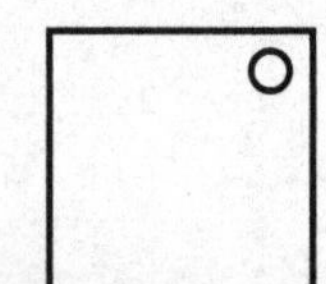

E.

19.

A.

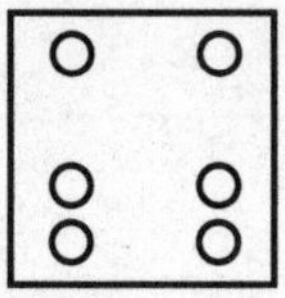

B.

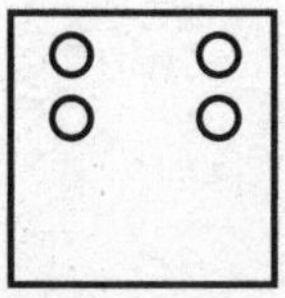

C.

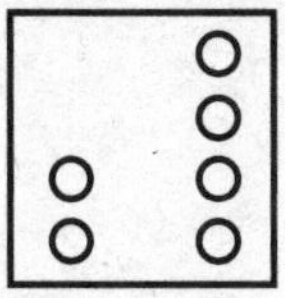

D.

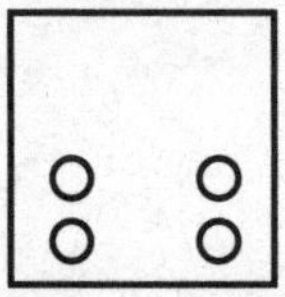

E.

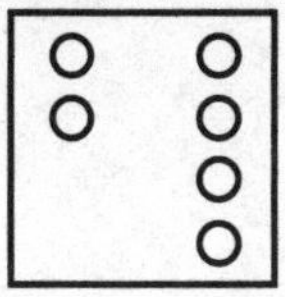

20. 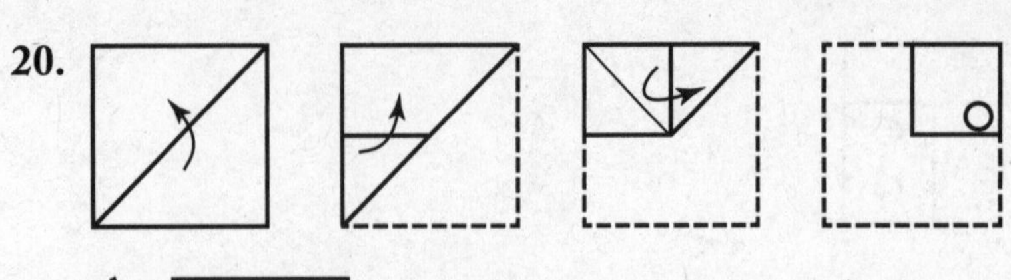

A. 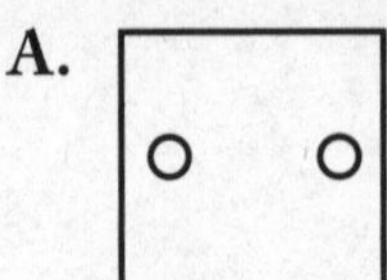

B. 

C. 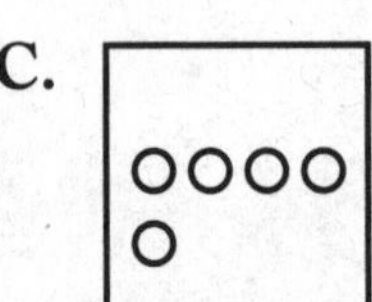

D. 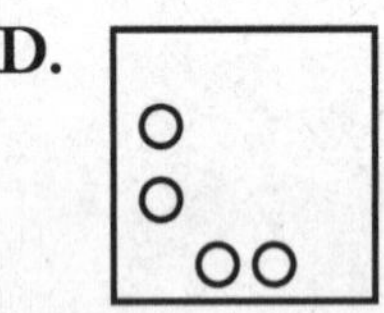

E. 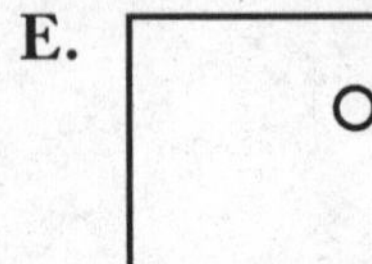

21.

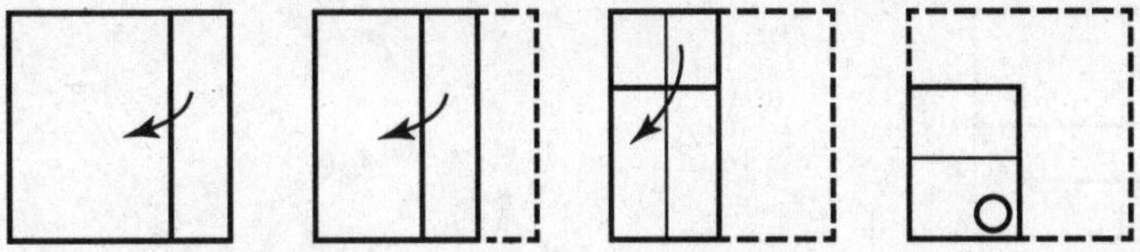

A.

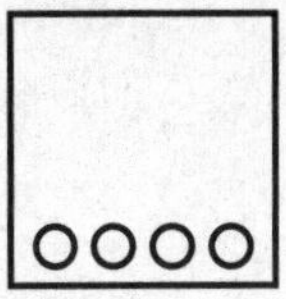

B.

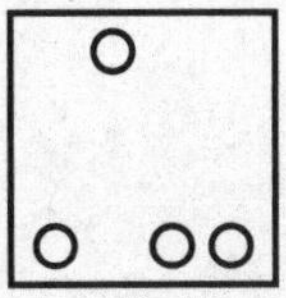

C.

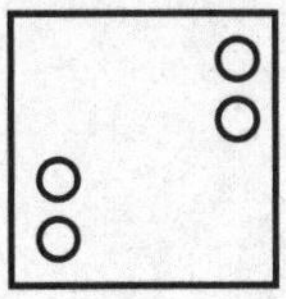

D.

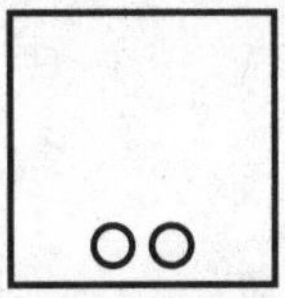

E.

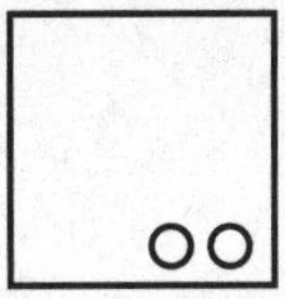

22. 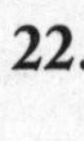

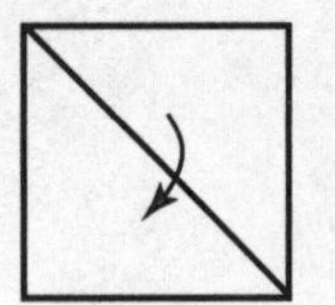 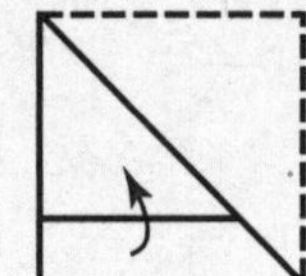 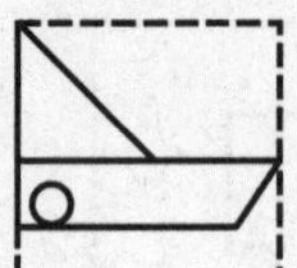

A. 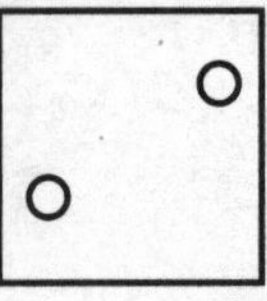

B. 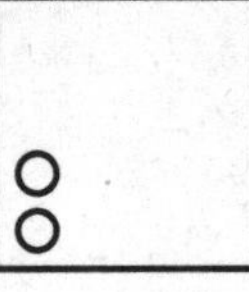

C. 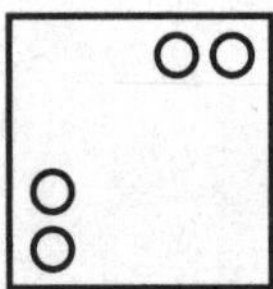

D. 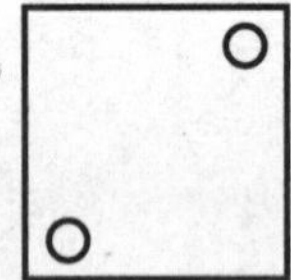

E. 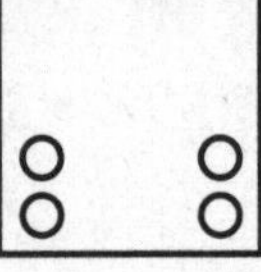

23. 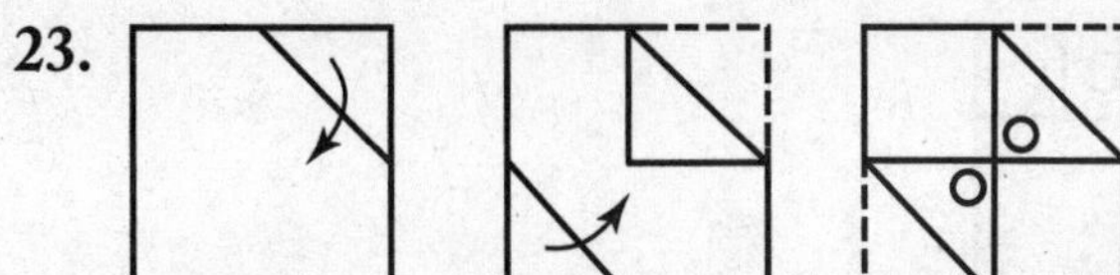

A. 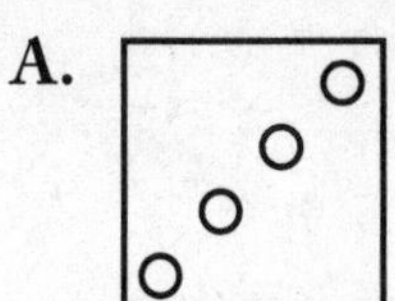

B. 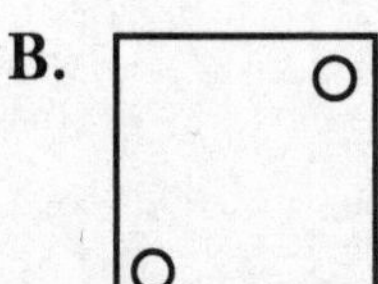

C. 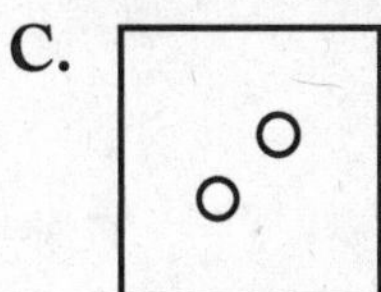

D. 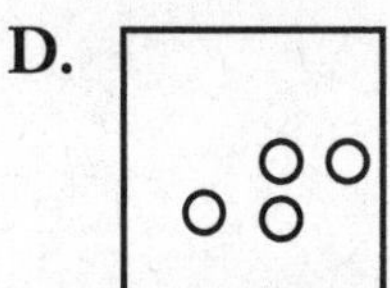

E. 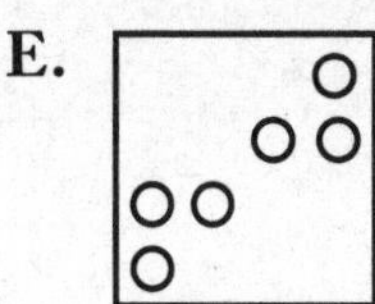

24. 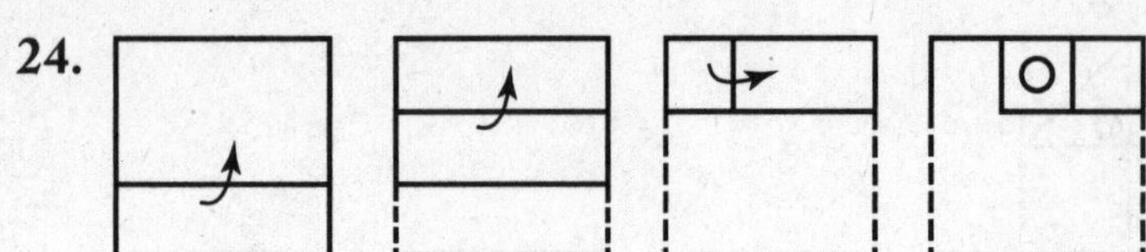

A.

B.

C.

D.

E.

25. 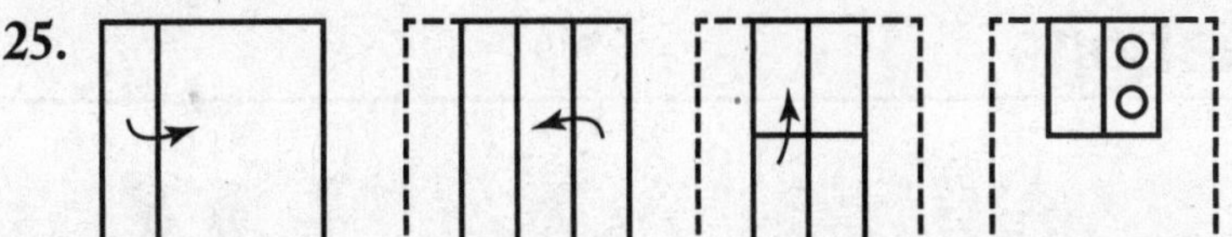

A.

B.

C.

D.

E.

Answer Key and Explanations

1. E	**6.** E	**11.** E	**16.** A	**21.** A
2. A	**7.** B	**12.** A	**17.** E	**22.** C
3. D	**8.** A	**13.** B	**18.** D	**23.** A
4. C	**9.** C	**14.** C	**19.** A	**24.** D
5. B	**10.** B	**15.** B	**20.** D	**25.** C

Figure Classification

1. **The correct answer is E.** The figures on either side of the line are reflections of each other.

2. **The correct answer is A.** An equilateral triangle is affixed to *every* edge of the figure.

3. **The correct answer is D.** Exactly one pair of diametrically opposed vertices are connected by a line segment in each figure.

4. **The correct answer is C.** The figures consist of a pair of parallel lines and a line that is perpendicular to them.

5. **The correct answer is B.** Each of the circles has an odd number of points on it. The circle in choice B has 7 points on it, which is an odd number.

6. **The correct answer is E.** Each figure has one pair of congruent sectors diametrically opposed across the center that are shaded.

7. **The correct answer is B.** Each figure has line segments passing through, on the outside, exactly two *consecutive* vertices of the figure.

8. **The correct answer is A.** The number of points inside each figure is a prime number. The figure in choice A has 7 points inside, which is prime.

9. **The correct answer is C.** Each figure is comprised of two concentric versions of itself, and both are either solid or dotted.

Figure Matrices

10. **The correct answer is B.** There are three characteristics of note in each row. First, two of the three cells contain figures that are NOT shaded. Second, if you subtract the number of figures in the first and second columns, you get the number of figures in the third column. And third, the type of figure in each of the three cells in a row are all different. So, the only option that meets all the needed characteristics is choice B.

11. **The correct answer is E.** The third cell in each row is obtained by lining up the parallel segments in the first two cells and then rotating that pair by 90 degrees.

12. **The correct answer is A.** Subtracting the number of shaded parts in the second cell from the number of shaded parts in the first cell gives you the number of parts of the figure in the third cell that must be shaded. And, of note is that each figure is divided into congruent parts, the number of which equals the number of sides of the figure. Following this scheme, the figure in the third cell in the third row must have only one part shaded.

13. **The correct answer is B.** The third cell in each row is obtained by embedding the figure in the first cell inside the figure in the second cell and shading the interior of the inside figure.

14. **The correct answer is C.** The third cell in each row is obtained by placing a figure of the same type as used in the other two cells in that row in each of the nine positions that do not have a figure in them in the other two cells.

15. **The correct answer is B.** The middle cell in each row is obtained by flipping the figure horizontally so that the effectively the shapes, with their shading, simply change positions.

16. **The correct answer is A.** The relationship between the first and second cell in each row is that each circle is replaced by a line segment emanating from its position directly across to the other side of the figure. So, the figure in the first cell of the bottom row must be a square with two circles—one above the upper-left vertex and one below the lower-right vertex.

17. **The correct answer is E.** Each row consists of a square with one circle along the outside of its perimeter, a square with two circles along the outside of its perimeter, and a square with three circles along the outside of its perimeter. It does not matter where these circles appear. The missing cell must be a square with three circles along its perimeter.

Paper Folding

18. **The correct answer is D.** Based on the folds and the location of the hole punch, only a single sheet is being punched. When unfolded, that hole will appear in the upper-right corner of the square sheet of paper.

19. **The correct answer is A.** Undoing the folds one at a time, starting with the horizontal fold, the higher of the two holes punched will occur in the upper-right corner as well as its current location. Then, undoing the next fold puts all three punches along the leftmost edge of the square sheet of paper as well. So, there are two columns consisting of three holes each along the left and right edges of the square sheet.

20. **The correct answer is D.** There are four sheets of paper through which the hole punch is punching. Unfolding the last fold shows the hole is punched in a small triangle, directly above a horizontal fold. So, when you undo that fold, there will be a hole directly above it and directly below it. Finally, each of those holes will appear along the bottom edge of the square sheet when undoing the last diagonal fold.

21. **The correct answer is A.** There are three sheets of paper through which the hole punch is punching. The final fold makes the top third of the folded paper overlap with the next third of that paper. Since the hole is punched in the lowest third, this fold will not produce additional locations of holes in the unfolded square sheet of paper. However, each of the other two folds will produce additional holes. These holes will appear along the bottom edge of the square sheet.

22. **The correct answer is C.** There are four sheets of paper through which the hole punch is punching. Undoing the last fold shows two holes in the leftmost column at the bottom. Then, undoing the last diagonal fold makes the holes appear in the upper right corner of the square sheet.

23. **The correct answer is A.** Each of the two small triangular folds meet in the middle of the square. Each of the two holes will also occur in the opposite corner of the square (top right and bottom left) when the paper is unfolded. So, there are four holes punched along the diagonal of the square extending from the lower-left vertex to the upper-right one.

24. **The correct answer is D.** There are six sheets being punched. Undoing the first fold shows two holes in the top third of the sheet, positioned in the upper-left corner and the middle of the top row. Undoing each of the other two folds results in replicating those holes in the second and third rows of the square sheet. Therefore, the result is two columns of three holes.

25. **The correct answer is C.** Since the holes are punched in the third column of four equally spaced columns on the sheet, the first fold of the sequence does not affect the location of the holes. The last fold puts holes in the bottom of the third column, resulting in the third column with four holes. Then, undoing the second fold places each of those holes in the rightmost column of the square sheet. So, when completely unfolded, the third and fourth columns of the square sheet have four holes punched.

Appendix A: Word List

A

abbreviate (verb) to make briefer, to shorten. *Because time was running out, the speaker had to abbreviate his remarks.* **abbreviation** (noun).

abrasive (adjective) irritating, grinding, rough. *The manager's rude, abrasive way of criticizing the workers was bad for morale.* **abrasion** (noun).

abridge (verb) to shorten, to reduce. *The Bill of Rights is designed to prevent Congress from abridging the rights of Americans.* **abridgment** (noun).

absolve (verb) to free from guilt, to exonerate. *The criminal jury absolved Mr. Callahan of the murder of his neighbor.* **absolution** (noun).

abstain (verb) to refrain, to hold back. *After his heart attack, William was warned by his doctor to abstain from smoking, drinking, and overeating.* **abstinence** (noun), **abstemious** (adjective).

accentuate (verb) to emphasize, to stress. *The overcast skies and chill winds only accentuate our gloomy mood.* **accentuation** (noun).

acrimonious (adjective) biting, harsh, caustic. *The election campaign became acrimonious, as the candidates traded insults and accusations.* **acrimony** (noun).

adaptable (adjective) able to be changed to be suitable for a new purpose. *Some scientists say that the mammals outlived the dinosaurs because they were more adaptable to a changing climate.* **adapt** (verb), **adaptation** (noun).

adulation (noun) extreme admiration. *The young actress received great adulation from critics and fans following her performance in the Broadway play.* **adulate** (verb), **adulatory** (adjective).

adversary (noun) an enemy or opponent. *When Germany became an American ally, the United States lost a major adversary.* **adversarial** (adjective).

adversity (noun) misfortune. *It's easy to be patient and generous when things are going well; a person's true character is revealed under adversity.* **adverse** (adjective).

aesthetic (adjective) relating to art or beauty. *Mapplethorpe's photos may be attacked on moral grounds, but no one questions their aesthetic value—they are beautiful.* **aestheticism** (noun).

affected (adjective) false, artificial. *At one time, Japanese women were taught to speak in an affected high-pitched voice, which was thought girlishly attractive.* **affect** (verb), **affectation** (noun).

aggressive (adjective) forceful, energetic, and attacking. *Some believe that a football player needs a more aggressive style of play than a soccer player.* **aggression** (noun).

alacrity (noun) promptness, speed. *Thrilled with the job offer, he accepted with alacrity—"Before they can change their minds!" he thought.* **alacritous** (adjective).

allege (verb) to state without proof. *Some have alleged that Foster was murdered, but all the evidence points to suicide.* **allegation** (noun).

alleviate (verb) to make lighter or more bearable. *Although no cure for AIDS has been found, doctors are able to alleviate the suffering of those with the disease.* **alleviation** (noun).

ambiguous (adjective) having two or more possible meanings. *The phrase, "Let's table that discussion" is ambiguous; some think it means, "Let's discuss it now," while others think it means, "Let's save it for later."* **ambiguity** (noun).

ambivalent (adjective) having two or more contradictory feelings or attitudes; uncertain. *She was ambivalent toward her impending marriage; at times she was eager to go ahead, while at other times she wanted to call it off.* **ambivalence** (noun).

amiable (adjective) likable, agreeable, friendly. *He was an amiable lab partner, always smiling, on time, and ready to work.* **amiability** (noun).

amicable (adjective) friendly, peaceable. *Although they agreed to divorce, their settlement was amicable, and they remained friends afterward.*

amplify (verb) to enlarge, expand, or increase. *Uncertain as to whether they understood, the students asked the teacher to amplify his explanation.* **amplification** (noun).

anachronistic (adjective) out of the proper time. *The reference, in Shakespeare's* Julius Caesar *to "the clock striking twelve" is anachronistic, since there were no striking timepieces in ancient Rome.* **anachronism** (noun).

anarchy (noun) absence of law or order. *For several months after the Nazi government was destroyed, there was no effective government in parts of Germany, and anarchy ruled.* **anarchic** (adjective).

anomaly (noun) something different or irregular. *Tiny Pluto, orbiting next to the giants Jupiter, Saturn, and Neptune, had long appeared to be an anomaly.* **anomalous** (adjective).

antagonism (noun) hostility, conflict, opposition. *As more and more reporters investigated the Watergate scandal, antagonism between Nixon and the press increased.* **antagonistic** (adjective), **antagonize** (verb).

antiseptic (adjective) fighting infection; extremely clean. *A wound should be washed with an antiseptic solution. The all-white offices were bare and almost antiseptic in their starkness.*

apathy (noun) lack of interest, concern, or emotion. *Tom's apathy toward his job could be seen in his lateness, his sloppy work, and his overall poor attitude.* **apathetic** (adjective).

arable (adjective) able to be cultivated for growing crops. *Rocky New England has relatively little arable farmland.*

arbiter (noun) someone able to settle disputes; a judge or referee. *The public is the ultimate arbiter of commercial value; it decides what sells and what doesn't.*

arbitrary (adjective) based on random or merely personal preference. *Both computers cost the same and had the same features, so in the end I made an arbitrary decision about which one to buy.*

arcane (adjective) little-known, mysterious, obscure. *Eliot's* Waste Land *is filled with arcane lore, including quotations in Latin, Greek, French, German, and Sanskrit.* **arcana** (noun, plural).

ardor (noun) a strong feeling of passion, energy, or zeal. *The young revolutionary proclaimed his convictions with an ardor that excited the crowd.* **ardent** (adjective).

arid (adjective) very dry; boring and meaningless. *The arid climate of Arizona makes farming difficult. Some find the law a fascinating topic, but for me it is an arid discipline.* **aridity** (noun).

ascetic (adjective) practicing strict self-discipline for moral or spiritual reasons. *The so-called Desert Fathers were hermits who lived an ascetic life of fasting, study, and prayer.* **asceticism** (verb).

assiduous (adjective) working with care, attention, and diligence. *Although Karen is not a naturally gifted math student, by assiduous study she managed to earn an A in trigonometry.* **assiduity** (noun).

astute (adjective) observant, intelligent, and shrewd. *The reporter's years of experience in Washington and his personal acquaintance with many political insiders made him an astute commentator on politics.*

atypical (adjective) not typical; unusual. *In* Hyde Park on Hudson, *Bill Murray, best known as a comic actor, gave an atypical dramatic performance.*

audacious (adjective) bold, daring, adventurous. *Her plan to cross the Atlantic single-handed in a 12-foot sailboat was audacious, if not reckless.* **audacity** (noun).

audible (adjective) able to be heard. *Although she whispered, her voice was picked up by the microphone, and her words were audible throughout the theater.* **audibility** (noun).

auspicious (adjective) promising good fortune; propitious. *The news that a team of British climbers had reached the summit of Everest seemed an auspicious sign for the reign of newly crowned Queen Elizabeth II.*

authoritarian (adjective) favoring or demanding blind obedience to leaders. *Despite Americans' belief in democracy, the American government has supported authoritarian regimes in other countries.* **authoritarianism** (noun)

B

belated (adjective) delayed past the proper time. *She called her mother on January 5th to offer her a belated "Happy New Year."*

belie (verb) to present a false or contradictory appearance. *Lena Horne's youthful appearance belied her long, distinguished career in show business.*

benevolent (adjective) wishing or doing good. *In his old age, Carnegie used his wealth for benevolent purposes, donating large sums to various libraries and schools.* **benevolence** (noun).

berate (verb) to scold or criticize harshly. *The judge angrily berated the two lawyers for their unprofessional behavior.*

bereft (adjective) lacking or deprived of something. *Bereft of parental love, orphans sometimes grow up to be insecure.*

bombastic (adjective) inflated or pompous in style. *Old-fashioned bombastic political speeches don't work on television, which demands a more intimate style of communication.* **bombast** (noun).

bourgeois (adjective) middle class or reflecting middle-class values. *The Dadaists of the 1920s produced art deliberately designed to offend bourgeois art collectors, with their taste for respectable, refined, uncontroversial pictures.* **bourgeois** (noun).

buttress (noun) something that supports or strengthens; a projecting structure of masonry or wood. *The endorsement of the American Medical Association is a powerful buttress for the claims made about this new medicine. The buttress on the south wall of the medieval castle was beginning to crumble.* **buttress** (verb).

C

camaraderie (noun) a spirit of friendship. *Spending long days and nights together on the road, the members of a traveling theater group develop a strong sense of camaraderie.*

candor (noun) openness, honesty, frankness. *In his memoir about the Vietnam War, former defense secretary McNamara described his mistakes with remarkable candor.* **candid** (adjective).

capricious (adjective) unpredictable, whimsical. *The pop star changes her image so many times that each new transformation now appears capricious rather than purposeful.* **caprice** (noun).

carnivorous (adjective) meat-eating. *The long, dagger-like teeth of the Tyrannosaurus make it obvious that this was a carnivorous dinosaur.* **carnivore** (noun).

carping (adjective) unfairly or excessively critical; querulous. *New York is famous for its demanding critics, but none is harder to please than the carping John Simon, said to have single-handedly destroyed many acting careers.* **carp** (verb).

catalytic (adjective) bringing about, causing, or producing some result. *The conditions for revolution existed in America by 1765; the disputes about taxation that arose later were the catalytic events that sparked the rebellion.* **catalyze** (verb).

caustic (adjective) burning, corrosive. *No one was safe when the satirist H. L. Mencken unleashed his caustic wit.*

censure (noun) blame, condemnation. *The news that the senator had harassed several women brought censure from many feminists.* **censure** (verb).

chaos (noun) disorder, confusion, chance. *The first few moments after the explosion were pure chaos: no one was sure what had happened, and the area was filled with people running and yelling.* **chaotic** (adjective).

circuitous (adjective) winding or indirect. *We drove to the cottage by a circuitous route so we could see as much of the surrounding countryside as possible.*

circumlocution (noun) speaking in a roundabout way; wordiness. *Legal documents often contain circumlocutions that make them difficult to understand.*

circumscribe (verb) to define by a limit or boundary. *Originally, the role of the executive branch of government was clearly circumscribed, but that role has greatly expanded over time.* **circumscription** (noun).

circumvent (verb) to get around. *When James was caught speeding, he tried to circumvent the law by offering the police officer a bribe.*

clandestine (adjective) secret, surreptitious. *As a member of the underground, Balas took part in clandestine meetings to discuss ways of sabotaging the Nazi forces.*

cloying (adjective) overly sweet or sentimental. *The deathbed scenes in the novels of Dickens are famously cloying: as Oscar Wilde said, "One would need a heart of stone to read the death of Little Nell without dissolving into tears . . . of laughter."*

cogent (adjective) forceful and convincing. *The committee members were won over to the project by the cogent arguments of the chairman.* **cogency** (noun).

cognizant (adjective) aware, mindful. *Cognizant of the fact that it was getting late, the master of ceremonies cut short the last speech.* **cognizance** (noun).

cohesive (adjective) sticking together, unified. *An effective military unit must be a cohesive team, all its members working together for a common goal.* **cohere** (verb), **cohesion** (noun).

collaborate (verb) to work together. *To create a truly successful movie, the director, writers, actors, and many others must collaborate closely.* **collaboration** (noun), **collaborative** (adjective).

colloquial (adjective) informal in language; conversational. *Some expressions from Shakespeare, such as the use of thou and thee, sound formal today but were colloquial English in Shakespeare's time.*

competent (adjective) having the skill and knowledge needed for a particular task; capable. *Any competent lawyer can draw up a will.* **competence** (noun).

complacent (adjective) smug, self-satisfied. *Until recently, American auto makers were complacent, believing that they would continue to be successful with little effort.* **complacency** (noun).

composure (noun) calm self-assurance. *The company's president managed to keep his composure during his speech even when the teleprompter broke down, leaving him without a script.* **composed** (adjective).

conciliatory (adjective) seeking agreement, compromise, or reconciliation. *As a conciliatory gesture, the union leaders agreed to postpone a strike and to continue negotiations with management.* **conciliate** (verb), **conciliation** (noun).

concise (adjective) expressed briefly and simply; succinct. *Less than a page long, the Bill of Rights is a concise statement of the freedoms enjoyed by all Americans.* **concision** (noun).

condescending (adjective) having an attitude of superiority toward another; patronizing. *"What a cute little car!" she remarked in a condescending style. "I suppose it's the nicest one someone like you could afford!"* **condescension** (noun).

condolence (noun) pity for someone else's sorrow or loss; sympathy. *After the sudden death of Princess Diana, thousands of messages of condolence were sent to her family.* **condole** (verb).

confidant (noun) someone entrusted with another's secrets. *No one knew about Jane's engagement except Sarah, her confidant.* **confide** (verb), **confidential** (adjective).

conformity (noun) agreement with or adherence to custom or rule. *In my high school, conformity was the rule: everyone dressed the same, talked the same, and listened to the same music.* **conform** (verb), **conformist** (noun, adjective).

consensus (noun) general agreement among a group. *Among Quakers, voting traditionally is not used; instead, discussion continues until the entire group forms a consensus.*

consolation (noun) relief or comfort in sorrow or suffering. *Although we miss our dog very much, it is a consolation to know that she died quickly, without suffering.* **console** (verb).

consternation (noun) shock, amazement, dismay. *When a voice in the back of the church shouted out, "I know why they should not be married!" the entire gathering was thrown into consternation.*

consummate (verb) to complete, finish, or perfect. *The deal was consummated with a handshake and the payment of the agreed-upon fee.* **consummate** (adjective), **consummation** (noun).

contaminate (verb) to make impure. *Chemicals dumped in a nearby forest had seeped into the soil and contaminated the local water supply.* **contamination** (noun).

contemporary (adjective) modern, current; from the same time. *I prefer old-fashioned furniture rather than contemporary styles. The composer Vivaldi was roughly contemporary with Bach.* **contemporary** (noun).

contrite (adjective) sorry for past misdeeds. *The public is often willing to forgive celebrities who are involved in some scandal, as long as they appear contrite.* **contrition** (noun).

conundrum (noun) a riddle, puzzle, or problem. *The question of why an all-powerful, all-loving God allows evil to exist is a conundrum many philosophers have pondered.*

convergence (noun) the act of coming together in unity or similarity. *A remarkable example of evolutionary convergence can be seen in the shark and the dolphin, two sea creatures that developed from different origins to become very similar in form.* **converge** (verb).

convoluted (adjective) twisting, complicated, intricate. *Tax law has become so convoluted that it's easy for people to accidentally violate it.* **convolute** (verb), **convolution** (noun).

corroborating (adjective) supporting with evidence; confirming. *A passerby who had witnessed the crime gave corroborating testimony about the presence of the accused person.* **corroborate** (verb), **corroboration** (noun).

corrosive (adjective) eating away, gnawing, or destroying. *Years of poverty and hard work had a corrosive effect on her beauty.* **corrode** (verb), **corrosion** (noun).

credulity (noun) willingness to believe, even with little evidence. *Con artists fool people by taking advantage of their credulity.* **credulous** (adjective).

criterion (noun) a standard of measurement or judgment. *In choosing a design for the new taxicabs, reliability will be our main criterion.* **criteria** (plural).

critique (noun) a critical evaluation. *The editor gave a detailed critique of the manuscript, explaining its strengths and its weaknesses.* **critique** (verb).

culpable (adjective) deserving blame, guilty. *Although he committed the crime, because he was mentally ill he should not be considered culpable for his actions.* **culpability** (noun).

cumulative (adjective) made up of successive additions. *Smallpox was eliminated only through the cumulative efforts of several generations of doctors and scientists.* **accumulation** (noun), **accumulate** (verb).

curtail (verb) to shorten. *The opening round of the golf tournament was curtailed by the severe thunderstorm.*

D

debased (adjective) lowered in quality, character, or esteem. *The quality of TV journalism has been debased by the many new tabloid-style talk shows.* **debase** (verb).

debunk (verb) to expose as false or worthless. *Magician James Randi loves to debunk psychics, mediums, clairvoyants, and others who claim supernatural powers.*

decorous (adjective) having good taste; proper, appropriate. *Prior to her visit to Buckingham Palace, the young woman was instructed to demonstrate the most decorous behavior.* **decorum** (noun).

decry (verb) to criticize or condemn. *The workers continued to decry the lack of safety in their factory.*

deduction (noun) a logical conclusion, especially a specific conclusion based on general principles. *Based on what is known about the effects of greenhouse gases on atmospheric temperature, scientists have made several deductions about the likelihood of global warming.* **deduce** (verb).

delegate (verb) to give authority or responsibility. *The president delegated the vice president to represent the administration at the peace talks.* **delegate** (noun).

deleterious (adjective) harmful. *About thirty years ago, scientists proved that working with asbestos could be deleterious to one's health, producing cancer and other diseases.*

delineate (verb) to outline or describe. *Naturalists had long suspected the fact of evolution, but Darwin was the first to delineate a process—natural selection—through which evolution could occur.* **delineation** (noun)

demagogue (noun) a leader who plays dishonestly on the prejudices and emotions of his followers. *Senator Joseph McCarthy was a demagogue who used the paranoia of the anti-Communist 1950s as a way of seizing fame and power in Washington.* **demagoguery** (noun).

demure (adjective) modest or shy. *The demure heroines of Victorian fiction have given way to today's stronger, more opinionated, and more independent female characters.*

denigrate (verb) to criticize or belittle. *The firm's new president tried to explain his plans for improving the company without appearing to denigrate the work of his predecessor.* **denigration** (noun).

depose (verb) to remove from office, especially from a throne. *Iran was once ruled by a monarch called the Shah, who was deposed in 1979.*

derelict (adjective) neglecting one's duty. *The train crash was blamed on a switchman who was derelict, having fallen asleep while on duty.* **dereliction** (noun).

derivative (adjective) taken from a particular source. *When a person first writes poetry, her poems are apt to be derivative of whatever poetry she most enjoys reading.* **derivation** (noun), **derive** (verb).

desolate (adjective) empty, lifeless, and deserted; hopeless, gloomy. *Robinson Crusoe was shipwrecked and had to learn to survive alone on a desolate island. The murder of her husband left Mary Lincoln desolate.* **desolation** (noun).

destitute (adjective) very poor. *Years of rule by a dictator who stole the wealth of the country had left the people of the Philippines destitute.* **destitution** (noun).

deter (verb) to discourage from acting. *The best way to deter crime is to ensure that criminals will receive swift and certain punishment.* **deterrence** (noun), **deterrent** (adjective).

detractor (noun) someone who belittles or disparages. *Neil Diamond has many detractors who consider his music boring, inane, and sentimental.* **detract** (verb).

deviate (verb) to depart from a standard or norm. *Having agreed upon a spending budget for the company, we mustn't deviate from it; if we do, we may run out of money soon.* **deviation** (noun).

devious (adjective) tricky, deceptive. *The CEO's devious financial tactics were designed to enrich his firm while confusing or misleading government regulators.*

didactic (adjective) intended to teach, instructive. *The children's TV show* Sesame Street *is designed to be both entertaining and didactic.*

diffident (adjective) hesitant, reserved, shy. *Someone with a diffident personality should pursue a career that involves little public contact.* **diffidence** (noun).

diffuse (verb) to spread out, to scatter. *The red dye quickly became diffused through the water, turning it a very pale pink.* **diffusion** (noun).

digress (verb) to wander from the main path or the main topic. *My high school biology teacher loved to digress from science into personal anecdotes about his college adventures.* **digression** (noun), **digressive** (adjective).

dilatory (adjective) delaying, procrastinating. *The lawyer used various dilatory tactics, hoping that his opponent would get tired of waiting for a trial and drop the case.*

diligent (adjective) working hard and steadily. *Through diligent efforts, the townspeople were able to clear away the debris from the flood in a matter of days.* **diligence** (noun).

diminutive (adjective) unusually small, tiny. *Children are fond of Shetland ponies because their diminutive size makes them easy to ride.* **diminution** (noun).

discern (verb) to detect, notice, or observe. *I could discern the shape of a whale off the starboard bow, but it was too far away to determine its size or species.* **discernment** (noun).

disclose (verb) to make known; to reveal. *Election laws require candidates to disclose the names of those who contribute large sums of money to their campaigns.* **disclosure** (noun).

discomfit (verb) to frustrate, thwart, or embarrass. *Discomfited by the interviewer's unexpected question, Peter could only stammer in reply.* **discomfiture** (noun).

disconcert (verb) to confuse or embarrass. *When the hallway bells began to ring halfway through her lecture, the speaker was disconcerted and didn't know what to do.*

discredit (verb) to cause disbelief in the accuracy of some statement or the reliability of a person. *Although many people still believe in UFOs, among scientists the reports of "alien encounters" have been thoroughly discredited.*

discreet (adjective) showing good judgment in speech and behavior. *Be discreet when discussing confidential business matters— don't talk among strangers on the elevator, for example.* **discretion** (noun).

discrepancy (noun) a difference or variance between two or more things. *The discrepancies between the two witnesses' stories show that one of them must be lying.* **discrepant** (adjective).

disdain (noun) contempt, scorn. *The professor could not hide his disdain for those students who were perpetually late to his class.* **disdain** (verb), **disdainful** (adjective).

disingenuous (adjective) pretending to be candid, simple, and frank. *When Texas billionaire H. Ross Perot ran for president, many considered his "jest plain folks" style disingenuous.*

disparage (verb) to speak disrespectfully about, to belittle. *Many political ads today both praise their own candidate and disparage his or her opponent.* **disparagement** (noun), **disparaging** (adjective).

disparity (noun) difference in quality or kind. *There is often a disparity between the kind of high-quality television people say they want and the low-brow programs they actually watch.* **disparate** (adjective).

disregard (verb) to ignore, to neglect. *If you don't write a will, when you die, your survivors may disregard your wishes about how your property should be handled.* **disregard** (noun).

disruptive (adjective) causing disorder, interrupting. *When the senator spoke at our college, angry demonstrators picketed, heckled, and engaged in other disruptive activities.* **disrupt** (verb), **disruption** (noun).

dissemble (verb) to pretend, to simulate. *When the police questioned her about the crime, she dissembled innocence.*

dissipate (verb) to spread out or scatter. *The windows and doors were opened, allowing the smoke that had filled the room to dissipate.* **dissipation** (noun).

dissonance (noun) lack of music harmony; lack of agreement between ideas. *Most modern music is characterized by dissonance, which many listeners find hard to enjoy. There is a noticeable dissonance between two common beliefs of most conservatives: their faith in unfettered free markets and their preference for traditional social values.* **dissonant** (adjective).

diverge (verb) to move in different directions. *Frost's poem* The Road Less Traveled *tells of the choice he made when "Two roads diverged in a yellow wood."* **divergence** (noun), **divergent** (adjective).

diversion (noun) a distraction or pastime. *During the two hours he spent in the doctor's waiting room, the game on his cell phone was a welcome diversion.* **divert** (verb).

divination (noun) the art of predicting the future. *In ancient Greece, people wanting to know their fate would visit the priests at Delphi, supposedly skilled at divination.* **divine** (verb).

divisive (adjective) causing disagreement or disunity. *Throughout history, race has been the most divisive issue in American society.*

divulge (verb) to reveal. *The people who count the votes for the Oscar awards are under strict orders not to divulge the names of the winners.*

dogmatic (adjective) holding firmly to a particular set of beliefs with little or no basis. *Believers in Marxist doctrine tend to be dogmatic, ignoring evidence that contradicts their beliefs.* **dogmatism** (noun).

dominant (adjective) greatest in importance or power. *Turner's* Frontier Thesis *suggests that the existence of the frontier had a dominant influence on American culture.* **dominate** (verb), **domination** (noun).

dubious (adjective) doubtful, uncertain. *Despite the chairman's attempts to convince the committee members that his plan would succeed, most of them remained dubious.* **dubiety** (noun).

durable (adjective) long lasting. *Denim is a popular material for work clothes because it is strong and durable.*

duress (noun) compulsion or restraint. *Fearing that the police might beat him, he confessed to the crime, not willingly but under duress.*

E

eclectic (adjective) drawn from many sources; varied, heterogeneous. *The Mellon family art collection is an eclectic one, including works ranging from ancient Greek sculptures to modern paintings.* **eclecticism** (noun).

efficacious (adjective) able to produce a desired effect. *Though thousands of people today are taking herbal supplements to treat depression, researchers have not yet proved them efficacious.* **efficacy** (noun).

effrontery (noun) shameless boldness. *The sports world was shocked when a professional basketball player had the effrontery to choke his head coach during a practice session.*

effusive (adjective) pouring forth one's emotions very freely. *Having won the Oscar for Best Actress, Sally Field gave an effusive acceptance speech in which she marveled, "You like me! You really like me!"* **effusion** (noun).

egotism (noun) excessive concern with oneself; conceit. *Robert's egotism was so great that all he could talk about was the importance—and the brilliance—of his own opinions.* **egotistic** (adjective).

egregious (adjective) obvious, conspicuous, flagrant. *It's hard to imagine how the editor could allow such an egregious error to appear.*

elated (adjective) excited and happy; exultant. *When the Washington Redskins' last, desperate pass was intercepted, the elated fans of the Philadelphia Eagles began to celebrate.* **elate** (verb), **elation** (noun).

elliptical (adjective) very terse or concise in writing or speech; difficult to understand. *Rather than speak plainly, she hinted at her meaning through a series of nods, gestures, and elliptical half sentences.*

elusive (adjective) hard to capture, grasp, or understand. *Though everyone thinks they know what "justice" is, when you try to define the concept precisely, it proves to be quite elusive.*

embezzle (verb) to steal money or property that has been entrusted to your care. *The church treasurer was found to have embezzled thousands of dollars by writing phony checks on the church bank account.* **embezzlement** (noun).

emend (verb) to correct. *Before the letter is mailed, please emend the two spelling errors.* **emendation** (noun).

emigrate (verb) to leave one place or country to settle elsewhere. *Millions of Irish emigrated to the New World in the wake of the great Irish famines of the 1840s.* **emigrant** (noun), **emigration** (noun).

eminent (adjective) noteworthy, famous. *Vaclav Havel was an eminent author before he was elected president of the Czech Republic.* **eminence** (noun).

emissary (noun) someone who represents another. *In an effort to avoid a military showdown, former President Jimmy Carter was sent as an emissary to Korea to negotiate a settlement.*

emollient (noun) something that softens or soothes. *She used a hand cream as an emollient on her dry, work-roughened hands.* **emollient** (adjective).

empathy (noun) imaginative sharing of the feelings, thoughts, or experiences of another. *It's easy for a parent to have empathy for the sorrow of another parent whose child has died.* **empathetic** (adjective).

empirical (adjective) based on experience or personal observation. *Although many people believe in ESP, scientists have found no empirical evidence of its existence.* **empiricism** (noun).

emulate (verb) to imitate or copy. *The British band Oasis admitted their desire to emulate their idols, the Beatles.* **emulation** (noun).

encroach (verb) to go beyond acceptable limits; to trespass. *By quietly seizing more and more authority, Robert Moses continually encroached on the powers of other government leaders.* **encroachment** (noun).

enervate (verb) to reduce the energy or strength of someone or something. *The extended exposure to the sun along with dehydration enervated the shipwrecked crew, leaving them almost too weak to spot the passing vessel.*

engender (verb) to produce, to cause. *Countless disagreements over the proper use of national forests have engendered feelings of hostility between ranchers and environmentalists.*

enhance (verb) to improve in value or quality. *New kitchen appliances will enhance your house and increase the amount of money you'll make when you sell it.* **enhancement** (noun).

enmity (noun) hatred, hostility, ill will. *Long-standing enmity, like that between the Protestants and Catholics in Northern Ireland, is difficult to overcome.*

enthrall (verb) to enchant or charm. *The Swedish singer Jenny Lind enthralled American audiences in the nineteenth century with her beauty and talent.*

ephemeral (adjective) quickly disappearing; transient. *Stardom in pop music is ephemeral; many of the top acts of ten years ago are forgotten today.*

equanimity (noun) calmness of mind, especially under stress. *FDR had the gift of facing the great crises of his presidency—the Depression and the Second World War—with equanimity and even humor.*

eradicate (verb) to destroy completely. *American society has failed to eradicate racism, although some of its worst effects have been reduced.*

espouse (verb) to take up as a cause; to adopt. *No politician in America today will openly espouse racism, although some behave and speak in racially prejudiced ways.*

euphoric (adjective) a feeling of extreme happiness and well-being; elation. *One often feels euphoric during the earliest days of a new love affair.* **euphoria** (noun).

evanescent (adjective) vanishing like a vapor; fragile and transient. *As she walked by, the evanescent fragrance of her perfume reached me for just an instant.*

exacerbate (verb) to make worse or more severe. *The roads in our town already have too much traffic; building a new shopping mall will exacerbate the problem.*

exasperate (verb) to irritate or annoy. *Because she was trying to study, Sharon was exasperated by the yelling of her neighbors' children.*

exculpate (verb) to free from blame or guilt. *When someone else confessed to the crime, the previous suspect was exculpated.* **exculpation** (noun), **exculpatory** (adjective).

exemplary (adjective) worthy to serve as a model. *The Baldrige Award is given to a company with exemplary standards of excellence in products and service.* **exemplar** (noun), **exemplify** (verb).

exonerate (verb) to free from blame. *Although the truck driver was suspected at first of being involved in the bombing, later evidence exonerated him.* **exoneration** (noun), **exonerative** (adjective).

expansive (adjective) broad and large; speaking openly and freely. *The LBJ Ranch is located on an expansive tract of land in Texas. Over dinner, she became expansive in describing her dreams for the future.*

expedite (verb) to carry out promptly. *As the flood waters rose, the governor ordered state agencies to expedite their rescue efforts.*

expertise (noun) skill, mastery. *The software company was eager to hire new graduates with programming expertise.*

expiate (verb) to atone for. *The president's apology to the survivors of the notorious Tuskegee experiments was his attempt to expiate the nation's guilt over their mistreatment.* **expiation** (noun).

expropriate (verb) to seize ownership of. *When the Communists came to power in China, they expropriated most businesses and turned them over to government-appointed managers.* **expropriation** (noun).

extant (adjective) currently in existence. *Of the seven ancient* Wonders of the World, *only the pyramids of Egypt are still extant.*

extenuate (verb) to make less serious. *Jeanine's guilt is extenuated by the fact that she was only twelve when she committed the theft.* **extenuating** (adjective), **extenuation** (noun).

extol (verb) to greatly praise. *At the party convention, speaker after speaker rose to extol their candidate for the presidency.*

extricate (verb) to free from a difficult or complicated situation. *Much of the humor in the TV show* I Love Lucy *comes in watching Lucy try to extricate herself from the problems she creates by fibbing or trickery.* **extricable** (adjective).

extrinsic (adjective) not an innate part or aspect of something; external. *The high price of old baseball cards is due to extrinsic factors, such as the nostalgia felt by baseball fans for the stars of their youth, rather than the inherent beauty or value of the cards themselves.*

exuberant (adjective) wildly joyous and enthusiastic. *As the final seconds of the game ticked away, the fans of the winning team began an exuberant celebration.* **exuberance** (noun).

F

facile (adjective) easy; shallow or superficial. *The one-minute political commercial favors a candidate with facile opinions rather than serious, thoughtful solutions.* **facilitate** (verb), **facility** (noun).

fallacy (noun) an error in fact or logic. *It's a fallacy to think that "natural" means "healthful"; after all, the deadly poison arsenic is completely natural.* **fallacious** (adjective).

felicitous (adjective) pleasing, fortunate, apt. *The sudden blossoming of the dogwood trees on the morning of Matt's wedding seemed a felicitous sign of good luck.* **felicity** (noun).

feral (adjective) wild. *The garbage dump was inhabited by a pack of feral dogs that had escaped from their owners and become completely wild.*

fervent (adjective) full of intense feeling; ardent, zealous. *In the days just after his religious conversion, his piety was at its most fervent.* **fervid** (adjective), **fervor** (noun).

flagrant (adjective) obviously wrong; offensive. *Nixon was forced to resign the presidency after a series of flagrant crimes against the U.S. Constitution.* **flagrancy** (noun).

flamboyant (adjective) very colorful, showy, or elaborate. *At Mardi Gras, partygoers compete to show off the most wild and flamboyant outfits.*

florid (adjective) flowery, fancy; reddish. *The grand ballroom was decorated in a florid style. Years of heavy drinking had given him a florid complexion.*

foppish (adjective) describing a man who is foolishly vain about his dress or appearance. *The foppish character of the 1890s wore bright-colored spats and a top hat; in the 1980s, he wore fancy suspenders and a shirt with a contrasting collar.* **fop** (noun).

formidable (adjective) awesome, impressive, or frightening. *According to his plaque in the Baseball Hall of Fame, pitcher Tom Seaver turned the New York Mets "from lovable losers into formidable foes."*

fortuitous (adjective) lucky, fortunate. *Although the mayor claimed credit for the falling crime rate, it was really caused by several fortuitous trends.*

fractious (adjective) troublesome, unruly. *Members of the British Parliament are often fractious, shouting insults and sarcastic questions during debates.*

fragility (noun) the quality of being easy to break; delicacy, weakness. *Because of their fragility, few stained-glass windows from the early Middle Ages have survived.* **fragile** (adjective).

fraternize (verb) to associate with on friendly terms. *Although baseball players aren't supposed to fraternize with their opponents, players from opposing teams often chat before games.* **fraternization** (noun).

frenetic (adjective) chaotic, frantic. *The floor of the stock exchange, filled with traders shouting and gesturing, is a scene of frenetic activity.*

frivolity (noun) lack of seriousness; levity. *The frivolity of the Mardi Gras carnival is in contrast to the seriousness of the religious season of Lent that follows.* **frivolous** (adjective).

frugal (adjective) spending little. *With our last few dollars, we bought a frugal dinner: a loaf of bread and a piece of cheese.* **frugality** (noun).

fugitive (noun) someone trying to escape. *When two prisoners broke out of the local jail, police were warned to keep an eye out for the fugitives.* **fugitive** (adjective).

G

gargantuan (adjective) huge, colossal. *The building of the Great Wall of China was one of the most gargantuan projects ever undertaken.*

genial (adjective) friendly, gracious. *A good host welcomes all visitors in a warm and genial fashion.*

grandiose (adjective) overly large, pretentious, or showy. *Among Hitler's grandiose plans for Berlin was a gigantic building with a dome several times larger than any ever built.* **grandiosity** (noun).

gratuitous (adjective) given freely or without cause. *Since her opinion was not requested, her harsh criticism of his singing seemed a gratuitous insult.*

gregarious (adjective) enjoying the company of others; sociable. *Naturally gregarious, Emily is a popular member of several clubs and a sought-after lunch companion.*

guileless (adjective) without cunning; innocent. *Deborah's guileless personality and complete honesty make it hard for her to survive in the harsh world of politics.*

gullible (adjective) easily fooled. *When the sweepstakes entry form arrived bearing the message, "You may be a winner!" my gullible neighbor tried to claim a prize.* **gullibility** (noun).

H

hackneyed (adjective) without originality, trite. *When someone invented the phrase, "No pain, no gain," it was clever, but now it is so commonly heard that it seems hackneyed.*

haughty (adjective) overly proud. *The fashion model strode down the runway, her hips thrust forward and a haughty expression, like a sneer, on her face.* **haughtiness** (noun).

hedonist (noun) someone who lives mainly to pursue pleasure. *Having inherited great wealth, he chose to live the life of a hedonist, traveling the world in luxury.* **hedonism** (noun), **hedonistic** (adjective).

heinous (adjective) very evil, hateful. *The massacre by Pol Pot of more than a million Cambodians is one of the twentieth century's most heinous crimes.*

hierarchy (noun) a ranking of people, things, or ideas from highest to lowest. *A cabinet secretary ranks just below the president and vice president in the hierarchy of the executive branch.* **hierarchical** (adjective).

hypocrisy (noun) a false pretense of virtue. *When the sexual misconduct of the television preacher was exposed, his followers were shocked at his hypocrisy.* **hypocritical** (adjective).

I

iconoclast (noun) someone who attacks traditional beliefs or institutions. *Comedian Stephen Colbert enjoys his reputation as an iconoclast, though people in power often resent his satirical jabs.* **iconoclasm** (noun), **iconoclastic** (adjective).

idiosyncratic (adjective) peculiar to an individual; eccentric. *Cyndi Lauper sings pop music in an idiosyncratic style, mingling high-pitched whoops and squeals with throaty gurgles.* **idiosyncrasy** (noun).

idolatry (noun) the worship of a person, thing, or institution as a god. *In Communist China, Chairman Mao was the subject of idolatry; his picture was displayed everywhere, and millions of Chinese memorized his sayings.* **idolatrous** (adjective).

impartial (adjective) fair, equal, unbiased. *If a judge is not impartial, then all of her rulings are questionable.* **impartiality** (noun).

impeccable (adjective) flawless. *The crooks printed impeccable copies of the Super Bowl tickets, making it impossible to distinguish them from the real ones.*

impetuous (adjective) acting hastily or impulsively. *Stuart's resignation was an impetuous act; he did it without thinking, and he soon regretted it.* **impetuosity** (noun).

impinge (verb) to encroach upon, touch, or affect. *You have a right to do whatever you want, so long as your actions don't impinge on the rights of others.*

implicit (adjective) understood without being openly expressed; implied. *Although most clubs had no rules excluding minorities, many had an implicit understanding that no member of a minority group would be allowed to join.*

impute (verb) to credit or give responsibility to; to attribute. *Although Helena's comments embarrassed me, I don't impute any ill will to her; I think she didn't realize what she was saying.* **imputation** (noun).

inarticulate (adjective) unable to speak or express oneself clearly and understandably. *A skilled athlete may be an inarticulate public speaker, as demonstrated by many post-game interviews.*

incisive (adjective) clear and direct expression. *Franklin settled the debate with a few incisive remarks that summed up the issue perfectly.*

incompatible (adjective) unable to exist together; conflicting. *Many people hold seemingly incompatible beliefs: for example, supporting the death penalty while believing in the sacredness of human life.* **incompatibility** (noun).

inconsequential (adjective) of little importance. *When the flat screen TV was delivered, it was a different shade of gray than I expected, but the difference was inconsequential.*

incontrovertible (adjective) impossible to question. *The fact that Alexandra's fingerprints were the only ones on the murder weapon made her guilt seem incontrovertible.*

incorrigible (adjective) impossible to manage or reform. *Lou is an incorrigible trickster, constantly playing practical jokes no matter how much his friends complain.*

incremental (adjective) increasing gradually by small amounts. *Although the initial cost of the Medicare program was small, the incremental expenses have grown to be very large.* **increment** (noun).

incriminate (verb) to give evidence of guilt. *The fifth amendment to the Constitution says that no one is required to reveal information that would incriminate him or her in a crime.* **incriminating** (adjective).

incumbent (noun) someone who occupies an office or position. *It is often difficult for a challenger to win a seat in Congress from the incumbent.* **incumbency** (noun), **incumbent** (adjective).

indeterminate (adjective) not definitely known. *The college plans to enroll an indeterminate number of students; the size of the class will depend on the number of applicants and how many accept offers of admission.* **determine** (verb).

indifferent (adjective) unconcerned, apathetic. *The mayor's small proposed budget for education suggests that he is indifferent to the needs of our schools.* **indifference** (noun).

indistinct (adjective) unclear, uncertain. *We could see boats on the water, but in the thick morning fog their shapes were indistinct.*

indomitable (adjective) unable to be conquered or controlled. *The world admired the indomitable spirit of Nelson Mandela; he remained courageous despite years of imprisonment.*

induce (verb) to cause. *The doctor prescribed a medicine that was supposed to induce a lowering of the blood pressure.* **induction** (noun).

ineffable (adjective) difficult to describe or express. *He gazed in silence at the sunrise over the Taj Mahal, his eyes reflecting an ineffable sense of wonder.*

inevitable (adjective) unable to be avoided. *Once the Japanese attacked Pearl Harbor, American involvement in World War II was inevitable.* **inevitability** (noun).

inexorable (adjective) unable to be deterred; relentless. *It's difficult to imagine how the mythic character of Oedipus could have avoided his evil destiny; his fate appears inexorable.*

ingenious (adjective) showing cleverness and originality. *The Post-it note is an ingenious solution to a common problem—how to mark papers without spoiling them.* **ingenuity** (noun).

inherent (adjective) naturally part of something. *Compromise is inherent in democracy, since everyone cannot get his or her way.* **inhere** (verb), **inherence** (noun).

innate (adjective) inborn, native. *Not everyone who takes piano lessons becomes a fine musician, which shows that music requires innate talent as well as training.*

innocuous (adjective) harmless, inoffensive. *I was surprised that Melissa took offense at such an innocuous joke.*

inoculate (verb) to prevent a disease by infusing with a disease-causing organism. *Pasteur found he could prevent rabies by inoculating patients with the virus that causes the disease.* **inoculation** (noun).

insipid (adjective) flavorless, uninteresting. *Some TV shows are so insipid that you can watch them while reading without missing a thing.* **insipidity** (noun).

insolence (noun) an attitude or behavior that is bold and disrespectful. *Some feel that news reporters who shout questions at the president are behaving with insolence.* **insolent** (adjective).

insular (adjective) narrow or isolated in attitude or viewpoint. *Americans are famous for their insular attitudes; they seem to think that nothing important has ever happened outside of their country.* **insularity** (noun).

insurgency (noun) uprising, rebellion. *The angry townspeople had begun an insurgency bordering on downright revolution; they were collecting arms, holding secret meetings, and refusing to pay certain taxes.* **insurgent** (adjective).

integrity (noun) honesty, uprightness; soundness, completeness. *"Honest Abe" Lincoln is considered a model of political integrity. Inspectors examined the building's support beams and foundation and found no reason to doubt its structural integrity.*

interlocutor (noun) someone taking part in a dialogue or conversation. *Annoyed by the constant questions from someone in the crowd, the speaker challenged his interlocutor to offer a better plan.* **interlocutory** (adjective).

interlude (noun) an interrupting period or performance. *The two most dramatic scenes in* King Lear *are separated, strangely, by a comic interlude starring the king's jester.*

interminable (adjective) endless or seemingly endless. *Addressing the United Nations, Castro announced, "We will be brief"—then delivered an interminable 4-hour speech.*

intransigent (adjective) unwilling to compromise. *Despite the mediator's attempts to suggest a fair solution, the two parties were intransigent, forcing a showdown.* **intransigence** (noun).

intrepid (adjective) fearless and resolute. *Only an intrepid adventurer is willing to undertake the long and dangerous trip by sled to the South Pole.* **intrepidity** (noun).

intrusive (adjective) forcing a way in without being welcome. *The legal requirement of a search warrant is supposed to protect Americans from intrusive searches by the police.* **intrude** (verb), **intrusion** (noun).

intuitive (adjective) known directly, without apparent thought or effort. *An experienced chess player sometimes has an intuitive sense of the best move to make, even if she can't explain it.* **intuit** (verb), **intuition** (noun).

inundate (verb) to flood; to overwhelm. *As soon as the playoff tickets went on sale, eager fans inundated the box office with orders.*

invariable (adjective) unchanging, constant. *When writing a book, it was her invariable habit to rise at 6 a.m. and work at her desk from 7 to 12.* **invariability** (noun).

inversion (noun) a turning backwards, inside-out, or upside-down; a reversal. *Latin poetry often features inversion of word order; for example, the first line of Virgil's* Aeneid: *"Arms and the man I sing."* **invert** (verb), **inverted** (adjective).

inveterate (adjective) persistent, habitual. *It's very difficult for an inveterate gambler to give up the pastime.* **inveteracy** (noun).

invigorate (verb) to give energy to, to stimulate. *As her car climbed the mountain road, Lucinda felt invigorated by the clear air and the cool breezes.*

invincible (adjective) impossible to conquer or overcome. *For three years at the height of his career, boxer Mike Tyson seemed invincible.*

inviolable (adjective) impossible to attack or trespass upon. *In the president's remote hideaway at Camp David, guarded by the Secret Service, his privacy is, for once, inviolable.*

irrational (adjective) unreasonable. *Richard knew that his fear of insects was irrational, but he was unable to overcome it.* **irrationality** (noun).

irresolute (adjective) uncertain how to act, indecisive. *The line in the ice cream shop grew as the irresolute child wavered between her two favorite ice cream flavors before finally choosing one.* **irresolution** (noun).

J

jeopardize (verb) to put in danger. *Terrorist attacks jeopardize the fragile peace in the Middle East.* **jeopardy** (noun).

juxtapose (verb) to put side by side. *Juxtaposing the two editorials revealed the enormous differences in the writers' opinions.* **juxtaposition** (noun).

L

languid (adjective) without energy; slow, sluggish, listless. *The hot, humid weather of late August can make anyone feel languid.* **languish** (verb), **languor** (noun).

latent (adjective) not currently obvious or active; hidden. *Although he had committed only a single act of violence, the examining psychiatrist said it's likely he always had a latent tendency toward violence.* **latency** (noun).

laudatory (adjective) giving praise. *The ads for the movie are filled with laudatory comments from critics.*

lenient (adjective) mild, soothing, or forgiving. *The judge was known for his lenient disposition; he rarely imposed long jail sentences on criminals.* **leniency** (noun).

lethargic (adjective) lacking energy; sluggish. *Visitors to the zoo are surprised that the lions appear so lethargic, but, in the wild, lions sleep up to 18 hours a day.* **lethargy** (noun).

liability (noun) an obligation or debt; a weakness or drawback. *The insurance company had a liability of millions of dollars after the town was destroyed by a tornado. Slowness afoot is a serious liability in an aspiring basketball player.* **liable** (adjective).

lithe (adjective) flexible and graceful. *The ballet dancer was almost as lithe as a cat.*

longevity (noun) length of life; durability. *The reduction in early deaths from infectious diseases is responsible for most of the increase in human longevity over the past two centuries.*

lucid (adjective) clear and understandable. *Hawking's* A Short History of the Universe *is a lucid explanation of modern scientific theories about the origin of the universe.* **lucidity** (noun).

lurid (adjective) shocking, gruesome. *While the serial killer was on the loose, the newspapers were filled with lurid stories about his crimes.*

M

malediction (noun) curse. *In the fairy tale "Sleeping Beauty," the princess is trapped in a death-like sleep because of the malediction uttered by an angry witch.*

malevolence (noun) hatred, ill will. *Critics say that Iago, the villain in Shakespeare's* Othello, *seems to exhibit malevolence with no real cause.* **malevolent** (adjective).

malinger (verb) to pretend incapacity or illness to avoid a duty or work. *During the labor dispute, hundreds of employees malingered, forcing the company to slow production and costing it millions in profits.*

malleable (adjective) able to be changed, shaped, or formed by outside pressures. *Gold is a very useful metal because it is so malleable. A child's personality is malleable and deeply influenced by the things his or her parents say and do.* **malleability** (noun).

mandate (noun) order, command. *The new policy of using only organic produce in the restaurant went into effect as soon as the manager issued his mandate about it.* **mandate** (verb), **mandatory** (adjective).

maturation (noun) the process of becoming fully grown or developed. *Free markets in the former Communist nations are likely to operate smoothly only after a long period of maturation.* **mature** (adjective and verb), **maturity** (noun).

mediate (verb) to act to reconcile differences between two parties. *During the baseball strike, both the players and the club owners were willing to have the president mediate the dispute.* **mediation** (noun).

mediocrity (noun) the state of being middling or poor in quality. *The New York Mets finished in ninth place in 1968 but won the world's championship in 1969, going from horrible to great in a single year and skipping mediocrity.* **mediocre** (adjective).

mercurial (adjective) changing quickly and unpredictably. *The mercurial personality of Robin Williams, with his many voices and styles, made him perfect for the role of the ever-changing genie in* Aladdin.

meticulous (adjective) very careful with details. *Repairing watches calls for a craftsperson who is patient and meticulous.*

mimicry (noun) imitation, aping. *The continued popularity of Elvis Presley has given rise to a class of entertainers who make a living through mimicry of "The King."* **mimic** (noun and verb).

misconception (noun) a mistaken idea. *Columbus sailed west with the misconception that he would reach the shores of Asia.* **misconceive** (verb).

mitigate (verb) to make less severe; to relieve. *Wallace certainly committed the assault, but the verbal abuse he'd received helps to explain his behavior and somewhat mitigates his guilt.* **mitigation** (noun).

modicum (noun) a small amount. *The plan for your new business is well designed; with a modicum of luck, you should be successful.*

mollify (verb) to soothe or calm; to appease. *Samantha tried to mollify the angry customer by promising him a full refund.*

morose (adjective) gloomy, sullen. *After Chuck's girlfriend dumped him, he lay around the house for a couple of days, feeling morose.*

mundane (adjective) everyday, ordinary, commonplace. *Moviegoers in the 1930s liked the glamorous films of Fred Astaire because they provided an escape from the mundane problems of life during the Great Depression.*

munificent (adjective) very generous; lavish. *Ted Turner's billion-dollar donation to the United Nations was one of the most munificent acts of charity in history.* **munificence** (noun).

mutable (adjective) likely to change. *A politician's reputation can be highly mutable, as seen in the case of Harry Truman—mocked during his lifetime, revered afterward.*

N

narcissistic (adjective) showing excessive love for oneself; egoistic. *Andre's room, decorated with photos of himself and the sports trophies he has won, suggests a narcissistic personality.* **narcissism** (noun).

nocturnal (adjective) of the night; active at night. *Travelers on the Underground Railroad escaped from slavery to the North by a series of nocturnal flights. The eyes of nocturnal animals must be sensitive in dim light.*

nonchalant (adjective) appearing to be unconcerned. *Unlike the other players on the football team who pumped their fists when their names were announced, John ran on the field with a nonchalant wave.* **nonchalance** (noun).

nondescript (adjective) without distinctive qualities; drab. *The bank robber's clothes were nondescript; none of the witnesses could remember their color or style.*

notorious (adjective) famous, especially for evil actions or qualities. *Warner Brothers produced a series of movies about notorious gangsters such as John Dillinger and Al Capone.* **notoriety** (noun).

novice (noun) beginner. *Lifting your head before you finish your swing is a typical mistake committed by the novice at golf.*

nuance (noun) a subtle difference or quality. *At first glance, Monet's paintings of water lilies all look much alike, but the more you study them, the more you appreciate the nuances of color and shading that distinguish them.*

nurture (verb) to nourish or help to grow. *The money given by the National Endowment for the Arts helps nurture local arts organizations throughout the country.* **nurture** (noun).

O

obdurate (adjective) unwilling to change; stubborn, inflexible. *Despite the many pleas he received, the governor was obdurate in his refusal to grant clemency to the convicted murderer.*

objective (adjective) dealing with observable facts rather than opinions or interpretations. *When a legal case involves a shocking crime, it may be hard for a judge to remain objective in his rulings.*

oblivious (adjective) unaware, unconscious. *Karen practiced her oboe with complete concentration, oblivious to the noise and activity around her.* **oblivion** (noun), **obliviousness** (noun).

obscure (adjective) little known; hard to understand. *Mendel was an obscure monk until decades after his death when his scientific work was finally discovered. Most people find the writings of James Joyce obscure; hence the popularity of books that explain his books.* **obscure** (verb), **obscurity** (noun).

obsessive (adjective) haunted or preoccupied by an idea or feeling. *His concern with cleanliness became so obsessive that he washed his hands twenty times every day.* **obsess** (verb), **obsession** (noun).

obsolete (adjective) no longer current; old-fashioned. *W. H. Auden said that his ideal landscape would include water wheels, wooden grain mills, and other forms of obsolete machinery.* **obsolescence** (noun).

obstinate (adjective) stubborn, unyielding. *Despite years of effort, the problem of drug abuse remains obstinate.* **obstinacy** (noun).

obtrusive (adjective) overly prominent. *Philip should sing more softly; his bass is so obtrusive that the other singers can barely be heard.* **obtrude** (verb), **obtrusion** (noun).

ominous (adjective) foretelling evil. *Ominous black clouds gathered on the horizon, for a violent storm was fast approaching.* **omen** (noun).

onerous (adjective) heavy, burdensome. *The hero Hercules was ordered to clean the Augean Stables, one of several onerous tasks known as "the labors of Hercules."* **onus** (noun).

opportunistic (adjective) eagerly seizing chances as they arise. *When Princess Diana died suddenly, opportunistic publishers quickly released books about her life and death.* **opportunism** (noun).

opulent (adjective) rich, lavish. *The mansion of newspaper tycoon Hearst is famous for its opulent decor.* **opulence** (noun).

ornate (adjective) highly decorated, elaborate. *Baroque architecture is often highly ornate, featuring surfaces covered with carving, sinuous curves, and painted scenes.*

ostentatious (adjective) overly showy, pretentious. *To show off his wealth, the millionaire threw an ostentatious party featuring a full orchestra, a famous singer, and tens of thousands of dollars' worth of food.*

ostracize (verb) to exclude from a group. *In Biblical times, those who suffered from the disease of leprosy were ostracized and forced to live alone.* **ostracism** (noun).

P

pallid (adjective) pale; dull. *Working all day in the coal mine had given him a pallid complexion. The new musical offers only pallid entertainment: the music is lifeless, the acting dull, the story absurd.*

parched (adjective) very dry; thirsty. *After two months without rain, the crops were shriveled and parched by the sun.* **parch** (verb).

pariah (noun) outcast. *Accused of robbery, he became a pariah; his neighbors stopped talking to him, and people he'd considered friends no longer called.*

partisan (adjective) reflecting strong allegiance to a particular party or cause. *The vote on the president's budget was strictly partisan: every member of the president's party voted yes, and all others voted no.* **partisan** (noun).

pathology (noun) disease or the study of disease; extreme abnormality. *Some people believe that high rates of crime are symptoms of an underlying social pathology.* **pathological** (adjective).

pellucid (adjective) very clear; transparent; easy to understand. *The water in the mountain stream was cold and pellucid. Thanks to the professor's pellucid explanation, I finally understand relativity theory.*

penitent (adjective) feeling sorry for past crimes or sins. *Having grown penitent, he wrote a long letter of apology, asking forgiveness.*

penurious (adjective) extremely frugal; stingy. *Haunted by memories of poverty, he lived in penurious fashion, driving a 12-year-old car and wearing only the cheapest clothes.* **penury** (noun).

perceptive (adjective) quick to notice, observant. *With his perceptive intelligence, Holmes was the first to notice the importance of this clue.* **perceptible** (adjective), **perception** (noun).

perfidious (adjective) disloyal, treacherous. *Although he was one of the most talented generals of the American Revolution, Benedict Arnold is remembered today as a perfidious betrayer of his country.* **perfidy** (noun).

perfunctory (adjective) unenthusiastic, routine, or mechanical. *When the play opened, the actors sparkled, but by the thousandth night their performance had become perfunctory.*

permeate (verb) to spread through or penetrate. *Little by little, the smell of gas from the broken pipe permeated the house.*

persevere (adjective) to continue despite difficulties. *Although several of her teammates dropped out of the marathon, Gail persevered.* **perseverance** (noun).

perspicacity (noun) keenness of observation or understanding. *Journalist Murray Kempton was famous for the perspicacity of his comments on social and political issues.* **perspicacious** (adjective).

peruse (verb) to examine or study. *It is wise to peruse a contract carefully before signing it.* **perusal** (noun).

pervasive (adjective) spreading throughout. *As news of the disaster reached the town, a pervasive sense of gloom could be felt.* **pervade** (verb).

phlegmatic (adjective) sluggish and unemotional in temperament. *It was surprising to see Tom, who is normally so phlegmatic, acting excited.*

placate (verb) to soothe or appease. *The waiter tried to placate the angry customer with the offer of a free dessert.* **placatory** (adjective).

plastic (adjective) able to be molded or reshaped. *Because it is highly plastic, clay is an easy material for beginning sculptors to use.*

plausible (adjective) apparently believable. *According to the judge, the defense attorney's argument was both powerful and plausible.* **plausibility** (noun).

polarize (verb) to separate into opposing groups or forces. *Controversial topics tend to polarize people, with many people voicing extreme views and few trying to find a middle ground.* **polarization** (noun).

portend (verb) to indicate a future event; to forebode. *According to folklore, red skies at dawn portend a day of stormy weather.*

potentate (noun) a powerful ruler. *The Tsar of Russia was one of the last hereditary potentates of Europe.*

pragmatism (noun) a belief in approaching problems through practical rather than theoretical means. *Roosevelt's approach to the Great Depression was based on pragmatism: "Try something," he said. "If it doesn't work, try something else."* **pragmatic** (adjective).

preamble (noun) an introductory statement. *The preamble to the Constitution begins with the famous words, "We the people of the United States of America..."*

precocious (adjective) mature at an unusually early age. *Picasso was so precocious as an artist that, at nine, he is said to have painted far better pictures than his teacher.* **precocity** (noun).

predatory (adjective) living by killing and eating other animals; exploiting others for personal gain. *The tiger is the largest predatory animal native to Asia. Microsoft has been accused of predatory business practices that prevent other software companies from competing with it.* **predation** (noun), **predator** (noun).

predilection (noun) a liking or preference. *To relax from his presidential duties, Kennedy had a predilection for spy novels featuring James Bond.*

predominant (adjective) greatest in numbers or influence. *Although hundreds of religions are practiced in India, the predominant faith is Hinduism.* **predominance** (noun), **predominate** (verb).

prepossessing (adjective) attractive. *Smart, lovely, and talented, she has all the prepossessing qualities that mark a potential movie star.*

presumptuous (adjective) going beyond the limits of courtesy or appropriateness. *The senator winced when the presumptuous young staffer addressed him as "Chuck."* **presume** (verb), **presumption** (noun).

pretentious (adjective) claiming excessive value or importance. *For a shoe salesman to call himself a "Personal Foot Apparel Consultant" seems awfully pretentious.* **pretension** (noun).

procrastinate (verb) to put off, to delay. *If you habitually procrastinate, try this technique: never touch a piece of paper without either filing it, responding to it, or throwing it out.* **procrastination** (noun).

profane (adjective) impure, unholy. *It is inappropriate and rude to use profane language in a church.* **profane** (verb), **profanity** (noun).

proficient (adjective) skillful, adept. *A proficient artist, Louise quickly and accurately sketched the scene.* **proficiency** (noun).

proliferate (verb) to increase or multiply. *Over the past twenty-five years, high-tech companies have proliferated in northern California, Massachusetts, and Seattle.* **proliferation** (noun).

prolific (adjective) producing many offspring or creations. *With more than 300 books to his credit, Isaac Asimov was one of the most prolific writers of all time.*

prominence (noun) the quality of standing out; fame. *Barack Obama rose to political prominence after his keynote address to the 2004 Democratic National Convention.* **prominent** (adjective).

promulgate (verb) to make public, to declare. *Lincoln signed the proclamation that freed the slaves in 1862, but he waited several months to promulgate it.*

propagate (verb) to cause to grow; to foster. *John Smithson's will left his fortune for the founding of an institution to propagate knowledge, without saying whether that meant a university, a library, or a museum.* **propagation** (noun).

propriety (noun) appropriateness. *The principal questioned the propriety of the discussion the teacher had with her students about another instructor's gambling addiction.*

prosaic (adjective) everyday, ordinary, dull. *"Paul's Case" tells the story of a boy who longs to escape from the prosaic life of a clerk into a world of wealth, glamour, and beauty.*

protagonist (noun) the main character in a story or play; the main supporter of an idea. *Leopold Bloom is the protagonist of James Joyce's great novel* Ulysses.

provocative (adjective) likely to stimulate emotions, ideas, or controversy. *The demonstrators began chanting obscenities, a provocative act that they hoped would cause the police to lose control.* **provoke** (verb), **provocation** (noun).

proximity (noun) closeness, nearness. *Neighborhood residents were angry over the proximity of the sewage plant to the local school.* **proximate** (adjective).

prudent (adjective) wise, cautious, and practical. *A prudent investor will avoid putting all of her money into any single investment.* **prudence** (noun), **prudential** (adjective).

pugnacious (adjective) combative, bellicose, truculent; ready to fight. *Ty Cobb, the pugnacious outfielder for the Detroit Tigers, got into more than his fair share of brawls, both on and off the field.* **pugnacity** (noun).

punctilious (adjective) very concerned about proper forms of behavior and manners. *A punctilious dresser like James would rather skip the party altogether than wear the wrong color tie.* **punctilio** (noun).

pundit (noun) someone who offers opinions in an authoritative style. *The Sunday morning talk shows are filled with pundits, each with his or her own theory about the week's political news.*

punitive (adjective) inflicting punishment. *The jury awarded the plaintiff one million dollars in punitive damages, hoping to teach the defendant a lesson.*

purify (verb) to make pure, clean, or perfect. *The new plant is supposed to purify the drinking water provided to everyone in the nearby towns.* **purification** (noun).

Q

quell (verb) to quiet, to suppress. *It took a huge number of police officers to quell the rioting.*

querulous (adjective) complaining, whining. *The nursing home attendant needed a lot of patience to care for the three querulous, unpleasant residents on his floor.*

R

rancorous (adjective) expressing bitter hostility. *Many Americans are disgusted by recent political campaigns, which seem more rancorous than ever before.* **rancor** (noun).

rationale (noun) an underlying reason or explanation. *Looking at the sad faces of his employees, it was hard for the company president to explain the rationale for closing the business.*

raze (verb) to completely destroy; demolish. *The old Coliseum building will soon be razed to make room for a new hotel.*

reciprocate (verb) to give and take mutually. *If you'll watch my children tonight, I'll reciprocate by taking care of yours tomorrow.* **reciprocity** (noun).

reclusive (adjective) withdrawn from society. *During the last years of her life, actress Greta Garbo led a reclusive existence, rarely appearing in public.* **recluse** (noun).

reconcile (verb) to make consistent or harmonious. *FDR's greatness as a leader can be seen in his ability to reconcile the demands and values of the varied groups that supported him.* **reconciliation** (noun).

recrimination (noun) a retaliatory accusation. *After the governor called his opponent unethical, his opponent angrily replied with recriminations that the governor was a hypocrite.* **recriminate** (verb), **recriminatory** (adjective).

recuperate (verb) to regain health after an illness. *Although Marie left the hospital two days after her operation, it took her a few weeks to fully recuperate.* **recuperation** (noun), **recuperative** (adjective).

redoubtable (adjective) inspiring respect, awe, or fear. *Johnson's knowledge, experience, and personal clout made him a redoubtable political opponent.*

refurbish (verb) to fix up; renovate. *It took three days' work by a team of carpenters, painters, and decorators to completely refurbish the apartment.*

refute (verb) to prove false. *The company invited reporters to visit their plant in an effort to refute the charges of unsafe working conditions.* **refutation** (noun).

relevance (noun) connection to the matter at hand; pertinence. *Testimony in a criminal trial may be admitted only if it has clear relevance to the question of guilt or innocence.* **relevant** (adjective).

remedial (adjective) serving to remedy, cure, or correct some condition. *Affirmative action can be justified as a remedial step to help minority members overcome the effects of past discrimination.* **remediation** (noun), **remedy** (verb).

remorse (noun) a painful sense of guilt over wrongdoing. *In Poe's story* The Tell-Tale Heart, *a murderer is driven insane by remorse over his crime.* **remorseful** (adjective).

remuneration (noun) pay. *In a civil lawsuit, the attorney often receives part of the financial settlement as his or her remuneration.* **remunerate** (verb), **remunerative** (adjective).

renovate (verb) to renew by repairing or rebuilding. *The television program* This Old House *shows how skilled craftspeople renovate houses.* **renovation** (noun).

renunciation (noun) the act of rejecting or refusing something. *King Edward VII's renunciation of the British throne was caused by his desire to marry an American divorcee, something he couldn't do as king.* **renounce** (verb).

replete (adjective) filled abundantly. *Graham's book is replete with wonderful stories about the famous people she has known.*

reprehensible (adjective) deserving criticism or censure. *Although Pete Rose's misdeeds were reprehensible, not all fans agree that he deserves to be excluded from the Baseball Hall of Fame.* **reprehend** (verb), **reprehension** (noun).

repudiate (verb) to reject, to renounce. *After it became known that Duke had been a leader of the Ku Klux Klan, most Republican leaders repudiated him.* **repudiation** (noun).

reputable (adjective) having a good reputation; respected. *Find a reputable auto mechanic by asking your friends for recommendations based on their own experiences.* **reputation** (noun), **repute** (noun).

resilient (adjective) able to recover from difficulty. *A professional athlete must be resilient, able to lose a game one day and come back the next with confidence and enthusiasm.* **resilience** (noun).

resplendent (adjective) glowing, shining. *In late December, midtown New York is resplendent with holiday lights and decorations.* **resplendence** (noun).

responsive (adjective) reacting quickly and appropriately. *The new director of the Internal Revenue Service has promised to make the agency more responsive to public complaints.* **respond** (verb), **response** (noun).

restitution (noun) return of something to its original owner; repayment. *Some Native American leaders are demanding that the U.S. government make restitution for the lands taken from them.*

revere (verb) to admire deeply, to honor. *Millions of people around the world revered Mother Teresa for her saintly generosity.* **reverence** (noun), **reverent** (adjective).

rhapsodize (verb) to praise in a wildly emotional way. *That critic is such a huge fan of Toni Morrison that she will surely rhapsodize over the writer's next novel.* **rhapsodic** (adjective).

S

sagacious (adjective) discerning, wise. *Only a leader as sagacious as Nelson Mandela could have united South Africa so successfully and peacefully.* **sagacity** (noun).

salvage (verb) to save from wreck or ruin. *After the hurricane destroyed her home, she was able to salvage only a few of her belongings.* **salvage** (noun), **salvageable** (adjective).

sanctimonious (adjective) showing false or excessive piety. *The sanctimonious prayers of the TV preacher were interspersed with requests that the viewers send him money.* **sanctimony** (noun).

scapegoat (noun) someone who bears the blame for others' acts; someone hated for no apparent reason. *Although Buckner's error was only one reason the Red Sox lost, many fans made him the scapegoat, booing him mercilessly.*

scrupulous (adjective) acting with extreme care; painstaking. *Disney theme parks are famous for their scrupulous attention to small details.* **scruple** (noun).

scrutinize (verb) to study closely. *The lawyer scrutinized the contract, searching for any sentence that could pose a risk for her client.* **scrutiny** (noun).

secrete (verb) to emit; to hide. *Glands in the mouth secrete saliva, a liquid that helps in digestion. The jewel thieves secreted the necklace in a tin box buried underground.*

sedentary (adjective) requiring much sitting. *When Officer Samson was given a desk job, she had trouble getting used to sedentary work after years on the street.*

sequential (adjective) arranged in an order or series. *The courses for the chemistry major are sequential; you must take them in order, since each course builds on the previous ones.* **sequence** (noun).

serendipity (noun) the act of lucky, accidental discoveries. *Great inventions sometimes come about through deliberate research and hard work, sometimes through pure serendipity.* **serendipitous** (adjective).

servile (adjective) like a slave or servant; submissive. *The tycoon demanded that his underlings behave in a servile manner, agreeing quickly with everything he said.* **servility** (noun).

simulated (adjective) imitating something else; artificial. *High-quality simulated gems must be examined under a magnifying glass to be distinguished from real ones.* **simulate** (verb), **simulation** (noun).

solace (verb) to comfort or console. *There was little the rabbi could say to solace the husband after his wife's death.* **solace** (noun).

spontaneous (adjective) happening without plan. *When the news of Kennedy's assassination broke, people everywhere gathered in a spontaneous effort to share their shock and grief.* **spontaneity** (noun).

spurious (adjective) false, fake. *The so-called Piltdown Man, supposed to be the fossil of a primitive human, turned out to be spurious, although who created the hoax is still uncertain.*

squander (verb) to use up carelessly, to waste. *Those who had made donations to the charity were outraged to learn that its director had squandered millions on fancy dinners and first-class travel.*

stagnate (verb) to become stale through lack of movement or change. *Having had no contact with the outside world for generations, Japan's culture gradually stagnated.* **stagnant** (adjective), **stagnation** (noun).

staid (adjective) sedate, serious, and grave. *This college is definitely not a "party school"; the students all work hard, and the campus has a reputation for being staid.*

stimulus (noun) something that excites a response or provokes an action. *The arrival of merchants and missionaries from the West provided a stimulus for change in Japanese society.* **stimulate** (verb).

stoic (adjective) showing little feeling, even in response to pain or sorrow. *A soldier must respond to the death of his comrades in stoic fashion, since the fighting will not stop for his grief.* **stoicism** (noun).

strenuous (adjective) requiring energy and strength. *Hiking in the foothills of the Rockies is fairly easy, but climbing the higher peaks can be strenuous.*

submissive (adjective) accepting the will of others; humble, compliant. *At the end of Ibsen's play* A Doll's House, *Nora leaves her husband and abandons the role of submissive housewife.*

substantiate (verb) verified or supported by evidence. *The charge that Nixon had helped to cover up crimes was substantiated by his comments about it on a series of audio tapes.* **substantiated** (adjective), **substantiation** (noun).

sully (verb) to soil, stain, or defile. *Nixon's misdeeds as president did much to sully the reputation of the American government.*

Appendix A: Word List

superficial (adjective) on the surface only; without depth or substance. *Her wound was superficial and required only a light bandage. His superficial attractiveness hides the fact that his personality is lifeless and his mind is dull.* **superficiality** (noun).

superfluous (adjective) more than is needed, excessive. *Once you've won the debate, don't keep talking; superfluous arguments will only bore and annoy the audience.*

suppress (verb) to put down or restrain. *As soon as the unrest began, thousands of helmeted police were sent into the streets to suppress the riots.* **suppression** (noun).

surfeit (noun) an excess. *Most American families have a surfeit of food and drink on Thanksgiving Day.* **surfeit** (verb).

surreptitious (adjective) done in secret. *Because Iraq avoided weapons inspections, many believed it had a surreptitious weapons development program.*

surrogate (noun) a substitute. *When the congressman died in office, his wife was named to serve the rest of his term as a surrogate.* **surrogate** (adjective).

sustain (verb) to keep up, to continue; to support. *Because of fatigue, he was unable to sustain the effort needed to finish the marathon.*

T

tactile (adjective) relating to the sense of touch. *The thick brush strokes and gobs of color give the paintings of van Gogh a strongly tactile quality.* **tactility** (noun).

talisman (noun) an object supposed to have magical effects or qualities. *Superstitious people sometimes carry a rabbit's foot, a lucky coin, or some other talisman.*

tangential (adjective) touching lightly; only slightly connected or related. *Having enrolled in a class on African-American history, the students found the teacher's stories about his travels in South America of only tangential interest.* **tangent** (noun).

tedium (noun) boredom. *For most people, watching the Weather Channel for 24 hours would be sheer tedium.* **tedious** (adjective).

temerity (noun) boldness, rashness, excessive daring. *Only someone who didn't understand the danger would have the temerity to try to climb Everest without a guide.* **temerarious** (adjective).

temperance (noun) moderation or restraint in feelings and behavior. *Most professional athletes practice temperance in their personal habits; too much eating or drinking, they know, can harm their performance.* **temperate** (adjective).

tenacious (adjective) clinging, sticky, or persistent. *Tenacious in pursuit of her goal, she applied for the grant unsuccessfully four times before it was finally approved.* **tenacity** (noun).

tentative (adjective) subject to change; uncertain. *A firm schedule has not been established, but the Super Bowl in 2019 has been given the tentative date of February 3.*

terminate (verb) to end, to close. *The Olympic Games terminate with a grand ceremony attended by athletes from every participating country.* **terminal** (noun), **termination** (noun).

terrestrial (adjective) of the earth. *Turtles are primarily aquatic reptiles, but tortoises are terrestrial.*

therapeutic (adjective) curing or helping to cure. *Hot-water spas were popular in the nineteenth century among the sickly, who believed that soaking in the water had therapeutic effects.* **therapy** (noun).

timorous (adjective) fearful, timid. *The cowardly lion approached the throne of the wizard with a timorous look on his face.*

toady (noun) someone who flatters a superior in hopes of gaining favor; a sycophant. *"I can't stand a toady!" declared the movie mogul. "Give me someone who'll tell me the truth—even if it costs him his job!"* **toady** (verb).

tolerant (adjective) accepting, enduring. *San Franciscans have a tolerant attitude about lifestyles: "Live and let live" seems to be their motto.* **tolerate** (verb), **toleration** (noun).

toxin (noun) poison. *DDT is a powerful toxin once used to kill insects but now banned in the United States because of the risk it poses to human life.* **toxic** (adjective).

tranquility (noun) freedom from disturbance or turmoil; calm. *She moved from New York City to rural Vermont seeking the tranquility of country life.* **tranquil** (adjective).

transgress (verb) to go past limits; to violate. *No one could fathom why the honor student transgressed by shoplifting hundreds of dollars of merchandise from his favorite clothing store.* **transgression** (noun).

transient (adjective) passing quickly. *Long-term visitors to this hotel pay a different rate than transient guests who stay for just a day or two.* **transience** (noun).

transitory (adjective) quickly passing. *Public moods tend to be transitory; people may be anxious and angry one month but relatively content and optimistic the next.* **transition** (noun).

translucent (adjective) letting some light pass through. *Panels of translucent glass let daylight into the room while maintaining privacy.*

transmute (verb) to change in form or substance. *In the Middle Ages, the alchemists tried to discover ways to transmute metals such as iron into gold.* **transmutation** (noun).

treacherous (adjective) untrustworthy or disloyal; dangerous or unreliable. *Nazi Germany proved to be a treacherous ally, first signing a peace pact with the Soviet Union, then invading. Be careful crossing the rope bridge; parts are badly frayed and treacherous.* **treachery** (noun).

tremulous (adjective) trembling or shaking; timid or fearful. *Never having spoken in public before, he began his speech in a tremulous, hesitant voice.*

trite (adjective) boring because of over-familiarity; hackneyed. *Her letters were filled with trite expressions, like "All's well that ends well" and "So far so good."*

truculent (adjective) aggressive, hostile, belligerent. *Hitler's truculent behavior in demanding more territory for Germany made it clear that war was inevitable.* **truculence** (noun).

truncate (verb) to cut off. *The poor copying job truncated the playwright's manuscript: the last page ended in the middle of a scene, halfway through the first act.*

turbulent (adjective) agitated or disturbed. *The night before the championship match, Serena Williams was unable to sleep, her mind turbulent with fears and hopes.* **turbulence** (noun).

U

unheralded (adjective) little known, unexpected. *In a year of big-budget, much-hyped, mega-movies, this unheralded foreign film has surprised everyone with its popularity.*

unpalatable (adjective) distasteful, unpleasant. *Although I agree with the candidate on many issues, I can't vote for her because I find her position on capital punishment unpalatable.*

unparalleled (adjective) with no equal; unique. *Tiger Woods's victory in the Masters golf tournament by a full twelve strokes was an unparalleled accomplishment.*

unstinting (adjective) giving freely and generously. *Eleanor Roosevelt was much admired for her unstinting efforts on behalf of the poor.*

untenable (adjective) impossible to defend. *The theory that this painting is a genuine van Gogh became untenable when the artist who actually painted it came forth.*

untimely (adjective) out of the natural or proper time. *The untimely death of a youthful Princess Diana seemed far more tragic than Mother Teresa's death from old age.*

unyielding (adjective) firm, resolute, obdurate. *Despite criticism, Mario Cuomo was unyielding in his opposition to capital punishment; he vetoed several death penalty bills as governor.*

usurper (noun) someone who takes a place or possession without the right to do so. *Kennedy's most devoted followers tended to regard later presidents as usurpers, holding the office they felt he or his brothers should have held.* **usurp** (verb), **usurpation** (noun).

utilitarian (adjective) purely of practical benefit. *The design of the Model T car was simple and utilitarian, lacking the luxuries found in later models.*

utopia (noun) an imaginary, perfect society. *Those who founded the Oneida community dreamed that it could be a kind of utopia—a prosperous state with complete freedom and harmony.* **utopian** (adjective).

V

validate (verb) to officially approve or confirm. *The election of the president is validated when the members of the Electoral College meet to confirm the choice of the voters.* **valid** (adjective), **validity** (noun).

variegated (adjective) spotted with different colors. *The brilliant, variegated appearance of butterflies makes them popular among collectors.* **variegation** (noun).

venerate (verb) to admire or honor. *In Communist China, Chairman Mao Zedong was venerated as an almost god-like figure.* **venerable** (adjective), **veneration** (noun).

verdant (adjective) green with plant life. *Southern England is famous for its verdant countryside filled with gardens and small farms.* **verdancy** (noun).

vestige (noun) a trace or remainder. *Today's tiny Sherwood Forest is the last vestige of a woodland that once covered most of England.* **vestigial** (adjective).

vex (verb) to irritate, annoy, or trouble. *It vexes me that she never helps with any chores around the house.* **vexation** (noun).

vicarious (adjective) experienced through someone else's actions by way of the imagination. *Great literature broadens our minds by giving us vicarious participation in the lives of other people.*

vindicate (verb) to confirm, justify, or defend. *Lincoln's Gettysburg Address was intended to vindicate the objectives of the Union in the Civil War.*

virtuoso (noun) someone very skilled, especially in an art. *Vladimir Horowitz was one of the great piano virtuosos of the twentieth century.* **virtuosity** (noun).

vivacious (adjective) lively, sprightly. *The role of Maria in* The Sound of Music *is usually played by a charming, vivacious young actress.* **vivacity** (noun).

volatile (adjective) quickly changing; fleeting, transitory; prone to violence. *Public opinion is notoriously volatile; a politician who is very popular one month may be voted out of office the next.* **volatility** (noun).

W

whimsical (adjective) based on a capricious, carefree, or sudden impulse or idea; fanciful, playful. *Dave Barry's* Book of Bad Songs *is filled with the kind of goofy jokes that are typical of his whimsical sense of humor.* **whim** (noun).

Z

zealous (adjective) filled with eagerness, fervor, or passion. *A crowd of the candidate's most zealous supporters greeted her at the airport with banners, signs, and a marching band.* **zeal** (noun), **zealot** (noun), **zealotry** (noun).

Appendix B: List of Synonyms and Antonyms

A

abbreviate
Synonyms—shorten, make concise
Antonyms—lengthen, elongate (to make longer)

abrasive
Synonyms—harsh, rough, irritating
Antonyms—smooth, soft, soothing

abstain
Synonyms—refrain, give up, hold back
Antonyms—give in, indulge (to allow oneself to partake or participate)

acclaim
Synonyms—praise, approve, applaud
Antonyms—blame, condemn, censure (to criticize)

accumulate
Synonyms—acquire, gain, hoard
Antonyms—diminish, give away, squander (to waste)

accuse
Synonyms—challenge, blame, incriminate (to attribute responsibility)
Antonyms—forgive, exonerate (to free from guilt)

adaptable
Synonyms—flexible, changeable
Antonyms—inflexible, rigid

adept
Synonyms—skillful, proficient, competent
Antonyms—inexperienced, incompetent, unskillful

adhere
Synonyms—attach, stick, follow, uphold
Antonyms—detach, disengage, reject

adversary
Synonyms—enemy, opponent, foe, nemesis (an arch enemy)
Antonyms—friend, collaborator, ally (one who collaborates)

adverse
Synonyms—bad, negative
Antonyms—good, positive

aggressive
Synonyms—combative, belligerent (hostile)
Antonyms—peaceful, conciliatory (easily makes amends)

agitate
Synonyms—irritate, anger, upset, stir
Antonyms—soothe, calm, pacify (to calm)

agreeable
Synonyms—pleasant, likeable, delightful
Antonyms—mean, unkind, unpleasant

ambiguous
Synonyms—unclear, vague
Antonyms—clear, straightforward

ambitious
Synonyms—determined, driven, motivated
Antonyms—lazy, unmotivated, unenthusiastic

ambivalent
Synonyms—indecisive, wishy-washy, unsure
Antonyms—decided, determined, sure

amplify
Synonyms—expand, heighten, enlarge
Antonyms—decrease, minimize, diminish

animated
Synonyms—energetic, lively, spirited
Antonyms—lazy, sluggish, depressed

animosity
Synonyms—hostility, resentment, hatred
Antonyms—kindness, friendliness, warmth, compassion (caring)

anomalous
Synonyms—odd, inconsistent, irregular, unusual
Antonyms—commonplace, ordinary, normal, regular

anonymous
Synonyms—nameless, unknown, unidentified
Antonyms—identified, known, recognized

antagonize
Synonyms—irritate, bother, annoy
Antonyms—help, aid, soothe

apathy
Synonyms—indifference, unconcern, disregard (lack of interest)
Antonyms—interest, concern

arbitrary
Synonyms—random, chance, inconsistent
Antonyms—steady, unchanging, reliable, predictable

arid
Synonyms—dry, barren, parched (lacking water)
Antonyms—humid, soaked, well-watered

attentive
Synonyms—interested, observant, aware
Antonyms—unaware, unconcerned, neglectful

astute
Synonyms— quick-witted, intelligent, smart
Antonyms—inept, foolish, slow-witted

atypical
Synonyms—not normal, uncommon, unnatural
Antonyms—normal, regular, common, typical

audacious
Synonyms—outrageous, bold, daring
Antonyms—meek, mild, quiet

audible
Synonyms—perceptible, discernible, distinct (able to be heard)
Antonyms—silent, indistinct (quiet or not able to be heard)

authentic
Synonyms— original, trustworthy, credible
Antonyms—corrupt, untrustworthy, fake

autonomous
Synonyms—independent, self-governing
Antonyms—dependent, helpless, subjugated (controlled by others)

B

baffle
Synonyms—confuse, stump, puzzle
Antonyms—clarify, elucidate (to make clear)

banal
Synonyms—usual, common, ordinary
Antonyms—unusual, different, special

barren
Synonyms—lifeless, empty, unfruitful (not able to support life)
Antonyms—productive, fruitful (able to support life)

belated
Synonyms—late, overdue
Antonyms—prompt, punctual (on time)

benevolent
Synonyms—kind, good-hearted
Antonyms—cruel, evil, malevolent (willing to cause harm)

benign
Synonyms— mild, peaceable, harmless
Antonyms—deadly, dangerous, harmful

berate
Synonyms— scold, criticize, reprimand (to scold or blame)
Antonyms—praise, encourage, uplift

bleak
Synonyms—grim, hopeless, desolate (deserted and empty)
Antonyms—hopeful, cheerful, encouraging

boisterous
Synonyms—noisy, loud, rambunctious (uncontrolled)
Antonyms—quiet, orderly, subdued (calm and under control)

bombastic
Synonyms—boastful, ostentatious (showy), pompous (full of oneself)
Antonyms—restrained, quiet, humble, reserved (private)

buttress
Synonyms—bolster, reinforce, support
Antonyms— weaken

C

cajole
Synonyms—coax, persuade, wheedle (to convince by asking nicely)
Antonyms—order, force, compel

camaraderie
Synonyms—friendship, companionship, togetherness
Antonyms—animosity, isolation

candid
Synonyms—truthful, straightforward, unrehearsed
Antonyms—dishonest, staged, set up

candor
Synonyms—honesty, directness, veracity (truthfulness)
Antonyms—insincerity, deceit, lying

capricious
Synonyms—willful, arbitrary, impulsive (acting without thought)
Antonyms—predictable, steady, sensible

captivate
Synonyms—dazzle, enchant, fascinate
Antonyms—bore, offend, repulse

caustic
Synonyms—burning, hurtful, sarcastic (cutting or mocking)
Antonyms—soothing, mild, innocuous (harmless)

chaos
Synonyms—disorder, confusion, pandemonium (an uproar or hubbub)
Antonyms—harmony, order, tranquility (peace)

circumvent
Synonyms—go around, avoid, elude (to get away from)
Antonyms—take on, confront, face

clandestine
Synonyms—secret, undercover, covert, surreptitious (hidden)
Antonyms—public, open, aboveboard, overt (open)

cloying
Synonyms—sticky, sentimental, clingy
Antonyms—independent, detached, cool

coerce
Synonyms—force, bully, pressure
Antonyms—coax, cajole, encourage

cogent
Synonyms—powerful, logical, persuasive
Antonyms—unconvincing, ineffective, illogical

cognizant
Synonyms—aware, informed, sentient (conscious)
Antonyms—ignorant, oblivious (not attentive)

coherent
Synonyms—understandable, clear
Antonyms—confused, meaningless

cohesive
Synonyms—close-knit, unified, interconnected
Antonyms—scattered, disorganized, fragmented

collaborate
Synonyms—work together, cooperate, join forces
Antonyms—separate, part ways, conflict

commend
Synonyms—praise, applaud, honor
Antonyms—criticize, put down, disapprove

compatible
Synonyms—harmonious, well-suited, congenial (friendly)
Antonyms—mismatched, clashing, incompatible

compel
Synonyms—force, require, pressure
Antonyms—discourage, prevent, dissuade (to advise against)

competent
Synonyms—skilled, qualified, proficient (good at)
Antonyms—inept, useless, bungling (prone to making mistakes)

complacent
Synonyms—self-satisfied, comfortable, smug (self-satisfied)
Antonyms—restless, dissatisfied, discontent

comply
Synonyms—obey, conform, follow
Antonyms—rebel, resist, defy

comprehensive
Synonyms—thorough, inclusive, complete
Antonyms—limited, partial, restricted

concise
Synonyms—short, to the point, succinct (brief)
Antonyms—rambling, long-winded, wordy

condescending
Synonyms—rude, snobbish
Antonyms—down-to-earth, friendly, kind

confident
Synonyms—sure, convinced, positive
Antonyms—insecure, shy, fearful

conform
Synonyms—comply, submit, follow
Antonyms—defy, disobey, flout (to go against or disregard)

conformity
Synonyms—compliance, submission
Antonyms—defiance, disobedience

congested
Synonyms—packed, jammed, blocked
Antonyms—empty, free, wide-open

congruent
Synonyms—alike, matching, harmonious (goes well together)
Antonyms—incompatible, mismatched, dissimilar

consensus
Synonyms—agreement, compromise, harmony
Antonyms—difference, disparity, confrontation

consequential
Synonyms—important, major, meaningful
Antonyms—trivial, insignificant

conservative
Synonyms—traditional, old-fashioned, conventional
Antonyms—progressive, adventurous, avant-garde (extremely modern)

constant
Synonyms—steady, persistent, incessant (unceasing)
Antonyms—irregular, occasional

constrain
Synonyms—hold back, restrict, inhibit (to slow down or prevent)
Antonyms—expand, develop, increase

consummate
Synonyms—ideal, perfect, superlative (the best)
Antonyms—inferior, awful, abysmal (very bad)

contaminate
Synonyms—pollute, spoil, taint (to spoil or damage)
Antonyms—purify, cleanse

contemporary
Synonyms—modern, up to date, new
Antonyms—old-fashioned, antique

contradict
Synonyms—disagree, oppose, challenge
Antonyms—support, concur (to agree)

conventional
Synonyms—usual, established, typical
Antonyms—uncommon, odd, original

converge
Synonyms—meet, come together, join
Antonyms—diverge, separate

convey
Synonyms—tell, express, communicate
Antonyms—hold back, contain

convoluted
Synonyms—complex, difficult
Antonyms—simple, uncomplicated, straightforward

corroborate
Synonyms—confirm, support, substantiate (to back up with evidence)
Antonyms—contradict, deny, challenge, refute

corrupt
Synonyms—dishonest, shady, crooked
Antonyms—truthful, honest, moral, upstanding

covert
Synonyms—secret, hidden, underground
Antonyms—open, public, exposed

criticize
Synonyms—disparage (to cut down), denigrate (to put down)
Antonyms—praise, commend

culpable
Synonyms—responsible, guilty, at fault
Antonyms—innocent, blameless

curtail
Synonyms—cut back, limit, shorten, restrict
Antonyms—increase, expand, lengthen

D

debased
Synonyms—corrupted, depraved (wicked)
Antonyms—upright, noble, dignified

decisive
Synonyms—determined, conclusive, sure
Antonyms—undetermined, indecisive, irresolute (unsure)

decorous
Synonyms—polite, proper, suitable
Antonyms—indecent, wrong, unsuitable

decry
Synonyms—devalue, disparage (to criticize), demean (to put down)
Antonyms—respect, approve, praise

deficient
Synonyms—lacking, insufficient, not enough
Antonyms—ample, adequate, enough

deficit
Synonyms—deficiency, loss, shortage
Antonyms—excess, surplus, sufficient amount

definite
Synonyms—certain, explicit, indubitable (not questionable)
Antonyms—uncertain, questionable, refutable

defy
Synonyms— disregard, flout (to go against)
Antonyms—obey, respect, follow

delete
Synonyms—remove, take away, expunge (to get rid of)
Antonyms—add, build up, create

deleterious
Synonyms—damaging, hurtful, injurious (harmful)
Antonyms—helpful, good for the health, beneficial, harmless

denigrate
Synonyms— malign, impugn, slander (to put down)
Antonyms— encourage, boost, celebrate

deplete
Synonyms—diminish, reduce, use up
Antonyms—fill, increase, enhance

deplore
Synonyms—despise, hate, undervalue
Antonyms—appreciate, accept, value

deprecate
Synonyms—ridicule, disparage (to criticize), denigrate (to put down)
Antonyms—commend, approve, bolster, support

deprive
Synonyms—take away, rob, remove
Antonyms—give, confer, bestow (to give)

desire
Synonyms—want, longing, craving
Antonyms—disinterest, apathy (lack of interest), repulsion (extreme dislike)

desolate
Synonyms—barren, lifeless, devoid (empty)
Antonyms—inhabited, lively, fruitful (productive)

destitute
Synonyms—poor, indigent (without money)
Antonyms—wealthy, secure, prosperous

destroy
Synonyms—eliminate, obliterate (to wipe out), raze (to completely destroy)
Antonyms—build, fix, improve

detach
Synonyms—remove, segregate, separate
Antonyms—join, put together, assemble

deter
Synonyms—stop, halt, hinder
Antonyms—aid, inspire, incite (to promote)

detractor
Synonyms—critic, enemy
Antonyms—supporter, benefactor, friend

detrimental
Synonyms—bad, harmful, unfavorable
Antonyms—positive, helpful, useful

devastate
Synonyms—destroy, wreck, annihilate (to demolish)
Antonyms—save, protect, expand, augment (to add to)

devious
Synonyms—dishonest, evil, duplicitous (scheming)
Antonyms—honest, forthright, righteous

diffuse
Synonyms—spread out, expanded, propagated (spread out)
Antonyms—condensed, confined, succinct (brief)

digress
Synonyms—stray, ramble, deviate (to go off in another direction)
Antonyms—focus, be direct, stay on course

diligent
Synonyms—hard-working, earnest, persistent
Antonyms—thoughtless, careless, lazy

diminish
Synonyms—decrease, dwindle, reduce
Antonyms—prolong, increase, enhance, extend

diminutive
Synonyms—petite, small, short
Antonyms—big, enormous, huge

dire
Synonyms—critical, very important, desperate, grave (serious)
Antonyms—trivial, unimportant, silly

disagree
Synonyms—conflict, go against, dissent (to differ in opinion)
Antonyms—agree, concur (to have the same opinion), acquiesce (to accept without protesting)

discern
Synonyms—recognize, distinguish, perceive
Antonyms—confuse, misunderstand, discombobulate (to confuse)

disclose
Synonyms—tell, expose, reveal, make known
Antonyms—suppress, hide, disavow (to deny)

discomfort
Synonyms—unpleasantness, irritation, pain, anguish (great pain)
Antonyms—comfort, peacefulness, ease

disconcerting
Synonyms—disturbing, unbalancing, upsetting
Antonyms—quieting, calming, comforting

discord
Synonyms—disharmony, conflict
Antonyms—harmony, peacefulness

discrepancy
Synonyms—variation, difference, incongruity (difference)
Antonyms—consistency, sameness, reliability

dismal
Synonyms—bleak, sad, horrible
Antonyms—bright, hopeful, encouraging

dismay
Synonyms—disappointment, discouragement, trepidation (anxiety or fear)
Antonyms—encouragement, security, confidence

dismiss
Synonyms—send away, discard, push aside
Antonyms—permit, allow, keep, maintain

disparage
Synonyms— mock, criticize, belittle (to put down)
Antonyms—lift up, support, encourage, sanction (to support)

disparate
Synonyms—at variance, contrasting, different
Antonyms—similar, invariable, like

disparity
Synonyms—imbalance, gap, inequity
Antonyms—equity, likeness, sameness

dispute
Synonyms—bicker, argue, contend
Antonyms—harmonize, agree, go along with

disruptive
Synonyms—disorderly, disturbing
Antonyms—unifying, peaceful, calming

disseminate
Synonyms—publicize, scatter, radiate, disperse
Antonyms—condense, conceal, hide

dissipate
Synonyms—deplete, use up, squander (to waste)
Antonyms—save, preserve, conserve (to save)

distinct
Synonyms—separate, clearly defined, explicit (obvious)
Antonyms—vague, unsure, ambiguous (poorly defined)

distorted
Synonyms—warped, bent out of shape, perverted
Antonyms—straight, pure, invariable

diverge
Synonyms—separate, deviate (to go off course)
Antonyms—converge, join

diverse
Synonyms—dissimilar, different, varied
Antonyms—conforming, uniform, similar

divide
Synonyms—split up, disjoin, partition (to cut up)
Antonyms—join, add, combine

divulge
Synonyms—bring to light, confess, tell
Antonyms—protect, suppress, hide, conceal

dominant
Synonyms—superior, controlling, main
Antonyms—subordinate, inferior, auxiliary (additional)

dominate
Synonyms—rule over, influence, overshadow
Antonyms—follow, submit, acquiesce (to go along with)

dubious
Synonyms—suspicious, doubtful, disputable
Antonyms—reliable, true, unambiguous

duplicitous
Synonyms—two-faced, shady, dishonest
Antonyms—trustworthy, reliable, truthful, honest

durable
Synonyms—rugged, tough, tenacious (persistent)
Antonyms—flimsy, fragile, weak

duress
Synonyms—hardship, suffering, threat
Antonyms—ease, support, peacefulness

E

endure
Synonyms—bear, withstand, suffer, tolerate, cope with
Antonyms—give up, surrender, cave in

effusive
Synonyms—expressive, gushing, unrestrained
Antonyms—reserved, restrained, aloof

egotism
Synonyms—narcissism, self-absorption (focusing only on one's self and one's own desires)
Antonyms—selflessness, compassion, thoughtfulness

elaborate
Synonyms—ornate, refined, complicated
Antonyms—plain, simple, uncomplicated

elated
Synonyms—thrilled, joyful, euphoric (extremely happy)
Antonyms—deflated, melancholy, disappointed

elusive
Synonyms—mysterious, puzzling, baffling (difficult to understand)
Antonyms—clear, understandable, concise (brief and clear)

eminent
Synonyms—prestigious, well-known, illustrious (well-known in a positive manner)
Antonyms—unimportant, ordinary, unknown

emulate
Synonyms—copy, mimic, act like
Antonyms—act independently

encompass
Synonyms—include, circumscribe, encircle
Antonyms—exclude, leave out, remove

enervate
Synonyms—weaken, incapacitate, drain
Antonyms—animate, empower, strengthen

engage
Synonyms—deal with, undertake, employ
Antonyms—avoid, repulse, ignore, fire

engender
Synonyms—incite, provoke, rouse (to move to action)
Antonyms—calm, discourage, hinder (to block or stop), dissuade (to advise against)

enhance
Synonyms—heighten, improve, increase
Antonyms—devalue, weaken, reduce, lessen, undermine (to weaken)

enrich
Synonyms—improve, enhance, aggrandize (to make bigger)
Antonyms—decrease, impoverish (to make poorer)

enthrall
Synonyms—charm, captivate, mesmerize (to capture the attention of)
Antonyms—bore, disgust, repel

eradicate
Synonyms—eliminate, destroy, get rid of
Antonyms—maintain, protect

erratic
Synonyms—irregular, unpredictable, volatile (explosive)
Antonyms—steadfast, predictable, regular

espouse
Synonyms—advocate, defend, support
Antonyms—disallow, reject, forsake (to abandon)

essential
Synonyms—necessary, requisite (required), indispensable (very much needed)
Antonyms—trivial, unnecessary, extra

euphoric
Synonyms—excited, thrilled, very happy
Antonyms—depressed, grieving, sorrowful

exacerbate
Synonyms—embitter, intensify, irritate
Antonyms— calm down, alleviate (to lesson), placate (to please)

exasperate
Synonyms—provoke, rile up, infuriate (to make angry)
Antonyms—mollify (to soothe), tranquilize (to calm down)

exclude
Synonyms—keep out, omit, ostracize (to ban someone from a group)
Antonyms—include, welcome, allow in

exculpate
Synonyms—forgive, excuse, acquit (to free from guilt)
Antonyms—punish, accuse, incriminate (to make appear responsible for a crime)

exempt
Synonyms—not required to, immune
Antonyms—responsible, required to

exonerate
Synonyms—hold blameless, vindicate (to free from guilt), exculpate (to free from guilt)
Antonyms—condemn, convict, hold accountable

expand
Synonyms—enlarge, increase, swell
Antonyms—decrease, minimize, reduce

expansive
Synonyms—all-inclusive, broad, widespread
Antonyms—exclusive, narrow, limited

expedite
Synonyms—quicken, hurry, hasten
Antonyms—delay, slow down, retard

expert
Synonyms—skilled, knowledgeable, experienced
Antonyms— amateur, inept (unskilled), novice (new at something)

extenuate
Synonyms—diminish, lessen
Antonyms—increase, worsen, exacerbate (to make worse)

extol
Synonyms—praise, exalt, acclaim (to rave about)
Antonyms—disapprove, condemn, disparage (to complain about)

extraneous
Synonyms—extra, not needed, unnecessary, irrelevant
Antonyms—vital, relevant

extricate
Synonyms—liberate, free
Antonyms—restrain, involve, constrain (to limit)

extrinsic
Synonyms—foreign, alien, external (outside)
Antonyms—native, natural, inherent (originating from within)

exuberant
Synonyms—cheerful, buoyant (high-spirited), ebullient (full of positive energy)
Antonyms—unenthusiastic, dull, lethargic (slow)

F

fabricate
Synonyms—manufacture, make up, formulate
Antonyms—disassemble, break apart

fallacy
Synonyms—falsehood, lie, deception
Antonyms—truth, fact, reality

fanatic
Synonyms—lunatic, zealot, radical (extremist)
Antonyms—conservative, disinterested party, unbeliever, infidel (non-believer)

fecund
Synonyms—propagating, fertile, fruitful (able to reproduce)
Antonyms—infertile, sterile, barren (unable to have children)

felicitous
Synonyms—appropriate, suitable, apropos (appropriate)
Antonyms—inopportune, poorly-timed, irrelevant

feral
Synonyms—wild, savage, untamed
Antonyms—tamed, mild-mannered, civilized

fervent
Synonyms—sincere, impassioned
Antonyms—unenthusiastic, unfeeling, dispassionate (unmoved)

flagrant
Synonyms—shameless, undisguised, brazen (brash)
Antonyms—obscure, contained, camouflaged (hidden)

flamboyant
Synonyms—glamorous, over-the-top, pretentious (showy)
Antonyms—refined, dull, common

forbid
Synonyms—prohibit, disallow, ban
Antonyms—facilitate, advance, admit (to allow)

formal
Synonyms—official, established, conventional
Antonyms—casual, informal, unofficial

forthright
Synonyms—sincere, honest, candid (open and direct)
Antonyms—dishonest, sneaky, lying

fortitude
Synonyms—courage, endurance, tenacity (persistence)
Antonyms—cowardice, laziness

foster
Synonyms—champion, support, nurture
Antonyms—neglect, halt, starve, deprive (to withhold support)

fragile
Synonyms—breakable, weak, frail
Antonyms—strong, durable, sturdy, rugged

frenetic
Synonyms—obsessive, overwrought (very upset), maniacal (frenzied, like a madman)
Antonyms—normal, balanced, calm

frivolity
Synonyms—whimsicality, silliness, childishness, playfulness
Antonyms—seriousness, sternness

frugal
Synonyms—economical, penny-pinching, thrifty
Antonyms—wasteful, spendthrift, lavish

furtive
Synonyms—secretive, clandestine (hidden), stealthy (done in a sneaky way)
Antonyms—candid, straightforward, overt (done in an obvious way)

futile
Synonyms—pointless, purposeless, trifling (having no value)
Antonyms—useful, worthwhile, efficacious (effective)

G

gargantuan
Synonyms—huge, gigantic, enormous
Antonyms—tiny, infinitesimal (infinitely small), minute (really small or insignificant)

generate
Synonyms—make, create, produce
Antonyms—end, terminate, destroy

genial
Synonyms—cordial, amiable, kindly (likeable)
Antonyms—disagreeable, unfriendly, surly (gruff)

grandiose
Synonyms—exaggerating, pompous (full of oneself), ostentatious (acting like a "show-off")
Antonyms—humble, lowly, unimposing (humble)

gratuitous
Synonyms—excessive, uncalled for, unnecessary
Antonyms—warranted, necessary, vital

greedy
Synonyms—gluttonous, insatiable (strong desire for selfish gain)
Antonyms—generous, giving, satisfied, metered (controlled)

gregarious
Synonyms—sociable, outgoing, good-natured
Antonyms—shy, introverted (turning inward to oneself), antisocial (unfriendly or aloof)

guileless
Synonyms—truthful, honest, straightforward
Antonyms—cunning, deceitful, tricky

gullible
Synonyms—simple, credulous (easily fooled)
Antonyms—sophisticated, skeptical, incredulous (unbelieving)

H

hackneyed
Synonyms—stale, common, trite (something overdone or constantly repeated)
Antonyms—original, fresh, authentic

haughty
Synonyms—snotty, narcissistic (focused on the self), arrogant (feeling superior to others)
Antonyms—humble, polite, self-effacing (humble)

heinous
Synonyms—wicked, repugnant (very bad), atrocious (awful)
Antonyms—honorable, wonderful, pleasing

heretic
Synonyms—pagan, unbeliever, iconoclast (one who goes against a belief system)
Antonyms—believer, loyalist, adherent (one who follows a belief system)

hesitate
Synonyms—pause, defer (to put off), balk (to refuse to move forward)
Antonyms—charge into, perform, hasten (to speed up)

honorable
Synonyms—well-regarded, law-abiding, esteemed (well-respected)
Antonyms—unethical, unjust, corrupt, dishonorable, base (lowly)

hypocrisy
Synonyms—phoniness, fraudulence (fakeness), duplicity (lying)
Antonyms—honesty, sincerity, genuineness

hypothetical
Synonyms—supposed, presumed, guessed
Antonyms—factual, actual, real

I

imitate
Synonyms—copy, mimic, impersonate (to act like someone), emulate (to strive to be like)
Antonyms—differ from, diverge from (to differ from)

immature
Synonyms—childish, infantile (like an infant)
Antonyms—experienced, mature, adult, seasoned (experienced)

impede
Synonyms—block, hinder, stymie (thwart)
Antonyms—facilitate, accelerate, bolster (to support), expedite (to speed up)

impersonate
Synonyms—mimic, copy, imitate (to act like)
Antonyms—differ from

impetuous
Synonyms—hasty, rash (acting with little thought)
Antonyms—cautious, thoughtful, planned

impulsive
Synonyms—unpredictable, erratic (irregular), hasty (acting quickly, without thought)
Antonyms—deliberate, planned, designed (well-thought-out)

inarticulate
Synonyms—stammering, incomprehensible, tongue-tied (not well-spoken)
Antonyms—intelligible, clear, understandable, eloquent (well-spoken)

incisive
Synonyms—clever, acute, sharp (quick-witted)
Antonyms—dull, half-witted, incompetent (not capable)

incompatible
Synonyms—opposite, clashing (conflicting), disparate (different)
Antonyms—suitable, harmonious, simpatico (compatible)

incongruent
Synonyms—unlike, conflicting, inconsistent
Antonyms—alike, equal, analogous (similar)

incontrovertible
Synonyms—irrefutable, unquestionable, sure
Antonyms—questionable, inconclusive, unconvincing

incorporate
Synonyms—include, join, merge, mix
Antonyms—exclude, divide, separate

incriminate
Synonyms— accuse, involve, blame
Antonyms—free, exonerate (to remove from guilt)

indecision
Synonyms—ambivalence, hesitancy, tentativeness
Antonyms—certainty, assurance, decisiveness

independent
Synonyms—self-determining, free, self-sufficient, liberated
Antonyms—dependent

indeterminate
Synonyms—inexact, inconclusive, imprecise (not accurate)
Antonyms—conclusive, definite, irrefutable (certain)

indict
Synonyms—accuse, condemn, blame
Antonyms—hold blameless, exonerate (to excuse), acquit (to find not guilty)

indifference
Synonyms—disinterest, apathy (lack of interest)
Antonyms—concern, involvement, interest

indistinct
Synonyms—poorly defined, murky (unclear), ambiguous (not clearly marked or understood)
Antonyms—obvious, well-defined, discernible (distinct)

induce
Synonyms—motivate, cause, instigate (to set in motion)
Antonyms—hinder, block, impede (to slow or stop), dissuade (to advise against)

inept
Synonyms—unskillful, clumsy, incompetent (not capable), bungling (prone to making mistakes)
Antonyms—skillful, masterful, competent (capable), dexterous (demonstrating skill)

inevitable
Synonyms—unavoidable, impending (happening soon), destined (bound by destiny to happen)
Antonyms—avoidable, unlikely, uncertain

infamous
Synonyms—disreputable (having a bad reputation), notorious (well-known in a negative way)
Antonyms—righteous, noble, goodly

informal
Synonyms—casual, unofficial, unfussy
Antonyms—fussy, formal, stiff (acting in a strict manner)

ingenious
Synonyms—gifted, intelligent, resourceful (clever)
Antonyms—foolish, dumb, dull-witted

inherent
Synonyms—built-in, natural, innate (found naturally within)
Antonyms—acquired, unnatural, learned

inhibit
Synonyms—constrain, suppress, restrain, prevent
Antonyms—assist, encourage, support

inhibited
Synonyms—shy, subdued, reserved (quiet or timid in manner)
Antonyms—outrageous, loud, boisterous (noisy)

initiate
Synonyms—start, begin, inaugurate (to implement)
Antonyms—end, finish, cease (to stop)

initiative
Synonyms—drive, motivation, gumption
Antonyms—idleness, laziness

innocuous
Synonyms—inoffensive, mild, harmless
Antonyms—offensive, shocking, wild

insipid
Synonyms—dull, tedious, boring
Antonyms—exciting, interesting, fun

insolence
Synonyms— crudeness, disrespect, impertinence (lack of respect)
Antonyms—respect, obedience, humility

instigate
Synonyms—start, initiate (to begin), foment (to stimulate to action)
Antonyms—suppress, not allow, dissuade (to advise against)

integrate
Synonyms—put together, merge, harmonize
Antonyms—separate, leave out, cast aside

intimidating
Synonyms—coercive, threatening, compelling
Antonyms—easy-going, non-threatening

intrepid
Synonyms—fearless, courageous, undaunted (unafraid)
Antonyms—cautious, fearful, afraid

inundate
Synonyms—overload, flood, overwhelm
Antonyms—relieve, lessen

invariable
Synonyms—unchanging, consistent, constant, steady
Antonyms—variable, changing, inconsistent, wavering

invigorate
Synonyms—energize, stimulate, enliven
Antonyms—drain, discourage, deflate

invincible
Synonyms—strong, unbeatable, indomitable (unable to be conquered)
Antonyms—weak, downtrodden, conquerable

irate
Synonyms—angry, furious, enraged
Antonyms—calm, peaceful, pacified (soothed)

irrational
Synonyms—illogical, nonsensical
Antonyms—rational, logical, sensible

irregular
Synonyms—variable, unsteady, inconsistent, unusual, variegated (full of variety)
Antonyms—regular, steady, predictable, consistent, normal, uniform

irresolute
Synonyms—uncertain, undecided, indecisive
Antonyms—resolute, certain, decisive

irritate
Synonyms—annoy, upset, aggravate
Antonyms—please, soothe, placate (to make happy)

J

jeopardize
Synonyms—endanger, threaten
Antonyms—protect, support, empower

jovial
Synonyms—happy, upbeat, good-natured
Antonyms—cranky, grumpy, glum (sullen)

judicious
Synonyms—thoughtful, cautious, prudent (wise)
Antonyms—reckless, ill-considered, imprudent (unwise)

K

keen
Synonyms—sharp, quick, astute (smart)
Antonyms—dull, slow, unintelligent

L

laborious
Synonyms—difficult, hard, demanding
Antonyms—easy, relaxed, undemanding

lackluster
Synonyms—dull, boring, uninteresting
Antonyms—brilliant, captivating, interesting

lament
Synonyms—mourn, regret, grieve
Antonyms—celebrate

languid
Synonyms—slow, sluggish, weak
Antonyms—energetic, vital, strong

languish
Synonyms—droop, decline, suffer
Antonyms—thrive, grow, flourish (to grow)

latent
Synonyms—unexpressed, inactive, hidden, undeveloped
Antonyms—expressed, active, actualized, developed

lavish
Synonyms—extravagant, posh, opulent (abundant)
Antonyms—poor, bare, understated, low-key

lax
Synonyms—relaxed, loose, permissive, lenient (not strict)
Antonyms—strict, tight, rigid

lazy
Synonyms—unmotivated, unenergetic, indolent (avoiding work)
Antonyms—driven, energetic, hardworking, industrious

legitimate
Synonyms—actual, real, verified (shown to be true)
Antonyms—illegitimate, false, fake, unreal

lenient
Synonyms—allowing, permissive, forgiving, lax (not strict)
Antonyms—strict, rigid, restrictive, punishing

lethargic
Synonyms—slow, lazy, sluggish, inactive
Antonyms—quick, energetic, vital, active

liability
Synonyms—obligation, debt, weakness, disadvantage
Antonyms—asset, strength, advantage

linger
Synonyms—stay, loiter, delay
Antonyms—leave, flee, rush, expedite (to hurry)

livid
Synonyms—angry, irate, furious
Antonyms—calm, pleased, contented

lofty
Synonyms—high, ambitious, pretentious (showy)
Antonyms—low, lowly, meager (very poor or not enough)

loquacious
Synonyms—talkative, chatty, wordy, garrulous (talkative)
Antonyms—silent, unresponsive, concise (brief), taciturn (unexpressive), terse (short)

lucid
Synonyms—clear, understandable, rational
Antonyms—unclear, muddled, confusing

M

malevolence
Synonyms—hatred, ill will, malice (intent to harm)
Antonyms—goodness, kindness, benevolence (good will)

malingering
Synonyms—lazy, shirking (avoiding duties)
Antonyms—hardworking, industrious

malignant
Synonyms—harmful, dangerous
Antonyms—beneficial, harmless, benign (not harmful)

malleable
Synonyms—changeable, bendable, pliable (easy to bend)
Antonyms—unchangeable, inflexible, rigid

mature
Synonyms—full-grown, developed, ripe
Antonyms—immature, undeveloped, underdeveloped

mediocre
Synonyms—unimpressive, ordinary, average, so-so
Antonyms—impressive, extraordinary, excellent, stellar (outstanding)

mercurial
Synonyms—ever-changing, unpredictable, fickle (not loyal), capricious (quick to change)
Antonyms—steady, constant, predictable

meticulous
Synonyms—neat, careful, detailed, precise (accurate)
Antonyms—messy, sloppy, imprecise (lacking accuracy)

misconception
Synonyms—misunderstanding, misperception, false belief
Antonyms—fact, truth

mitigate
Synonyms—reduce, lessen, relieve
Antonyms—worsen, exacerbate (to make more severe)

moderate
Synonyms—mild, medium, average
Antonyms—extreme, excessive, intense

modicum
Synonyms—bit, tidbit, morsel (a tiny amount)
Antonyms—load, large amount

mollify
Synonyms—soothe, calm, pacify (to calm)
Antonyms—enrage, aggravate, irritate, anger

moribund
Synonyms—dying, ending, declining, terminal (at the end)
Antonyms—vital, thriving, alive, living

morose
Synonyms—negative, dark, sullen (gloomy)
Antonyms—positive, happy, cheerful

mundane
Synonyms—ordinary, commonplace, everyday
Antonyms—extraordinary, unique, original

munificent
Synonyms—generous, lavish, liberal (giving freely)
Antonyms—stingy, miserly, withholding

mutable
Synonyms—changeable, flexible, malleable (able to be changed)
Antonyms—inflexible, rigid, steadfast

N

naive
Synonyms—innocent, trusting, newcomer
Antonyms—experienced, sophisticated

narcissistic
Synonyms—self-absorbed, conceited, selfish
Antonyms—generous, altruistic (helping others)

nebulous
Synonyms—vague, unclear
Antonyms—precise, specific, well-defined

neglect
Synonyms—forget, abandon, overlook
Antonyms—nurture, care for, foster

nemesis
Synonyms—arch enemy, opponent, adversary
Antonyms—best friend, collaborator, ally (friend)

nocturnal
Synonyms—nighttime, vampirish
Antonyms—daytime, diurnal (during the day)

nonchalant
Synonyms—casual, relaxed, laid-back
Antonyms—formal, stiff, uptight

notorious
Synonyms—disreputable (having a bad reputation), infamous (well-known for a bad reason)
Antonyms—unknown, unfamiliar, unheard of

novel
Synonyms—new, unique, imaginative
Antonyms—ordinary, everyday, unoriginal

novice
Synonyms—beginner, trainee, neophyte (new learner)
Antonyms—expert, authority, professional

nurture
Synonyms—care for, foster, protect
Antonyms—neglect, abandon, ignore, harm

O

objective
Synonyms—fair, unbiased, open-minded
Antonyms—prejudiced, partial, subjective (biased)

obliterate
Synonyms—demolish, eliminate, eradicate (wipe out)
Antonyms—assemble, build, create

oblivious
Synonyms—unresponsive, unaware, forgetting
Antonyms—mindful, conscious, alert

obscure
Synonyms—unknown, minor, unseen
Antonyms—famous, prominent, recognized

obsolete
Synonyms—outdated, irrelevant, archaic (old)
Antonyms—contemporary, current, trendy, modern

obstinate
Synonyms—stubborn, headstrong, obdurate (stubborn), tenacious (determined)
Antonyms—obedient, yielding (giving in), accommodating (eager to please others)

obtrusive
Synonyms—obvious, prominent, blatant (highly noticeable)
Antonyms—ordinary, unremarkable, inconspicuous (unnoticeable)

occlude
Synonyms—block, obstruct, impede (to hold back)
Antonyms—assist, facilitate, ease

omnipotent
Synonyms—supreme, invincible (unstoppable)
Antonyms—powerless, weak, helpless

onerous
Synonyms—burdensome, tedious (repetitive and boring), arduous (difficult and demanding)
Antonyms—easy, effortless, trouble-free

opinionated
Synonyms—inflexible, unbending, dogmatic (having rigid opinions)
Antonyms—mellow, easygoing, laid-back

opponent
Synonyms—rival, foe, challenger
Antonyms—friend, colleague, teammate, ally (friend)

opportune
Synonyms—well-timed, advantageous (helpful)
Antonyms—inconvenient, unfortunate

optimistic
Synonyms—hopeful, positive, sanguine (confident)
Antonyms—pessimistic, gloomy

opulent
Synonyms—lavish, luxurious, sumptuous (expensive)
Antonyms—inadequate, meager (very poor or not enough), impoverished (poor)

ordinary
Synonyms—common, usual, regular, normal
Antonyms—extraordinary, exceptional, unique

ornate
Synonyms—lavish, bejeweled, adorned (decorated)
Antonyms—plain, simple, basic

orthodox
Synonyms—conventional, mainstream, usual
Antonyms—innovative, pioneering, ground-breaking

ostentatious
Synonyms—flashy, flamboyant, pretentious (showy)
Antonyms—modest, down-to-earth, humble

ostracize
Synonyms—banish, ignore, cast out
Antonyms—welcome, include, embrace

overt
Synonyms—open, unconcealed, blatant (obvious)
Antonyms—hidden, covert (concealed), clandestine (secret)

P

parched
Synonyms—dry, dehydrated, waterless
Antonyms—wet, saturated, drenched

pariah
Synonyms—outcast, untouchable, exile
Antonyms—insider, hero, idol

passion
Synonyms—enthusiasm, zeal, delight
Antonyms—indifference, apathy (lack of interest)

passive
Synonyms—sluggish, lifeless, inert (inactive)
Antonyms—active, lively, energetic

pathetic
Synonyms—pitiful, wretched, lame
Antonyms—admirable, excellent, worthy

penitent
Synonyms—sorry, apologetic, contrite (sorry)
Antonyms—unrepentant, shameless, unremorseful

perceptive
Synonyms—insightful, observant
Antonyms—insensitive, oblivious (unaware)

perish
Synonyms—die, pass away, expire
Antonyms—live, survive, endure

perplexing
Synonyms—puzzling, bewildering, mystifying
Antonyms—simple, effortless, trouble-free, clear, understandable

persevere
Synonyms—persist, continue, keep on
Antonyms—quit, surrender, give up

perturb
Synonyms—annoy, disturb, bother
Antonyms—please, delight, gratify (make happy)

pervasive
Synonyms—omnipresent, all-encompassing (found everywhere)
Antonyms—contained, limited

pessimistic
Synonyms—gloomy, negative
Antonyms—optimistic, hopeful

pious
Synonyms—religious, reverent
Antonyms—disrespectful, heretical (going against established beliefs)

placate
Synonyms—soothe, pacify, appease (to calm down)
Antonyms—enrage, anger, infuriate (to anger)

placid
Synonyms—calm, peaceful, easygoing
Antonyms—anxious, stressed, agitated (upset)

plausible
Synonyms—believable, possible, likely
Antonyms—improbable, far-fetched, questionable

popular
Synonyms—appealing, well-liked, admired
Antonyms—disliked, ill-favored, unpopular

potent
Synonyms—powerful, strong, effective
Antonyms—weak, unsuccessful, incapable

practical
Synonyms—useful, sensible, no-nonsense
Antonyms—unrealistic, unreasonable, impractical

precede
Synonyms—lead, go before
Antonyms—follow, trail

predatory
Synonyms—aggressive, rapacious (out to kill)
Antonyms—harmless, passive (inactive)

predominant
Synonyms—major, principal, most common
Antonyms—secondary, insignificant

pretentious
Synonyms—showy, conceited, self-important
Antonyms—practical, down-to-earth, humble

privilege
Synonyms—advantage, benefit
Antonyms—disadvantage, drawback, shortcoming

procrastinate
Synonyms—postpone, delay
Antonyms—advance, proceed, progress, hurry

proficient
Synonyms—skilled, talented, capable
Antonyms—incompetent, clumsy, inept (unskilled)

proliferate
Synonyms—increase, flourish, spread, thrive (to do well)
Antonyms—reduce, diminish, dwindle

propagate
Synonyms—spread, transmit, publicize
Antonyms—suppress, hold back

propensity
Synonyms—tendency, inclination, penchant (tendency)
Antonyms—reluctance, aversion (dislike)

proponent
Synonyms—supporter, advocate, fan
Antonyms—opponent, foe, antagonist (enemy)

propriety
Synonyms—respectability, politeness
Antonyms—rudeness, discourtesy

prosaic
Synonyms—dull, ordinary, commonplace
Antonyms—inspiring, stirring, exciting

prosperous
Synonyms—wealthy, affluent, abundant
Antonyms—unsuccessful, disadvantaged

proximity
Synonyms—closeness, convenience, nearness
Antonyms—distance, remoteness

prudent
Synonyms—wise, cautious, practical
Antonyms—foolish, risky, reckless

punitive
Synonyms—penalizing, disciplinary, retaliatory (punishing)
Antonyms—rewarding, incentivizing, inducing (encouraging), enticing (tempting)

purify
Synonyms—cleanse, distill, filter, sanitize
Antonyms—soil, pollute, muddy

Q

quell
Synonyms—crush, defeat, conquer, suppress
Antonyms—incite, provoke, inflame, encourage

querulous
Synonyms—difficult, irritable, argumentative, cantankerous (argumentative)
Antonyms—amiable, friendly, good-natured, genial (likeable)

quarrelsome
Synonyms—querulous, cranky, grouchy, bad-tempered
Antonyms—affable, likable, good-humored, kind

quiescent
Synonyms—quiet, sluggish, passive (inactive), dormant (inactive)
Antonyms—active, lively, energetic, vigorous

R

random
Synonyms—accidental, haphazard, chance, casual
Antonyms—predictable, intentional, planned, on purpose

rational
Synonyms—sane, normal, coherent (makes sense)
Antonyms—unreasonable, absurd, illogical

rebut
Synonyms—deny, disprove, invalidate
Antonyms—accept, believe, recognize, support

recede
Synonyms—ebb, diminish, draw back
Antonyms—advance, press forward, progress

reclusive
Synonyms—isolated, solitary, withdrawn
Antonyms—outgoing, friendly, sociable

reconcile
Synonyms—reunite, resolve, bring together
Antonyms—separate, split, break up

recuperate
Synonyms—recover, get well, improve
Antonyms—decline, weaken, deteriorate (to get worse)

refined
Synonyms—polished, developed, cultivated
Antonyms—coarse, crude, rough

remedy
Synonyms—cure, restore, fix
Antonyms—worsen, aggravate, exacerbate (make worse)

remorse
Synonyms—guilt, sorrow, regret, shame
Antonyms—indifference, hard-heartedness, pride

remote
Synonyms—distant, isolated, far
Antonyms—close, nearby

renovate
Synonyms—renew, refresh, repair
Antonyms—demolish, destroy

renounce
Synonyms—reject, abandon, deny
Antonyms—accept, embrace

replete
Synonyms—full, stuffed, plentiful
Antonyms—hungry, empty, bare

reprehensible
Synonyms—criminal, wicked, disgraceful
Antonyms—honorable, noble, praiseworthy

repress
Synonyms—restrain, control, suppress, stifle (to hold back)
Antonyms—express, release, free (to let go)

reputable
Synonyms—trustworthy, dependable, respectable, legitimate
Antonyms—questionable, shady, dishonest

resilient
Synonyms—flexible, elastic, rebounding
Antonyms—rigid, unyielding, stiff

resplendent
Synonyms—dazzling, magnificent, glorious, stunning
Antonyms—unimpressive, ordinary, forgettable

restrain
Synonyms—control, confine, hold back
Antonyms—free, release, liberate

retain
Synonyms—keep, save, preserve
Antonyms—discard, throw away, let go

revere
Synonyms—admire, respect, esteem (to regard highly)
Antonyms—disapprove, dislike, object to

robust
Synonyms—healthy, strong, vigorous
Antonyms—weak, feeble, frail

routine
Synonyms—usual, ordinary, normal
Antonyms—exceptional, uncommon

rupture
Synonyms—break, burst, rip open
Antonyms—heal, mend, repair

S

sagacious
Synonyms—wise, shrewd, learned, perceptive
Antonyms—foolish, thoughtless, irrational

saturate
Synonyms—soak, flood, inundate (to overwhelm)
Antonyms—dehydrate, desiccate (to dry)

scrutinize
Synonyms—examine, inspect, analyze
Antonyms—ignore, disregard, overlook

secrete
Synonyms—conceal, hide, stash
Antonyms—reveal, disclose, divulge (to reveal)

sedentary
Synonyms—inactive, immobile, lethargic (slow)
Antonyms—active, lively, energetic

sequential
Synonyms—in order, chronological (sorted by time)
Antonyms—disordered, chaotic, random

serene
Synonyms—calm, peaceful, tranquil
Antonyms—busy, lively, hectic

skeptical
Synonyms—doubtful, unconvinced, disbelieving
Antonyms—persuaded, converted, won over

solace
Synonyms—comfort, support, relief
Antonyms—irritation, annoyance, hurt

soporific
Synonyms—dull, sleep-inducing, monotonous (boring)
Antonyms—stimulating, exciting, lively, energizing

sparse
Synonyms—limited, scarce, inadequate, scant (a small amount)
Antonyms—abundant, plentiful, profuse (in good supply)

spontaneous
Synonyms—unplanned, spur-of-the-moment, impromptu (unplanned)
Antonyms—structured, deliberate, premeditated (planned)

squander
Synonyms—waste, spend, misuse
Antonyms—save, keep, conserve (to save)

stagnant
Synonyms—still, inactive, inert (not active)
Antonyms—moving, mobile, dynamic

sterile
Synonyms—antiseptic, disinfected, sanitary
Antonyms—contaminated, dirty, soiled

stimulate
Synonyms—encourage, motivate, inspire
Antonyms—discourage, dampen, stifle (to hold back)

strenuous
Synonyms—taxing, straining, demanding, arduous (difficult)
Antonyms—easy, effortless, painless

strict
Synonyms—firm, exacting, rigorous
Antonyms—lenient, relaxed, easygoing

submissive
Synonyms—obedient, passive (inactive), compliant (willing to obey)
Antonyms—assertive, pushy, aggressive

substantial
Synonyms—considerable, extensive, sizeable, significant
Antonyms—minor, insignificant, limited

substantiate
Synonyms—verify, prove, corroborate (to prove)
Antonyms—disprove, refute, invalidate

subtle
Synonyms—slight, understated, delicate
Antonyms—obvious, noticeable, apparent

sullen
Synonyms—brooding, grim, gloomy
Antonyms—cheerful, smiling, joyful

summon
Synonyms—call, beckon, gather
Antonyms—dismiss, release

superficial
Synonyms—shallow, surface
Antonyms—deep, profound, meaningful

superfluous
Synonyms—extra, surplus (more than is needed)
Antonyms—indispensable, necessary, vital, essential

supply
Synonyms—provide, give, contribute
Antonyms—remove, take away, deprive (to withhold from)

support
Synonyms—maintain, encourage, sustain (to keep going)
Antonyms—abandon, ignore, forsake (to abandon)

suppress
Synonyms—prevent, repress (to hold down), stifle (to hold back), constrain (to limit)
Antonyms—spread, express, distribute

surge
Synonyms—rush, flow, pour, gush
Antonyms—stagnate, stand still, pool (to gather in one place)

surplus
Synonyms—extra, spare, leftover
Antonyms—basic, essential

surreptitious
Synonyms—secret, sneaky, stealthy (sneaky), covert (hidden)
Antonyms—open, honest, direct

surrogate
Synonyms—substitute, replacement, stand-in
Antonyms—real, permanent, genuine

sustain
Synonyms—support, maintain, keep going
Antonyms—quit, stop, give up, abandon

T

tame
Synonyms—domestic, friendly, docile (obedient)
Antonyms—wild, untamed, feral (not domesticated)

tardy
Synonyms—late, slow, delayed
Antonyms—prompt, punctual, timely

tedious
Synonyms—boring, dull, dreary, monotonous (boring)
Antonyms—interesting, motivating, fascinating

temperate
Synonyms—moderate, pleasant, mild
Antonyms—extreme, severe, intense

temperamental
Synonyms—unpredictable, moody, volatile (explosive)
Antonyms—reliable, dependable, even-tempered

tenacious
Synonyms—stubborn, persistent, determined
Antonyms—unsure, hesitant, irresolute (undecided)

tentative
Synonyms—cautious, hesitant, uncertain
Antonyms—sure, definite, secure

tenuous
Synonyms—weak, flimsy, fragile
Antonyms—strong, sound, robust (strong)

tense
Synonyms—worried, anxious, stressed, uptight
Antonyms—relaxed, calm, tranquil, peaceful

terminate
Synonyms—end, finish, conclude, cease
Antonyms—begin, commence, originate

terse
Synonyms—abrupt, brief, concise (to the point), brusque (abrupt)
Antonyms—rambling, long-winded, wordy

therapeutic
Synonyms—healing, beneficial, helpful
Antonyms—harmful, destructive, unsafe, detrimental (harmful)

tolerant
Synonyms—broadminded, understanding, forbearing (patient)
Antonyms—intolerant, unforgiving, rigid, impatient

toxic
Synonyms—poisonous, deadly, lethal (deadly)
Antonyms—harmless, safe

tranquil
Synonyms—peaceful, calm, relaxing, serene (peaceful)
Antonyms—noisy, chaotic, frenzied

transgression
Synonyms—wrongdoing, disobedience, offense
Antonyms—good deed, kindness, favor

transient
Synonyms—temporary, brief, fleeting, short-lived
Antonyms—permanent, lasting, eternal, enduring

translucent
Synonyms—clear, transparent, see-through
Antonyms—opaque, dense, thick

treacherous
Synonyms—unsafe, dangerous, hazardous, perilous (dangerous)
Antonyms—harmless, safe, risk-free

trepidation
Synonyms—fear, anxiety, apprehension (fear)
Antonyms—composure, level-headedness, equanimity (calmness)

trivial
Synonyms—minor, insignificant, petty, negligible (not important)
Antonyms—crucial, essential, important, necessary, vital

truncate
Synonyms—shorten, abbreviate, trim
Antonyms—lengthen, extend, elongate (to make longer)

turbulent
Synonyms—chaotic, confused, tumultuous (in turmoil)
Antonyms—orderly, calm

U

unheralded
Synonyms—unannounced, unpredicted, unexpected
Antonyms—forecasted, foretold, expected

uniform
Synonyms—unchanging, unvarying, standardized, homogeneous (the same)
Antonyms—different, dissimilar, unlike, diverse (different)

unpalatable
Synonyms—unpleasant, distasteful, disagreeable
Antonyms—enjoyable, pleasing, satisfying

unparalleled
Synonyms—matchless, unequaled, incomparable, supreme
Antonyms—common, ordinary, everyday, regular

unstinting
Synonyms—generous, giving
Antonyms—stingy, tightfisted

untenable
Synonyms—indefensible, unreasonable
Antonyms—justifiable, understandable

utilitarian
Synonyms—useful, practical, functional
Antonyms—ineffective, nonfunctional

utopian
Synonyms—perfect, ideal
Antonyms—problematic, flawed

V

vague
Synonyms—unclear, hazy, indistinct (not clear)
Antonyms—definite, distinct, evident (clear)

valid
Synonyms—legitimate, reasonable, sensible, official
Antonyms—invalid, illegitimate, unsound, fallacious (not true)

validate
Synonyms—confirm, approve, certify, authorize
Antonyms—invalidate, cancel, disapprove, deny

verdant
Synonyms—green, lush, luxuriant
Antonyms—bare, stripped, withered

versatile
Synonyms—adaptable, resourceful, multitalented
Antonyms—limited, narrow, restricted

vex
Synonyms—annoy, pester, irritate, exasperate (frustrate)
Antonyms—please, satisfy, calm

virtuoso
Synonyms—expert, master, ace, whiz
Antonyms—amateur, beginner, dabbler, hobbyist

viscous
Synonyms—thick, sticky, gluey
Antonyms—thin, runny

vital
Synonyms—essential, fundamental, crucial
Antonyms—unimportant, insignificant, trivial

vitality
Synonyms—energy, liveliness, durability
Antonyms—weariness, sluggishness, lethargy (lack of energy)

vivacious
Synonyms—lively, cheerful, spirited
Antonyms— slow, languid (lacking energy), lethargic (slow)

vivid
Synonyms—bright, vibrant, colorful
Antonyms—dull, dreary, faded, lackluster (dull)

volatile
Synonyms—explosive, unpredictable, unstable
Antonyms— calm, placid (calm), inert (inactive)

voluntary
Synonyms—unpaid, honorary, pro bono (done without pay)
Antonyms—paid, compensated, remunerated (paid)

vulnerable
Synonyms—unprotected, in danger, at risk
Antonyms—secure, protected

W

wane
Synonyms—diminish, decline, fade
Antonyms—increase, develop, wax (to fade or decline)

waver
Synonyms—hesitate, fluctuate, vacillate (to be indecisive)
Antonyms—decide, resolve, choose

whimsical
Synonyms—fanciful, quirky, eccentric (unusual)
Antonyms—normal, regular, ordinary

wordy
Synonyms—rambling, long-winded, verbose (full of words)
Antonyms—concise (brief), taciturn (quiet), reticent (quiet)

Y

youthful
Synonyms—young, vigorous, vital
Antonyms—aged, decrepit (old), infirm (ill)

Z

zeal
Synonyms—enthusiasm, passion, eagerness
Antonyms—disinterest, indifference, apathy (lack of interest)

zealous
Synonyms—eager, passionate, fervent (full of passion)
Antonyms— bored, lethargic (slow), listless (lacking energy)

Appendix C: Study Guides and Answer Sheets

Study Guide: Spelling

Much spelling must be learned, but the following list presents some of the most useful spelling rules and some of the most common exceptions to those rules. You may want to review these rules before taking the Spelling Drill and as you continue to prepare for your exam. Try to learn them all!

Twenty-Four Spelling Rules

1. *i* before *e*
   Except after *c*
   Or when sounded like *ay*
   As in *neighbor* or *weigh.*
   Exceptions: Neither, leisure, foreigner, seized, weird, heights.
2. If a word ends in *y* preceded by a vowel, keep the *y* when adding a suffix.
   Examples: day, days; attorney, attorneys
3. If a word ends in *y* preceded by a consonant, change the *y* to *i* before adding a suffix.
   Examples: try, tries, tried; lady, ladies

   Exceptions: To avoid double *i*, retain the *y* before *-ing* and *-ish.*
   Examples: fly, flying; baby, babyish
4. Silent *e* at the end of a word is usually dropped before a suffix beginning with a vowel.
   Examples: dine + ing = dining
   locate + ion = location
   use + able = usable
   offense + ive = offensive

   Exceptions: Words ending in *ce* and *ge* retain *e* before *-able* and *-ous* in order to retain the soft sounds of *c* and *g*.
   Examples: peace + able = peaceable
   courage + ous = courageous

5. Silent *e* is usually kept before a suffix beginning with a consonant.
   Examples: care + less = careless
   late + ly = lately
   one + ness = oneness
   game + ster = gamester

6. Some exceptions must simply be memorized. Some exceptions to the last two rules are *truly, duly, awful, argument, wholly, ninth, mileage, dyeing, acreage, canoeing.*

7. A word of one syllable that ends in a single consonant preceded by a single vowel doubles the final consonant before a suffix beginning with a vowel or before the suffix *-y*.
   Examples: hit, hitting; drop, dropped; big, biggest; mud, muddy; **but:** *help, helping* because *help* ends in two consonants; *need, needing, needy* because the final consonant is preceded by two vowels.

8. A word of more than one syllable that accents the last syllable and that ends in a single consonant preceded by a single vowel doubles the final consonant when adding a suffix beginning with a vowel.
   Examples: begin, beginner; admit, admitted; **but:** *enter, entered* because the accent is not on the last syllable.

9. A word ending in *er* or *ur* doubles the *r* in the past tense if the word is accented on the last syllable.
   Examples: occur, occurred; prefer, preferred; transfer, transferred

10. A word ending in *er* does not double the *r* in the past tense if the accent falls before the last syllable.
    Examples: answer, answered; offer, offered; differ, differed

11. When *-full* is added to the end of a noun, the final *l* is dropped.
    Examples: cheerful, cupful, hopeful

12. All words beginning with *over* are one word.
    Examples: overcast, overcharge, overhear

13. All words with the prefix *self-* are hyphenated.
    Examples: self-control, self-defense, self-evident

14. The letter *q* is always followed by *u*.
    Examples: quiz, bouquet, acquire

15. Numbers from twenty-one to ninety-nine are hyphenated.

16. *Per cent* is *never* hyphenated. It may be written as one word (*percent*) or as two words (*per cent*).

17. *Welcome* is one word with one *l*.

18. *All right* is always two words. *Alright* is a nonstandard form of English and should not be used.

19. *Already* means "prior to some specified time." *All ready* means "completely ready."
Example: By the time I was *all ready* to go to the play, the tickets were *already* sold out.

20. *Altogether* means "entirely." *All together* means "in sum" or "collectively."
Example: There are *altogether* too many people to seat in this room when we are *all together*.

21. *Their* is the possessive of *they*.
They're is the contraction for *they are*.
There means *at that place*.
Example: *They're* going to put *their* books over *there*.

22. *Your* is the possessive of *you*.
You're is the contraction for *you are*.
Example: *You're* certainly planning to leave *your* muddy boots outside.

23. *Whose* is the possessive of *who*.
Who's is the contraction for *who is*.
Example: Do you know *who's* ringing the doorbell or *whose* car is in the street?

24. *Its* is the possessive of *it*. *It's* is the contraction for it is.
Example: *It's* I who lost the letter and *its* envelope.

Study Guide: Grammar

Capitalization Rules

Capitalize words that fall into the following categories:

The first word of every sentence, line of poetry, or direct quotation:

- The teacher scowled as he entered the room.
- "How do I love thee? Let me count the ways."
- Jenn said, "My homework is on the desk."

Proper nouns:

- Tom Anderson; Aurora Ochoa (people)
- Nebraska; Paris; Australia (states, cities, countries/continents)
- Dad; Mommy; Grandma (kinship names)
- Fluffy; Odie; Lassie (pets)

Titles that come before proper nouns:

- Uncle Jack; Mrs. Fisher; Captain Jordan Smith; President Donald Trump

Note: Titles that are not paired with a proper noun are not capitalized.

- My uncle; the captain; the president

Proper adjectives (adjectives derived from proper nouns):

- French cooking, Aztec architecture, Italian sculpture, Mendelian genetics

Names of organizations, companies and businesses, and special buildings:

- Rotary Club; Prudential Life Insurance Company; McDonald's; Sears Tower; Grand Central Station

Months, days of the week, and all holidays:

- January, May September
- Labor Day; Boxing Day; Rosh Hashana
- Sunday, Wednesday, Friday

Note: Seasons (spring, summer, fall/autumn, winter) are not capitalized.

Historical events, wars and battles, and historical eras:

- the Boston Tea Party; The Great Depression; the Industrial Revolution
- the Spanish-American War; The Battle of Britain; World War I
- the Dark Ages, the Renaissance; the Roaring Twenties

Geographical areas:

- Our family likes the Northwest more than the East.
- Hallie grew up in the Midwest.
- The plane flew over the Arctic Circle.

Note: The words north, south, east, *and* west *are not capitalized when they refer to a direction:*

- We were driving east.
- Head west to the corner of Hollywood and Vine.
- She moved from the north side of town.

School subjects that are languages or that have level numbers:

- He is taking Russian.
- She will take Mixed Media Art I and Algebra II next semester.

Note: Do not capitalize other subjects.

- I plan to take art and algebra.

Titles of books, documents, stories, poems, musical works, art works, and plays:

- *The Odyssey* (epic [poem])
- "The Cold Equations" (short story)
- "Annabel Lee" (poem)
- the *Mona Lisa* (painting)
- *Les Misérables* (novel, play, musical, and movie)

*Note: Internal prepositions, conjunctions, and articles (*a, an, *and* the*) are not capitalized.*

- "We Are the Champions"
- *Pride and Prejudice*
- "Ode to a Nightingale"

Note: Prepositions of four or more letters are frequently capitalized.

- *Gone With the Wind*
- *What About Bob?*

Languages, Ethnicities, and Nationalities:

- French, Spanish, English, Latin
- Aborigines; Inuit; Romanies
- Asian; South African, European

Punctuation Rules

Commas

Use commas in the following instances.

To separate three or more words in a list or series:

- The dog likes toys, bones, and biscuits.

To separate two or more adjectives that come before a noun when *and* can be substituted without changing the meaning:

- Debbie had a calm, gentle demeanor.
- The cat had long, soft, white fur.

Note: Do not use a comma if:

1. the adjectives together express a single idea,
   - The boy had a bright blue ball.

or

2. the noun is a compound made up of an adjective and a noun.
   - A majestic bald eagle soared above us.

To set off appositives or appositive phrases:

- Ernest Hemingway, a great American novelist, was born in 1899.

Note: Do not use commas when the appositive or appositive phrase is essential to the meaning of the sentence:

- The novelist Ernest Hemingway was born in 1899.

To set off nonessential phrases and clauses:

- My English professor, who has an odd sense of humor, has been teaching for some 40 years.

Note: Do not use commas when the phrase or clause is essential to the meaning of the sentence:

- The professor who teaches my English class has an odd sense of humor.

To separate independent clauses joined by a coordinating conjunction in a compound sentence:

- Mom lives in New York, and my sister lives in Los Angeles.
- Some people like baseball, but others prefer hockey.

To set off transitional expressions (*however, therefore, nevertheless*) and independent comments (*of course, by the way, I think*) from the rest of the sentence:

- We shall try, nevertheless, to meet the deadline.
- I knew, of course, that he was hiding something.

To set off an introductory word, phrase, or clause at the beginning of a sentence:

- Yes, I'd be happy to give you a ride.
- After some years, the committee decided to approve the plan to rebuild.
- Because she is shy, Lauren is often uncomfortable speaking in front of others.

To set off a word in direct address:

- Thanks, friends, for all your help.
- How was your vacation, Antoine?

To set off the question tag in a tag question:

- You won't travel there again, will you?
- It snowing again, isn't it?

To introduce or set off a quotation:

- The queen said, "Let them eat cake!"
- "I really don't care how long we stay," she smirked, "as long as we make an entrance."

To close the salutation in a personal letter and the complimentary close in a business or personal letter:

- Dear Simone,
- Sincerely, Robert Jones

To set off titles and degrees:

- Margaret Bolsterli, Ph.D.
- Bryson Frye, Esq.

To separate sentence elements that might be read incorrectly without the comma:

- As we entered, in the shadows we could see a dark figure.
- What time shall we eat, Aunt Martha?

To set off the month and day from the year in full dates:

- The next meeting will be held on June 25, 2020.

To set off the year in full dates:

- The next meeting will be held on June 25, 2020, at City Hall.

Note: Do not use a comma when only the month and year appear:

- The next meeting will be held in June 2020.

To separate the city and state in an address:

- Jenny Green
  111 Meadow Lane
  Boston, MA 02116

Note: If the address is inserted into text, add a second comma after the state:

- Akron, Ohio, is their home.

Apostrophes and Hyphens

Use an apostrophe and an *s* to form the possessive of a singular noun.

- girl + *s* =girl's Charles + *s* = Charles's

Use an apostrophe to form the possessive of a plural noun that ends in *s*.

- girls + *s* = girls' cities + *s* = cities'

Use an apostrophe and an *s* to form the possessive of a plural noun that does not end in *s*.

- women + *s* = women's mice + *s* = mice's

Note: Do not use an apostrophe in a possessive pronoun.

- These skates are hers.
- Theirs are in the car.

Use an apostrophe to replace letters that have been omitted in a contraction.

(A contraction is formed by combining two words into one and leaving out one or more letters.)

- it is = it's
- you + are = you're

Note: Don't confuse it's with the possessive pronoun its.

Use a hyphen in compound numbers.

- sixty-five
- one hundred forty-two

Use a hyphen or hyphens in certain compound nouns. (Consult a dictionary to be sure.)

- great-uncle
- sister-in-law
- attorney-at-law
- editor-in-chief

Use a hyphen in certain compound adjectives when they appear before a noun. (Consult a dictionary to be sure.)

- She asked an open-ended question (BUT—The question she asked was open ended.)
- We bought high-quality silk.

Use a hyphen in adverb + adjective compounds and adverb + participle compounds when they appear before a noun.

- He took a much-needed vacation. (BUT—The vacation he took was much needed.)
- It is a high-jumping kangaroo.

Note: When the adverb in an adjective or participle combination ends in -ly, the compound is not hyphenated, regardless of its location in the sentence.

- It is a highly sought position. (The position was highly sought.)
- It was a mildly amusing joke. (The joke was mildly amusing.)

Quotation Marks and Italics

Use quotation marks before and after a direct quotation.

- "I am going to the café after I visit the bookstore," said Jillian.

Use quotation marks around each part of an interrupted quotation.

- "She was," explained John, "always searching for the nearest bookstore."

Use a comma or commas to separate a phrase such as *he said* from the quotation itself. (Place the commas outside opening quotation marks but inside closing quotation marks.)

- Beth said, "Jill has more books than any person I know."
- "She finally received her VIP card from her local bookstore," Libby added.

Place a period inside the closing quotation marks.

- Ian declared, "We should all shop at local bookstores more often."

Place a question mark or an exclamation mark inside the quotation marks when it is part of the quotation.

- Justin asked, "Don't you prefer to have them delivered to your home?"

Place a question mark or an exclamation mark outside the quotation marks when it is part of the entire sentence but not part of the quotation.

- Did Greg say, "The big online retailers put local bookstores out of business"?

Use quotation marks for the title of a short story, essay, poem, song, magazine or newspaper article, or book chapter.

- "The Gift of the Magi" (short story)
- "Blue Suede Shoes" (song)
- "The Raven" (poem)

Use italics (or underlining) to identify the title of a book, play, film, television series, magazine, or newspaper.

- *Where the Red Fern Grows* (book)
- The Adventures of Huckleberry Finn (book)
- *National Geographic* (magazine)
- *The Daily News* (newspaper)

Semicolon and Colons

Use a semicolon to join parts of a compound sentence when a conjunction such as *and*, *but*, or *or* is not used. (A compound sentence has two or more simple sentences that are joined by a conjunction.)

- We traveled through many states during the summer; our favorite stops were in Montana and Idaho.
- Lucas was born in Germany in 1982; he moved to the United States in 2015.
- Samuel likes classical music; he plays the violin.

Use a colon to introduce a list of items that ends a sentence. (To properly introduce a list, a complete sentence should be used before the colon. The phrases *such as the following*, *such as these*, or *as follows* are often used to introduce lists.)

- Sylvester always had two things on his grocery list: milk and cereal.
- Einstein's relativity theory advanced new ideas about the following concepts:
    - Time
    - Space
    - Mass
    - Motion

Use a colon to separate the hour from the minute when writing the time of day.

- Jose's train left Princeton at 10:05 A.M. and arrived in New York City at 2:30 P.M.

Use a colon after the salutation of a business letter.

- To whom it may concern:
- Dear Ms. Williams:

Abbreviation Rules

Abbreviate the titles Mr., Mrs., Ms., and Dr. before a person's name.

- Mr. John Kennedy
- Dr. Ann Sperry
- Ms. Shannon Danko

Abbreviate the professional or academic degrees that follow a person's name, as well as the titles Jr. and Sr.

- Harry Young, M.D.
- Thomas Diaz, Ph.D.
- Ed Wilson Jr.

Abbreviate names of organizations and businesses using capital letters and no periods.

- AAA
- AT&T
- NBC
- YMCA

Write abbreviations that are pronounced letter by letter (initialisms) or as words (acronyms) using capital letters and no periods.

- NASA—National Aeronautics and Space Administration
- DARE—Drug Abuse Resistance Education
- MVP—Most valuable player
- FBI—Federal Bureau of Investigation

Use the abbreviations a.m. (*ante meridiem*, before noon) and p.m. (*post meridiem*, after noon) for exact times.

- 6:15 a.m.
- 5:30 p.m.

Abbreviate systems of chronology in capital letters without periods:

- BC—before Christ OR BCE—before the Common Era
- AD—anno Domini (in the year of [our]Lord) OR CE—Common Era

Abbreviate calendar items only in charts and lists.

- Mon. Wed. Thurs. Fri. Jan. Mar. Nov.

Abbreviate units of measure in scientific writing. (Use periods with abbreviations of English units but not metric units.)

- inch—in.
- foot (feet)—ft.
- grams—g
- liters—l

Use roadway abbreviations in mailing addresses. Spell them out everywhere else.

- Street—St.
- Avenue—Ave.
- Road—Rd.
- Court—Ct.

Use two-letter postal codes for state names in addresses. Spell them out everywhere else.

- Alabama—AL
- Alaska—AK
- Arizona—AZ
- Arkansas—AR
- California—CA
- Delaware—DE
- Florida—FL
- Georgia—GA
- Indiana—IN
- Maryland—MD

Number Rules

Spell out numbers you can write in one or two words.

- There are twenty-six boys in the P.E. class.
- The arena holds fifty-five hundred people.

Note: If the number is greater than 999,999, use figures followed by the word million or billion, and so on, even if the number could be written in two words.

- 1 million
- 280 billion
- 3.2 trillion

Use numerals for numbers of more than two words.

- The distance between the two cities is 150 miles.

Spell out any number that begins a sentence or reword the sentence so that it doesn't begin with a number:

- Five thousand, one hundred and ninety-three fans attended the game.
- Attendance at the game was 5,193.

Numbers of the same kind should be written in the same way. If one number must be written as a numeral, write all numbers as numerals.

- On August 28, 464 students voted for the new mascot, and 420 students voted against it.

Spell out ordinal numbers (first, second, third, etc.) under one hundred.

- The eighth of December will be the couple's thirty-fourth wedding anniversary.

Use words to write the time of day unless you are using a.m. or p.m.

- I usually go for a walk at five o'clock in the morning. I return home at a quarter to six.
- The first school bell rang at 7:45 a.m., and the last one rang at 3:00 p.m.

Use numerals to write dates, house numbers, street numbers above ninety-nine, apartment and room numbers, telephone numbers, amounts of money more than two words, and percentages.

- On May 1, 2019, I met Emily at 36 West 49th Street in Apartment 5G.
- Her telephone number is 555-6688.
- I found 150 dollars in my couch cushions.
- The book's original price was $23.95.
- The store offered 50% discounts.

Study Guide: Math

Numbers & Numeration

Order of Operations

PEMDAS — Parentheses, Exponents, Multiplication, Division, Addition, Subtraction

Factors/Factoring

Prime number: A number that has no other factors other than itself and 1.

Greatest common factor (GCF): The greatest factor that divides two numbers.

Least common multiple (LCM): The smallest positive integer that is divisible by two integers.

Conversions

To convert a fraction to a decimal, divide the fraction's numerator by its denominator.

To convert a percentage to a decimal, divide the percentage by 100.

To convert a percentage to a fraction, use the percentage as the numerator of a fraction with 100 as the denominator and simplify or reduce as needed.

To convert a decimal to a percentage, multiply the decimal by 100.

Measurements & Equivalents

Length

1 foot = 12 inches

1 yard = 3 feet

1 meter = 100 centimeters

1 kilometer = 1,000 meters

Weight

1 pound = 16 ounces

1 kilogram = 1,000 grams

Liquid

1 cup = 8 ounces

1 pint = 2 cups

1 quart = 2 pints or 4 cups

1 gallon = 4 quarts

Geometry

Formulas

Area of a circle: $A = \pi r^2$

Area of a rectangle: $A = bh$ or lw

Area of a square: $A = s^2$

Area of a triangle: $A = \frac{1}{2}bh$

Circumference of a circle: $C = 2\pi r$ or πd

Perimeter of a rectangle: $A = 2l + 2w$ or $2(l + w)$

Perimeter of a square: $A = 4s$

Diameter of a circle: $d = 2r$

Volume of a rectangular solid: $V = lwh$

Pythagorean theorem: $a^2 + b^2 = c^2$

Angle Rules

Right angles measure 90°.

Complementary angles add up to 90°.

Supplementary angles add up to 180°.

The sum of the interior angles of a triangle is 180°.

The sum of the interior angles of a quadrilateral is 360°.

Statistics & Probability

Measurements of Central Tendency:

Referring to a set of numbers:

Mean (or Average) = Sum of the numbers in the set ÷ The amount of numbers in the set

Median = Middle number in a list of values ordered from lowest to highest

Mode = The value that appears most often in the set of numbers

Study Guide: Analogies

Analogy questions test your ability to see a relationship between two words and to apply that relationship to other words.

To solve an analogy problem, follow these five steps:

1. Define the initial terms.
2. Describe the initial relationship.
3. Eliminate incorrect answers.
4. Refine the initial relationship, if necessary.
5. Choose the best of the remaining answer choices.

Remember: The key to answering verbal analogy questions lies in the relationship between the first two words!

The Six Most Common Analogy Relationships

1. Characteristic (e.g., *hard* to *rock*)
2. Purpose (e.g., *shovel* to *dig*)
3. Antonym (e.g., *cruelty* to *kindness*)
4. Part to whole (e.g., *brick* to *wall*)
5. Whole to part (e.g., *pie* to *slice*)
6. Degree (e.g., *cool* to *frigid*)

Other Analogy Relationships

- Cause and effect (e.g., *spark* to *flame*)
- Effect and cause (e.g., *excellence* to *practice*)
- Association (e.g., *puck* to *hockey*)
- Sequence (e.g., *prologue* to *epilogue*)
- Function (e.g., *manager* to *employee*)
- Synonym (e.g., *sad* to *morose*)

If you have difficulty figuring out the relationship between the word pairs, try turning the analogy pairs into sentences to help you see the connection. Then fit the answer pairs into the same sentence until you find the one that works best.

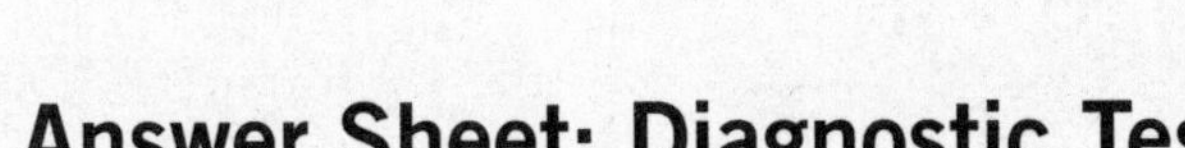

Answer Sheet: Diagnostic Test

Reading

1. Ⓐ Ⓑ Ⓒ Ⓓ	5. Ⓐ Ⓑ Ⓒ Ⓓ	9. Ⓐ Ⓑ Ⓒ Ⓓ	13. Ⓐ Ⓑ Ⓒ Ⓓ	17. Ⓐ Ⓑ Ⓒ Ⓓ
2. Ⓐ Ⓑ Ⓒ Ⓓ	6. Ⓐ Ⓑ Ⓒ Ⓓ	10. Ⓐ Ⓑ Ⓒ Ⓓ	14. Ⓐ Ⓑ Ⓒ Ⓓ	18. Ⓐ Ⓑ Ⓒ Ⓓ
3. Ⓐ Ⓑ Ⓒ Ⓓ	7. Ⓐ Ⓑ Ⓒ Ⓓ	11. Ⓐ Ⓑ Ⓒ Ⓓ	15. Ⓐ Ⓑ Ⓒ Ⓓ	19. Ⓐ Ⓑ Ⓒ Ⓓ
4. Ⓐ Ⓑ Ⓒ Ⓓ	8. Ⓐ Ⓑ Ⓒ Ⓓ	12. Ⓐ Ⓑ Ⓒ Ⓓ	16. Ⓐ Ⓑ Ⓒ Ⓓ	20. Ⓐ Ⓑ Ⓒ Ⓓ

Verbal Skills

21. Ⓐ Ⓑ Ⓒ Ⓓ	24. Ⓐ Ⓑ Ⓒ Ⓓ	27. Ⓐ Ⓑ Ⓒ	30. Ⓐ Ⓑ Ⓒ Ⓓ	33. Ⓐ Ⓑ Ⓒ Ⓓ
22. Ⓐ Ⓑ Ⓒ Ⓓ	25. Ⓐ Ⓑ Ⓒ	28. Ⓐ Ⓑ Ⓒ Ⓓ	31. Ⓐ Ⓑ Ⓒ Ⓓ	34. Ⓐ Ⓑ Ⓒ Ⓓ
23. Ⓐ Ⓑ Ⓒ Ⓓ	26. Ⓐ Ⓑ Ⓒ	29. Ⓐ Ⓑ Ⓒ Ⓓ	32. Ⓐ Ⓑ Ⓒ Ⓓ	35. Ⓐ Ⓑ Ⓒ Ⓓ

Written Expression/Language

36. Ⓐ Ⓑ Ⓒ Ⓓ	38. Ⓐ Ⓑ Ⓒ Ⓓ	40. Ⓐ Ⓑ Ⓒ Ⓓ	42. Ⓐ Ⓑ Ⓒ Ⓓ	44. Ⓐ Ⓑ Ⓒ Ⓓ
37. Ⓐ Ⓑ Ⓒ Ⓓ	39. Ⓐ Ⓑ Ⓒ Ⓓ	41. Ⓐ Ⓑ Ⓒ Ⓓ	43. Ⓐ Ⓑ Ⓒ Ⓓ	45. Ⓐ Ⓑ Ⓒ Ⓓ

Math

46. Ⓐ Ⓑ Ⓒ Ⓓ	50. Ⓐ Ⓑ Ⓒ Ⓓ	54. Ⓐ Ⓑ Ⓒ Ⓓ	58. Ⓐ Ⓑ Ⓒ Ⓓ	62. Ⓐ Ⓑ Ⓒ Ⓓ
47. Ⓐ Ⓑ Ⓒ Ⓓ	51. Ⓐ Ⓑ Ⓒ Ⓓ	55. Ⓐ Ⓑ Ⓒ Ⓓ	59. Ⓐ Ⓑ Ⓒ Ⓓ	63. Ⓐ Ⓑ Ⓒ Ⓓ
48. Ⓐ Ⓑ Ⓒ Ⓓ	52. Ⓐ Ⓑ Ⓒ Ⓓ	56. Ⓐ Ⓑ Ⓒ Ⓓ	60. Ⓐ Ⓑ Ⓒ Ⓓ	64. Ⓐ Ⓑ Ⓒ Ⓓ
49. Ⓐ Ⓑ Ⓒ Ⓓ	53. Ⓐ Ⓑ Ⓒ Ⓓ	57. Ⓐ Ⓑ Ⓒ Ⓓ	61. Ⓐ Ⓑ Ⓒ Ⓓ	65. Ⓐ Ⓑ Ⓒ Ⓓ

Quantitative Skills

66. Ⓐ Ⓑ Ⓒ Ⓓ	68. Ⓐ Ⓑ Ⓒ Ⓓ	70. Ⓐ Ⓑ Ⓒ Ⓓ
67. Ⓐ Ⓑ Ⓒ Ⓓ	69. Ⓐ Ⓑ Ⓒ Ⓓ	71. Ⓐ Ⓑ Ⓒ Ⓓ

Ability

72. Ⓐ Ⓑ Ⓒ Ⓓ Ⓔ	73. Ⓐ Ⓑ Ⓒ Ⓓ Ⓔ	74. Ⓐ Ⓑ Ⓒ Ⓓ Ⓔ	75. Ⓐ Ⓑ Ⓒ Ⓓ Ⓔ

Answer Sheet: Chapter 2 Drills

Reading—Comprehension

1. Ⓐ Ⓑ Ⓒ Ⓓ	16. Ⓐ Ⓑ Ⓒ Ⓓ	31. Ⓐ Ⓑ Ⓒ Ⓓ	46. Ⓐ Ⓑ Ⓒ Ⓓ	61. Ⓐ Ⓑ Ⓒ Ⓓ
2. Ⓐ Ⓑ Ⓒ Ⓓ	17. Ⓐ Ⓑ Ⓒ Ⓓ	32. Ⓐ Ⓑ Ⓒ Ⓓ	47. Ⓐ Ⓑ Ⓒ Ⓓ	62. Ⓐ Ⓑ Ⓒ Ⓓ
3. Ⓐ Ⓑ Ⓒ Ⓓ	18. Ⓐ Ⓑ Ⓒ Ⓓ	33. Ⓐ Ⓑ Ⓒ Ⓓ	48. Ⓐ Ⓑ Ⓒ Ⓓ	63. Ⓐ Ⓑ Ⓒ Ⓓ
4. Ⓐ Ⓑ Ⓒ Ⓓ	19. Ⓐ Ⓑ Ⓒ Ⓓ	34. Ⓐ Ⓑ Ⓒ Ⓓ	49. Ⓐ Ⓑ Ⓒ Ⓓ	64. Ⓐ Ⓑ Ⓒ Ⓓ
5. Ⓐ Ⓑ Ⓒ Ⓓ	20. Ⓐ Ⓑ Ⓒ Ⓓ	35. Ⓐ Ⓑ Ⓒ Ⓓ	50. Ⓐ Ⓑ Ⓒ Ⓓ	65. Ⓐ Ⓑ Ⓒ Ⓓ
6. Ⓐ Ⓑ Ⓒ Ⓓ	21. Ⓐ Ⓑ Ⓒ Ⓓ	36. Ⓐ Ⓑ Ⓒ Ⓓ	51. Ⓐ Ⓑ Ⓒ Ⓓ	66. Ⓐ Ⓑ Ⓒ Ⓓ
7. Ⓐ Ⓑ Ⓒ Ⓓ	22. Ⓐ Ⓑ Ⓒ Ⓓ	37. Ⓐ Ⓑ Ⓒ Ⓓ	52. Ⓐ Ⓑ Ⓒ Ⓓ	67. Ⓐ Ⓑ Ⓒ Ⓓ
8. Ⓐ Ⓑ Ⓒ Ⓓ	23. Ⓐ Ⓑ Ⓒ Ⓓ	38. Ⓐ Ⓑ Ⓒ Ⓓ	53. Ⓐ Ⓑ Ⓒ Ⓓ	68. Ⓐ Ⓑ Ⓒ Ⓓ
9. Ⓐ Ⓑ Ⓒ Ⓓ	24. Ⓐ Ⓑ Ⓒ Ⓓ	39. Ⓐ Ⓑ Ⓒ Ⓓ	54. Ⓐ Ⓑ Ⓒ Ⓓ	69. Ⓐ Ⓑ Ⓒ Ⓓ
10. Ⓐ Ⓑ Ⓒ Ⓓ	25. Ⓐ Ⓑ Ⓒ Ⓓ	40. Ⓐ Ⓑ Ⓒ Ⓓ	55. Ⓐ Ⓑ Ⓒ Ⓓ	70. Ⓐ Ⓑ Ⓒ Ⓓ
11. Ⓐ Ⓑ Ⓒ Ⓓ	26. Ⓐ Ⓑ Ⓒ Ⓓ	41. Ⓐ Ⓑ Ⓒ Ⓓ	56. Ⓐ Ⓑ Ⓒ Ⓓ	71. Ⓐ Ⓑ Ⓒ Ⓓ
12. Ⓐ Ⓑ Ⓒ Ⓓ	27. Ⓐ Ⓑ Ⓒ Ⓓ	42. Ⓐ Ⓑ Ⓒ Ⓓ	57. Ⓐ Ⓑ Ⓒ Ⓓ	72. Ⓐ Ⓑ Ⓒ Ⓓ
13. Ⓐ Ⓑ Ⓒ Ⓓ	28. Ⓐ Ⓑ Ⓒ Ⓓ	43. Ⓐ Ⓑ Ⓒ Ⓓ	58. Ⓐ Ⓑ Ⓒ Ⓓ	73. Ⓐ Ⓑ Ⓒ Ⓓ
14. Ⓐ Ⓑ Ⓒ Ⓓ	29. Ⓐ Ⓑ Ⓒ Ⓓ	44. Ⓐ Ⓑ Ⓒ Ⓓ	59. Ⓐ Ⓑ Ⓒ Ⓓ	74. Ⓐ Ⓑ Ⓒ Ⓓ
15. Ⓐ Ⓑ Ⓒ Ⓓ	30. Ⓐ Ⓑ Ⓒ Ⓓ	45. Ⓐ Ⓑ Ⓒ Ⓓ	60. Ⓐ Ⓑ Ⓒ Ⓓ	75. Ⓐ Ⓑ Ⓒ Ⓓ

Reading—Comprehension

1. Ⓐ Ⓑ Ⓒ Ⓓ	16. Ⓐ Ⓑ Ⓒ Ⓓ	31. Ⓐ Ⓑ Ⓒ Ⓓ	46. Ⓐ Ⓑ Ⓒ Ⓓ	61. Ⓐ Ⓑ Ⓒ Ⓓ
2. Ⓐ Ⓑ Ⓒ Ⓓ	17. Ⓐ Ⓑ Ⓒ Ⓓ	32. Ⓐ Ⓑ Ⓒ Ⓓ	47. Ⓐ Ⓑ Ⓒ Ⓓ	62. Ⓐ Ⓑ Ⓒ Ⓓ
3. Ⓐ Ⓑ Ⓒ Ⓓ	18. Ⓐ Ⓑ Ⓒ Ⓓ	33. Ⓐ Ⓑ Ⓒ Ⓓ	48. Ⓐ Ⓑ Ⓒ Ⓓ	63. Ⓐ Ⓑ Ⓒ Ⓓ
4. Ⓐ Ⓑ Ⓒ Ⓓ	19. Ⓐ Ⓑ Ⓒ Ⓓ	34. Ⓐ Ⓑ Ⓒ Ⓓ	49. Ⓐ Ⓑ Ⓒ Ⓓ	64. Ⓐ Ⓑ Ⓒ Ⓓ
5. Ⓐ Ⓑ Ⓒ Ⓓ	20. Ⓐ Ⓑ Ⓒ Ⓓ	35. Ⓐ Ⓑ Ⓒ Ⓓ	50. Ⓐ Ⓑ Ⓒ Ⓓ	65. Ⓐ Ⓑ Ⓒ Ⓓ
6. Ⓐ Ⓑ Ⓒ Ⓓ	21. Ⓐ Ⓑ Ⓒ Ⓓ	36. Ⓐ Ⓑ Ⓒ Ⓓ	51. Ⓐ Ⓑ Ⓒ Ⓓ	66. Ⓐ Ⓑ Ⓒ Ⓓ
7. Ⓐ Ⓑ Ⓒ Ⓓ	22. Ⓐ Ⓑ Ⓒ Ⓓ	37. Ⓐ Ⓑ Ⓒ Ⓓ	52. Ⓐ Ⓑ Ⓒ Ⓓ	67. Ⓐ Ⓑ Ⓒ Ⓓ
8. Ⓐ Ⓑ Ⓒ Ⓓ	23. Ⓐ Ⓑ Ⓒ Ⓓ	38. Ⓐ Ⓑ Ⓒ Ⓓ	53. Ⓐ Ⓑ Ⓒ Ⓓ	68. Ⓐ Ⓑ Ⓒ Ⓓ
9. Ⓐ Ⓑ Ⓒ Ⓓ	24. Ⓐ Ⓑ Ⓒ Ⓓ	39. Ⓐ Ⓑ Ⓒ Ⓓ	54. Ⓐ Ⓑ Ⓒ Ⓓ	69. Ⓐ Ⓑ Ⓒ Ⓓ
10. Ⓐ Ⓑ Ⓒ Ⓓ	25. Ⓐ Ⓑ Ⓒ Ⓓ	40. Ⓐ Ⓑ Ⓒ Ⓓ	55. Ⓐ Ⓑ Ⓒ Ⓓ	70. Ⓐ Ⓑ Ⓒ Ⓓ
11. Ⓐ Ⓑ Ⓒ Ⓓ	26. Ⓐ Ⓑ Ⓒ Ⓓ	41. Ⓐ Ⓑ Ⓒ Ⓓ	56. Ⓐ Ⓑ Ⓒ Ⓓ	71. Ⓐ Ⓑ Ⓒ Ⓓ
12. Ⓐ Ⓑ Ⓒ Ⓓ	27. Ⓐ Ⓑ Ⓒ Ⓓ	42. Ⓐ Ⓑ Ⓒ Ⓓ	57. Ⓐ Ⓑ Ⓒ Ⓓ	72. Ⓐ Ⓑ Ⓒ Ⓓ
13. Ⓐ Ⓑ Ⓒ Ⓓ	28. Ⓐ Ⓑ Ⓒ Ⓓ	43. Ⓐ Ⓑ Ⓒ Ⓓ	58. Ⓐ Ⓑ Ⓒ Ⓓ	73. Ⓐ Ⓑ Ⓒ Ⓓ
14. Ⓐ Ⓑ Ⓒ Ⓓ	29. Ⓐ Ⓑ Ⓒ Ⓓ	44. Ⓐ Ⓑ Ⓒ Ⓓ	59. Ⓐ Ⓑ Ⓒ Ⓓ	74. Ⓐ Ⓑ Ⓒ Ⓓ
15. Ⓐ Ⓑ Ⓒ Ⓓ	30. Ⓐ Ⓑ Ⓒ Ⓓ	45. Ⓐ Ⓑ Ⓒ Ⓓ	60. Ⓐ Ⓑ Ⓒ Ⓓ	75. Ⓐ Ⓑ Ⓒ Ⓓ

Answer Sheet Chapter 2 Drills

Reading—HSPT Vocabulary

1. Ⓐ Ⓑ Ⓒ Ⓓ	16. Ⓐ Ⓑ Ⓒ Ⓓ	31. Ⓐ Ⓑ Ⓒ Ⓓ	46. Ⓐ Ⓑ Ⓒ Ⓓ	61. Ⓐ Ⓑ Ⓒ Ⓓ
2. Ⓐ Ⓑ Ⓒ Ⓓ	17. Ⓐ Ⓑ Ⓒ Ⓓ	32. Ⓐ Ⓑ Ⓒ Ⓓ	47. Ⓐ Ⓑ Ⓒ Ⓓ	62. Ⓐ Ⓑ Ⓒ Ⓓ
3. Ⓐ Ⓑ Ⓒ Ⓓ	18. Ⓐ Ⓑ Ⓒ Ⓓ	33. Ⓐ Ⓑ Ⓒ Ⓓ	48. Ⓐ Ⓑ Ⓒ Ⓓ	63. Ⓐ Ⓑ Ⓒ Ⓓ
4. Ⓐ Ⓑ Ⓒ Ⓓ	19. Ⓐ Ⓑ Ⓒ Ⓓ	34. Ⓐ Ⓑ Ⓒ Ⓓ	49. Ⓐ Ⓑ Ⓒ Ⓓ	64. Ⓐ Ⓑ Ⓒ Ⓓ
5. Ⓐ Ⓑ Ⓒ Ⓓ	20. Ⓐ Ⓑ Ⓒ Ⓓ	35. Ⓐ Ⓑ Ⓒ Ⓓ	50. Ⓐ Ⓑ Ⓒ Ⓓ	65. Ⓐ Ⓑ Ⓒ Ⓓ
6. Ⓐ Ⓑ Ⓒ Ⓓ	21. Ⓐ Ⓑ Ⓒ Ⓓ	36. Ⓐ Ⓑ Ⓒ Ⓓ	51. Ⓐ Ⓑ Ⓒ Ⓓ	66. Ⓐ Ⓑ Ⓒ Ⓓ
7. Ⓐ Ⓑ Ⓒ Ⓓ	22. Ⓐ Ⓑ Ⓒ Ⓓ	37. Ⓐ Ⓑ Ⓒ Ⓓ	52. Ⓐ Ⓑ Ⓒ Ⓓ	67. Ⓐ Ⓑ Ⓒ Ⓓ
8. Ⓐ Ⓑ Ⓒ Ⓓ	23. Ⓐ Ⓑ Ⓒ Ⓓ	38. Ⓐ Ⓑ Ⓒ Ⓓ	53. Ⓐ Ⓑ Ⓒ Ⓓ	68. Ⓐ Ⓑ Ⓒ Ⓓ
9. Ⓐ Ⓑ Ⓒ Ⓓ	24. Ⓐ Ⓑ Ⓒ Ⓓ	39. Ⓐ Ⓑ Ⓒ Ⓓ	54. Ⓐ Ⓑ Ⓒ Ⓓ	69. Ⓐ Ⓑ Ⓒ Ⓓ
10. Ⓐ Ⓑ Ⓒ Ⓓ	25. Ⓐ Ⓑ Ⓒ Ⓓ	40. Ⓐ Ⓑ Ⓒ Ⓓ	55. Ⓐ Ⓑ Ⓒ Ⓓ	70. Ⓐ Ⓑ Ⓒ Ⓓ
11. Ⓐ Ⓑ Ⓒ Ⓓ	26. Ⓐ Ⓑ Ⓒ Ⓓ	41. Ⓐ Ⓑ Ⓒ Ⓓ	56. Ⓐ Ⓑ Ⓒ Ⓓ	71. Ⓐ Ⓑ Ⓒ Ⓓ
12. Ⓐ Ⓑ Ⓒ Ⓓ	27. Ⓐ Ⓑ Ⓒ Ⓓ	42. Ⓐ Ⓑ Ⓒ Ⓓ	57. Ⓐ Ⓑ Ⓒ Ⓓ	72. Ⓐ Ⓑ Ⓒ Ⓓ
13. Ⓐ Ⓑ Ⓒ Ⓓ	28. Ⓐ Ⓑ Ⓒ Ⓓ	43. Ⓐ Ⓑ Ⓒ Ⓓ	58. Ⓐ Ⓑ Ⓒ Ⓓ	73. Ⓐ Ⓑ Ⓒ Ⓓ
14. Ⓐ Ⓑ Ⓒ Ⓓ	29. Ⓐ Ⓑ Ⓒ Ⓓ	44. Ⓐ Ⓑ Ⓒ Ⓓ	59. Ⓐ Ⓑ Ⓒ Ⓓ	74. Ⓐ Ⓑ Ⓒ Ⓓ
15. Ⓐ Ⓑ Ⓒ Ⓓ	30. Ⓐ Ⓑ Ⓒ Ⓓ	45. Ⓐ Ⓑ Ⓒ Ⓓ	60. Ⓐ Ⓑ Ⓒ Ⓓ	75. Ⓐ Ⓑ Ⓒ Ⓓ

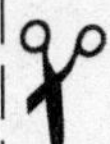

Answer Sheet: Chapter 3 Drills

Spelling

1. Ⓐ Ⓑ Ⓒ Ⓓ
2. Ⓐ Ⓑ Ⓒ Ⓓ
3. Ⓐ Ⓑ Ⓒ Ⓓ
4. Ⓐ Ⓑ Ⓒ Ⓓ
5. Ⓐ Ⓑ Ⓒ Ⓓ
6. Ⓐ Ⓑ Ⓒ Ⓓ
7. Ⓐ Ⓑ Ⓒ Ⓓ
8. Ⓐ Ⓑ Ⓒ Ⓓ
9. Ⓐ Ⓑ Ⓒ Ⓓ
10. Ⓐ Ⓑ Ⓒ Ⓓ
11. Ⓐ Ⓑ Ⓒ Ⓓ
12. Ⓐ Ⓑ Ⓒ Ⓓ
13. Ⓐ Ⓑ Ⓒ Ⓓ
14. Ⓐ Ⓑ Ⓒ Ⓓ
15. Ⓐ Ⓑ Ⓒ Ⓓ
16. Ⓐ Ⓑ Ⓒ Ⓓ
17. Ⓐ Ⓑ Ⓒ Ⓓ
18. Ⓐ Ⓑ Ⓒ Ⓓ
19. Ⓐ Ⓑ Ⓒ Ⓓ
20. Ⓐ Ⓑ Ⓒ Ⓓ
21. Ⓐ Ⓑ Ⓒ Ⓓ
22. Ⓐ Ⓑ Ⓒ Ⓓ
23. Ⓐ Ⓑ Ⓒ Ⓓ
24. Ⓐ Ⓑ Ⓒ Ⓓ
25. Ⓐ Ⓑ Ⓒ Ⓓ
26. Ⓐ Ⓑ Ⓒ Ⓓ
27. Ⓐ Ⓑ Ⓒ Ⓓ
28. Ⓐ Ⓑ Ⓒ Ⓓ
29. Ⓐ Ⓑ Ⓒ Ⓓ
30. Ⓐ Ⓑ Ⓒ Ⓓ
31. Ⓐ Ⓑ Ⓒ Ⓓ
32. Ⓐ Ⓑ Ⓒ Ⓓ
33. Ⓐ Ⓑ Ⓒ Ⓓ
34. Ⓐ Ⓑ Ⓒ Ⓓ
35. Ⓐ Ⓑ Ⓒ Ⓓ
36. Ⓐ Ⓑ Ⓒ Ⓓ
37. Ⓐ Ⓑ Ⓒ Ⓓ
38. Ⓐ Ⓑ Ⓒ Ⓓ
39. Ⓐ Ⓑ Ⓒ Ⓓ
40. Ⓐ Ⓑ Ⓒ Ⓓ
41. Ⓐ Ⓑ Ⓒ Ⓓ
42. Ⓐ Ⓑ Ⓒ Ⓓ
43. Ⓐ Ⓑ Ⓒ Ⓓ
44. Ⓐ Ⓑ Ⓒ Ⓓ
45. Ⓐ Ⓑ Ⓒ Ⓓ
46. Ⓐ Ⓑ Ⓒ Ⓓ
47. Ⓐ Ⓑ Ⓒ Ⓓ
48. Ⓐ Ⓑ Ⓒ Ⓓ
49. Ⓐ Ⓑ Ⓒ Ⓓ
50. Ⓐ Ⓑ Ⓒ Ⓓ
51. Ⓐ Ⓑ Ⓒ Ⓓ
52. Ⓐ Ⓑ Ⓒ Ⓓ
53. Ⓐ Ⓑ Ⓒ Ⓓ
54. Ⓐ Ⓑ Ⓒ Ⓓ
55. Ⓐ Ⓑ Ⓒ Ⓓ
56. Ⓐ Ⓑ Ⓒ Ⓓ
57. Ⓐ Ⓑ Ⓒ Ⓓ
58. Ⓐ Ⓑ Ⓒ Ⓓ
59. Ⓐ Ⓑ Ⓒ Ⓓ
60. Ⓐ Ⓑ Ⓒ Ⓓ
61. Ⓐ Ⓑ Ⓒ Ⓓ
62. Ⓐ Ⓑ Ⓒ Ⓓ
63. Ⓐ Ⓑ Ⓒ Ⓓ
64. Ⓐ Ⓑ Ⓒ Ⓓ
65. Ⓐ Ⓑ Ⓒ Ⓓ
66. Ⓐ Ⓑ Ⓒ Ⓓ
67. Ⓐ Ⓑ Ⓒ Ⓓ
68. Ⓐ Ⓑ Ⓒ Ⓓ
69. Ⓐ Ⓑ Ⓒ Ⓓ
70. Ⓐ Ⓑ Ⓒ Ⓓ
71. Ⓐ Ⓑ Ⓒ Ⓓ
72. Ⓐ Ⓑ Ⓒ Ⓓ
73. Ⓐ Ⓑ Ⓒ Ⓓ
74. Ⓐ Ⓑ Ⓒ Ⓓ
75. Ⓐ Ⓑ Ⓒ Ⓓ

Answer Sheet Chapter 3 Drills

Capitalization and Punctuation

1. Ⓐ Ⓑ Ⓒ Ⓓ
2. Ⓐ Ⓑ Ⓒ Ⓓ
3. Ⓐ Ⓑ Ⓒ Ⓓ
4. Ⓐ Ⓑ Ⓒ Ⓓ
5. Ⓐ Ⓑ Ⓒ Ⓓ
6. Ⓐ Ⓑ Ⓒ Ⓓ
7. Ⓐ Ⓑ Ⓒ Ⓓ
8. Ⓐ Ⓑ Ⓒ Ⓓ
9. Ⓐ Ⓑ Ⓒ Ⓓ
10. Ⓐ Ⓑ Ⓒ Ⓓ
11. Ⓐ Ⓑ Ⓒ Ⓓ
12. Ⓐ Ⓑ Ⓒ Ⓓ
13. Ⓐ Ⓑ Ⓒ Ⓓ
14. Ⓐ Ⓑ Ⓒ Ⓓ
15. Ⓐ Ⓑ Ⓒ Ⓓ
16. Ⓐ Ⓑ Ⓒ Ⓓ
17. Ⓐ Ⓑ Ⓒ Ⓓ
18. Ⓐ Ⓑ Ⓒ Ⓓ
19. Ⓐ Ⓑ Ⓒ Ⓓ
20. Ⓐ Ⓑ Ⓒ Ⓓ
21. Ⓐ Ⓑ Ⓒ Ⓓ
22. Ⓐ Ⓑ Ⓒ Ⓓ
23. Ⓐ Ⓑ Ⓒ Ⓓ
24. Ⓐ Ⓑ Ⓒ Ⓓ
25. Ⓐ Ⓑ Ⓒ Ⓓ
26. Ⓐ Ⓑ Ⓒ Ⓓ
27. Ⓐ Ⓑ Ⓒ Ⓓ
28. Ⓐ Ⓑ Ⓒ Ⓓ
29. Ⓐ Ⓑ Ⓒ Ⓓ
30. Ⓐ Ⓑ Ⓒ Ⓓ
31. Ⓐ Ⓑ Ⓒ Ⓓ
32. Ⓐ Ⓑ Ⓒ Ⓓ
33. Ⓐ Ⓑ Ⓒ Ⓓ
34. Ⓐ Ⓑ Ⓒ Ⓓ
35. Ⓐ Ⓑ Ⓒ Ⓓ
36. Ⓐ Ⓑ Ⓒ Ⓓ
37. Ⓐ Ⓑ Ⓒ Ⓓ
38. Ⓐ Ⓑ Ⓒ Ⓓ
39. Ⓐ Ⓑ Ⓒ Ⓓ
40. Ⓐ Ⓑ Ⓒ Ⓓ
41. Ⓐ Ⓑ Ⓒ Ⓓ
42. Ⓐ Ⓑ Ⓒ Ⓓ
43. Ⓐ Ⓑ Ⓒ Ⓓ
44. Ⓐ Ⓑ Ⓒ Ⓓ
45. Ⓐ Ⓑ Ⓒ Ⓓ
46. Ⓐ Ⓑ Ⓒ Ⓓ
47. Ⓐ Ⓑ Ⓒ Ⓓ
48. Ⓐ Ⓑ Ⓒ Ⓓ
49. Ⓐ Ⓑ Ⓒ Ⓓ
50. Ⓐ Ⓑ Ⓒ Ⓓ
51. Ⓐ Ⓑ Ⓒ Ⓓ
52. Ⓐ Ⓑ Ⓒ Ⓓ
53. Ⓐ Ⓑ Ⓒ Ⓓ
54. Ⓐ Ⓑ Ⓒ Ⓓ
55. Ⓐ Ⓑ Ⓒ Ⓓ
56. Ⓐ Ⓑ Ⓒ Ⓓ
57. Ⓐ Ⓑ Ⓒ Ⓓ
58. Ⓐ Ⓑ Ⓒ Ⓓ
59. Ⓐ Ⓑ Ⓒ Ⓓ
60. Ⓐ Ⓑ Ⓒ Ⓓ
61. Ⓐ Ⓑ Ⓒ Ⓓ
62. Ⓐ Ⓑ Ⓒ Ⓓ
63. Ⓐ Ⓑ Ⓒ Ⓓ
64. Ⓐ Ⓑ Ⓒ Ⓓ
65. Ⓐ Ⓑ Ⓒ Ⓓ
66. Ⓐ Ⓑ Ⓒ Ⓓ
67. Ⓐ Ⓑ Ⓒ Ⓓ
68. Ⓐ Ⓑ Ⓒ Ⓓ
69. Ⓐ Ⓑ Ⓒ Ⓓ
70. Ⓐ Ⓑ Ⓒ Ⓓ
71. Ⓐ Ⓑ Ⓒ Ⓓ
72. Ⓐ Ⓑ Ⓒ Ⓓ
73. Ⓐ Ⓑ Ⓒ Ⓓ
74. Ⓐ Ⓑ Ⓒ Ⓓ
75. Ⓐ Ⓑ Ⓒ Ⓓ

Usage

1. Ⓐ Ⓑ Ⓒ Ⓓ	16. Ⓐ Ⓑ Ⓒ Ⓓ	31. Ⓐ Ⓑ Ⓒ Ⓓ	46. Ⓐ Ⓑ Ⓒ Ⓓ	61. Ⓐ Ⓑ Ⓒ Ⓓ
2. Ⓐ Ⓑ Ⓒ Ⓓ	17. Ⓐ Ⓑ Ⓒ Ⓓ	32. Ⓐ Ⓑ Ⓒ Ⓓ	47. Ⓐ Ⓑ Ⓒ Ⓓ	62. Ⓐ Ⓑ Ⓒ Ⓓ
3. Ⓐ Ⓑ Ⓒ Ⓓ	18. Ⓐ Ⓑ Ⓒ Ⓓ	33. Ⓐ Ⓑ Ⓒ Ⓓ	48. Ⓐ Ⓑ Ⓒ Ⓓ	63. Ⓐ Ⓑ Ⓒ Ⓓ
4. Ⓐ Ⓑ Ⓒ Ⓓ	19. Ⓐ Ⓑ Ⓒ Ⓓ	34. Ⓐ Ⓑ Ⓒ Ⓓ	49. Ⓐ Ⓑ Ⓒ Ⓓ	64. Ⓐ Ⓑ Ⓒ Ⓓ
5. Ⓐ Ⓑ Ⓒ Ⓓ	20. Ⓐ Ⓑ Ⓒ Ⓓ	35. Ⓐ Ⓑ Ⓒ Ⓓ	50. Ⓐ Ⓑ Ⓒ Ⓓ	65. Ⓐ Ⓑ Ⓒ Ⓓ
6. Ⓐ Ⓑ Ⓒ Ⓓ	21. Ⓐ Ⓑ Ⓒ Ⓓ	36. Ⓐ Ⓑ Ⓒ Ⓓ	51. Ⓐ Ⓑ Ⓒ Ⓓ	66. Ⓐ Ⓑ Ⓒ Ⓓ
7. Ⓐ Ⓑ Ⓒ Ⓓ	22. Ⓐ Ⓑ Ⓒ Ⓓ	37. Ⓐ Ⓑ Ⓒ Ⓓ	52. Ⓐ Ⓑ Ⓒ Ⓓ	67. Ⓐ Ⓑ Ⓒ Ⓓ
8. Ⓐ Ⓑ Ⓒ Ⓓ	23. Ⓐ Ⓑ Ⓒ Ⓓ	38. Ⓐ Ⓑ Ⓒ Ⓓ	53. Ⓐ Ⓑ Ⓒ Ⓓ	68. Ⓐ Ⓑ Ⓒ Ⓓ
9. Ⓐ Ⓑ Ⓒ Ⓓ	24. Ⓐ Ⓑ Ⓒ Ⓓ	39. Ⓐ Ⓑ Ⓒ Ⓓ	54. Ⓐ Ⓑ Ⓒ Ⓓ	69. Ⓐ Ⓑ Ⓒ Ⓓ
10. Ⓐ Ⓑ Ⓒ Ⓓ	25. Ⓐ Ⓑ Ⓒ Ⓓ	40. Ⓐ Ⓑ Ⓒ Ⓓ	55. Ⓐ Ⓑ Ⓒ Ⓓ	70. Ⓐ Ⓑ Ⓒ Ⓓ
11. Ⓐ Ⓑ Ⓒ Ⓓ	26. Ⓐ Ⓑ Ⓒ Ⓓ	41. Ⓐ Ⓑ Ⓒ Ⓓ	56. Ⓐ Ⓑ Ⓒ Ⓓ	71. Ⓐ Ⓑ Ⓒ Ⓓ
12. Ⓐ Ⓑ Ⓒ Ⓓ	27. Ⓐ Ⓑ Ⓒ Ⓓ	42. Ⓐ Ⓑ Ⓒ Ⓓ	57. Ⓐ Ⓑ Ⓒ Ⓓ	72. Ⓐ Ⓑ Ⓒ Ⓓ
13. Ⓐ Ⓑ Ⓒ Ⓓ	28. Ⓐ Ⓑ Ⓒ Ⓓ	43. Ⓐ Ⓑ Ⓒ Ⓓ	58. Ⓐ Ⓑ Ⓒ Ⓓ	73. Ⓐ Ⓑ Ⓒ Ⓓ
14. Ⓐ Ⓑ Ⓒ Ⓓ	29. Ⓐ Ⓑ Ⓒ Ⓓ	44. Ⓐ Ⓑ Ⓒ Ⓓ	59. Ⓐ Ⓑ Ⓒ Ⓓ	74. Ⓐ Ⓑ Ⓒ Ⓓ
15. Ⓐ Ⓑ Ⓒ Ⓓ	30. Ⓐ Ⓑ Ⓒ Ⓓ	45. Ⓐ Ⓑ Ⓒ Ⓓ	60. Ⓐ Ⓑ Ⓒ Ⓓ	75. Ⓐ Ⓑ Ⓒ Ⓓ

Answer Sheet Chapter 3 Drills

Composition and Expression

1. Ⓐ Ⓑ Ⓒ Ⓓ
2. Ⓐ Ⓑ Ⓒ Ⓓ
3. Ⓐ Ⓑ Ⓒ Ⓓ
4. Ⓐ Ⓑ Ⓒ Ⓓ
5. Ⓐ Ⓑ Ⓒ Ⓓ
6. Ⓐ Ⓑ Ⓒ Ⓓ
7. Ⓐ Ⓑ Ⓒ Ⓓ
8. Ⓐ Ⓑ Ⓒ Ⓓ
9. Ⓐ Ⓑ Ⓒ Ⓓ
10. Ⓐ Ⓑ Ⓒ Ⓓ
11. Ⓐ Ⓑ Ⓒ Ⓓ
12. Ⓐ Ⓑ Ⓒ Ⓓ
13. Ⓐ Ⓑ Ⓒ Ⓓ
14. Ⓐ Ⓑ Ⓒ Ⓓ
15. Ⓐ Ⓑ Ⓒ Ⓓ
16. Ⓐ Ⓑ Ⓒ Ⓓ
17. Ⓐ Ⓑ Ⓒ Ⓓ
18. Ⓐ Ⓑ Ⓒ Ⓓ
19. Ⓐ Ⓑ Ⓒ Ⓓ
20. Ⓐ Ⓑ Ⓒ Ⓓ
21. Ⓐ Ⓑ Ⓒ Ⓓ
22. Ⓐ Ⓑ Ⓒ Ⓓ
23. Ⓐ Ⓑ Ⓒ Ⓓ
24. Ⓐ Ⓑ Ⓒ Ⓓ
25. Ⓐ Ⓑ Ⓒ Ⓓ
26. Ⓐ Ⓑ Ⓒ Ⓓ
27. Ⓐ Ⓑ Ⓒ Ⓓ
28. Ⓐ Ⓑ Ⓒ Ⓓ
29. Ⓐ Ⓑ Ⓒ Ⓓ
30. Ⓐ Ⓑ Ⓒ Ⓓ
31. Ⓐ Ⓑ Ⓒ Ⓓ
32. Ⓐ Ⓑ Ⓒ Ⓓ
33. Ⓐ Ⓑ Ⓒ Ⓓ
34. Ⓐ Ⓑ Ⓒ Ⓓ
35. Ⓐ Ⓑ Ⓒ Ⓓ
36. Ⓐ Ⓑ Ⓒ Ⓓ
37. Ⓐ Ⓑ Ⓒ Ⓓ
38. Ⓐ Ⓑ Ⓒ Ⓓ
39. Ⓐ Ⓑ Ⓒ Ⓓ
40. Ⓐ Ⓑ Ⓒ Ⓓ
41. Ⓐ Ⓑ Ⓒ Ⓓ
42. Ⓐ Ⓑ Ⓒ Ⓓ
43. Ⓐ Ⓑ Ⓒ Ⓓ
44. Ⓐ Ⓑ Ⓒ Ⓓ
45. Ⓐ Ⓑ Ⓒ Ⓓ
46. Ⓐ Ⓑ Ⓒ Ⓓ
47. Ⓐ Ⓑ Ⓒ Ⓓ
48. Ⓐ Ⓑ Ⓒ Ⓓ
49. Ⓐ Ⓑ Ⓒ Ⓓ
50. Ⓐ Ⓑ Ⓒ Ⓓ
51. Ⓐ Ⓑ Ⓒ Ⓓ
52. Ⓐ Ⓑ Ⓒ Ⓓ
53. Ⓐ Ⓑ Ⓒ Ⓓ
54. Ⓐ Ⓑ Ⓒ Ⓓ
55. Ⓐ Ⓑ Ⓒ Ⓓ
56. Ⓐ Ⓑ Ⓒ Ⓓ
57. Ⓐ Ⓑ Ⓒ Ⓓ
58. Ⓐ Ⓑ Ⓒ Ⓓ
59. Ⓐ Ⓑ Ⓒ Ⓓ
60. Ⓐ Ⓑ Ⓒ Ⓓ
61. Ⓐ Ⓑ Ⓒ Ⓓ
62. Ⓐ Ⓑ Ⓒ Ⓓ
63. Ⓐ Ⓑ Ⓒ Ⓓ
64. Ⓐ Ⓑ Ⓒ Ⓓ
65. Ⓐ Ⓑ Ⓒ Ⓓ
66. Ⓐ Ⓑ Ⓒ Ⓓ
67. Ⓐ Ⓑ Ⓒ Ⓓ
68. Ⓐ Ⓑ Ⓒ Ⓓ
69. Ⓐ Ⓑ Ⓒ Ⓓ
70. Ⓐ Ⓑ Ⓒ Ⓓ
71. Ⓐ Ⓑ Ⓒ Ⓓ
72. Ⓐ Ⓑ Ⓒ Ⓓ
73. Ⓐ Ⓑ Ⓒ Ⓓ
74. Ⓐ Ⓑ Ⓒ Ⓓ
75. Ⓐ Ⓑ Ⓒ Ⓓ

Answer Sheet: Chapter 4 Drills

Math

1. Ⓐ Ⓑ Ⓒ Ⓓ
2. Ⓐ Ⓑ Ⓒ Ⓓ
3. Ⓐ Ⓑ Ⓒ Ⓓ
4. Ⓐ Ⓑ Ⓒ Ⓓ
5. Ⓐ Ⓑ Ⓒ Ⓓ
6. Ⓐ Ⓑ Ⓒ Ⓓ
7. Ⓐ Ⓑ Ⓒ Ⓓ
8. Ⓐ Ⓑ Ⓒ Ⓓ
9. Ⓐ Ⓑ Ⓒ Ⓓ
10. Ⓐ Ⓑ Ⓒ Ⓓ
11. Ⓐ Ⓑ Ⓒ Ⓓ
12. Ⓐ Ⓑ Ⓒ Ⓓ
13. Ⓐ Ⓑ Ⓒ Ⓓ
14. Ⓐ Ⓑ Ⓒ Ⓓ
15. Ⓐ Ⓑ Ⓒ Ⓓ
16. Ⓐ Ⓑ Ⓒ Ⓓ
17. Ⓐ Ⓑ Ⓒ Ⓓ
18. Ⓐ Ⓑ Ⓒ Ⓓ
19. Ⓐ Ⓑ Ⓒ Ⓓ
20. Ⓐ Ⓑ Ⓒ Ⓓ
21. Ⓐ Ⓑ Ⓒ Ⓓ
22. Ⓐ Ⓑ Ⓒ Ⓓ
23. Ⓐ Ⓑ Ⓒ Ⓓ
24. Ⓐ Ⓑ Ⓒ Ⓓ
25. Ⓐ Ⓑ Ⓒ Ⓓ
26. Ⓐ Ⓑ Ⓒ Ⓓ
27. Ⓐ Ⓑ Ⓒ Ⓓ
28. Ⓐ Ⓑ Ⓒ Ⓓ
29. Ⓐ Ⓑ Ⓒ Ⓓ
30. Ⓐ Ⓑ Ⓒ Ⓓ
31. Ⓐ Ⓑ Ⓒ Ⓓ
32. Ⓐ Ⓑ Ⓒ Ⓓ
33. Ⓐ Ⓑ Ⓒ Ⓓ
34. Ⓐ Ⓑ Ⓒ Ⓓ
35. Ⓐ Ⓑ Ⓒ Ⓓ
36. Ⓐ Ⓑ Ⓒ Ⓓ
37. Ⓐ Ⓑ Ⓒ Ⓓ
38. Ⓐ Ⓑ Ⓒ Ⓓ
39. Ⓐ Ⓑ Ⓒ Ⓓ
40. Ⓐ Ⓑ Ⓒ Ⓓ
41. Ⓐ Ⓑ Ⓒ Ⓓ
42. Ⓐ Ⓑ Ⓒ Ⓓ
43. Ⓐ Ⓑ Ⓒ Ⓓ
44. Ⓐ Ⓑ Ⓒ Ⓓ
45. Ⓐ Ⓑ Ⓒ Ⓓ
46. Ⓐ Ⓑ Ⓒ Ⓓ
47. Ⓐ Ⓑ Ⓒ Ⓓ
48. Ⓐ Ⓑ Ⓒ Ⓓ
49. Ⓐ Ⓑ Ⓒ Ⓓ
50. Ⓐ Ⓑ Ⓒ Ⓓ
51. Ⓐ Ⓑ Ⓒ Ⓓ
52. Ⓐ Ⓑ Ⓒ Ⓓ
53. Ⓐ Ⓑ Ⓒ Ⓓ
54. Ⓐ Ⓑ Ⓒ Ⓓ
55. Ⓐ Ⓑ Ⓒ Ⓓ
56. Ⓐ Ⓑ Ⓒ Ⓓ
57. Ⓐ Ⓑ Ⓒ Ⓓ
58. Ⓐ Ⓑ Ⓒ Ⓓ
59. Ⓐ Ⓑ Ⓒ Ⓓ
60. Ⓐ Ⓑ Ⓒ Ⓓ
61. Ⓐ Ⓑ Ⓒ Ⓓ
62. Ⓐ Ⓑ Ⓒ Ⓓ
63. Ⓐ Ⓑ Ⓒ Ⓓ
64. Ⓐ Ⓑ Ⓒ Ⓓ
65. Ⓐ Ⓑ Ⓒ Ⓓ
66. Ⓐ Ⓑ Ⓒ Ⓓ
67. Ⓐ Ⓑ Ⓒ Ⓓ
68. Ⓐ Ⓑ Ⓒ Ⓓ
69. Ⓐ Ⓑ Ⓒ Ⓓ
70. Ⓐ Ⓑ Ⓒ Ⓓ
71. Ⓐ Ⓑ Ⓒ Ⓓ
72. Ⓐ Ⓑ Ⓒ Ⓓ
73. Ⓐ Ⓑ Ⓒ Ⓓ
74. Ⓐ Ⓑ Ⓒ Ⓓ
75. Ⓐ Ⓑ Ⓒ Ⓓ

Math

1. Ⓐ Ⓑ Ⓒ Ⓓ	16. Ⓐ Ⓑ Ⓒ Ⓓ	31. Ⓐ Ⓑ Ⓒ Ⓓ	46. Ⓐ Ⓑ Ⓒ Ⓓ	61. Ⓐ Ⓑ Ⓒ Ⓓ
2. Ⓐ Ⓑ Ⓒ Ⓓ	17. Ⓐ Ⓑ Ⓒ Ⓓ	32. Ⓐ Ⓑ Ⓒ Ⓓ	47. Ⓐ Ⓑ Ⓒ Ⓓ	62. Ⓐ Ⓑ Ⓒ Ⓓ
3. Ⓐ Ⓑ Ⓒ Ⓓ	18. Ⓐ Ⓑ Ⓒ Ⓓ	33. Ⓐ Ⓑ Ⓒ Ⓓ	48. Ⓐ Ⓑ Ⓒ Ⓓ	63. Ⓐ Ⓑ Ⓒ Ⓓ
4. Ⓐ Ⓑ Ⓒ Ⓓ	19. Ⓐ Ⓑ Ⓒ Ⓓ	34. Ⓐ Ⓑ Ⓒ Ⓓ	49. Ⓐ Ⓑ Ⓒ Ⓓ	64. Ⓐ Ⓑ Ⓒ Ⓓ
5. Ⓐ Ⓑ Ⓒ Ⓓ	20. Ⓐ Ⓑ Ⓒ Ⓓ	35. Ⓐ Ⓑ Ⓒ Ⓓ	50. Ⓐ Ⓑ Ⓒ Ⓓ	65. Ⓐ Ⓑ Ⓒ Ⓓ
6. Ⓐ Ⓑ Ⓒ Ⓓ	21. Ⓐ Ⓑ Ⓒ Ⓓ	36. Ⓐ Ⓑ Ⓒ Ⓓ	51. Ⓐ Ⓑ Ⓒ Ⓓ	66. Ⓐ Ⓑ Ⓒ Ⓓ
7. Ⓐ Ⓑ Ⓒ Ⓓ	22. Ⓐ Ⓑ Ⓒ Ⓓ	37. Ⓐ Ⓑ Ⓒ Ⓓ	52. Ⓐ Ⓑ Ⓒ Ⓓ	67. Ⓐ Ⓑ Ⓒ Ⓓ
8. Ⓐ Ⓑ Ⓒ Ⓓ	23. Ⓐ Ⓑ Ⓒ Ⓓ	38. Ⓐ Ⓑ Ⓒ Ⓓ	53. Ⓐ Ⓑ Ⓒ Ⓓ	68. Ⓐ Ⓑ Ⓒ Ⓓ
9. Ⓐ Ⓑ Ⓒ Ⓓ	24. Ⓐ Ⓑ Ⓒ Ⓓ	39. Ⓐ Ⓑ Ⓒ Ⓓ	54. Ⓐ Ⓑ Ⓒ Ⓓ	69. Ⓐ Ⓑ Ⓒ Ⓓ
10. Ⓐ Ⓑ Ⓒ Ⓓ	25. Ⓐ Ⓑ Ⓒ Ⓓ	40. Ⓐ Ⓑ Ⓒ Ⓓ	55. Ⓐ Ⓑ Ⓒ Ⓓ	70. Ⓐ Ⓑ Ⓒ Ⓓ
11. Ⓐ Ⓑ Ⓒ Ⓓ	26. Ⓐ Ⓑ Ⓒ Ⓓ	41. Ⓐ Ⓑ Ⓒ Ⓓ	56. Ⓐ Ⓑ Ⓒ Ⓓ	71. Ⓐ Ⓑ Ⓒ Ⓓ
12. Ⓐ Ⓑ Ⓒ Ⓓ	27. Ⓐ Ⓑ Ⓒ Ⓓ	42. Ⓐ Ⓑ Ⓒ Ⓓ	57. Ⓐ Ⓑ Ⓒ Ⓓ	72. Ⓐ Ⓑ Ⓒ Ⓓ
13. Ⓐ Ⓑ Ⓒ Ⓓ	28. Ⓐ Ⓑ Ⓒ Ⓓ	43. Ⓐ Ⓑ Ⓒ Ⓓ	58. Ⓐ Ⓑ Ⓒ Ⓓ	73. Ⓐ Ⓑ Ⓒ Ⓓ
14. Ⓐ Ⓑ Ⓒ Ⓓ	29. Ⓐ Ⓑ Ⓒ Ⓓ	44. Ⓐ Ⓑ Ⓒ Ⓓ	59. Ⓐ Ⓑ Ⓒ Ⓓ	74. Ⓐ Ⓑ Ⓒ Ⓓ
15. Ⓐ Ⓑ Ⓒ Ⓓ	30. Ⓐ Ⓑ Ⓒ Ⓓ	45. Ⓐ Ⓑ Ⓒ Ⓓ	60. Ⓐ Ⓑ Ⓒ Ⓓ	75. Ⓐ Ⓑ Ⓒ Ⓓ

Answer Sheet: Chapter 5 Drills

Analogies

1. Ⓐ Ⓑ Ⓒ Ⓓ	16. Ⓐ Ⓑ Ⓒ Ⓓ	31. Ⓐ Ⓑ Ⓒ Ⓓ	46. Ⓐ Ⓑ Ⓒ Ⓓ	61. Ⓐ Ⓑ Ⓒ Ⓓ
2. Ⓐ Ⓑ Ⓒ Ⓓ	17. Ⓐ Ⓑ Ⓒ Ⓓ	32. Ⓐ Ⓑ Ⓒ Ⓓ	47. Ⓐ Ⓑ Ⓒ Ⓓ	62. Ⓐ Ⓑ Ⓒ Ⓓ
3. Ⓐ Ⓑ Ⓒ Ⓓ	18. Ⓐ Ⓑ Ⓒ Ⓓ	33. Ⓐ Ⓑ Ⓒ Ⓓ	48. Ⓐ Ⓑ Ⓒ Ⓓ	63. Ⓐ Ⓑ Ⓒ Ⓓ
4. Ⓐ Ⓑ Ⓒ Ⓓ	19. Ⓐ Ⓑ Ⓒ Ⓓ	34. Ⓐ Ⓑ Ⓒ Ⓓ	49. Ⓐ Ⓑ Ⓒ Ⓓ	64. Ⓐ Ⓑ Ⓒ Ⓓ
5. Ⓐ Ⓑ Ⓒ Ⓓ	20. Ⓐ Ⓑ Ⓒ Ⓓ	35. Ⓐ Ⓑ Ⓒ Ⓓ	50. Ⓐ Ⓑ Ⓒ Ⓓ	65. Ⓐ Ⓑ Ⓒ Ⓓ
6. Ⓐ Ⓑ Ⓒ Ⓓ	21. Ⓐ Ⓑ Ⓒ Ⓓ	36. Ⓐ Ⓑ Ⓒ Ⓓ	51. Ⓐ Ⓑ Ⓒ Ⓓ	66. Ⓐ Ⓑ Ⓒ Ⓓ
7. Ⓐ Ⓑ Ⓒ Ⓓ	22. Ⓐ Ⓑ Ⓒ Ⓓ	37. Ⓐ Ⓑ Ⓒ Ⓓ	52. Ⓐ Ⓑ Ⓒ Ⓓ	67. Ⓐ Ⓑ Ⓒ Ⓓ
8. Ⓐ Ⓑ Ⓒ Ⓓ	23. Ⓐ Ⓑ Ⓒ Ⓓ	38. Ⓐ Ⓑ Ⓒ Ⓓ	53. Ⓐ Ⓑ Ⓒ Ⓓ	68. Ⓐ Ⓑ Ⓒ Ⓓ
9. Ⓐ Ⓑ Ⓒ Ⓓ	24. Ⓐ Ⓑ Ⓒ Ⓓ	39. Ⓐ Ⓑ Ⓒ Ⓓ	54. Ⓐ Ⓑ Ⓒ Ⓓ	69. Ⓐ Ⓑ Ⓒ Ⓓ
10. Ⓐ Ⓑ Ⓒ Ⓓ	25. Ⓐ Ⓑ Ⓒ Ⓓ	40. Ⓐ Ⓑ Ⓒ Ⓓ	55. Ⓐ Ⓑ Ⓒ Ⓓ	70. Ⓐ Ⓑ Ⓒ Ⓓ
11. Ⓐ Ⓑ Ⓒ Ⓓ	26. Ⓐ Ⓑ Ⓒ Ⓓ	41. Ⓐ Ⓑ Ⓒ Ⓓ	56. Ⓐ Ⓑ Ⓒ Ⓓ	71. Ⓐ Ⓑ Ⓒ Ⓓ
12. Ⓐ Ⓑ Ⓒ Ⓓ	27. Ⓐ Ⓑ Ⓒ Ⓓ	42. Ⓐ Ⓑ Ⓒ Ⓓ	57. Ⓐ Ⓑ Ⓒ Ⓓ	72. Ⓐ Ⓑ Ⓒ Ⓓ
13. Ⓐ Ⓑ Ⓒ Ⓓ	28. Ⓐ Ⓑ Ⓒ Ⓓ	43. Ⓐ Ⓑ Ⓒ Ⓓ	58. Ⓐ Ⓑ Ⓒ Ⓓ	73. Ⓐ Ⓑ Ⓒ Ⓓ
14. Ⓐ Ⓑ Ⓒ Ⓓ	29. Ⓐ Ⓑ Ⓒ Ⓓ	44. Ⓐ Ⓑ Ⓒ Ⓓ	59. Ⓐ Ⓑ Ⓒ Ⓓ	74. Ⓐ Ⓑ Ⓒ Ⓓ
15. Ⓐ Ⓑ Ⓒ Ⓓ	30. Ⓐ Ⓑ Ⓒ Ⓓ	45. Ⓐ Ⓑ Ⓒ Ⓓ	60. Ⓐ Ⓑ Ⓒ Ⓓ	75. Ⓐ Ⓑ Ⓒ Ⓓ

Antonyms

1. Ⓐ Ⓑ Ⓒ Ⓓ	16. Ⓐ Ⓑ Ⓒ Ⓓ	31. Ⓐ Ⓑ Ⓒ Ⓓ	46. Ⓐ Ⓑ Ⓒ Ⓓ	61. Ⓐ Ⓑ Ⓒ Ⓓ
2. Ⓐ Ⓑ Ⓒ Ⓓ	17. Ⓐ Ⓑ Ⓒ Ⓓ	32. Ⓐ Ⓑ Ⓒ Ⓓ	47. Ⓐ Ⓑ Ⓒ Ⓓ	62. Ⓐ Ⓑ Ⓒ Ⓓ
3. Ⓐ Ⓑ Ⓒ Ⓓ	18. Ⓐ Ⓑ Ⓒ Ⓓ	33. Ⓐ Ⓑ Ⓒ Ⓓ	48. Ⓐ Ⓑ Ⓒ Ⓓ	63. Ⓐ Ⓑ Ⓒ Ⓓ
4. Ⓐ Ⓑ Ⓒ Ⓓ	19. Ⓐ Ⓑ Ⓒ Ⓓ	34. Ⓐ Ⓑ Ⓒ Ⓓ	49. Ⓐ Ⓑ Ⓒ Ⓓ	64. Ⓐ Ⓑ Ⓒ Ⓓ
5. Ⓐ Ⓑ Ⓒ Ⓓ	20. Ⓐ Ⓑ Ⓒ Ⓓ	35. Ⓐ Ⓑ Ⓒ Ⓓ	50. Ⓐ Ⓑ Ⓒ Ⓓ	65. Ⓐ Ⓑ Ⓒ Ⓓ
6. Ⓐ Ⓑ Ⓒ Ⓓ	21. Ⓐ Ⓑ Ⓒ Ⓓ	36. Ⓐ Ⓑ Ⓒ Ⓓ	51. Ⓐ Ⓑ Ⓒ Ⓓ	66. Ⓐ Ⓑ Ⓒ Ⓓ
7. Ⓐ Ⓑ Ⓒ Ⓓ	22. Ⓐ Ⓑ Ⓒ Ⓓ	37. Ⓐ Ⓑ Ⓒ Ⓓ	52. Ⓐ Ⓑ Ⓒ Ⓓ	67. Ⓐ Ⓑ Ⓒ Ⓓ
8. Ⓐ Ⓑ Ⓒ Ⓓ	23. Ⓐ Ⓑ Ⓒ Ⓓ	38. Ⓐ Ⓑ Ⓒ Ⓓ	53. Ⓐ Ⓑ Ⓒ Ⓓ	68. Ⓐ Ⓑ Ⓒ Ⓓ
9. Ⓐ Ⓑ Ⓒ Ⓓ	24. Ⓐ Ⓑ Ⓒ Ⓓ	39. Ⓐ Ⓑ Ⓒ Ⓓ	54. Ⓐ Ⓑ Ⓒ Ⓓ	69. Ⓐ Ⓑ Ⓒ Ⓓ
10. Ⓐ Ⓑ Ⓒ Ⓓ	25. Ⓐ Ⓑ Ⓒ Ⓓ	40. Ⓐ Ⓑ Ⓒ Ⓓ	55. Ⓐ Ⓑ Ⓒ Ⓓ	70. Ⓐ Ⓑ Ⓒ Ⓓ
11. Ⓐ Ⓑ Ⓒ Ⓓ	26. Ⓐ Ⓑ Ⓒ Ⓓ	41. Ⓐ Ⓑ Ⓒ Ⓓ	56. Ⓐ Ⓑ Ⓒ Ⓓ	71. Ⓐ Ⓑ Ⓒ Ⓓ
12. Ⓐ Ⓑ Ⓒ Ⓓ	27. Ⓐ Ⓑ Ⓒ Ⓓ	42. Ⓐ Ⓑ Ⓒ Ⓓ	57. Ⓐ Ⓑ Ⓒ Ⓓ	72. Ⓐ Ⓑ Ⓒ Ⓓ
13. Ⓐ Ⓑ Ⓒ Ⓓ	28. Ⓐ Ⓑ Ⓒ Ⓓ	43. Ⓐ Ⓑ Ⓒ Ⓓ	58. Ⓐ Ⓑ Ⓒ Ⓓ	73. Ⓐ Ⓑ Ⓒ Ⓓ
14. Ⓐ Ⓑ Ⓒ Ⓓ	29. Ⓐ Ⓑ Ⓒ Ⓓ	44. Ⓐ Ⓑ Ⓒ Ⓓ	59. Ⓐ Ⓑ Ⓒ Ⓓ	74. Ⓐ Ⓑ Ⓒ Ⓓ
15. Ⓐ Ⓑ Ⓒ Ⓓ	30. Ⓐ Ⓑ Ⓒ Ⓓ	45. Ⓐ Ⓑ Ⓒ Ⓓ	60. Ⓐ Ⓑ Ⓒ Ⓓ	75. Ⓐ Ⓑ Ⓒ Ⓓ

Synonyms

1. Ⓐ Ⓑ Ⓒ Ⓓ	16. Ⓐ Ⓑ Ⓒ Ⓓ	31. Ⓐ Ⓑ Ⓒ Ⓓ	46. Ⓐ Ⓑ Ⓒ Ⓓ	61. Ⓐ Ⓑ Ⓒ Ⓓ
2. Ⓐ Ⓑ Ⓒ Ⓓ	17. Ⓐ Ⓑ Ⓒ Ⓓ	32. Ⓐ Ⓑ Ⓒ Ⓓ	47. Ⓐ Ⓑ Ⓒ Ⓓ	62. Ⓐ Ⓑ Ⓒ Ⓓ
3. Ⓐ Ⓑ Ⓒ Ⓓ	18. Ⓐ Ⓑ Ⓒ Ⓓ	33. Ⓐ Ⓑ Ⓒ Ⓓ	48. Ⓐ Ⓑ Ⓒ Ⓓ	63. Ⓐ Ⓑ Ⓒ Ⓓ
4. Ⓐ Ⓑ Ⓒ Ⓓ	19. Ⓐ Ⓑ Ⓒ Ⓓ	34. Ⓐ Ⓑ Ⓒ Ⓓ	49. Ⓐ Ⓑ Ⓒ Ⓓ	64. Ⓐ Ⓑ Ⓒ Ⓓ
5. Ⓐ Ⓑ Ⓒ Ⓓ	20. Ⓐ Ⓑ Ⓒ Ⓓ	35. Ⓐ Ⓑ Ⓒ Ⓓ	50. Ⓐ Ⓑ Ⓒ Ⓓ	65. Ⓐ Ⓑ Ⓒ Ⓓ
6. Ⓐ Ⓑ Ⓒ Ⓓ	21. Ⓐ Ⓑ Ⓒ Ⓓ	36. Ⓐ Ⓑ Ⓒ Ⓓ	51. Ⓐ Ⓑ Ⓒ Ⓓ	66. Ⓐ Ⓑ Ⓒ Ⓓ
7. Ⓐ Ⓑ Ⓒ Ⓓ	22. Ⓐ Ⓑ Ⓒ Ⓓ	37. Ⓐ Ⓑ Ⓒ Ⓓ	52. Ⓐ Ⓑ Ⓒ Ⓓ	67. Ⓐ Ⓑ Ⓒ Ⓓ
8. Ⓐ Ⓑ Ⓒ Ⓓ	23. Ⓐ Ⓑ Ⓒ Ⓓ	38. Ⓐ Ⓑ Ⓒ Ⓓ	53. Ⓐ Ⓑ Ⓒ Ⓓ	68. Ⓐ Ⓑ Ⓒ Ⓓ
9. Ⓐ Ⓑ Ⓒ Ⓓ	24. Ⓐ Ⓑ Ⓒ Ⓓ	39. Ⓐ Ⓑ Ⓒ Ⓓ	54. Ⓐ Ⓑ Ⓒ Ⓓ	69. Ⓐ Ⓑ Ⓒ Ⓓ
10. Ⓐ Ⓑ Ⓒ Ⓓ	25. Ⓐ Ⓑ Ⓒ Ⓓ	40. Ⓐ Ⓑ Ⓒ Ⓓ	55. Ⓐ Ⓑ Ⓒ Ⓓ	70. Ⓐ Ⓑ Ⓒ Ⓓ
11. Ⓐ Ⓑ Ⓒ Ⓓ	26. Ⓐ Ⓑ Ⓒ Ⓓ	41. Ⓐ Ⓑ Ⓒ Ⓓ	56. Ⓐ Ⓑ Ⓒ Ⓓ	71. Ⓐ Ⓑ Ⓒ Ⓓ
12. Ⓐ Ⓑ Ⓒ Ⓓ	27. Ⓐ Ⓑ Ⓒ Ⓓ	42. Ⓐ Ⓑ Ⓒ Ⓓ	57. Ⓐ Ⓑ Ⓒ Ⓓ	72. Ⓐ Ⓑ Ⓒ Ⓓ
13. Ⓐ Ⓑ Ⓒ Ⓓ	28. Ⓐ Ⓑ Ⓒ Ⓓ	43. Ⓐ Ⓑ Ⓒ Ⓓ	58. Ⓐ Ⓑ Ⓒ Ⓓ	73. Ⓐ Ⓑ Ⓒ Ⓓ
14. Ⓐ Ⓑ Ⓒ Ⓓ	29. Ⓐ Ⓑ Ⓒ Ⓓ	44. Ⓐ Ⓑ Ⓒ Ⓓ	59. Ⓐ Ⓑ Ⓒ Ⓓ	74. Ⓐ Ⓑ Ⓒ Ⓓ
15. Ⓐ Ⓑ Ⓒ Ⓓ	30. Ⓐ Ⓑ Ⓒ Ⓓ	45. Ⓐ Ⓑ Ⓒ Ⓓ	60. Ⓐ Ⓑ Ⓒ Ⓓ	75. Ⓐ Ⓑ Ⓒ Ⓓ

Verbal Logic and Verbal Classification

1. Ⓐ Ⓑ Ⓒ Ⓓ
2. Ⓐ Ⓑ Ⓒ Ⓓ
3. Ⓐ Ⓑ Ⓒ Ⓓ
4. Ⓐ Ⓑ Ⓒ Ⓓ
5. Ⓐ Ⓑ Ⓒ Ⓓ
6. Ⓐ Ⓑ Ⓒ Ⓓ
7. Ⓐ Ⓑ Ⓒ Ⓓ
8. Ⓐ Ⓑ Ⓒ Ⓓ
9. Ⓐ Ⓑ Ⓒ Ⓓ
10. Ⓐ Ⓑ Ⓒ Ⓓ
11. Ⓐ Ⓑ Ⓒ Ⓓ
12. Ⓐ Ⓑ Ⓒ Ⓓ
13. Ⓐ Ⓑ Ⓒ Ⓓ
14. Ⓐ Ⓑ Ⓒ Ⓓ
15. Ⓐ Ⓑ Ⓒ Ⓓ
16. Ⓐ Ⓑ Ⓒ Ⓓ
17. Ⓐ Ⓑ Ⓒ Ⓓ
18. Ⓐ Ⓑ Ⓒ Ⓓ
19. Ⓐ Ⓑ Ⓒ Ⓓ
20. Ⓐ Ⓑ Ⓒ Ⓓ
21. Ⓐ Ⓑ Ⓒ Ⓓ
22. Ⓐ Ⓑ Ⓒ Ⓓ
23. Ⓐ Ⓑ Ⓒ Ⓓ
24. Ⓐ Ⓑ Ⓒ Ⓓ
25. Ⓐ Ⓑ Ⓒ Ⓓ
26. Ⓐ Ⓑ Ⓒ Ⓓ
27. Ⓐ Ⓑ Ⓒ Ⓓ
28. Ⓐ Ⓑ Ⓒ Ⓓ
29. Ⓐ Ⓑ Ⓒ Ⓓ
30. Ⓐ Ⓑ Ⓒ Ⓓ
31. Ⓐ Ⓑ Ⓒ Ⓓ
32. Ⓐ Ⓑ Ⓒ Ⓓ
33. Ⓐ Ⓑ Ⓒ Ⓓ
34. Ⓐ Ⓑ Ⓒ Ⓓ
35. Ⓐ Ⓑ Ⓒ Ⓓ
36. Ⓐ Ⓑ Ⓒ Ⓓ
37. Ⓐ Ⓑ Ⓒ Ⓓ
38. Ⓐ Ⓑ Ⓒ Ⓓ
39. Ⓐ Ⓑ Ⓒ Ⓓ
40. Ⓐ Ⓑ Ⓒ Ⓓ
41. Ⓐ Ⓑ Ⓒ Ⓓ
42. Ⓐ Ⓑ Ⓒ Ⓓ
43. Ⓐ Ⓑ Ⓒ Ⓓ
44. Ⓐ Ⓑ Ⓒ Ⓓ
45. Ⓐ Ⓑ Ⓒ Ⓓ
46. Ⓐ Ⓑ Ⓒ Ⓓ
47. Ⓐ Ⓑ Ⓒ Ⓓ
48. Ⓐ Ⓑ Ⓒ Ⓓ
49. Ⓐ Ⓑ Ⓒ Ⓓ
50. Ⓐ Ⓑ Ⓒ Ⓓ
51. Ⓐ Ⓑ Ⓒ Ⓓ
52. Ⓐ Ⓑ Ⓒ Ⓓ
53. Ⓐ Ⓑ Ⓒ Ⓓ
54. Ⓐ Ⓑ Ⓒ Ⓓ
55. Ⓐ Ⓑ Ⓒ Ⓓ
56. Ⓐ Ⓑ Ⓒ Ⓓ
57. Ⓐ Ⓑ Ⓒ Ⓓ
58. Ⓐ Ⓑ Ⓒ Ⓓ
59. Ⓐ Ⓑ Ⓒ Ⓓ
60. Ⓐ Ⓑ Ⓒ Ⓓ
61. Ⓐ Ⓑ Ⓒ Ⓓ
62. Ⓐ Ⓑ Ⓒ Ⓓ
63. Ⓐ Ⓑ Ⓒ Ⓓ
64. Ⓐ Ⓑ Ⓒ Ⓓ
65. Ⓐ Ⓑ Ⓒ Ⓓ
66. Ⓐ Ⓑ Ⓒ Ⓓ
67. Ⓐ Ⓑ Ⓒ Ⓓ
68. Ⓐ Ⓑ Ⓒ Ⓓ
69. Ⓐ Ⓑ Ⓒ Ⓓ
70. Ⓐ Ⓑ Ⓒ Ⓓ
71. Ⓐ Ⓑ Ⓒ Ⓓ
72. Ⓐ Ⓑ Ⓒ Ⓓ
73. Ⓐ Ⓑ Ⓒ Ⓓ
74. Ⓐ Ⓑ Ⓒ Ⓓ
75. Ⓐ Ⓑ Ⓒ Ⓓ

Answer Sheet: Chapter 6 Drills

HSPT Quantitative Skills

Sequence

1. Ⓐ Ⓑ Ⓒ Ⓓ	6. Ⓐ Ⓑ Ⓒ Ⓓ	11. Ⓐ Ⓑ Ⓒ Ⓓ	16. Ⓐ Ⓑ Ⓒ Ⓓ	21. Ⓐ Ⓑ Ⓒ Ⓓ
2. Ⓐ Ⓑ Ⓒ Ⓓ	7. Ⓐ Ⓑ Ⓒ Ⓓ	12. Ⓐ Ⓑ Ⓒ Ⓓ	17. Ⓐ Ⓑ Ⓒ Ⓓ	22. Ⓐ Ⓑ Ⓒ Ⓓ
3. Ⓐ Ⓑ Ⓒ Ⓓ	8. Ⓐ Ⓑ Ⓒ Ⓓ	13. Ⓐ Ⓑ Ⓒ Ⓓ	18. Ⓐ Ⓑ Ⓒ Ⓓ	23. Ⓐ Ⓑ Ⓒ Ⓓ
4. Ⓐ Ⓑ Ⓒ Ⓓ	9. Ⓐ Ⓑ Ⓒ Ⓓ	14. Ⓐ Ⓑ Ⓒ Ⓓ	19. Ⓐ Ⓑ Ⓒ Ⓓ	24. Ⓐ Ⓑ Ⓒ Ⓓ
5. Ⓐ Ⓑ Ⓒ Ⓓ	10. Ⓐ Ⓑ Ⓒ Ⓓ	15. Ⓐ Ⓑ Ⓒ Ⓓ	20. Ⓐ Ⓑ Ⓒ Ⓓ	25. Ⓐ Ⓑ Ⓒ Ⓓ

Quantitative Reasoning

26. Ⓐ Ⓑ Ⓒ Ⓓ	31. Ⓐ Ⓑ Ⓒ Ⓓ	36. Ⓐ Ⓑ Ⓒ Ⓓ	41. Ⓐ Ⓑ Ⓒ Ⓓ	46. Ⓐ Ⓑ Ⓒ Ⓓ
27. Ⓐ Ⓑ Ⓒ Ⓓ	32. Ⓐ Ⓑ Ⓒ Ⓓ	37. Ⓐ Ⓑ Ⓒ Ⓓ	42. Ⓐ Ⓑ Ⓒ Ⓓ	47. Ⓐ Ⓑ Ⓒ Ⓓ
28. Ⓐ Ⓑ Ⓒ Ⓓ	33. Ⓐ Ⓑ Ⓒ Ⓓ	38. Ⓐ Ⓑ Ⓒ Ⓓ	43. Ⓐ Ⓑ Ⓒ Ⓓ	48. Ⓐ Ⓑ Ⓒ Ⓓ
29. Ⓐ Ⓑ Ⓒ Ⓓ	34. Ⓐ Ⓑ Ⓒ Ⓓ	39. Ⓐ Ⓑ Ⓒ Ⓓ	44. Ⓐ Ⓑ Ⓒ Ⓓ	49. Ⓐ Ⓑ Ⓒ Ⓓ
30. Ⓐ Ⓑ Ⓒ Ⓓ	35. Ⓐ Ⓑ Ⓒ Ⓓ	40. Ⓐ Ⓑ Ⓒ Ⓓ	45. Ⓐ Ⓑ Ⓒ Ⓓ	50. Ⓐ Ⓑ Ⓒ Ⓓ

Geometric and Nongeometric Comparisons

51. Ⓐ Ⓑ Ⓒ Ⓓ	56. Ⓐ Ⓑ Ⓒ Ⓓ	61. Ⓐ Ⓑ Ⓒ Ⓓ	66. Ⓐ Ⓑ Ⓒ Ⓓ	71. Ⓐ Ⓑ Ⓒ Ⓓ
52. Ⓐ Ⓑ Ⓒ Ⓓ	57. Ⓐ Ⓑ Ⓒ Ⓓ	62. Ⓐ Ⓑ Ⓒ Ⓓ	67. Ⓐ Ⓑ Ⓒ Ⓓ	72. Ⓐ Ⓑ Ⓒ Ⓓ
53. Ⓐ Ⓑ Ⓒ Ⓓ	58. Ⓐ Ⓑ Ⓒ Ⓓ	63. Ⓐ Ⓑ Ⓒ Ⓓ	68. Ⓐ Ⓑ Ⓒ Ⓓ	73. Ⓐ Ⓑ Ⓒ Ⓓ
54. Ⓐ Ⓑ Ⓒ Ⓓ	59. Ⓐ Ⓑ Ⓒ Ⓓ	64. Ⓐ Ⓑ Ⓒ Ⓓ	69. Ⓐ Ⓑ Ⓒ Ⓓ	74. Ⓐ Ⓑ Ⓒ Ⓓ
55. Ⓐ Ⓑ Ⓒ Ⓓ	60. Ⓐ Ⓑ Ⓒ Ⓓ	65. Ⓐ Ⓑ Ⓒ Ⓓ	70. Ⓐ Ⓑ Ⓒ Ⓓ	75. Ⓐ Ⓑ Ⓒ Ⓓ

Answer Sheet Chapter 6 Drills

TACHS Ability Questions

1. Ⓐ Ⓑ Ⓒ Ⓓ Ⓔ	6. Ⓐ Ⓑ Ⓒ Ⓓ Ⓔ	11. Ⓐ Ⓑ Ⓒ Ⓓ Ⓔ	16. Ⓐ Ⓑ Ⓒ Ⓓ Ⓔ	21. Ⓐ Ⓑ Ⓒ Ⓓ Ⓔ
2. Ⓐ Ⓑ Ⓒ Ⓓ Ⓔ	7. Ⓐ Ⓑ Ⓒ Ⓓ Ⓔ	12. Ⓐ Ⓑ Ⓒ Ⓓ Ⓔ	17. Ⓐ Ⓑ Ⓒ Ⓓ Ⓔ	22. Ⓐ Ⓑ Ⓒ Ⓓ Ⓔ
3. Ⓐ Ⓑ Ⓒ Ⓓ Ⓔ	8. Ⓐ Ⓑ Ⓒ Ⓓ Ⓔ	13. Ⓐ Ⓑ Ⓒ Ⓓ Ⓔ	18. Ⓐ Ⓑ Ⓒ Ⓓ Ⓔ	23. Ⓐ Ⓑ Ⓒ Ⓓ Ⓔ
4. Ⓐ Ⓑ Ⓒ Ⓓ Ⓔ	9. Ⓐ Ⓑ Ⓒ Ⓓ Ⓔ	14. Ⓐ Ⓑ Ⓒ Ⓓ Ⓔ	19. Ⓐ Ⓑ Ⓒ Ⓓ Ⓔ	24. Ⓐ Ⓑ Ⓒ Ⓓ Ⓔ
5. Ⓐ Ⓑ Ⓒ Ⓓ Ⓔ	10. Ⓐ Ⓑ Ⓒ Ⓓ Ⓔ	15. Ⓐ Ⓑ Ⓒ Ⓓ Ⓔ	20. Ⓐ Ⓑ Ⓒ Ⓓ Ⓔ	25. Ⓐ Ⓑ Ⓒ Ⓓ Ⓔ

NOTES

NOTES

NOTES

NOTES

NOTES

NOTES

NOTES

NOTES

NOTES

NOTES

NOTES

NOTES